THE NEW CULTS

WALTER MARTIN, M.A.
Director of the Christian Research Institute
Anaheim, California
General Editor

with

Gretchen Passantino

and

The Research Staff of the Christian Research Institute
Cal Beisner
Todd Ehrenborg
Carole Hausmann
Elliot Miller
Gretchen Passantino
Robert Passantino
Kurt Van Gorden
John Weldon

Vision House

Santa Ana, California 92705

THE NEW CULTS

Copyright © 1980 by Vision House Publishers
Santa Ana, California 92705

Library of Congress Catalog Card Number 80-52210
ISBN 0-88449-016-5

Second printing, February 1981

Printed in the United States of America.

WORKS BY WALTER MARTIN

BOOKS

Kingdom of the Cults
Jehovah of the Watchtower
The Rise of the Cults
The Maze of Mormonism
Essential Christianity
Screwtape Writes Again

BOOKLETS

Mormonism
Jehovah's Witnesses
Christian Science
Herbert W. Armstrong
Abortion: Is It Always Murder?
The Riddle of Reincarnation

CONTENTS

PREFACE

Never before in religious history have so many people become so rapidly aware of the dangers of cultism. In the aftermath of the horror of Jonestown, Guyana, and the Peoples' Temple massacre of some 912 men, women, and children, the whole world reeled in disbelief. The word "cult" evoked fear and disgust everywhere as what was once feared could happen in such extremist groups did in fact happen. Of course, not all cults are the same or have the same potential for self-destruction as the Jonestown Cult, though some, like The Way International and The Children of God, have what has been properly termed a "siege mentality," which under the proper conditions could very well trigger violence or mass suicide. The new cults constitute a genuine threat in many areas, not only to their own physical well-being, psychological well-being, and spiritual well-being, but to the Christian church as well. Many of these cults prey on the young and uninformed, and we ignore them only at great risk to ourselves and our church.

In 1965 I produced the first contemporary comprehensive textbook on the cults, *Kingdom of the Cults*. In 1976 and 1980 I updated and revised my handbook on the cults, *The Rise of the Cults*. Both of these books have helped Christians to evangelize and understand cultists and their arguments against Christianity. However, neither of them dealt with the wave of new cults sweeping the United States—and the world, for that matter—in the last few years. The Mormons and Jehovah's Witnesses are familiar to us after years of contact, but many Christians have been finding recently that strange new religious movements have been sweeping through the world at an alarming rate. Now, along with the white shirts and neat ties of the Mormons we find the saffron robes of the Hare Krishnas, the seductive low-cut blouses of the Children of God, the shining faces of the Moonies, and the mysterious, occultic gazes of the Ascended Masters.

Until now, no one has compiled reliable, documented, and easy-to-understand information about many of these groups in one place. A simple understanding of the contents of this book will enable a Christian to understand these cults, to be able to answer their deviant doctrines, and to be able to lovingly present the gospel of our Lord and Savior, Jesus Christ, to the new cultists.

The format of this book is clear and uncomplicated. We have endeavored to show the basic teachings of the particular cult as their teachings oppose Christianity, and then the Bible's answers to such teachings. We have dealt with the essential areas of Christian faith: God, Christ, Man, Sin, and Salvation. It is on these essential areas that our salvation rests. Since many of the cults hold similar doctrinal deviations in common, it is inevitable that there is some overlapping of material. We have designed each chapter to be complete in itself, containing all necessary information and Christian doctrine. However, even with some repetition, the reader will find that the doctrinal evidence is presented with specific relevance for the individual cult's deviations from the gospel. Consequently, some chapters deal more completely with one or more doctrines than others. All, however, cover the essentials, and each can be studied by itself.

We have documented our statements with quotations from the cultic material itself, and we have tried to use quotes from cultic literature that is easily obtainable.

Amidst the controversy concerning the psychological bondage of some of these cults has arisen the practice called "deprogramming." Many well-meaning Christians and non-Christians have actually kidnapped adult cult members and have subjected them to endless hours of "counterbrainwashing" to convince them to leave their cult. I cannot stand behind such practices. It is true that cultists have been blinded by the "god of this age," but it is also true that they have the right to make up their own minds, and we should not stoop to unchristian tactics to accomplish God's ends. The truth has nothing to fear from lies, and we do not need to "counterbrainwash" anyone who truly wants a personal relationship with the eternal God. Therefore, this book is decidedly *not* a manual on deprogramming.

I am indebted to the research staff at Christian Research Institute, and particularly to Gretchen Passantino, for sound research and cogent written analyses showing real concern not only for theological accuracy but also for the individuals misled by the various cultic groups under consideration. The countless families fragmented by cultic infiltration, the lost children, the agony of broken marriages directly traceable to cults is now commonplace. The tide must be turned if we are to be true to our Christian commitment.

The cults in America are multiplying faster than we can imagine. It is our hope that the following pages will help you to know what these particular cults believe, how to respond to them as Christians, and how to share with them the good news of Jesus Christ. It is only as the Christian church is aroused to the challenge of these new cultic systems, and responds properly, that positive steps to evangelize and combat them can be implemented. The new cults have rushed into the vacuum of confusion and unbelief so characteristic of the last two decades of our history, and the impact has been formidable. Let us resolve to resist this invasion of alien thought and doctrine, knowing that "when the enemy shall come in like a flood, the Lord will raise up a standard against him."

Walter Martin
San Juan Capistrano, California
April, 1980

CHAPTER
1

THE DECEPTION
OF THE NEW CULTS*

What does a young man with a shaved head and a saffron robe have to do with a young girl dressed in old hippy clothes? What charisma exudes from both a tiny, long-haired, robed Indian man and a tall, good-looking, well-dressed Englishman? These individuals are all part of the cultic revolution sweeping through our nation, recruiting members from all walks of life, preaching their unique gospels to a world jaded and cynical from the turbulent years of the sixties and seventies. The Hare Krishna youth and the young girl in the Children of God are both selling a religious experience, a subjective and metaphysical journey focusing on the self. Maharishi Mahesh Yogi and Roy Masters both claim to be exclusive deposits of heavenly wisdom, the source of spiritual ecstasy. There are many other modern-day messiahs, some more appealing than others.

However, all of these religious leaders have one primary thing in common: they take biblical Christianity and change it into a clever counterfeit of the real thing. The Bible itself declares that we, as Christians, should "not believe every spirit, but test the spirits to see whether they are from God, because many false prophets have gone out into the world" (1 John 4:1). Jesus told His disciples that at the end they should "Watch out that no one deceives you. For many will

*Researched by Robert and Gretchen Passantino.

come in my name, claiming, 'I am the Christ,' and will deceive many...and many false prophets will appear and deceive many people" (Matthew 24:4,5,11).

The specific cults we are dealing with in this volume are also distinct from such established cults as Jehovah's Witnesses, Mormons, and Christian Science.[1] The impact of the new cults on American society is relatively new, and they seem less accepted than the older cults, even by the secular community. The groups we will discuss produce lifestyles and personal commitment substantially different from mainline Protestant, Catholic, evangelical, and charismatic churches. They are not to be envied for their ability to cause their followers to "fit the mold" of a particular cultic dogma.

We will be investigating the claims of such groups as: The Way International (leader: Victor Paul Wierwille), Hinduism, Hare Krishna, Transcendental Meditation (leader: Maharishi Mahesh Yogi), Erhard Seminar Training (leader: Werner Erhard), The Children of God (leader: David "Moses" Berg), The "I AM" Ascended Masters, Silva Mind Control, The Church of the Living Word (leader: John Robert Stevens), The Foundation of Human Understanding (leader: Roy Masters), Nichiren Shoshu Buddhism, The Local Church of Witness Lee, and Reincarnation. In addition, we will investigate other Eastern philosophical and religious phenomena in conjunction with our study of Hare Krishna and Transcendental Meditation.

Although we will review the particular group's background, development, history, and group structure, we will focus on the theological aberrations of the particular sect. What does the group believe about Scripture? What about God? Who is He? Who is Jesus? What is man and how can he relate to God? Each of the groups deviates in some way from the Bible in its doctrines of God, Jesus Christ, man, sin, salvation, and Scripture.

As evangelical Christians, persuaded of the veracity of the

Word of God in all matters, both spiritual and temporal, we are using the Bible as our standard by which all claims are tested. Far from holding ourselves as the final judge of truth and error, we acknowledge that this right belongs only to the Lord of the Universe, the God of the Bible, and to His Word as he has communicated it to us in the Bible.

We also believe that God has endowed mankind, His highest creation, with a rational mind by which he is to judge and test the world he lives in. We believe that man is fallen and in sin, but is still able to use the rationality that God gave him in the beginning. The regenerate man is able to not only rationally apprehend reality, but is also in harmony with God's reality and is therefore able to relate on a personal level with his Creator. The natural, fallen man is unable to relate to God not because he is mentally deficient, but because he is spiritually deficient. He can come to the same reasoned conclusions, based on the evidence, that a Christian can come to, but he is not able to rise above his fallen (dead) spiritual nature except in faith and under the regenerating power of the Holy Spirit.

These presuppositions form the basis of our present analysis of the new cults. We have analyzed the new cults on the basis of the evidence and are confident that any rational man, Christian or not, can read this material and come to the same rational conclusions we have presented. However, the non-Christian cannot be forced by the evidence to which he intellectually assents to become a Christian. he must want, in his innermost being, to submit to God's will and to repent of his self-centered life. This is only accomplished by the power and grace of God. The evidence presented here will not save anyone. But it will give non-Christians the evidence they need to determine the differences between Christianity and the new cults, between God's way and man's way. From that point on, we need to pray and ask God the Holy Spirit to use us and our words to minister spiritually to our loved ones in the new cults, and for them to have a heartfelt desire to turn to God. This book is therefore a tool for evangelism, and can be quite effective in the hands of a concerned Christian submitted to the will of God.

God commands us to make reasoned examination of evidence a part of our multifaceted evangelism of the lost. In Acts, we read that the Apostle Paul reasoned with non-Christians. In Acts 17:17, Luke tells us, "So he [Paul] reasoned in the synagogue with the Jews and the God-fearing Greeks, as well as in the marketplace day by day with those who happened to be there." God commands us in 1 Peter 3:15 to "always be prepared to give an answer to everyone who asks you to give the reason for the hope that you have." Paul instructed Titus (2:1) to teach everything in accord with sound doctrine, and Jude 3 reminds us all to "contend for the faith that God has once for all entrusted to the saints." Christianity is a reasonable faith, one of which we as Christians should be proud and willing to defend. We do not have blind, objectless faith. Our faith must be *in* something or someone. We do not believe in spite of the evidence; instead, the evidence points us toward the Savior of the world, Jesus Christ.

"Contending for the faith" is known as *apologetics*. Apologetics means a reasoned defense of one's beliefs or convictions. Our English word comes from the Greek *apologia,* which is found in 1 Peter 3:15, quoted above. The new cults have claimed to be spokesmen of God and have claimed to be compatible with Christianity. They are not. In fact, they assail some of the foundational doctrines of Christianity for which we are commanded to "give an answer" or in effect practice apologetics. We must answer the challenge of the cults and we must answer that challenge according to the guidelines God has given us in His Word.

God's Word, the Bible, is infallible in all that it proclaims, whether spiritual or temporal. We can trust it in all points to accurately represent reality and truth. This does not mean that every word in the Bible is truth, for the Bible contains the words of good and bad men, of holy and fallen angels, and of God Himself. However, it is *God's* record, and we can trust that He has preserved for us exactly what these men, angels, and demons have said. What Satan said to Eve in the Garden of Eden, for example, was a lie. But we can trust God that His record, the Bible, has accurately preserved what Satan said. Of course, when God Himself speaks in the Bible, whether directly or through His human servants, we can trust that He is telling only truth, for in Him there is no lie (Titus 1:2; Hebrews 6:18).

Our standard in examining the beliefs of the new cults is the Bible. It will be the final arbiter in the cults' challenge to Christianity. The Bible declares that certain articles of Christian faith are essential to salvation—namely, the Being and nature of God, the Person and work of Christ, His sacrificial death and bodily resurrection, man's natural condition and opportunity for salvation, the means of salvation, and Christ's ultimate return and reconciliation of all things to the Father. These are the areas we must examine in our journey through the labyrinth of cultic doctrine. Does the group support the doctrine of the trinity of God, the deity of Christ, the substitutionary atonement, the bodily resurrection of Christ, salvation by grace, and the second coming of Christ? If, upon examining the literature of the group, we find that it denies these essential doctrines, then we must classify it as a cult, seriously at variance with God's Word.

Paul warned Timothy that in the last days there would be all sorts of false teachers, who would have a form of godliness but would deny true allegiance to the God of the Bible. These are men who "oppose the truth—men of depraved minds, who, as far as the faith is concerned, are rejected" (2 Timothy 3:8; cf. 3:5-9). We must beware of the false teachers while at the same time having compassion on their followers, who have (perhaps unknowingly) been duped into following men while they think they are following God. We will examine each cult concerning its teaching on God, man, and salvation. We will examine what each cult teaches concerning the above doctrines, and if we find that they err on the essential matters of Christian belief as taught clearly in the Bible, we will know that they are false teachers and not servants of God.

By "cult," we mean a group, religious in nature, which surrounds a leader or a group of teachings which either denies or misinterprets essential biblical doctrine. Most cults have a single leader, or a succession of leaders, who claim to represent God's voice on earth and who claim authority greater than that of the Bible. The cultic teaching claims to be in harmony with the Bible but denies one or more of the cardinal doctrines presented therein. Members are generally not given the freedom to accept or reject any of the group's teachings on its own merits. The follower must blindly accept all of the teachings of the group or else risk "divine disfavor"—often including expulsion from the group.

Irving Zaretsky and Mark Leone, in *Religious Movements in Contemporary America,* have some interesting observations on cultism from a sociological point of view. As sociologists, they have evaluated some of the different characteristics of a cult. They state:

> These groups produce life styles and personal commitment substantially different from mainline institutional churches, and they are uniquely successful at influencing the life-ways of their members . . . they cater to a reaffirmed religious zeal founded on personalized theologies made to fit the needs of an ever-expanding and diversified following. They provide a framework wherein ecstatic religious experiences for the individual are reintroduced and provided with purpose and justification. . . .While originally drawing from the margins of society in age distribution, economic and social status, *they are now successfully making inroads in middle America.*[2]

Zaretsky and Leone go on to list 26 characteristics of the

cults, many of which we have also noted and which we believe are sometimes unique to cults.

CHARACTERISTICS OF THE CULTS

Although each of the cults we study in this book is relatively new on the American scene, all of them are a significant factor in the rise of cultism in America. What often seems amazing to the observer of the cult scene is the magnitude of the impact made by these new cults despite the fact that their membership is much smaller than recognized Protestantism and Catholicism. Collectively, the cult membership in the United States may reach close to 20 million. When we compare this to the vast numbers of unchurched or mainline-churched Americans, we can see that a distinct minority, the cults, is significantly affecting the majority. We shall now examine some of the characteristics which unify contemporary cults—characteristics which provide some of the impetus to this thriving movement.

Zaretsky and Leone are among the few cult observers who, like we, have noticed that most of the contemporary cults are in some way offshoots of nineteenth-century American Protestantism. Even those cults which claim another religion as their source (the Hare Krishnas, for example), usually are generically related to groups which were in America in the last century. Mormonism began in 1830, Jehovah's Witnesses in 1874, Christian Science in 1866, etc. The century was one of social and religious turmoil, and the repercussions of rationalism were being felt in all areas of life, including religion. It was a time in which people could and did believe almost anything. In many ways, those decades are paralleled by the years following the emergence of relativism in this century. It is not unusual, therefore, that today's new cults can trace their roots to the cults of the last century. Beyond these roots, what common denominators do we discover among the new cults?

1. Cults, new as well as old, are usually started by strong

and dynamic leaders who are in complete control of their followers. The power such leaders exercise is said to be supernatural and to come from either personal revelation or personal "anointing" from some idea of God.

2. All cults possess some Scripture that is either added to or which replaces the Bible as God's Word. The Hare Krishnas claim to be compatible with the Bible, and yet add the Hindu Scriptures to their canon as the "highest" revelations from God—even though they directly contradict the Bible. The Unification Church believes that *Divine Principle* by Sun Myung Moon is today's "Bible." All of the cults we will examine in some way add to or change the Bible.

3. The new cults have rigid standards for membership and accept no members who will not become integrally involved in the group. (It is true that the Children of God maintain close contact with what could be termed "nominal" members, but our investigation shows that these are not members at all, but are usually sources of financial gain to the Children of God and good publicity spokesmen.) Those who dare to deviate from the cult's norm are immediately disciplined and, if unrepentant, ostracized completely from the group and its members. We shall see in later discussion that this excommunication can have devastating effect on cultists whose entire lives revolve around the cult. Faced with a future of no friends, no productive activity, and no approval from God, most erring cult members repent immediately.

4. Cultists often become members of one cult after membership in one or more other cults. As we shall discuss later, the factors which draw a person into a cult are usually represented in many cults, and thus it is not unusual for a person to leave one cult for another.

5. The new cults are actively evangelistic and spend much of their time in proselytizing new converts. This feature is perhaps the most publicly prominent feature of the new cults, with the exception of the money-solicitation activities

of some of the new cults. One of the reasons behind this drive for converts lies in the almost-insatiable drive of the cult to have some outward display showing that it is truly in God's favor. Some might even attribute this to a leader's own ego gratification.

Another reason for the cultists' zeal in obtaining new members concerns some cults' requirements for salvation. Some cults teach that effective evangelization is a mark of a truly dedicated member, one who is proud of his organization. The cults deny, in one form or another, salvation by God's grace alone. The cults add something, some kind of work, to God's grace in order to achieve approval from God. Often one of the "works" necessary for salvation is that of witnessing of one's cultic faith to the world. Finally, Zaretsky and Leone give another reason for the strong membership drives of the cults:

> Proselytizing follows from the fact that these are often not the natal churches of individuals; rather, they receive the bulk of their adherents in adult life. The immediate family of a member often does not belong to the church. . . .Anyone is a potential convert. But in statistical fact, as opposed to ideological ideal, these churches cater to narrowly defined and homogeneous groups of people.[3]

6. Often we find that the leaders or officials of the new cults are not professional clergymen. They may be self-selected through some inner "revelation," selected by the leader or governing body of the cult, or chosen by the group as a whole. However, they are seldom schooled in Bible college or seminary, and most have not even attended extensive schooling within the cult, if the cult provides "schooling."

The primary prerequisite for becoming an important voice within a cult is, surprisingly, the ability to be a follower. One must obey each and every tenet of the cult and must exemplify, in every way, ideal cult membership. Then and only then is one in a position to rise within the organization.

7. All the new cults have a system of doctrine and practice which is in some state of flux. This system is rarely discussed or taught specifically, and sessions spent to learn the system are infrequent, if they occur at all. However, each member is expected to learn this system of practice and doctrine, and can be ostracized for not adhering to it. This is partly in order to preserve the necessity for a living group and a living leader, who can change the "revelations" at will. For example, among established cults, Jehovah's Witnesses are a prime example. At one time in their history vaccinations were said to be sinful, and anyone guilty of accepting a vaccination was ostracized. Now, supposedly, there is "new light," and vaccinations are acceptable.

8. In harmony with Christian theology, the new cults all believe that there is continual, ongoing communication from God. However, the cults differ from the biblical Christian church in believing that their new "revelations" can contradict and even at times supersede God's first revelation, the Bible. As Christians, however, we believe that the Bible is the standard by which all supposed revelation is tested. The interpretation of these new revelations characterizes the new cults and forms an integral part of the proselytizing of the groups. The cults emphasize experience rather than theological reasoning, and new revelation is just one form of new experience.

9. The new cults claim to have truth not available to any other groups or individuals. Usually this new truth is said to be a "restoration" of the "pure" Christianity which was, according to them, corrupted at some time in early church history. With this claim to exclusivity comes a definite aloofness from the rest of the world. The particular cult is the only bastion of truth, and as such is the only haven for truth-seekers. This logically develops to a dangerous state of isolation for the cult:

> Cults create fortified boundaries, confining their members in various ways and attacking those who would leave as defec-

tors, deserters or traitors; they recruit new members with ruthless energy and raise enormous sums of money, and they tend to view the outside world with increasing hostility and distrust as the organization ossifies.[4]

10. The last major characteristic of the new cults concerns cultic vocabulary.[5] Each cult has an initiate vocabulary by which it describes the truths of its revelation. Sometimes the "in words" of a particular cult are the words of orthodox Christianity, but invested with new meanings. Thus, for example, The Way International uses the term "Jesus Christ" to mean a man named Jesus who is definitely not God incarnate. At other times the cult may coin new words or phrases. The Children of God, for example, talk about "Ffing" when they mean soliciting money for sex, or prostitution.

Although different cult experts would perhaps add to or subtract from the above list of cultic characteristics, we have presented here all of the essential marks which distinguish many of the new cults from the rest of society and from the biblical Christian church. By using these warning signals, we can be prepared to identify and to evangelize these new cults which are springing up continuously in America today.

INGREDIENTS FOR CULTIC GROWTH

Through the centuries since the founding of the Christian church, we have witnessed repeated waves of heresy sweeping across the mainstream of the church. In New Testament times, corruption in the church usually came from Jewish believers who were unwilling to give up their legalism, or else from former Gentiles, who were reluctant to leave the old gods and the old sacrifices behind when they aligned themselves with the Christ and His church. In the early centuries, the church fathers contended with those who sought to change the biblical teachings on God (usually by relegating Christ to some position inferior to that of the Father).

The nineteenth century in America saw another surge of heresy within the body of Christ. Spawned particularly by "the age of reason" and existentialism, the ecstatic revelations of nineteenth-century visionaries produced scores of new cults, some of which, like the Mormons and Jehovah's Witnesses, are still with us in great numbers.

Today we are experiencing another rise of cults, a rise which was predicted by us more than 25 years ago and which has mushroomed in the last ten years to proportions undreamed-of in most churches. To what can we attribute this sudden fascination with fringe religion? Are we suddenly faced with a population that is unable to think rationally? Are people spurning the values, beliefs, and answers of traditional churches because traditional churches are unable to meet their needs? Can we focus on some of the factors which have contributed to this move, and can we work to remedy the shortcomings within the Christian church? We must understand some of the impetus behind the current move toward the cults in order to understand cultists and to meet with renewed vigor the challenge of the cults.

We have been able to isolate five dominant ingredients in the American culture of the last two decades which we believe have contributed significantly to the growth and advancement of the new cults. Having discussed previously some of the characteristics of the cults, we will now present the sources of some of those characteristics.

1. Perhaps the most significant instigator of the religious rebellion we are now faced with is American Christianity as represented in mainline denominations and Catholicism. We must face up to the fact that many of our American churches have failed in many instances to meet the needs of their constituents. American Christianity has almost reached the point where it is something distinct from biblical Christianity. With the influx of theological liberalism, or "modernism," and existential theology, many American churches now bear little resemblance to the vibrant, Christ-

centered church of the New Testament.

Although the pilgrimage to liberalism had its beginning in the early 1800s, the last 30 years have seen a pilgrimage of hundreds of pastors and church-related teachers to the Meccas of Tillichian and Bultmannian belief. Of the major denominations in the United States, hardly any are free from the taint of shallow liberalism. The Catholic Church in America, long considered a bastion of religious conservatism, today has clerics who range in belief from those who are not even sure God exists to those who wish to embrace evangelical Protestants as equal and full brothers in the true family of God.

Lest anyone think that we desire the Christian church to return to the "dark ages" of belief and practice, let us clarify what we mean by liberalism.

We are not opting for a Christianity that refuses to recognize the world around it, which refuses to benefit and learn from science and the secular world (oblivious to any good that those groups can provide the gospel) and which prefers to keep its mind in the thirteenth century. Neither are we opting for a Christianity that compromises the essentials of our faith—which retains, in the face of antireligious attack, only the name of Christianity, and discards all the biblical truths that should distinguish Christianity from anything man-made.

By liberalism, we mean that general attitude which recognizes no sacred truth, no beliefs that must be preserved at all costs from erosion by the world. Liberalism does not put Christ first, but actually puts the *self* first. Christ, as revealed in Scripture and testified to in our hearts by the Holy Spirit, must be the final Judge and standard by which everything else stands or falls.

The liberal, however, has set himself and human reason as that infallible judge. Whatever the self can be convinced of must therefore be truth. Truth is not objective and immutable, in the final analysis of the liberal view. Truth changes as the self's understanding changes, and the self lives in changes. The liberal usually will not ascribe to the Bible the title of the only and complete revelation of God. The liberal usually will not ascribe to Jesus the titles He ascribed to Himself: "the way, the truth, and the life" (John 14:6). Instead, in a world of relativism, liberalism's Christianity takes its place alongside many of the other religions in the world, with no greater claim to truth or reality than any other.

Is it any wonder, then, that Americans feel no reason to stay in the established churches, to believe the established standards? If the Lord Jesus Christ and Christianity are just one way among many equally good ways, then why shouldn't one try as many ways as he pleases? Why should he remain loyal to a Christ who can provide no more sure answers than he himself possesses?

More dangerously, however, many people are seeking desperately (but in the wrong places) for objective, permanent value in life. They are crying out for certainty and truth. They are not satisfied with a religion which can neither correspond to reality nor give some assurance of ultimate truth.

The new cults offer that security, even if it is a false security. The new cults and their dynamic leaders claim to know the truth, claim to be able to provide answers for all of life's many questions. Searching, seeking people seem inexorably drawn toward the false light of the new cults. Although for a time the new cult members seem to feel that security they were so desperately seeking, it is also true that many later leave, disillusioned and still empty-handed in their grasp for ultimate truth. It is at this point that the mainline churches must be willing to drop their pseudointellectualism and liberal theology which cannot conceive of a god greater than their own minds and to pick up once again the God of the Scriptures, of historic Christianity, who alone can reveal perfect and eternal truth. We will then have something to offer the searching person, something he will never have to abandon in despair, as he did his former cult.

2. Isolationism is the second major ingredient in the new cultic emphasis of this decade. It is closely related to self-centeredness, our third ingredient; and with rebelliousness, our fourth ingredient. In fact, when we see the effects of isolationist thought, we will see that it prepares us for the receptivity of our fifth ingredient, the importation and adoption of Eastern religious thought into our way of life.

Beginning in the last century and mushrooming into dominance in this century is an acute sense of isolationism. Isolationism teaches that the particular person, group, or even nation must look out for its own interests and must not interfere with any other person (or group or nation). In sociological terms we could refer to "cultural norms," the idea that each culture has its own ethics with which we must not interfere, recognizing that all ethics are determined by particular cultures: there are no absolute ethics. Selfishly we could refer to isolationism as "each man for himself."

This isolationism is widely accepted in America today. It is from this concept that many of our catch phrases come, such as "Do your own thing," "If it feels good, do it," "Whatever you say," "Give me some space," and other seemingly nonsocial expressions. It is also from this concept that the extreme self-centeredness of the sixties and seventies developed. Not only do we find each man fighting for himself, but we also find each man aggressively marching to expand and enrich his own kingdom *at the expense of others.* People refuse to get involved on behalf of others and even victimize others if by so doing their own ends are attained. This is known as the "me, my, and mine" syndrome, which enthrones selfishness and rejects altruism as weakness or stupidity.

However, man can never be truly happy with isolationist tendencies. In Genesis, God saw the man that He had made and declared, "It is not good for the man to be alone"

(2:18). As Christians, we are taught that none of us is sufficient in himself, for "God has combined the members of the body [of Christ] and has given greater honor to the parts that lacked it, so that there should be no division in the body, but that its parts should have equal concern for each other. If one part suffers, every part suffers with it; if one part is honored, every part rejoices with it. Now you are the body of Christ, and each one of you is a part of it" (1 Corinthians 12:24b-27).

When people are forced into isolation from one another, they cry out in loneliness as they look for human contact and interpersonal relationships. They are, as one psychiatrist rightly observed, "the lonely crowd." Many who are attracted to the new cults are attracted because the new cults offer social contact, offer human interaction, and claim to banish loneliness. The *group* is all-important in the cults, and each member is made to feel that he is an integral, necessary part of the whole. Often identical dress, vocabulary, and mannerisms reinforce this idea of "togetherness."

However, the clannishness of the cults is not ultimately satisfying, since it is based on an enforced sociability rather than on a togetherness created by true love and devotion that is kept together by the supernatural bonds of the Holy Spirit, as in true Christianity.

The sociability of the cults ultimately reverts to the same isolationism it supposedly seeks to destroy. The members are isolated from the rest of society, from their elevated spiritual leaders, and from each other. In other words, they are separated by those very outward trappings which were supposed to do away with isolation!

3. Cult leaders are also separated from others by their self-centered isolationism. Self-centeredness is one effect of isolationism. It can be brought on by an elevated self-image, a belief that God has specially anointed one to a position spiritually superior to everyone else. One can then

understandably insist that everything be done for his own benefit. One of the marks of a cultic leader is his near-self-deification.

Today's American society actively promotes the self-deification of the individual. So much of our culture reflects the current belief that the self is the most important single entity in the universe. One of the results of this is the overabundance of books on today's best-seller lists which are generally called "self-help" books. As never before, people are turning all their attention to themselves—wanting to improve their looks, their success, their finances, their health, their sex life, etc. Advertisers play on this self-preoccupation in the vast majority of advertisements we are surrounded with daily. Is it any wonder, then, that Americans begin to be their own gods, begin to use their own feelings and standards as their absolute ethic? People in this predicament find it hard to submit to an objective authority such as the Bible, which flatly declares that all have sinned and have fallen short of the glory of God (Romans 3:23).

As Christians, we need to balance the judgment of God toward man with the love of God toward man, both of which are presented in the Bible. While non-Christians must recognize that they are sinners in need of a Savior, we should go further and bring them the good news that they have a Savior—God Himself, who loved them so much that He died for them (John 3:16; Acts 20:28). It is true that we are all sinners, but it is also true that in Christ we can have new meaning in our lives, and can appropriate the great Gift that God gave to us in Jesus Christ. Paul said, ". . . I consider everything a loss compared to the surpassing greatness of knowing Christ Jesus my Lord, for whose sake I have lost all things. I consider them rubbish, that I may gain Christ and be found in Him, not having a righteousness of my own that comes from the law, but that which is through faith in Christ—the righteousness that comes from God and is by faith" (Philippians 3:8,9).

4. Another ingredient somewhat related to isolationism is the intense rebelliousness we have observed among many of our young people in the last two decades. Beginning with the "rock 'n roll" era of the early fifties, the youth of America have become increasingly disillusioned with their parents' values and unwilling to submit to those values. Because of a newly dominant feeling that the self is the ultimate judge of what is right and wrong, young people have reexamined all the values passed down to them from the adult population. In their examination of these traditional values, the youth have lacked an objective ethical standard and have therefore found no reason to keep those values. Thus, many of our youth today are valueless; truth and morality have become completely subjective. We see a generation without a sense of history—cut off from the past, alienated from the present, and having a fragmented concept of the future. The "now" generation is in reality a lost generation.

One of the hardest-hit of the traditional values is that of religion in American life. Once the central focus of the average family, religion has now been relegated to obscurity in many American families. Either the family is not religious at all, or it considers religious belief and expression to be very personal, and not for sharing with other family members. What is right for one family member in religion may not be right for another, the thought decrees. Individual experience has become the validation of religious truth.

Christians need to recognize this subjectivism and be sure that it has not permeated their Christian faith. We believe that Jesus rose from the dead and is the only way to God because we can demonstrate that Christianity is historically verifiable and rational: it corresponds to reality. We have eternal life and have become a part of the real Christian church through a vital encounter and personal relationship with Jesus Christ. We must be careful not to deny the reasonableness of Christianity, while at the same time we must remember that Christian experience is also personal and spiritual. We can offer to the subjective mind of today's society a faith that is familiar in its emphasis and yet superior in its objective verification.

The subjectivism of American youth has spawned a rebelliousness which is far beyond what has been experienced in previous generations in the United States. Youth is not willing to accept what an adult says simply because the adult is an adult and "knows everything." Youth wants its own answers and will not settle for so-called "hand-me-down" values or religion.

The rebellious actions of youth in the sixties and early seventies is especially symbolized by the campus riots, which started in protest of educational tunnel vision, according to the students, and ended by protesting almost everything from atomic energy to the Vietnam War.

The new cults have borrowed from that sense of rebellion and the youthful rejection of the values and religions of the adult population. The mecca of the new cults includes freedom from oppression, fighting for "the cause," and rejection of the traditionalism of parents. The sexual liberty in the Children of God cult reflects the changing sexual attitudes of this generation: the rejection of the previous generation's attitudes of sexual fidelity to one's legal spouse. The apparent disdain for authority prevalent in young Americans today is reflected in elevation of the self at the expense of others.

However, rather than just borrowing from the climate of the day, the new cults have gone further in making a strange union between subjectivism and absolutes. While most of these cults promote the idea that there are no absolute ethics, as the "older generation" teaches, most new cults also teach their own set of ethics— as absolute as any in the Bible or American traditional society. If one breaks the ethics of his own cult, he can expect no mercy from his cult peers and leaders. This paradoxical marriage between relativism and absolutism is perhaps only possible in our present society, which has recently been conditioned to accept contradictory ideas. This breakdown in consistency brings us to our last major ingredient in the new cultic wave of the seventies.

5. Whether Eastern religious and philosophical influences came *before* the relativism of these decades, *with* it, or *after* is unsure. We can be certain, however, that relativism and Eastern thought go hand-in-hand.

As we shall see in our discussion of the Eastern cults (see Chapter 3), the basic tenet of Eastern thought is that all is God and God is all. Thus the individual in some mystical and ultimate sense is God. This is in direct harmony with the self-centeredness we discussed above, and it can easily be seen that the two ideas are closely related.

In addition, Eastern thought, because of this basic tenet, has developed two additional major tenets. If all is God and God is all, it follows that all is good, if God is good. However, in the material world around us we see many things which do not appear to be good or a reflection of something we would call God, or would ascribe to His nature. Therefore, the Eastern mind makes a leap of blind faith and accepts contradictions. The Eastern mind-set can accept that good and bad are equally powerful, equally eternal, and indeed that one cannot exist without the other. From this we get the dualism of Zoroastrianism and the Chinese principle of yin and yang and the Eastern "puzzles" so popular here today, such as the contemplation of the question, "What is the sound of one hand clapping?"

The second major tenet stemming from the pantheism (God is all) of Eastern thought concerns the reality of the material world. In Eastern thought, the sight of evil and suffering is dealt with not only through acceptance of contradictions, but through a denial of the validity of man's senses. Many people in Eastern religions either reject what appears to be evil or try to attribute evil to one's own "karma," or what one deserves based on one's actions in this and previous lives. The line between reality and fantasy is very vague in the Eastern mind, and the objective existence of matter is sometimes hard to accept. Because of this, the Eastern mind continually turns inward, to the "God within." Again, this is a reflection of the self-centeredness we have already noted.

Because it bears such a close relationship to the isolationism of our Western culture today, Eastern thought is very attractive to the Western mind. With an Eastern orientation, one does not have to make sense of the world, one does not have to logically and rationally analyze one's beliefs and motives. One can keep his entire attention turned inward, and can occupy his time in self-worship instead of orienting himself toward an objective God and toward others who have been created by that God.

We cannot stress strongly enough the Eastern influence on today's religious behavior. From Alan Watts of several years ago to Rev. Moon's Unification Church today, Eastern religion has permeated much of the American religious scene. We shall discuss this thoroughly in later chapters.

These, then, are the five major influences on the growth of the new cults today. A weak and liberal church, isolationist tendencies resulting in self-centeredness and rebellion, and the importation of Eastern thought have all had their part in preparing this generation to be receptive to the call of the new cults.

By successfully combating these concepts and by offering a better alternative—the true Christ and true Christianity—we can win souls from the ranks of the new cults and return to a vital, growing, and living Christianity which is a testimony to the world of the power of Jesus Christ, who said, "Let your light shine before men, that they may see your good deeds and praise your Father in heaven" (Matthew 5:16).

THE LANGUAGE OF THE NEW CULTS

Before we talk about the specific cults and their doctrines in contrast to Christianity, we need to understand the role of semantics in cultic exclusivism. Semantics concerns *meaning in language*. What is meant by words in their context? How do idioms, specialized language, and figures of speech affect our ability to communicate with others and to understand others? In the world of the cults, religious terms are bandied about with little concern for their original and orthodox meanings. Each cult has its own definitions for the terms we consider fundamental to explaining our faith. Jesus to Silva Mind Control is a spirit guide; to the Hare Krishnas He is one of many avatars, or incarnations of God; to the members of the Way He is a lesser god; and to the Children of God He was sexually prolific and even engaged in homosexual activities.

From this we can see how very important it is for us to define our terms and to understand what those terms mean to the cultists with whom we deal. We will never communicate the gospel if the person with whom we are sharing is unable to understand what we mean because he has a preconceived, incorrect definition of the terms central to our discussion.

The problem of cultic semantics is one of the reasons the Christian church is just now beginning to wake up to the dangers of these inroads into orthodoxy. For years, complacent Christians ignored the cults, assuming that because they used the same terminology as orthodoxy, they were compatible with orthodoxy. We have talked with Hare Krishnas, for example, who have insisted that their religion is compatible with Christianity while at the same time insisting just as strongly that Krishna was the greatest incarnation of God and that we are all part of God.

A real shock faces the average Christian when he attempts to overcome the semantic barrier between himself and the cultist. The shock is that the Christian will discover that he is ill-equipped to explain what he believes in simple terms, and he will then be faced with the need to study his beliefs in earnest, perhaps for the first time! This can become a real benefit. We have trained many people to minister to the cults, and all of them have agreed that the important element to successful cult evangelism is a good knowledge of Christian doctrine and the ability to communicate that doctrine on a simple level. Unless one is willing to submit to the command of Scripture to "correctly handle the word of truth" (2 Timothy 2:15) and to study our faith, he would do best to avoid confrontation with a cultist.

We have become too complacent in our faith, and the mysticism of Eastern thought has even permeated the church to the extent that some Christians often feel they need not learn or study anything in depth about Jesus, that faith is anti-intellectual and that fully understanding God's Word is unimportant. On the contrary, we are repeatedly commanded to learn of the One who died for us. Hebrews 11:6 declares that we must believe that God exists before we can come to Him. How can we come to Him if we do not know who He is? How can we offer the hope of salvation to a cultist if we are unable to tell him who is saving him? We must remember the lengths to which Christ went to explain the Father to the people of his day. Jesus Christ is the exact representation of God to man (Hebrews 1:3; Colossians 1:15), and we must be able to explain who He is to those we wish to evangelize.

There are basically two types of vocabulary with which one must be familiar if he is to successfully communicate with a cultist. The first vocabulary of a cult consists of those words which it has in common with Christianity and other religions, but which it has redefined in the light of the particular cult's new revelations. This vocabulary might include such words as "God," "Jesus," "Trinity," etc. In the book *Essential Christianity* all the basic terms and concepts of the Christian faith are carefully and clearly defined and shown in Scripture. We will deal with these areas in our specific discussions of the cults in this book, also.

The second vocabulary of the cults consists of those words which have little or no meaning at all except for the meaning ascribed to them by the particular cult. "Avatar" in Eastern thought has no direct relationship to any Christian term. "Twigs," in the vocabulary of The Way, refers to a particular level of church administration. Numerous examples of this unique vocabulary will be discussed under the particular cult in which the words occur.

To communicate effectively with a cultist, then, one must be sure that he can define his own religious vocabulary to the cultist's satisfaction, and he must also be sure that he understands the cultist's vocabulary. In other words, he must understand both *that which is general* and *that which is unique* to the particular cult being confronted.

We cannot afford to assume that the cultist understands our vocabulary. We cannot ignore the real semantical problem that is present in each conversation with a cultist. We need to be sure that the gospel we are presenting corresponds with the gospel of the Scriptures, and that the cultist understands the differences between what he believes and what the Scriptures teach.

Language is the center of our relationship with other human beings. Without it we would be little better than the animals. We can join our thoughts, our emotions, and our lives through the medium of language. We had better not, as Christians, deny the cultist the opportunity of understanding the Bible we believe and comparing it rigorously with his own belief system.

CHAPTER NOTES

1. See *Kingdom of the Cults,* by Walter Martin, for treatment of these classical cults, as well as his separate books on several of the more prominent ones (see Bibliography for complete listing).

2. Irving Zaretsky and Mark Leone, *Religious Movements in Contemporary America* (Princeton: Princeton University Press, 1974) p. xxiii.

3. Ibid., p. xxlv.

4. L.J. West and R. Delgado, "Psyching Out the Cults' Collective Mania," in *The Los Angeles Times,* Nov. 26, 1978, VII, p. 1.

5. See the section on cultic semantics later in this chapter.

CHAPTER
2

THE WAY INTERNATIONAL*

HISTORY

The Way International, headquartered in New Knoxville, Ohio, was founded by a dynamic, longtime minister, Victor Paul Wierwille. Wierwille, born in 1916, is from New Knoxville and returned there with his cult several years ago.

Wierwille grew up in the Evangelical and Reformed Church and was first ordained by that denomination. He says that he felt his first calling to the ministry when he was only eight years old:

> My first recollection for considering a Christian calling in life is when I was around eight years old. The family church in New Knoxville was celebrating its annual Mission Festival service and a guest speaker, Dr. Lowman of Cincinnati, was present for the occasion. . . . As my mother and I walked past the ministers, Dr. Lowman put his hands on my shoulders in a friendly manner and asked me, "And what do you want to be when you grow up?" Without hesitation I replied, "Well, I would like to be a minister like you." Of course that was a boy's response to an adult's question, but considering the course of events of my life, this experience remains vivid in my memory.[1]

After high school graduation, Wierwille received a bachelor's degree from the Mission House College and

---

* Researched by Kurt Van Gorden.

Seminary at Plymouth, Wisconsin. He then studied at both the University of Chicago and Princeton Theological Seminary, in New Jersey. In 1941, the Evangelical and Reformed Church ordained Wierwille into the ministry. His first church was in Payne, Ohio, but discontent with the ministry and a feeling of inadequacy brought him to the brink of resigning from the ministry the next year.

From here, Wierwille's account of his life differs from the research we have done. Wierwille has claimed to have studied Greek, to have taken every correspondence course Moody Bible Institute offered, and to have furthered his education in other ways. Wierwille says that during this time in his life, when he generally held to a liberal view of Scripture, he was despondent and felt that the negative in his life greatly outweighed the positive.[2] An encounter with Christian lecturer and author Rosalind Rinker renewed his interest in the Bible and gave him the impetus for study which culminated in the unique theology of The Way Ministry.

Wierwille is quoted as saying, "I took everything I could take at the Moody Bible Institute, too, through their correspondence courses."[3] However, an inquiry to Moody Bible Institute resulted in a letter from director Paul D. Wieland in which Wieland states that Moody's records (from its inception in 1901 to the present) show no record of Wierwille completing *any* courses at all.

Although Wierwille was urged to study Greek at Princeton Theological Seminary, that school's record of his attendance (he graduated in 1941 with a master of theology degree) shows that he took no Greek courses at all! His misuse of Greek in his theology (which we will discuss later) is perhaps attributable to this lack in Greek study. According to James F. Armstron, Registrar at Princeton, his "degree represented advanced study in the field of preaching, and contained no work in the Greek language."[4]

In 1948, Wierwille received his Th.D. from Pikes Peak Seminary, a reputed degree mill in Manitou Springs, Colorado. In a letter from the Colorado Commission on Higher Education, a state official says that Pikes Peak Seminary had no resident instruction, no published list of faculty, and no accreditation, and that no agency of government supervised it. It offered its degree programs by "extramural" methods, involving the sending of book reviews and papers by mail. The degrees, this Commission official says, have no status except with the institution which conferred them. The institution itself, say state authorities, consisted only of a single residence that doubled as the headquarters of the operation.[5]

Aside from Wierville's apparent schooling difficulties, the future cult leader underwent a spiritual crisis during the period from 1941 to 1942. In 1942, at the end of this spiritual depression, he claimed that God the Father spoke to him audibly and declared that he (Wierwille) was in a position to possess the first accurate knowledge of the Bible since the first century, if he were willing to teach that knowledge to others.[6] As we noted in our first chapter, a claim to secret divine knowledge is one of the prominent and consistent features of the cultic realm.[7] We can see that even as early as 1942, Wierwille was on the road to forming his own cult, with himself as God's chosen leader.

In the same year, Wierwille began a weekly radio program, taught a Bible message each week in his public appearances, and preached in his church on Sundays. This necessitated his preparing at least three new messages each week, a fact of which he is proud, evidently feeling that this quantity of messages is in some way correlative to quality of message![8]

In most cult leaders, we find an early discontent with established religion and conventional understanding of the Scriptures. Often the cult leader is not satisfied with a normal interpretation of Scripture, and instead looks for a hidden or secret meaning, unknown to the general public, but which, when understood, unlocks all of the "secrets" of

God's revelation. Wierwille is a prime example of this. In his own words, he relates his frustration with established religion, established Bible teachers, and what he would term a surface-level understanding of the Bible.

> The more I worked the Bible, the more I began to see that the greatness of God's power lay in the Holy Spirit field. Thus I began a thorough search from Genesis to Revelation on the Holy Spirit until I knew from memory all 385 verses in the New Testament on the Holy Spirit, but I could never pattern these verses nor find anyone to put them together for me. This search for knowledge on the Holy Spirit led me from pillar to post—looking everywhere and anywhere for understanding. I studied everything I could find in the Roman Catholic church and in the Protestant churches. I endeavored to find the answers which would make the Bible fit and which would fit with the Bible, but my quest seemed like it led nowhere. Even though I studied and received tremendous knowledge of God's Word, there were many, many tantalizing Scriptures that I could not understand nor meaningfully fit together.[9]

The self-centeredness we also discussed before can be seen in the above statement, where Wierwille says, ''I endeavored to find the answers which would make the Bible fit and which would fit with the Bible. . . .'' It is another mark of the cults, and especially of cult leaders, to test everything by their own ideas, rather than testing all ideas by the Bible, the objective standard of truth. It is significant that Wierwille wanted to make the Bible fit answers before he was willing to make the answers fit the Bible. When one abandons the sanctity of Scripture and allows for the possibility of changing Scripture, he has no objective religious guide by which to check himself. When we discuss Wierwille's theology, we will see how he arbitrarily changes the plain meanings of many biblical verses to suit his own ideas.

The cult leader is also unwilling to learn from recognized

Christian leaders. He rapidly evolves to the point of feeling that any outside counsel is worthless. Wierwille felt so strongly that many biblical teachers and scholars were useless that he threw away over 3000 books from his biblical library, preferring to trust his own interpretation and study of God's Word unchecked by any other authority.[10]

It is difficult to pin down the actual date of the founding of The Way International. Certainly Wierwille's teaching activities were forerunners of his present organization, and they began in 1942. In the mid-1940s, Wierwille's wife was allegedly miraculously healed of rheumatic fever, and this is pinpointed by Wierwille as the time his healing ministry began.[11]

Wierwille places great importance on the date in November of 1950 when, he says, "Stiles led me into the manifestation of speaking in tongues...and from that day in 1950 my life and ministry began to change very rapidly."[12] It was not long after that, in 1953, that Wierwille taught his first "Power for Abundant Living" course, the basic introduction to Way theology which is the best-known training tool of The Way today. The name "The Way International" was first used in 1958, and in that same time period the entire group and operations were moved to their present location in New Knoxville, Ohio. Wierwille resides at the 150-acre Way farm in New Knoxville, and conducts the majority of his teaching there.

The period from 1950 through 1958 is not discussed in detail by Wierwille or his followers, but we do know that during 1955 Dr. Wierwille and his family traveled to England and India. Evidently it was during that trip that Wierwille began to be openly opposed to institutionalized churches. In 1957, Wierwille said that he decided to resign from his pastorate in Van Wert, Ohio, in order to devote all of his attention to his teaching ministry.

Whether his resignation was motivated by his knowledge of an official Evangelical and Reformed denomination investigation of his ministry is unknown. We do know, however, "that a committee had been appointed prior to this meeting and they were prepared to come in with a recommendation that he be removed from the ministerial roles of the Church. . . .I do recall merely from hearsay that he had been on a tour of some of the mission stations of our church and came back and was quite critical of them and sought to undermine them."[13]

Whenever we date the founding of the Way International, we know that it was a relatively small and insignificant group until the early seventies, when it grew tremendously through recruiting of young people from the Jesus movement.[14]

THE WAY TODAY

The Way Biblical Research Center is located on 150 acres of farmland near New Knoxville, Ohio. There are dozens of permanent housing units where Dr. Wierwille's close followers live. Dr. Wierwille and his family make their home on the farm, too. The Way owns other property throughout the United States, including two schools where their followers are taught the Word according to Wierwille.

The two schools were bought from other churches. One, The Way College of Emporia, Kansas, was formerly a Presbyterian college, while the other was a former Roman Catholic health spa in Rome City, Indiana.

Although membership figures are not made public by the cult, 1977 figures could be as high as 50,000 active members, most of whom have taken the *Power for Abundant Living* course. Missionairies of The Way are said to be in all 50 states and 51 foreign countries.[15] The almost–phenomenal recent growth of the group is due, in part, to the zealous proselytizing by active Way missionaries (called WOW ambassadors—"The Word Over the World"). An example of this fierce evangelism was reported in a Way publication.

One day last fall, when the sun rose on Wake County, North Carolina, there was more light than the folks of that area had seen in their lifetime as a new outreach of God's Word began.

In 13 weeks, 9945 families were introduced to the Biblical research and teaching books published by The Way International! Of this total, 5856 families took advantage of the opportunity and listened to a 20-minute presentation of the books, oriented toward God's Word. 2223 of these families purchased books and now have keys to abundant living from the accuracy and integrity of God's Word in their homes for regular study. As a result of follow-up work several persons took the foundational class on Power for Abundant Living. Many more attended Twig fellowships and public explanation meetings. Nine salespeople from The Way International's new Marketing Department, coordinated by Jerry Jacks, accomplished this witnessing feat in 91 days.[16]

As we discussed in Chapter 1, the missionary zeal of the cults is tremendous, and the missionary activities of The Way are no exception.

ORGANIZATIONAL STRUCTURE

Wierwille has organized his group around the symbol of a tree. The Way functions like a tree, with roots, trunk, branches, limbs, twigs, and leaves. With the authoritarian attitude prevalent in the cults, the first authority in The Way is Victor Paul Wierwille himself, who is called, with his associates, the "roots" of the Way "tree." The "trunk" is a conglomeration of national organizations. "Branches" are statewide units, and "limbs" are the city units. Each city unit, or limb, is divided into smaller "twigs," which are home Bible-study groups. The smallest units on The Way tree are the individual members themselves, who are referred to as "leaves."[17]

Although Wierwille declares that The Way is not a church, religious sect, or Protestant denomination, The

Way has over 60 ordained ministers, some of whom are women. Wierwille's aversion to organized religion and his assumption that only in The Way is religious truth to be found is evident in the following quote:

> The Way International is a biblical research and teaching organization concerned with setting before men and women of all ages the inherent accuracy of the Word of God (the Bible) so that everyone who so desires may know the power of God in his life. The Way is not a church, nor is it a denomination or a religious sect of any sort. Its followers are people of every culture and ethnic background who all their lives have hungered for purpose, for meaning, for answers to life's enigmas, and for the power that would lead them into the fulness of Christ's promise: "I am come that ye might have life, and that ye might have it more abundantly" (John 10:10).[18]

In addition to familiar missionary fields, The Way conducts an extensive missionary program in prisons and schools.[19]

Within the missionary program of The Way are two types of missionaries. The full-time missionaries work for a full year setting up *Power for Abundant Living* courses throughout the world. They are only allowed to work part-time to support themselves and are called WOW Ambassadors (Word Over the World Ambassadors). This title expresses the ultimate goal of The Way: to overcome the world with its unique message. In 1975, there were 2077 WOW Ambassadors, and that number has grown by the hundreds each year since then.[20] The other missionaries for The Way are high school and college students who work for The Way as missionaries during school breaks and summer vacations.[21]

The annual convention of the cult is called the *Rock of Ages* and was attended by 12,000 people in 1976. Each participant at the convention was called a "Christ."[22]

The publishing arm of The Way is called the American

Christian Press and is also in New Knoxville, Ohio. The American Christian Press publishes and distributes Dr. Wierwille's seven books: *Jesus Christ Is Not God; Power for Abundant Living; Receiving the Holy Spirit Today; The Bible Tells Me So; The Word's Way; The New Dynamic Church;* and *God's Magnified Word.*[23] In addition to the books published here, the Press also publishes an assortment of small doctrinal and evangelistic booklets and pamphlets as well as a colorful periodical, *The Way Magazine.*

THE WAY DOCTRINE

As we discuss the beliefs of each of the cults in this book, we will present those beliefs from their sources and then examine those beliefs in the light of what the Christian church believes and teaches. We will be discussing three main areas of belief: God, man, and salvation. As a prelude to these three areas, we will discuss each cult's belief about the Bible.

The Bible

Although The Way and its leader, Victor Paul Wierwille, say that they accept the Bible as God's Word, we find from our investigation that they have a very different view of the Bible and its contents from that of most Christian Bible scholars.

In contradiction of most responsible scholarship, Dr. Wierwille asserts that the New Testament was originally written in Aramaic, a language which is somewhat related to Hebrew but very different from the Greek language in which the New Testament was actually written.[24]

Responsible scholarship recognizes that Wierwille's assertion is without adequate support. In a letter to Christian Research Institute, Dr. Edwin Yamauchi, an expert in Mediterranean Studies and Ancient Languages, discounted Wierwille's assertion concerning the New Testament. Dr. Yamauchi is a specialist in Mandaic, an eastern Aramaic dialect, and is the author of *Mandaic Incantation Texts*.[25] In his lengthy letter, Dr. Yamauchi commented extensively on the assertions of George M. Lamsa, an Aramaic man whose translation of the New Testament from Aramaic is used by Wierwille, and who taught Aramaic for The Way.[26] Dr. Yamauchi wrote:

As many laymen have heard, the Old Testament was written in Hebrew, with the exception of a few passages in Ezra and Daniel written in Aramaic, and the New Testament was written in Greek. Most are probably aware that Jesus spoke Aramaic, a Semitic language which is kindred to Hebrew. . . .

In the light of the claims advanced by Lamsa for Syriac, it should be underlined that Syriac is an eastern and not a western dialect of Aramaic,[27] and indeed that it is "a form of Aramaic that emerges toward the beginning of the third century A.D." (Fitzmyer, *The Languages and Palestine. . .*, p. 525 (cf. fn. 1). Cf. A Jeffery, "Aramaic," *The Interpreter's Dictionary of the Bible I* (New York: Abingdon Press, 1962), p. 189; C. F. Pfeiffer, ed., *The Biblical World* (Grand Rapids: Baker Book House, 1966), p. 56; C. Brockelmann, *Syrische Grammatik* (Leipzig: *Verlag Enzyklopadie,* 1962). As such it is one of the least suitable of the Aramaic dialects to use for a reconstruction of the Jewish Palestinian Aramaic used by Jesus. . . .

Lamsa's contention that the Septuagint "was never officially read by the Jews in Palestine who spoke Aramaic and read Hebrew" (Lamsa, p. ix.) is flatly contradicted by the discovery of Septuagint fragments at Qumran and the quotations from the Septuagint in the New Testament, which are even more numerous than quotations from the Masoretic type texts. The suggestion of Lamsa that one can revise the Old Testament text on the basis of the ambiguities in either the consonants or vocalization of the Syriac Peshitta text is pure fantasy (*Ibid.*, pp. xiv-xvi.). . . .In contrast to Lamsa, who minimizes the dialectical differences between late, eastern Syriac and early, western Aramaic, Fitzmyer warns us: "We should be suspicious of philological arguments about the

Aramaic substratum when they depend on texts and dialects of Aramaic that come from a later date (e.g., from the third century A.D. or later), precisely because a new phase of the language begins about that time with clear geographical distinctions (J.A. Fitzmyer, review of M. Black, *An Aramaic Approach to the Gospels and Acts,* in *The Catholic Biblical Quarterly, XXX* [1968], 419).

Yamauchi's argument is two-pronged. He is first asserting that the New Testament was written in Greek, not Aramaic, and that the Jews of Jesus' time were familiar with Greek. Second, he is arguing that whether the New Testament was written in Aramaic or not (which, he states, it was not), Lamsa is in no position to argue from the Aramaic of eastern Syria, since that form of Aramaic was not known at the time of Christ and in fact did not develop until the beginning of the third century A.D. Too, Yamauchi points out, eastern Syriac Aramaic has some significant differences between it and early Palestinian Aramaic which make it impossible to pose philological arguments based on similarities.

In addition to a wrong conception of the original form of the New Testament, Wierwille does not have a proper understanding of the science of biblical hermeneutics—that is, understanding a passage in its context and taking into consideration its language, grammar, historical setting, and relation to other passages. We shall review Wierwille's method of hermeneutics to understand how he arrives at the faulty theology he claims is biblical.

To understand the Bible the Wierwille way, one must remember, according to him, that the Gospels (Matthew, Mark, Luke, and John) are actually supposed to be in the Old Testament. Wierwille says that the New Testament begins with the Book of Acts.

The records in the Gospels are addressed at times to Israel and at other times to the Gentiles, but never to the Church of God. One of the greatest errors in the translation of the Bible was placing the four Gospels in the New Testament. The Gospels logically belong in the Old Testament.[28]

Although Wierwille says that one must correctly handle his interpretation of the Bible, and must be sure that his interpretation is in harmony with the context of the Scriptures, we find that in trying to prove his doctrines, he breaks the very hermeneutical rules he sets down! He seems to be trying to both appease accepted scholarship methods and at the same time search for some sort of biblical support for his doctrines, even if that means ignoring the rules of interpretation. So that we can be sure that Wierwille understands some of the basics of interpretation, let us allow him to speak for himself:

> Truth is truth; it is "thus saith the Lord." What we think does not make any difference. The reason we have opinions is that we do not "rightly divide" The Word. If the Word of God is rightly divided, we have the true Word; when it is wrongly divided, we have error. When we wrongly divide The Word we are working for Satan. . . .[29]

> Anyone can take the Word of God and make it mean exactly what he wants by taking it out of its context or by adding to it or by deleting certain words. . . .

> A person can prove anything from the Bible by isolating a text or by changing it around. Anyone can substantiate a theological viewpoint by manipulating Scripture.[30]

Wierwille manipulates Scripture. Throughout his writings, we find inconsistent interpretation methods. Usually Wierwille quotes directly from the King James Version of the Bible. But, if this disagrees with what Dr. Wierwille believes, he often adds words to it in brackets. If he cannot stretch his brackets to fit the King James, he looks to his own interpretation of the Greek text for support. If he cannot find manufactured support in the Greek, he tries to find it in the Aramaic (Lamsa's Aramaic Version).

What happens when the King James, Greek, and Aramaic

refuse to fit Wierwille's theology? He retreats to biblical and church history in an effort to show that history has preserved what he terms the original meaning, although *all* texts of the Scriptures have evidently "lost" it! His treatment of history is no better than his treatment of language and Scripture.[31]

The Trinity

The Way and Victor Paul Wierwille do not believe in the Christian and biblical doctrine of the Trinity. In fact, they believe that the doctrine of the Trinity is from pagan religious sources and was never thought of in Christian or Jewish contexts. In this argument, Wierwille commits the fallacy of guilt by association. He asserts that since some pagan cultures had a trinity of sorts, any concept of trinity must, by association, be pagan itself.

> Long before the founding of Christianity the idea of a triune god or a god-in-three-persons was a common belief in ancient religions. Although many of these religions had many minor deities, they distinctly acknowledged that there was one supreme God who consisted of three persons or essences. The Babylonians used an equilateral triangle to represent this three-in-one god now the symbol of the modern three-in-one believers.[32]

Wierwille has wrongly assumed that the Christian Trinity is just like so-called pagan trinities and that both ideas came from the same source. In order to find out if the doctrine of the Trinity is true, we do not look to see if it resembles paganism, but to the Bible, to see if God teaches it in His Word. Pagans also believe in the concept of God. Does that mean that God must not be true? Pagans sleep. Does that mean that sleeping is wrong? We must not dismiss an idea merely because it is held in common with those of whom we may not approve.

Secondly, Wierwille has not presented the issue fairly regarding the types of trinities believed in by pagan cultures.

Although many pagan beliefs included belief in a triad or unity of gods, we know of no pagan belief in God which is actually analogous to the Christian Trinity. Many other religions believe in a plurality of gods, three of whom may be the chief gods. Other religions believe in a Father God, Mother God, and Son God. Still other religions believe that one God has three main attributes, aspects, or forms which are sometimes referred to as different gods, or given different names.

However, it is only in Christianity that we have the unique revelation of God as Trinity. By Trinity, we mean that within the nature of the one eternal God (Isaiah 43:10), there are three eternal, distinct Persons (Luke 3:21,22): the Father (2 Peter 1:17), the Son (John 1:1,14), and the Holy Spirit (Acts 5:3,4). These three Persons are the one God (Matthew 28:19). Christianity does not teach a plurality of Gods; the Bible informs us that there is only one God, has always been only one God, and always will be only one God (Isaiah 43:10; 45:22). However, the Scriptures just as clearly declare that this one God exists in three eternal Persons: the Father, the Son, and the Holy Spirit. We do not confound or confuse the Persons. The Father is not the Son, the Son is not the Holy Spirit, and the Holy Spirit is not the Father. However, each of the Persons shares equally in the one divine nature.

The Bible does not ask us to thoroughly comprehend all that it reveals. It only asks us to *believe* what it has revealed. We do not understand how our corruptible bodies will be resurrected into incorruptible bodies at the resurrection. Paul tried to give us a picture of this by telling us about how a seed becomes a plant (1 Corinthians 15:35-49), but we still do not know exactly how or why the resurrection will take place. However, we know from evidence that we can believe the Bible. The Bible tells us that our bodies will be resurrected and we believe it because the Bible says it, and we know we can trust the Bible.

In the same way, we do not understand how God can be one and exist in three Persons. We know that it is not illogical, but is instead simply beyond the realm of our understanding as to *how* God exists in this way. We must simply take the words of Scripture, understand what we can, believe all of it, and present it as accurately as we can. Too often cultists err in their doctrines because they try to make every doctrine completely humanly comprehensible. We must never forget that God has declared, ". . .my thoughts are not your thoughts, neither are your ways my ways. . . .As the heavens are higher than the earth, so are my ways higher than your ways and my thoughts than your thoughts" (Isaiah 55:8,9). God has given us intellect and reasoning ability. But we must also remember that we are finite and corruptible. We cannot know everything now as we will know it then. We must allow God to speak for Himself, and we must believe what He tells us about Himself. We will discuss more about the Trinity as we discuss the doctrines of The Way concerning Jesus and the Holy Spirit.

The "trinities" propagated by other religions are not like the Christian Trinity at all, and thus they cannot be compared with the Trinity on the level Wierwille compares them. He must address himself to the texts in the Scriptures which speak on the subject of the nature of God. We will examine that area in the following section.

Wierwille rejects the Trinity for several reasons. First, he does not believe that Jesus Christ is God in human form. In fact, he has written an entire book on the subject, *Jesus Christ Is Not God*. In addition, Wierwille does not believe that the Holy Spirit is a Person separate from the Father. In a twist to the unitarian position on the Godhead, Wierwille distinguishes between the Holy Spirit and the holy spirit! The Holy Spirit is the same in person as the Father, and is merely another name for the Father. The holy spirit is that immaterial power which God the Father makes available to those who wish to become Christians. It is not personal and is, of course, not God. In this point he agrees with Jehovah's Witnesses.

The Bible, which is God's revealed Word and will, does not once mention the word "trinity," although biblically there are three: (1) God, who is Holy Spirit, the Father of our Lord Jesus Christ, (2) Jesus Christ, the Son of God, and the son of man, and (3) the holy spirit, God's gift, which God made available on the day of Pentecost.[33]

The gift from The Holy Spirit, the Giver, is *pneuma hagion,* holy spirit, power from on high, spiritual abilities, enablements. This power is spirit in contrast to the sense. Spirit is holy as opposed to the flesh, which is called by God unholy. God is Holy Spirit and God can only give that which He is; therefore, the gift from the Giver is of necessity holy and spirit.[34]

We will discuss both the deity of Christ and the deity and personality of the Holy Spirit separately below.

The Nature of God

As well as rejecting the doctrine of the Trinity, Wierwille has also erred in his assessment of other attributes of God. For example, Wierwille believes that whatever God is able to do, He is willing to do. Stated another way, if God does not do something, he must be neither willing nor able to do it.

One more great truth is that God's ability always equals God's willingness. Many people say that God is willing, but he is not able; others say He is able, but not willing. This may be true of men, but not of God. A man may have the ability and lack the willingness, or have the willingness and lack the ability. For instance, let's say I am stranded along the highway with a flat tire and need a jack. You come along that highway, stop and say, "Hello, what can I do for you?" And I say, "Well, I need a jack"; but you do not have a jack either. You are willing to help me, but you lack the ability. On the other hand, let's say you would come along the highway and you do have a jack, but you will not let me use it; then you have the ability, but you lack the willingness. This is never true with God. God's ability always equals His willingness—they are always harmonious. What God is able to do, He is willing to do; and what He is willing to do, He is able to do.[35]

Luke 1:37 stands in stark contrast to Wierwille's false assumption: "For nothing is impossible with God." The Bible declares clearly that God is all-powerful, meaning that within God resides all power: He is capable of whatever may be accomplished.[36]

Within the world of the cults, we often find that a cult leader's theology is contradictory. A theology of human origin is very difficult to keep free from error. So it is that we find Wierwille seeming to contradict himself by declaring that man's strength of belief can stop God's actions. If man's belief can stop God's actions, does this mean that God is no longer *willing* to take that action, according to Wierwille's system? This seems to be the case, and yet Wierwille has created problems for himself in introducing this new factor to limit God's power. Let us see an example of man limiting God.

God's actions are limited by man's believing. And Mary the mother of Jesus was the first woman who believed to the extent that God could create soul-life in her so that she could bring forth God's only-begotten Son. . . .[37]

Was God willing to have His Son born before Mary "believed" enough? If He was willing, then why wasn't Jesus born earlier, if God performs whatever He is willing to do? And if He was not willing, then why was he *ever* willing? What made Him willing? What made Him able? What made Mary believing enough? What was the final agent in the conception of Jesus? Wierwille is not able to answer these questions logically with his personal modifications of God's nature.

Scripture shows us clearly that God was quite able to do

some things which He never actually did. An example of this occurs in Luke 3:8:

> . . .And do not begin to say to yourselves, "We have Abraham as our father." For I tell you that out of these stones God can raise up children for Abraham.

Whether this passage is hyperbolic or not, we still see that God has the ability to do something that He chose not to do.

Christ

As one investigates the beliefs of The Way, he is immediately struck with the most obvious difference in belief between Christianity and The Way. The Way does not believe that Jesus Christ is true deity. By this one position, Wierwille and his followers have separated themselves from biblical truth and have aligned themselves with cultic doctrine. Ultimately, all cults deny in some way the absolute deity of Christ. The Way is no exception.

In his book entitled *Jesus Christ Is Not God,* Wierwille tries to defend his unitarian (one-Person-is-God) doctrine. Wierwille even tries to assert that the Gospel of John was written expressly to disprove the idea that Jesus is God: ". . .The Gospel of John established the truth of God's Word that Jesus Christ was the Son of God, not "God the Son" or 'God Himself.' "[38] We will analyze the Gospel of John in our general discussion of the deity of Christ, following our review of Wierwille's position on the nature of the Son. We should note, however, that the Gospel of John, perhaps more than any other book in the New Testament, clearly and repeatedly asserts the unqualified divinity of Christ.

Wierwille very clearly states his teaching on Christ's lack of deity:

> Those who teach that Jesus Christ is God and God is Jesus Christ will never stand approved in "rightly dividing" God's Word, for there is only one God, and "thou shalt have no

other gods." The Bible clearly teaches that Jesus Christ was a man conceived by the Holy Spirit, God, whose life was without blemish and without spot, a lamb from the flock, thereby being the perfect sacrifice. Thus he became our redeemer.[39]

As we shall discuss in more depth below, Wierwille (as with most cultists) misunderstands the doctrine of the Trinity. We agree that there is only one true God. The Bible repeatedly affirms this. However, the Bible also affirms that the one true God eternally exists in three distinct Persons—the Father, the Son (or Word), and the Holy Spirit. These three Persons are the one God. Christians do not believe in three gods; we believe in *one* God in three Persons. We are not contradicting ourselves when we assert that fact. To contradict ourselves, we would have to assert that we believe in one god and three gods; or else one Person and three Persons. However, we believe in one God subsisting as three Persons.

Dr. Wierwille's twisted logic manipulates the Scriptures in order to allow him to deny the deity of Christ. He postulates that since Jesus is called the Son of God 50 times in the New Testament and God only four times,* He must be the Son of God and not God the Son. The game, for Wierwille, is ended with a score of 50 to 4!

> . . .we note that Jesus Christ is directly referred to as the "Son of God" in more than 50 verses in the New Testament; he is called "God" in four. (Never is he called "God the Son.") By sheer weight of this evidence alone, 50 to 4, the truth should be evident.[40]

We did not exist before the world began. Neither did Jesus Christ. However, in God's foreknowledge, redemption was a reality since God foreknew that the deeds of Adam would be followed by the accomplishments of Jesus Christ. Jesus Christ was with God (in His foreknowledge) before the foun-

---

* The truth of the matter is that the deity of Christ is asserted many, many times throughout the New Testament (not just four times, as Wierwille claims).

dation of the world. Jesus Christ did not exist. This dissimilarity alone proves that God the Son and the Son of God are not an identity.[41]

Note that in the above quotes Wierwille has cleverly built himself an escape for any verse produced to assert the deity of Christ. If we show him a verse that seems to clearly show that Jesus Christ existed eternally, he will merely say that God the Father *foreknew* Him eternally. If he is unable to use that ruse, he can always say that, even if the text *seems to say* that Jesus is God, it is outweighed by the 50 verses which say he is the *Son of God* (a term which only Wierwille and other antitrinitarians consider incompatible with Christ's deity). Wierwille has built a tautalogical argument—an illogical premise which no amount of evidence can ever possibly change.

In responsible scholarship, instead of making unwarranted presuppositions (as Wierwille has), one looks openly and objectively at all the evidence, and does not say more than the evidence warrants. In addition, responsible scholarship takes all alternatives into account, not presuming that one's own persuasion is necessarily correct. Wierwille has failed the test of responsible scholarship by his faulty logic, and we shall soon see that he has also failed the test of the Scriptures. Jesus *is* God the Son, and the Scriptures clearly teach this fact.

The Biblical Doctrine of Christ

We must look to the Bible to find out the true nature of Jesus Christ. Does the Bible teach that there is a Person called the Son who is distinct in Person from the Father and the Holy Spirit and yet the same in essence or nature—in other words, who is truly God?

If we can show that Jesus is God, then we know that by necessity He had no beginning, although Wierwille says that Jesus' beginning was His birth.[42] We shall see that the Bible declares Christ to be as eternal as the Father and the Holy

Spirit, although distinct from them in Person.

First, is Jesus a Person distinct from the Father and the Holy Spirit? The New Testament abounds with verses showing a subject-object relationship between the Father and the Son, as in John 17, where Jesus is praying to the Father, showing this distinction in Person while affirming their essential unity: "Father, the time has come. Glorify your Son, that your Son may glorify you. For you granted him authority over all people that he might give eternal life to all those you have given him. . . .And now, Father, glorify me in your presence with the glory I had with you before the world began" (John 17:1b,2,5). Jesus is a Person distinct from the Father.

The Gospel of John also provides us with a verse showing the clear distinction in Person between the Son and the Holy Spirit, while affirming their essential unity. John 14:16,17a says, "And I will ask the Father, and he will give you another Counselor to be with you forever—the Spirit of truth." Although Jesus calls the Holy Spirit another Counselor, making a distinction between Himself and the Spirit, He uses a word in the Greek for "another" *(allos)* which implies that the two are *of the same nature*—in other words, another *of the same kind.* We can see here that Jesus and the Holy Spirit are Persons (Counselors) and are of the same nature, but are nevertheless distinct from each other as Persons.

Second, does the New Testament teach that Jesus is God in nature? Is He of the same essence as the Father? Does the Bible state that Jesus is God? We must digress for a moment to comment on Wierwille's strange method of determining doctrine—his "doctrinal scoreboard." If Jesus does have the nature of God—if He is God—then it does not matter how many times He is called other titles—He is still God. If the Bible clearly calls Jesus God only once, that settles the issue. God does not have to repeat Himself; His Word is perfect and accurate. If God declares something once in His

Word, we are under just as much obligation to believe it as when he declares something ten times, or 30 times, or 100 times.

To see the weakness of Wierwille's reasoning, we need only examine the other titles of Jesus. Wierwille says Jesus is not God because he is called the Son 50 times and God four times. Now let us try Wierwille's technique on some other titles of Jesus. He is called the Son of David 16 times and the Son of Man 88 times. If Wierwille is right in claiming that Jesus is what He is called the most, then Jesus is no longer the Son of David (50 to 16) and not even the Son of God (88 to 50), but only the Son of Man! Obviously, Wierwille's reasoning is empty.

Now let us address the question of the deity of Christ. When we speak of the deity of Christ, we speak of the eternal existence of the second Person of the Trinity, variously called the Word, the Son, etc. This Person has all the nature and attributes of deity. He is just as much God as the Father and the Holy Spirit. He has never ceased being God and will always be God. However, at a point in time the eternal Word assumed a nature in addition to His divine nature—namely, the nature of a man. He became man (John 1:14) and assumed all the nature and attributes of unfallen humanity without ceasing to be truly God. He was, however, only one Person—a divine Person with two natures, that of God and that of man. Although the Person and the divine nature exist eternally, the human nature began at a certain point in the womb of the virgin and was subject to time in the sense that it grew to human maturity and eventually died (by crucifixion). However, Christ's body has been glorified and resurrected and is no longer susceptible to corruption. He has an immortal, resurrected body. The second Person of the Trinity, the divine Logos (Word), possesses two distinct but united natures, the divine and the human, forever. We shall see the Scriptures concerning this as we progress in our discussion of the deity of

Christ.

John 1:1: In the beginning was the Word, and the Word was with God, and the Word was God.

Contrary to Wierwille's belief that the Gospel of John denies the deity of Christ, we find that this Gospel begins with an affirmation of Christ's deity. The Word (Jesus—v. 14) is expressly declared to be God. Wierwille has two ways of denying the clear wording of John 1:1. First, he argues that the Word only existed in God's foreknowledge ("was with God"). Second, he claims that the first use of the term "Word" refers to God, the second use of the term to Jesus, and the third use of the term again to God ("the Word was God"). He says,

> In the beginning was the Word (God), and the (revealed) Word was with *(pros)*† God (with Him in his foreknowledge, yet independent of Him), and the Word was God.[43]

There is no grammatical, exegetical, contextual, or reasonable purpose for interposing 12 new words into the original verse of 17 words. Wierwille has simply fabricated his theory: the words are not there either implicitly or explicitly. If this verse was supposed to be speaking of Jesus Christ as the Logos (Word) merely in God's foreknowledge, or thought, then why didn't John write, "In the beginning was God, and the thought was with God, and God was God"? John did not write it that way because that is not what Scripture teaches. John 1:14 clearly tells us who the Word is—Jesus Christ Himself:

> And the Word became flesh and lived for a while among us. We have seen his glory, the glory of the one and only Son, who came from the Father, full of grace and truth

John 1:1 is one of the clear verses in the New Testament expressing the absolute deity of Christ. The construction is very clear and has been discussed by many of the world's great Greek and Bible scholars. We might paraphrase the

---

† Greek for "face to face" or "with."

verse something like the following: "Before anything came into existence, the Word was already in existence. He enjoyed a close relationship to God, and what God was, the Word was."

The last clause of the verse is of special importance to us: "the Word was God." In Greek, this is often referred to as a qualitative anarthrous predicate nominative construction. In other words, the word for God in the Greek, *theos,* is a predicate nominative, a noun which describes for us the subject of the passage, which is the Word. *Theos* is anarthrous in the Greek, meaning that it occurs with no article. Because of this and its location in the clause (before the verb in the Greek), it becomes qualitative. That is, it describes a quality about the subject of the passage, the Word. Therefore we find from this clause that the Word (described as the Son of God in verse 14) has all of the qualities, or nature, or attributes, of God. Since we know that there is only One who is God (Isaiah 44:6; 45:21-23; John 17:3; 1 Timothy 2:5; etc.), we know that One who has the nature of God must be God. Therefore, John 1:1 clearly tells us that Jesus is God.

John 5:18: For this reason the Jews tried all the harder to kill him; not only was he breaking the Sabbath, but he was even calling God his own Father, making himself equal with God.

In John 5:18 we find an interesting incident in Jesus' life. The Jews were upset because Jesus was doing miracles on the Sabbath day, actions which they believed were breaking the command to do no work on the Sabbath. If that were not bad enough, they became enraged when Jesus gave them the reason for His actions. He claimed to be able to "loose" the commands on the Sabbath because of his unique relationship with God the Father. The phrase "his own father" could be translated better as "his own unique father," with the "unique" relating to the equality of nature that He and His Father shared. The word translated "breaking" or "loosing" literally means to lift the restriction of the Sabbath. Since the Sabbath restrictions were instituted by God, only God could lift those restrictions. Jesus claimed that authority, verse 18 says, and even more than that, He claimed that authority because of his unique relationship with the Father. The Jews understood immediately the connotation of Jesus' statement, and sought to kill Him for blasphemy. They reasoned, how could He be claiming to be God when He is a man? This same thought is echoed in John 10:33, where Jesus was in danger of being stoned by the Jews because He asserted His deity. John tells us in 5:18 that Jesus' loosing of the Sabbath restrictions and His claiming such a unique relationship with the Father showed His essential equality with the Father. Again, John is asserting the fact that Jesus Christ is God.

John 8:58,59: "I tell you the truth," Jesus answered, "before Abraham was born, I am!" At this, they picked up stones to stone him, but Jesus hid himself, slipping away from the temple grounds.

In this passage, Jesus claimed to be God by referring to one of God's titles in the Old Testament and claiming that title for Himself. He was debating with the Jews concerning His messianic claims. The Jews taunted him, referring to His youth, as though He were presumptuous in declaring that He was greater than Abraham and that Abraham had rejoiced over Him. They challenged Jesus to identify Himself. He responded by calling Himself the "I Am," the divine name of God from Exodus 3:14 and numerous other passages in the Old Testament.

In Exodus 3, we find Moses talking with Jehovah concerning his mission to the Jews—to lead them out of bondage in Egypt. Moses was worried that the Jews would not listen to him.

> Moses said to God, "Suppose I go to the Israelites and say to them, 'The God of your fathers has sent me to you,' and they ask me, 'What is his name?' Then what shall I tell them?"

God said to Moses, "I am who I am. This is what you are
to say to the Israelites: I AM has sent me to you.' "[44]

In John 8:58, Jesus was claiming that same title for Himself.
He was declaring that He was eternal and was in fact the
eternal God, the God who had spoken to Moses so long ago,
the God of Abraham, Isaac, and Jacob. That the Jews
understood Jesus' claim is evident: in verse 59 they tried to
stone Him for blasphemy, as in John 5:18. John 8:58 states
emphatically that Jesus is God.

*John 20:28: Thomas said to him, "My Lord and my
God!"*

Of the many verses in the New Testament asserting the
deity of Christ, this verse is one of the easiest to understand.
The Apostle Thomas was not sure that Jesus had risen from
the dead. He had earlier declared to the other disciples,
"Unless I see the nail marks in his hands and put my finger
where the nails were, and put my hand into his side, I will
not believe it" (John 20:25). Jesus appeared the next week
to Thomas and the other disciples. He challenged Thomas
to touch Him and "stop doubting and believe." Thomas's
immediate response to the risen Lord occurs in verse 28, in
stark simplicity, as he calls Jesus "my Lord and my God!"

Thomas was a good Jew. He was monotheistic; he believed in only one true God. He knew what Christ had claimed
for Himself. He knew that the resurrection validated that
claim. He was faced with the evidence for the resurrection.
He could only acknowledge what he now knew to be true:
Jesus was his Lord and his God. Jesus approved of
Thomas's declaration, saying in verse 29, "Because you
have seen me, you have believed; blessed are those who have
not seen and yet have believed." Unless Thomas broke the
first commandment ("You shall have no other gods before
me"—Exodus 20:3), and Jesus approved of his breaking it,
we can be assured that Jesus is truly God, the God of the Bible, the God in whom we believe. Surely Dr. Wierwille is not
willing to say that an apostle committed blasphemy with

Jesus' blessings! John 20:28 clearly contradicts Wierwille's false view of Christ and establishes irrefutably the deity of Christ.

There are many other verses in the New Testament which establish that Jesus is God incarnate. We could discuss them for many pages.[45] However, as we said at the beginning of this section, God only has to declare something once for it to be true. We must believe what He has said in spite of our own presuppositions and our own man-made theology. The Bible asserts Christ's deity, and this we believe. Wierwille and The Way are wrong in asserting that Jesus is not God. This puts them outside the framework of Christianity and in the world of the cults.

The Virgin Birth

Victor Paul Wierwille and The Way deny the historic doctrine of the virgin birth of Jesus Christ. But even in this denial, their own position is contradictory. The first method they use to deny the virgin birth is by saying that Mary was impregnated in much the same way that a cow is impregnated by a bull. The second way they deny the virgin birth is by saying that Joseph had sexual relations with Mary from just after the conception of Jesus until and after his birth. Even if they taught that Jesus was conceived while Mary was a virgin (hardly possible with their "bull-cow" analogy), she could hardly have had a virgin *birth* if she had been having sexual relations with Joseph before then.

On the conception of Christ, Wierwille has this to say:

Luke 1:35: And the angel answered and said unto her, The Holy Ghost‡ shall come upon thee, and the power of the Highest shall overshadow thee: therefore also that Holy thing which shall be born of thee shall be called the Son of God.

The word "overshadow" means "to cover": "the power of the Highest shall cover thee." In the animal kingdom we speak of a bull covering a cow, meaning the sexual position

---

‡ Remember that for Wierwille the Holy Ghost is another name for the Father.

for conception. The same meaning is evident in human beings.[46]

This bears no relationship at all to the biblical doctrine of the conception of Christ. Instead, it almost reminds us of the old Mormon doctrine, § in which the god of the Mormons had sexual relations with Mary to produce Jesus!

On the contrary, the Bible says that Mary had no sexual relations with anyone—the Father, the Holy Ghost, or Joseph—before Jesus was born. Matthew 1:23 informs us that "a virgin shall be with child." Mary would hardly be a virgin if she were "covered" as a bull "covers" a cow!

On Joseph's relationship to Mary while she was pregnant, Wierwille says:

> If it said a virgin shall bring forth a son your Bible would fall to pieces. It says plainly that Mary was a virgin only at the time of conception, not at Jesus' birth; the theory of virgin birth has been a theological assumption and erroneous teaching. The Bible said in verse 20 that God told Joseph, "Take unto thee thy wife." When Joseph took her unto himself he lived with her as a husband lives with a wife. She was a virgin when she conceived by God, but when Joseph took her unto himself she was no longer a virgin. The divine conception made Mary no longer a virgin.[47]

When we examine the passage Wierwille was referring to (Matthew 1:18-25), we see that it refutes his contentions completely. First, Matthew 1:23 *does* say that a virgin shall bring forth a son. Let us examine the verse in detail:

> Behold, a virgin shall be with child and shall bring forth a son, and they shall call his name Emmanuel, which being interpreted is, God with us (KJV).

Wierwille is under the impression, perhaps, that the phrase "and shall bring forth a son" is not connected with the subject "a virgin." This would be the only way he could try to

---

§ The Mormons, however, say that God the Father has a body of flesh and bone.

say that the verse does not say a virgin shall bring forth a son. However, if "a virgin" is not the subject of the second phrase, then what is? The only possible antecedent is "a virgin," occurring in the immediate context. Grammatically, "a virgin" must be the subject of both "shall be with child" and "shall bring forth a son." The Bible *does* say that the virgin will bring forth a son, and that is exactly what Mary did.

Finally, perhaps Wierwille neglected to read the last verse of Matthew 1. Despite all of his invalid arguments to try to show that Joseph and Mary had sexual relations before Jesus was born, Matthew 1:25 directly contradicts Wierwille.

> And [Joseph] knew her not till she had brought forth her firstborn son; and he called his name Jesus.

The biblical precedent for the term "to know" one's spouse shows us that the term means to know in an intimate, sexual way. Matthew 1:25 makes it very plain that Joseph and Mary did not have any sexual relations until after the birth of Jesus Christ.

As we shall see below, Wierwille's belief concerning the virgin birth is only one of his strange teachings based on a confused understanding of the Bible. We find in our study of the cults that when a cult leader dismisses one portion of Scripture, or reinterprets it according to his own presuppositions, he is more than likely to dismiss or misconstrue a multitude of other passages also. Dr. J. Gresham Machen, a famous scholar and champion of the virgin birth and the inerrancy of the Bible, commented on the importance of the virgin birth:

> But the two elements of Christian truth belong logically together; the supernatural Person of our Lord belongs logically with His redemptive work; the virgin birth belongs logically with the Cross. Where one aspect is given up, the other will not logically remain; and where one is accepted, the

other will naturally be accepted, too. There may be halfway positions for a time, but they are in unstable equilibrium and will not long be maintained.[48]

In this same pattern of progression, Wierwille not only denies the biblical doctrine of the virgin birth, but he also denies the biblical crucifixion. We shall turn now to our analysis of Wierwille's beliefs concerning the crucifixion of Christ.

The Crucifixion

The Way is aggressive in its unbiblical assessment of the crucifixion of Jesus Christ. In clear terms, Wierwille asserts that Jesus could not be God and die for our sins on the cross. He says,

> To understand our redemption through Christ our passover, we must know that the perfect sacrifice had to be a man and not God. . . .
> The Word of God says that Jesus Christ was dead for 72 hours. How could Jesus Christ be God, for God cannot die? He is Alpha and Omega.[49]

We have already clearly answered Wierwille's disclaimer of Christ's deity. However, the question he raises concerning Jesus' death and deity is one often raised by cultists. How could Jesus be God and yet die? Does God die?

Of course God does not die, and yet Jesus did die, and He was and is God. The confusion experienced by Wierwille, the followers of The Way, and other cultists ☆ comes from two mistaken ideas concerning 1) the nature of the God-man, theologically known as the hypostatic union, and 2) the nature of death among men. Let us look at both concepts in the light of what the Bible actually teaches.

To understand Christ's incarnation, we must understand how God became flesh, as John 1:14 tells us. As we mentioned in our discussion of the deity of Christ, the eternal

---

☆ Jehovah's Witnesses, for example, use this same idea to question the deity of Christ.

Logos (Word) at a point in time assumed a nature *in addition to* His eternal divine nature; he assumed the nature of a perfect man. He became man and assumed all the nature and attributes of humanity, without ceasing to be truly God. He was, however, only one Person—a divine Person with two natures, that of God and that of man. Although the Person and the divine nature have existed eternally, the *human* nature and body began at a certain point and was subject to the limitations of time and space. On the cross the human body and human nature of Jesus died (became devoid of bios—physical, biological life). However, His divine *Person* endures eternally, having no ending or beginning. In fact, while Wierwille correctly ascribes the title "Alpha and Omega" to the Father as God, we find that Revelation 22:13 quotes *Jesus* as saying, "I am the Alpha and the Omega, the Beginning and the End."

God did not die on the cross: the human nature of the God-man ceased its biological functioning. Philippians 2:5-11 clearly explains the two natures in Christ, His death and resurrection, while maintaining His eternal deity:

This mind be constantly having in you. (This is the mind) which is also in Christ Jesus, who has always been and at present continues to subsist in that mode of being in which He gives outward expression of His essential nature, that of absolute deity, which expression comes from and is truly representative of His inner being (that of absolute deity), and who did not after weighing the facts, consider it a treasure to be clutched and retained at all hazards, this being on an equality with deity (in the expression of the divine essence), but himself He emptied, himself He made void, having taken the outward expression of a bondslave, which expression comes from and is truly representative of His nature (as deity), entering into a new state of existence, that of mankind. And being found to be in outward guise as man, He stooped very low, having become obedient (to God the Father) to the extent of death, even such a death as that upon a cross. Because of which voluntary act of supreme self-renunciation

God also supereminently exalted Him to the highest rank and power, and graciously bestowed upon Him the Name, the name which is above every name, in order that in recognition of the Name (all which the Lord Jesus is in His Person and work) which Jesus possesses, every knee should bow, of things in heaven, of things on earth, and of things under the earth, and in order that every tongue should plainly and openly agree to the fact that Jesus Christ is Lord, resulting in the glory of God the Father.[50]

The second problem which The Way has with the death of Christ is a result of The Way's misunderstanding of death itself. As with many other cultists, The Way members think that the dead are unconscious, or "asleep" or insentient. This dogma is often called "soul sleep"—a form of conditional immortality. Taking such verses as Ecclesiastes 9:5 and others out of context, The Way argues that the dead are, at best, unconscious. It is indeed ludicrous to conceive of an omnipotent God ruling the universe for three days in an unconscious state. However, both the Old and New Testaments teach clearly that the dead are conscious. Death is neither annihilation nor "sleep."#

In the same Book of Ecclesiastes we read: "Then shall the dust return to the earth as it was, and the spirit shall return unto God who gave it" (12:7 KJV). The verse misconstrued by The Way and other cults is referring to the appearance of a man's body after death, when it knows nothing and is no longer functioning biologically. Taken in context, we see that Ecclesiastes 3:20 refers to the outward appearance of death, while the very next verse, 21, refers to the state of the soul: "All go unto one place; all are of the dust, and all turn to dust again. Who knoweth the spirit of man that goeth upward, and the spirit of the beast that goeth downward to the earth?" (Ecclesiastes 3:20,21 KJV).

In 2 Corinthians 5:6-8 we find that the Christian leaves his

See a thorough discussion of soul sleep in *Kingdom of the Cults,* Appendix 1, pages 359-422.

body at death, and his spirit (or soul) remains conscious and comes into the presence of God. The verses read:

> Therefore we are always confident and know that as long as we are at home in the body we are away from the Lord. We live by faith, not by sight. We are confident, I say, and would prefer to be away from the body and at home with the Lord.

This clear teaching from Scripture is reiterated in Philippians 1:23, where Paul asserts that he is in a quandary, having a desire to die (which is to be present with the Lord) and a desire to stay in his body (to help his fellow Christians). He says, "I am torn between the two: I desire to depart and be with Christ, which is better by far; but it is more necessary for you that I remain in the body."

Clearly, Scripture strongly affirms the conscious existence of the soul or spirit of man after death.

An interesting deviation from the Gospel records concerning the crucifixion of Christ is Wierwille's assertion that four persons were crucified with Christ, rather than two, as is commonly held.

> According to the accurate Word of God, how many men were crucified with Jesus? Two malefactors plus two thieves makes four people. All the teaching that we have had saying Jesus was on the center cross with one culprit to the right and the other to the left is proven faulty. The reason we have believed this is that rather than reading The Word, we believed the paintings we have seen. When a person goes to the Word of God and sees the narrative development of Matthew and Luke on an identical situation, he sees very plainly that there were four crucified with Jesus.[51]

However, John 19:32,33 is very clear about the number of criminals crucified with Jesus. The New International Version reflects the force of the original well when it says, "The soldiers therefore came and broke the legs of the first man who had been crucified with Jesus, and then those of the other. But when they came to Jesus and found that he was already dead, they did not break his legs." The more traditional King James Version also supports the fact that only two men were crucified with Jesus. It says, "Then came the soldiers, and broke the legs of the first, and of the other which was crucified with him. But when they came to Jesus, and saw that he was dead already, they broke not his legs." No amount of linguistic manipulation on The Way's part alters the clear biblical fact that *two* people were crucified alongside Jesus.

The Holy Spirit

In addition to denying both the deity of Christ and the Trinity, Wierwille also denies the unique personality (and thus deity) of the Holy Spirit. Unlike most people who deny the personality of the Holy Spirit and confuse Him with the Person of the Father (such people are usually known as modalists), Wierwille does not have the same confusion of persons when it comes to the Son. In church history, a heresy prevalent in the third century known as modalism confused the personal distinctions among the Persons of the Trinity, and instead taught that the Father, Son, and Holy Spirit were merely different "modes" or manifestations of the one Person of God.**

However, Wierwille joins with the Jehovah's Witnesses in teaching a personal distinction between the Persons of the Father and the Son (although denying the deity of the Son) and yet confusing the Persons of the Father and the Holy Spirit. Jehovah's Witnesses confuse the Holy Spirit with the Father by claiming that the Holy Spirit is an "impersonal force" of the Father which is neither divine nor personal. ††
Wierwille incorrectly reasons that since the Father is both holy and spirit, He is called the Holy Spirit. Wierwille manufactures an additional "holy spirit" by declaring that the gift given to men by God is a "holy spirit" to replace

---

** See Appendix, "The Local Church of Witness Lee," for a thorough discussion of modalism.

†† See *Kingdom of the Cults, Jehovah of the Watchtower,* or *Rise of the Cults* for information on the beliefs of Jehovah's Witnesses.

man's spirit, which ceased at the fall.

The Giver is God, the Spirit. His gift is spirit. Failure to recognize the difference between the Giver and His gift has caused no end of confusion in the Holy Spirit field of study as well as in the understanding of the new birth. . . .

The gift is holy spirit, pneuma hagion, which is an inherent spiritual ability, dunamis, power from on high. This gift is "Christ in you, the hope of glory" with all its fullness.[52]

When we examine the New Testament usage of *pneuma hagion* (Holy Spirit), we see that when referring to God, the phrase becomes a specific title, a two-word title which cannot be broken and twisted as it is by The Way, and which refers specifically to the third Person of the Trinity. The Father is holy, and He is spirit (spiritual in nature), but that does not mean that the Father assumes the title *the Holy Spirit*, which is reserved for the third Person of the Trinity. While it is true that the words "Holy Spirit" in the Greek text often appear without the article "the," this does not mean that English translations should exclude the definite article. W.E. Vine, Greek scholar and author of the *Expository Dictionary of New Testament Words*, states:

The use or absence of the article in the original where the Holy Spirit is spoken of cannot always be decided by grammatical rules, nor can the presence or absence of the article alone determine whether the reference is to the Holy Spirit. Examples where the Person is meant when the article is absent are Matthew 22:43. . .Acts 4:25 R.V. (absent in some texts); 19:2,6; Rom. 14:17; I Cor. 2:4; Gal. 5:25 (twice); I Pet. 1:2. Sometimes the absence is to be accounted for by the fact that *Pneuma* (like *Theos*) is substantially a proper name, e.g., in John 7:39. As a general rule the article is present where the subject of the teaching is the Personality of the Holy Spirit, e.g., John 14:26, where He is spoken of in distinction from the Father and the Son. See also 15:26 and cp. Luke 3:22.[53]

There are numerous Scriptures which assert the personality of the Holy Spirit and His deity. The personality of the

Holy Spirit is clearly shown when He is directly quoted in such verses as Acts 13:2 and Hebrews 3:7ff. His distinction from the Persons of the Father and the Son are especially clear in Luke 3:21,22: "When all the people were being baptized, Jesus was baptized too. And as he was praying, heaven was opened and the Holy Spirit descended on him in bodily form like a dove. And a voice came from heaven: 'You are my Son, whom I love; with you I am well pleased.' " Matthew 28:19 reminds us to baptize in the name of the Father, and of the Son, and of the Holy Spirit. The deity of the Holy Spirit is affirmed in his being identified with Jehovah in such verses as Isaiah 6: 8-10 compared with Acts 28:25-27; Jeremiah 31:31-34 with Hebrews 10:15,16; and 2 Peter 1:20,21 with 2 Timothy 3:16. Acts 5:3,4 also identifies the Holy Spirit as God.

When we speak of the Trinity, we are speaking of three distinct Persons—the Father, the Son, and the Holy Spirit— all of whom are *one* God sharing *one* divine nature.

Mankind

In The Way theology, man is a very confusing conglomeration of body, soul, and spirit. According to Wierwille,[54] man was originally body (physical) and soul (breath or life) and spirit (that part of man that communicates with God). However, at the fall, man completely lost his "spirit" and reverted to no more than an animal with a body and soul (life).

Rather than teaching the orthodox belief, taught in the Bible, that man's spirit (or immaterial part) is fallen and corrupt, but still functioning, Wierwille says:

> The spirit disappeared. The reason the spirit was called dead is that it was no longer there. Their entire spiritual connection with God was lost. From that very day Adam and Eve were just body and soul—as any other animal.[55]

What does dead mean? Man appeared to be lively. He had body and soul, but was dead in trespasses and sins because he had no spirit. . . . Man is conceived and born in sin because he has no spirit.[56]

This absence of spirit, Wierwille says, continued right up until the Day of Pentecost, when God gave the "gift" of "holy spirit" to the believers. As we have already seen, Wierwille denies what the Bible teaches about the Holy Spirit.

He also denies the Bible's teaching that man has always had a spirit, which is either corrupt and in sin or else in right relationship to God through belief in God's ultimate gift, Jesus Christ. Several verses in both the Old Testament and the New Testament assert the existence of man's spirit, and his unique standing apart from the animals. Job 32:8 says, "But it is the spirit in a man, the breath of the Almighty, that gives him understanding." Psalm 32:2 declares, "Blessed is the man whose sin the Lord does not count against him and in whose spirit is no deceit." Ecclesiastes 12:7 refers to death: ". . .and the dust returns to the ground it came from, and the spirit returns to God who gave it."‡‡ Mary, the mother of Jesus, declared in Luke 1:47, ". . .my spirit rejoices in God my Savior. . . ." Man's spirit could be responsive to God long before the Day of Pentecost, and the above verses make it clear that man did indeed have a spirit quite distinct in nature from that of the animals (see Ecclesiastes 3:21).

Wierwille has also failed to deal adequately with John 20:21,22: "Again Jesus said, 'Peace be with you! As the Father has sent me, I am sending you.' And with that he breathed on them and said, 'Receive the Holy Spirit.' " If the "holy spirit" referred to here is the "gift" from God to man, to replace the spirit he "lost" in the fall, as Wierwille says, then how is Wierwille to deal with the fact that Jesus gave the disciples "holy spirit" *before* the Day of Pentecost?

‡‡For a discussion of the Hebrew words and their meanings, see R. Laird Harris, *Man: God's Eternal Creation* (Chicago: Moody Press, 1971), pages 8-15.

Wierwille's way with the doctrine of man is not the Bible's way, for it reveals an ignorance of biblical teaching on man and his relationship with God. It is not surprising, then, that Wierwille also denies that man is conscious after death, either in God's presence or in hell. As we discussed in our section on the two natures in Christ, Wierwille's teaching of "soul sleep" (the idea that man is "asleep" or effectively nonexistent at death) is fallacious and is contradicted by the Scriptures we discussed there.

Salvation

The Way teaches a salvation that is not biblical. One of the signs of cultism is the teaching that salvation requires human works in addition to God's grace. The Way teaches that salvation is guaranteed only by physical, vocal confession of faith and ultimately by speaking in tongues. Wierwille declares, ". . .now that person is going to change lordships when he confesses with his mouth a new Lord—Jesus Christ."[57] Concerning tongues, Wierwille states, ". . .the only visible and audible proof that a man has been born again and filled with the gift from the Holy Spirit is *always* that he speaks in a tongue or tongues."[58]

In addition to The Way's erroneous teaching on salvation itself, The Way teaches that a person can obtain a "spirit" from either God or Satan:

> The Word of God tells us that there are two spiritual fathers and, therefore, two possible sources for seed: God, the Father of our Lord and Savior Jesus Christ, and the devil, the god of this world. Thus a person can spiritually be born of either one of these two fathers.[59]

> It is possible for a man of body and soul to go through life and never be born again of either seed. A person does not always make a choice.[60]

Apparently, one can be a child of the devil, or a child of God, or an "orphan," so to speak. The fate of the "orphans" is unclear in The Way theology, but we have already seen that the hypothesis that man has no spirit and needs to obtain one from God (or the devil) is completely unbiblical.

Another problem with The Way theology concerning salvation is the teaching that one's spirit, after conversion to Christ, can never sin.

. . .Do we sin in the spirit? No. But in body and soul we fall.[61]

The Bible knows no such dichotomy between the body and soul or spirit. A person sins, and a person is responsible to God. Even as Christians, we sin in conscious acts against God.

Nowhere in the Bible do we find that man is lost and separated from God because he "lost" a part of his nature, i.e., his spirit. We find instead that man is separated from God because he deliberately corrupted a part of his nature through sin. It is *sin* which separates man and God; it is not the supposed "absence of man's spirit." Romans 3:23 reminds us that all men have sinned, and are thus away from God. Romans 6:23 asserts that man has a choice of coming to God and receiving eternal life, or of staying away from him and inheriting "death" (see also John 3:36). The Bible says that there is only one way to rid oneself of sin, and that is through the redemption of Christ:

He himself bore our sins in his body on the tree, so that we might die to sins and live for righteousness; by his wounds you have been healed.[62]

Jesus Christ desires us to come to Him for His freely given and all-sufficient grace (see Matthew 11:28-30 and John 3:16). Although no verbal confession is necessary for salvation (Ephesians 2:8-10), the mark of the believer is his public dedication to Christ (Romans 4:1-3,23-25). Tongues have more than one function in the New Testament (see 1 Corinthians 12 and 14; Acts 10; etc.), but none of these is to seal one's salvation. The gift of speaking in tongues is given to the person who is a believer already, and is for the edification of the believer and the church. It is not some badge of acceptance without which one has no assurance of salvation.

CONCLUSION

Members of The Way must be shown in love the true identity of the Lord Jesus (Titus 2:13) and urged to test Wierwille's claims and teachings by Scripture. Only in this way can they see Him who is "the way, the truth, and the life" and be freed from the bondage that now obscures the glorious light of the gospel of Christ.

CHAPTER NOTES

1. *Twenty-fifth Anniversary Souvenir Booklet* (New Knoxville, OH: The Way, Incorporated, 1967).

2. Ibid., pp. 6, 7, 9.

3. Elena Whiteside, *The Way: Living in Love* (New Knoxville, OH: American Christian Press, 1970), p. 175.

4. From a letter by James F. Armstrong, Registrar, Princeton Theological Seminary, dated July 13, 1976, on file at Christian Research Institute.

5. *Christianity Today* magazine, Nov. 21, 1975, pp. 19, 20.

6. *National Courier* magazine, Apr. 1, 1977, p. 4.

7. See Chapter 1.

8. *Twenty-fifth Anniversary Souvenir Booklet,* p. 10.

9. Ibid., p. 10.

10. Victor Paul Wierwille, *Power for Abundant Living* (New Knoxville, OH: American Christian Press, 1971), p. 120.

11. *Twenty-fifth Anniversary Souvenir Booklet,* p. 13.

12. Ibid., p. 12.

13. From a personal letter from Paul E. Rohrbaugh, former president of the Northwest Ohio Synod of the Evangelical and Reformed Church, letter dated Sept. 8, 1971.

14. See *Time* magazine, June 21, 1971, p. 62; and *Life* magazine, May 14, 1971, p. 78.

15. *National Courier* magazine, Apr. 1, 1977, p. 4.

16. *The Way* magazine, May 1976, p. 11.

17. *This Is the Way* (New Knoxville, OH), side 1.

18. Ibid., side 1.

19. Ibid., side 1.

20. *The Way* magazine, Nov./Dec. 1975, p. 26.

21. *The Way* magazine, July/Aug. 1976, p. 9.

22. *The Way* magazine, Nov./Dec. 1976, p. 20.

23. An eighth title by Wierwille, *Are the Dead Alive Now?* is published by the Devin-Adair Co., in Old Greenwich, CT.

24. *Twenty-fifth Anniversary Souvenir Booklet,* p. 17, and *Power for Abundant Living,* pp. 127-28.

25. American Oriental Society, New Haven, CT, 1967.

26. *Twenty-fifth Anniversary Souvenir Booklet,* p. 17.

27. Eastern Syriac Aramaic is the kind spoken by Lamsa and used by him in his New Testament studies.

28. *Power for Abundant Living,* pp. 207-11.

29. Wierwille, *The New Dynamic Church* (New Knoxville, OH: American Christian Press, 1971), pp. 190-91.

30. *Power for Abundant Living,* p. 118.

31. See, for example, his intricate manipulation of Matthew 28:19 in *Jesus Christ*

Is Not God, pp. 19-20.

32. Ibid., p. 11.

33. *Jesus Christ Is Not God,* p. 123.

34. Wierwille, *Receiving the Holy Spirit Today,* pp. 3-5.

35. *Power for Abundant Living,* pp. 21-22.

36. Of course, God is not capable of the *logically impossible.* He cannot make Himself go out of existence; He cannot make a square circle, etc.

37. Wierwille, *The Word's Way,* p. 5.

38. *Jesus Christ Is Not God,* p. 16.

39. Ibid., p. 79.

40. Ibid., p. 30.

41. Ibid., pp. 28-30.

42. Ibid., p. 82.

43. Ibid., chap. 2.

44. Exodus 3:13,14.

45. See, for example, Romans 9:5; Colossians 2:9; 1:15-17; Titus 2:13; 2 Peter 1:1; etc.

46. *The Word's Way,* p. 164.

47. *The Way* magazine, Dec. 1970, p. 6.

48. J. Gresham Machen, *The Virgin Birth of Christ* (Grand Rapids: Baker Book House, 1930), p. 391.

49. *Jesus Christ Is Not God,* pp. 76-77.

50. Kenneth Wuest, *The New Testament: An Expanded Translation* (Grand Rapids: Eerdmans Publishing Company, 1961), pp. 462-63.

51. Wierwille, *Power for Abundant Living,* pp. 162-63.

52. Wierwille, *Receiving the Holy Spirit Today,* pp. 3-5.

53. W.E. Vine, *Expository Dictionary of New Testament Words* (Old Tappan, NJ: Revell, 1940), Vol. IV, p. 63.

54. See Wierwille, *Jesus Christ Is Not God,* pp. 58-63.

55. Wierwille, *Power for Abundant Living,* p. 258.

56. Ibid., p. 270.

57. Wierwille, *Power for Abundant Living,* pp. 296-97.

58. Wierwille, *Receiving the Holy Spirit Today,* p. 148.

59. Wierwille, *The Word's Way,* p. 58.

60. Ibid., p. 60.

61. Wierwille, *Power for Abundant Living,* p. 313.

62. 1 Peter 2:24

CHAPTER
3

HINDUISM: HARE KRISHNA AND TRANSCENDENTAL MEDITATION (TM)*

INTRODUCTION

Non-Christian cults have been flourishing in the United States for generations. However, the last ten years have witnessed the explosive growth of new-age cults with their roots in Eastern Hinduism. Today we see around us a proliferation of gurus, swamis, and various sects from the East and especially from India.

There are so many hundreds of Eastern cults with members in America that it would be impossible for us to cover them all. Before we finished our study of the ones in existence now, there would be six or seven new ones springing up throughout the country, at the rate of one or two per month. Many are short-lived. Others are very small, with as few as 20 members. Some, however, grow and eventually rise to prominence, joining the ranks of the successful Eastern cults in America.

We will examine the roots of all of these cults, of Indian Hinduism, and of two of the largest and best-known Eastern cults in America—Transcendental Meditation (TM)

★ Researched by Elliot Miller.

and Hare Krishna (ISKCON). The beliefs of these two cults are viewed by us as representative of the general beliefs of the majority of the Eastern cults popular in America today. Since TM and ISKCON are so well-known, they have been reviewed and criticized by others, including Christians. We hope that our review of them will add to the body of evangelical literature which is available to Christians to help them in responding biblically to the challenge presented by TM and ISKCON.*

Because we are dealing with a parent religious system (Hinduism) and two of its offspring (TM and ISKCON), we will not be able to follow our standard format in all points. However, we will still cover all of the essential areas of discussion, including the cults' history, structure, and authority as well as their doctrines of God, Christ, mankind, and salvation.

HINDUISM

The Hinduism we see today in its various forms of expression both here and in the East is the product of a five-thousand-year gradual evolution. Bruce J. Nicholls summarizes the origin and structure of Hinduism:

> Of all the world's great religions, Hinduism is the most difficult to define. It did not have any one founder. . . . It has many scriptures which are authoritative but none that is exclusively so. Hinduism is "more like a tree that has *grown* gradually than like a building that has been *erected* by some great architect at some definite point in time."[1]

Hindus themselves refer to their religion as the "eternal system," or *sanatana dharma*. The term "Hindu" was coined by the Persians, after the "Indus" or "Sindu" River.

Orthodox Hinduism encompasses a variety of sects with diversified beliefs, practices, and traditions. In keeping with Hinduism's monistic world view (which we will discuss

---

* See Bibliography for listings of other Christian and non-Christian treatments of TM and ISKCON, as well as of Hinduism.

below), these sects are not considered by Hinduism to be wrong or heretical, but merely to be different perspectives of the One Eternal System *(sanatana dharma)*.

> The different Hindu sects, while practically appearing as different religions, in reality regard themselves as but different sects and divisions of the One Eternal Religion of India, of which each, of course, considers itself the best and most favored channel of expression and interpretation.[2]

After the Aryans invaded India and conquered the Dravidians, there was a gradual merging of the two peoples' cultures and religious beliefs. Estimates put the origin of the Hindu sacred scriptures, the Vedas, at around the last half of the second millennium B.C. The Vedas, meaning "wisdom" or "knowledge," are the earliest scriptures of Hinduism and provide the foundation for the entire Hindu religion.

Vedic development was in two directions: ritualistic and philosophical. The simple worship of the Vedic gods was transformed into an elaborate sacrificial ritual which benefits the worshiper only if the intricate ritual is followed exactly. It is from this direction of worship that the priestly class of hinduism, the *Brahmins,* arose. The priest occupied a position above even that of the gods, since he could control the gods through the religious rites. The philosophical development of the Vedic tradition was in protest against the ritualistic movement. Philosophic followers centered their religious practice in the mystical and symbolic meaning of the rites, and were largely unconcerned with the forms of the rituals.

These Hindu philosophers began to delve behind the relatively simple, anthropomorphic gods to the underlying power or substance behind the gods. From this contemplation arose the Hindu beliefs in monism and pantheism.[3] This range of belief encompasses simple pantheism, the idea that all is God and God is all; traditional monism, the idea that the universe is essentially one in substance or being; and finally a belief close to atheism, which sees the material universe as the only reality and, denying a personal or active God, simply dispenses with religion. Buddhism embraces this implication of Hindu philosophy.

Pantheism is defined as the belief that God is essentially one with all of reality, while the word "monism" indicates the belief that all of reality exists as a unified whole.

The Upanishads are the concluding portions of the Vedas and contain the developed essence of Vedic teaching. They are the foundations of Hinduism as we know it today. The Upanishads teach that all men can achieve the divine state if they strive for it. The individual personality is denied, being considered part of the world of illusion, or *maya,* and deification involves the shedding of *maya,* the merging and the obliteration of the self in the sea of the One Reality, God.

> As the flowing rivers disappear in the sea, losing their name and form, thus a wise man, freed from name and form, goes to the divine person who is beyond all.[4]

The Upanishads teach that every aspect of the universe, both animate and inanimate, shares the same essentially divine nature. There is actually only one Self in the universe.[5] Approximately 700 B.C. a system for enterpreting the Vedas, called Vedanta, was established, and it remains the leading school of Hindu philosophy in India today.

Central to understanding Hinduism is an understanding of the mutually dependent Hindu doctrines of *karma* and *samsara.*

> *Karma* operates as an inexorable law of retributive justice. It is an internal law of nature, independent of the decrees of God or the gods.[6]

According to the law of karma, a man is the result of his own past. Whatever a man sows, he will also reap. It is seen as the law of cause and effect on a moral plane. If one does good, he will escape the human condition (which is illusion), and return to the divine state. If a man does bad, he will remain in bondage to the human condition, being born again and again until he has worked out his bad karma. This belief in the rebirth or the transmigration of the soul which we call reincarnation is known in Hinduism as *samsara*. Not only men but all animals are engaged in the wheel of samsara, passing from one level of life to another.

The Hindu hope is the realization of the immortality of the soul, either in its individuality or in its absorption into *Brahman*. The body is the prison house of the soul and therefore any idea of an eternal union of the body and soul is an embarrassment and anathema. There is no place whatever for the idea of the resurrection of the body in the Hindu scheme of things.[7]

The formation of the Bhagavad-Gita marked a turning point in Hinduism. The *Bhagavad-Gita* is one portion of a Hindu epic and consists of a dialogue between Arjuna, the warrior-prince, and his charioteer, Krishna, who is the disguised incarnation of the Hindu god Vishnu. The Bhagavad-Gita (Gita) is the most important and favorite Hindu scripture. The dialogue summarizes the main points of Hindu philosophy and religious thought. The Gita presents a clear theism (perhaps better termed heno-theism—belief in many gods, one of whom is supreme over all others) that is new to Hinduism and marks a divergence of Hinduism from the pantheistic monism of the Upanishads.

The Gita is the philosophical basis of popular Hinduism. The book was probably written around 200 B.C. and reached its present form around 200 A.D. During this period the concept of the *avatar*, or incarnation of deity, was introduced and became very popular. The avatars are the warrior gods who triumph over sin and evil by becoming what could be termed redeemers within the evil world of maya. The avatar concept, which grew out of the theistic movement within Hinduism, was a result of the Hindus' desires to make God personal and immanent, or approachable. The central figure of the Gita is the avatar called Krishna. This incarnated being bears little resemblance to the incarnation of God in Jesus Christ presented to us in the Bible. Krishna was capable of (and indeed performed) many acts of violence and immorality. Hinduism does not deny the acts attributed to Krishna, but they deny that, for an avatar, these acts are immoral.

> . . .the violation of religious laws by the gods and the daring acts of the glorious do not bring any stains, as fire is not stained by feeding on impure substances. But those that are not gods should never commit such deeds, even in thought. If a man foolishly drinks poison in imitation of Siva, he is sure to die. The words of the gods are true, but their acts are sometimes true and sometimes not.[8]

There are three major paths to salvation discussed in the Gita and recognized generally by all Hindus today. These methods of attaining salvation are *karma marga* (method), which is the way of disinterested action; *bhakti marga,* the way of devotion; and *jnana marga,* which is the path of knowledge or mystical insight.

Those who hold to the monistic philosophy of Vedanta use jnana as a means of achieving their self-realization through intuitive awareness, a desire to break free from the delusions of maya and perceive that their true selves are God, thus transcending the world of distinction and duality, which they consider to be illusion.

Those Hindus who are theistic (or henotheistic) and believe that God is a personal being (albeit one with the universe), follow the path of bhakti (devotion) in hopes of freeing themselves of their bad karma through their devotions to God. In this pursuit they rely heavily on the grace of God, as they describe it. When they speak of the grace of God, they are not referring to the Christian concept of total absolution of all sins, but rather to something that will help them in the process of working for their own salvation through good works. Their good works bring them a part of the way—an essential part of the way—and from that point on the grace of God carries them the rest of the way.

The old school of ritualistic Hinduism is concerned with karma marga. Elaborate sacrificial ritual is the prominent feature of this discipline, and the outward form of such ritual is more important than the inward substance. Disciples engage in lifelong disciplines in harmony with the methods prescribed by their teachers from the Vedic tradition.

Around 800 A.D., Vedantic Hinduism enjoyed a great revival in India, which continues today. The common people, bored with a thousand years of dry, intellectual, philosophical Buddhism, were hungry for a religion that was more alive. The *Brahma-Sutra,* the earliest Vedantic work, was supplemented at this time by the *Sariraka-Bhasya,* a commentary on the Brahma-Sutra by *Shri Sankaracharya,* who is regarded by the Vedantists as one of the greatest philosophers that the world has ever produced.[9]

The Vedanta philosophy makes use of the Upanishads, the Bhagavad-Gita, and the Brahma-Sutra in expressing its philosophy. Sankaracharya (Shankara) was its "father," and his commentary is said to express a mind at least as great as those of Plato and Aquinas combined.[10] The impact of Shankara on modern Hindu thought is described by Ainslie T. Embree:

> One measure of this influence is that it is very difficult for anyone—either Hindu or non-Hindu—to read Indian religious texts without unconsciously seeing them through the general interpretation given by Shankara.[11]

Shankara's philosophy accurately represents the main tendency of the Upanishads. However, he tries to interpret them as though they all present a consistent, unified teaching, which is simply not true. There are enough shades of ambiguity within the Upanishads to provide a quasi-legitimate stand from which all the varying schools within Hinduism are able to cite particular passages in support of their doctrines. Other passages are blatantly contradictory.

For Shankara, worship of a personal God has its place in the spiritual growth of the common individual. This worship will ultimately be transcended when the individual realizes that there is no difference between himself and God, and that therefore there is no one to worship. The consistent cry of the Vedantist school is that the Absolute is not a person. While Shankara insisted that the Brahman (the supreme One) was devoid of all attributes, yet within him existed Being, Consciousness, and Bliss as essential features.[12] In Shankara's monism, there is no question of a relationship between Brahman and the world, since there is no difference between the two, and it takes two to make a relationship. The world we appear to see is a mistake—it is maya. We mistake Brahman for the world. If all that exists is Brahman, then it must be Brahman that is making this mistake in judgment. This is precisely what Shankara affirms.[13]

Although plurality does not exist, Shankara assigns the quality of relative truth to it. Since the things perceived in maya are real to those who perceive them, to this degree they have reality in them. On this basis Shankara sees good in the world of maya. In fact, he even places the personal God within this category.[14] The doctrines of reincarnation and karma also have this relative degree of reality. As long as the individual appears to exist within maya, he is subject to such laws. When he awakens to the fact that all is one, he is no longer bound to them and they cease to have any relative reality.

For Shankara, jnana marga (knowledge or mystical insight) is the supreme road to salvation; bhakti marga (devotion) only helps in certain cases, and is never a sufficient path to salvation in itself.[15] Remember, since all is one and all is God, salvation is not salvation at all, but merely realizing that one is part of the all-inclusive, impersonal One. Good and bad lose all absolute meaning and become relative to whatever is helpful or hindering in realizing oneness with the infinite.[16]

While Shankara was the philosopher of popular Vedantism, he was not able to transform the religious system into a vital system that would satisfy the needs of the common people for a personal relationship with God. Bhakti devotee Ramanuja modified the theology of Vedanta to accommodate a theistic idea for the people. Ramanuja identified the supreme spirit with Vishnu, one of the three personalities of the Hindu trinity. Brahma and Shiva, who were normally considered to be distinct gods within the Hindu trinity, became separate manifestations of Vishnu. Ramanuja's doctrine has been labeled qualified monism, since he taught that God, souls, and matter were all of one basic identity and yet maintained eternal distinctions among themselves. Souls and matter, according to Ramanuja, relate to God as the body relates to the spirit. In Ramanuja's scheme, salvation did not involve the disappearance of the individual self as it did in Shankara's scheme; instead, it involved a release from the limiting barriers of the physical body.

While Vedanta has been the most influential philosophy among the intellectuals of India, the majority of common Hindu men and women are henotheistic or theistic, and worship incarnations of gods and local deities. There are three basic groups into which the various Hindu sects can be classified: 1) the abstract monists, who are followers of Advaita monism, and are few in number. They refuse to personify Brahman; 2) the Vishnuites, or Vaishnavas, who are devoted to the god Vishnu; and 3) the Shivaites, or Shaivas, who are devoted to the god Shiva. Vaishnavas consider Vishnu to have incarnated in the form of his avatars, or manifestations in the flesh. Chief among these are Rama and Krishna.

As we shall see in our discussion, TM can be loosely aligned with the Advaita monism, and ISKCON with the Vishnuites.

HARE KRISHNA (ISKCON)

In the fifteenth century a great revival of devotion to Krishna began. The principal figure in this religious fervor was a man named Chaitanya, who is considered the founding father of ISKCON. Reared in the province of Bengal, where Vaishnavas (Vishnuites) were strongly opposed, Chaitanya hesitated at first to identify himself with the movement, but was soon overwhelmed by his devotion to Krishna. He formed a bhakti movement devoted to Krishna and soon possessed some of the most devoted and ecstatic followers of any religious movement in India. His followers were noted for their continual chanting of the name of Krishna and their communal singing and dancing. Chaitanya's theology basically resembled that of Ramanuja. In the catechism of the Krishna faith, the following dialogue between Chaitanya and a high official of the kingdom of Orissa is recorded:

Question: Which knowledge is the highest of all?
Answer: There is no knowledge but devotion to Krishna.

Question: What is the highest glory in all types of glory?
Answer: Being reputed to be Krishna's devotee.

Question: What is counted wealth among human possessions?
Answer: He is immensely wealthy who has love for Radha-Krishna.

Question: What is the heaviest of all sorrows?
Answer: There is no sorrow except separation from Krishna.

Question: Who is considered liberated among those who

	are liberated?
Answer:	He is the foremost of the liberated who practices devotion to Krishna.
Question:	What is the highest good of all creatures?
Answer:	There is none except the society of those who are devoted to Krishna.
Question:	Among objects of meditation, which should creatures meditate on?
Answer:	The supreme meditation is on the lotus-feet of Radha-Krishna.
Question:	What is chief among the objects of worship?
Answer:	The name of the most adorable couple, Radha-Krishna.[17]

It is obvious that Chaitanya was immersed in the worship and consciousness of Krishna, even as the members of the Hare Krishna movement today strive also to be. In India, as in America, the followers of Krishna are noted for the two perpendicular marks upon their foreheads, which signify their slavery to Krishna and their involvement in the Krishna bhakti movement.

The Hare Krishnas as we know them today, the International Society for Krishna Consciousness, started in the sixties in New York. Seventy-year-old Prabhupada, born Abhay Charan De, an immigrant from India, began quietly gathering disciples among Greenwich Village's counterculture. He followed (and led his own disciples) in the footsteps of the original Krishna bhakti devotees of Chaitanya's day.

His Divine Grace, A.C. Bhaktivedanta Swami Prabhupada, was born in Calcutta, India, in 1896 (d. 1978). He studied philosophy, business, English, and economics. In 1959 he left his family and devoted himself entirely to Krishna devotion under Siddhartha Goswami. Goswami spread the teachings of Chaitanya, which Prabhupada adopted and which are promulgated today by ISKCON devotees.

Prabhupada claimed to be in the direct line of holy teachers from Lord Chaitanya.

One of his first American supporters was poet Allen Ginsberg, and one of his most famous supporters was former Beatle George Harrison. Today the publications of Prabhupada are the focal point of devotee learning, propagation, and evangelism. The ISKCON periodical, *Back to Godhead,* is the best-known of ISKCON publications, although Prabhupada's prolific pen produced hundreds of publications since the mid-sixties, all of which call devotees to higher and more complete worship of Krishna. Today there are over 100 temples, farms, and centers of worship for ISKCON, where members lead rigid ascetic lives of devotion to Krishna. Recently, missionary activities have been increasing in Prabhupada's native country, India, although the total number of Indian converts has been surprisingly small.

Sankirtana refers to the Hare Krishna mantra, or chant, which ISKCON members chant almost continuously. This is said to be the recommended means for achieving "the mature stage of love of God in this age of Kali, or quarrel" and consists of chanting "Hare Krishna, Hare Krishna, Krishna Krishan, Hare Hare, Hare Rama, Hare Rama, Rama Rama, Hare Hare."[18]

The Sankirtana is the core of Krishna worship in ISKCON. It is supposed to be so powerful that in and of itself it can produce divine influence wherever it is said. It is chanted in the streets for the benefit of all citizens. In each of the ISKCON centers, sankirtana is repeated several times daily, and all other activity is lower in importance.[19]

ISKCON hosts Sunday feasts and other festivals as evangelism tools. Each feast consists of 10 to 15 courses of vegetarian Indian dishes. Programs of plays, chanting, and games enliven the feasts.[20]

To become a member of an ISKCON center means to relinquish one's association with the outside world.

To live in ISKCON as an initiated student, one agrees to accept four rules: no meat-eating, no illicit sex, no intoxicants and no gambling. The disciples perform devotional service, duties and chanting in a life-routine characterized by simple living and high thinking.[21]

. . .after studying and working in a temple for one year, the student may be awarded the title of *bhukti-sastri*, or ordained minister, with further responsibilities and with advancement of service. He may finally take the renounced order, called *sannyasa*, and receive the title *svami*.[22]

Devotees are not allowed to bring their old beliefs and ideas into ISKCON. The thoughts of the deceptive, maya world are anathema to proper Krishna consciousness. Prabhupada even called the ISKCON initiation process "washing your brain, because you have so much stool in your brain. We are sweepers engaged on behalf of God to wash the stool from your brain. We have to do it."[23] All who have not embraced the devotion to Krishna are called fools.[24]

The solicitation tactics of the ISKCON devotees are considered objectionable by most outside the group. The main source of revenue for the cult is from donations solicited by whatever means necessary from the unsuspecting public. Deceit is sometimes part of the fund-raising tactics of ISKCON.[25]

TRANSCENDENTAL MEDITATION

Transcendental Meditation (TM) is a spiritual practice called a yoga which is presented to the Western world as a "scientific" way of reducing stress and finding peace within oneself. It promises increased creativity and relaxation. But far from being a scientific method of relaxation, TM is union with Brahman, the Hindu concept of God, or, in TM founder Maharishi Mahesh Yogi's terms, "Being" or the "Science of Creative Intelligence."[26] Appealing to the Western consciousness, TM offers ultimate results with minimal effort.

The TM exercise consists of a short period (initially) of quiet meditation consisting of emptying the mind and continually repeating one's personal mantra, which is the name of a Hindu deity. The repeating of the mantra results in worshiping the Hindu deity.

In his book *The Science of Being and Art of Living,* Marharishi summarizes his teaching as "the summation of both the practical wisdom of integrated life advanced by the Vedic Rishis of ancient India and the growth of scientific thinking in the present-day Western world."[27]

Maharishi Mahesh Yogi was the student of Swami Brahmananda Saraswati, Jagadguru, Bhagwan Shankaracharya, commonly known as Guru Dev (Divine Teacher).[28] Guru Dev was considered to be an avatar, or manifestation of the divine Being. Mahareshi was commissioned to fulfill Guru Dev's plan to spread his teachings to the world, and in 1958 he founded the Spiritual Regeneration Movement, five years after the death of Guru Dev.

Maharishi remained strictly devoted to the service of Guru Dev until Guru Dev died. For two years after Guru Dev's death, Mararishi remained in seclusion in the Himalayas. On a visit to a temple in South India a man persuaded Maharishi to give a series of lectures, after which he continued to teach in India until 1958.

After a short teaching tour in the Far East, Maharishi came to Hawaii in 1959 and then to San Francisco in April of that year. The American organization of the Spiritual Regeneration Movement began in Los Angeles in midsummer 1959. Its first president was Dr. John Hislop, who was soon replaced by Charles Lutes, a salesman. The SRM was dissolved in June of 1977. The Students International Meditation Society (SIMS) was begun in 1965. Since then the International Meditation Society (IMS) was founded to offer courses to the general public, and the American Foundation for the Science of Creative Intelligence (AFSCI) was established for expansion in the business world. Maharishi's goal is to have one initiator into TM for every 1000 people in the world. There are currently over a million people who have been taught the meditation technique in the United States. TM is taught in over 90 countries, and there are close to 400 World Plan teaching centers in the United States, as well as 80 in Canada. TM has made powerful inroads into government-funded facilities (schools, prisons, etc.) until it was recently denied such access in the state of New Jersey (to be discussed below).

In 1975 Maharishi announced the dawn of the Age of Enlightenment, promising that crime and other social ills would decrease if at least one percent of a city's population were meditators. TM's growth has occurred in spite of expensive initiation fees (fees range from $150.00 for a college student to $200.00 for a single adult to $300.00 for families).

However, over the past two years there have been solid indications that Maharishi and TM's public credibility have been waning, and with it their hopes of effecting their world plan. The most significant of these factors was a ruling in October 1977 by a New Jersey Federal Court. The ruling barred TM from that state's schools and thereby set a precedent for the rest of the nation. Charging that separation of church and state was being violated, eight taxpayers, a New Jersey clergyman, the Americans United for Separation of Church and State, and the Spiritual Counterfeits Project of Berkeley California brought suit.

U.S. District Judge H. Curtis Meanor stated in his decision, "The teaching of SCI/TM and the puja are religious in nature; no other inference is 'permissible' or reasonable. . . .Although defendants have submitted well over 1500 pages of briefs, affidavits and deposition testimony in opposing plaintiffs' motion for summary judgment, defendants have failed to raise the slightest doubt as to the facts or as to the religious nature of the teaching of the Science of Creative Intelligence and the *puja*. The teaching of the SCI/TM course in New Jersey public high schools violates the establishment clause of the First Amendment, and its teaching must be enjoined."[29]

The New Jersey court case has hindered TM's efforts at getting government funding for prisoner rehabilitation programs. The summer of 1979 marked the last date before which appeal could have been filed in the matter, and since TM has declined to appeal the judge's decision, it stands invincible. Understanding the Western mentality, Maharishi had succeeded for a time in convincing many people that his program was a secular, scientific exercise. However, the documentation showing TM to be religious in nature is overwhelming, and it can clearly be seen that TM is a religious practice, and not science at all.

Many people have become disillusioned with TM because it does not live up to all of its claims.[30] In 1975, Jeanette Towery, Ph.D., conducted a study at the University of California at Berkeley to test the TM claims to change psychological functions and to thereby enhance one's ability to deal with today's problems.

> The results of this study suggest that the practice of TM does not lead to increased Cognitive Flexibility or greater Field Independence. These two variables refer to relatively stable, structural modes of thought and perception, respectively. It may be that TM practice does not produce an impact sufficient enough in depth to modify structural characteristics of human functioning. . . .[31]

Adverse effects of TM are noted by others.[32] Another factor which detracts from TM's claims is that in the studies which it cites to support its claims, there have been a significant lack of control groups (standard procedure in medical and psychological experiments).

Even if it were established that the meditation produces beneficial results, it would remain unproved that the overall effect upon the individual from TM is spiritually, mentally, or physically harmless, or that it works for the reasons claimed. The method is based on the Hindu mantric philosophy, and this only leads a person away from a true, biblical knowledge of God. We conclude with the words of Dr. George Domino of the University of Arizona, "The claim that meditation leads to increased creativity is not supported."[33]

Throughout the seventies, Marharishi has continued to affirm "We are not a religion,"[34] and this has been the proclamation of the entire TM movement. Because of this claim, Jewish, Protestant, and Catholic leaders have endorsed TM to their congregations, and many practice it themselves. But TM is Hinduism. Its origin, initiation rite, nature, practice, and theory are all religious at the core. TM stems from the Shankara tradition of Vedanta Hinduism. The Vedas, which Maharishi openly acknowledges as the source of TM, claim to have a divine origin and to be divine revelation. Maharishi studied under Guru Dev, who was one of the four central religious leaders of India and was said to be an avatar. The word yoga (Maharishi calls himself a yogi, or teacher of yoga) comes from the Sanskrit "yug" or "yoke," and has always implied a technique to achieve union with God. The fact that TM has been ruled religious in a court of law should be sufficient for anyone to see its religious nature.

The initiation rite itself, where the meditation is taught, is a Hindu ceremony worshiping the Hindu deities and offering them sacrifices of fruit, flowers, and cloth. The initiator sings a hymn to Guru Dev, identifying him with the Hindu trinity of Brahma, Vishnu, and Shiva, and concludes the ceremony by bowing before the altar, gesturing to the initiate to bow down with him. It is only after this ceremony has been performed that one may receive his mantra to meditate upon.[35]

Maharishi teaches his initiators that through this ceremony the initiate's mind is brought under the influence of "Being."[36] Taking advantage of the fact that the initiation ceremony is in Sanskrit, instructors explain to all who inquire that the puja is merely a ceremony of gratitude to the line of instructors responsible for passing down the tradition of the mantras, and compare it to bringing an apple to a teacher. But this is not true, for the mantra itself is also religious. The *American Heritage Dictionary* defines "mantra" as: "A sacred formula believed to embody the divinity invoked and to possess magical power. It is used in prayer and incantation." Maharishi himself admits that the use of the mantra invokes gods and spirits from the spirit world.[37] In the past, Maharishi has made many references to the religious nature of TM.[38]

Contrary to TM's current claims, TM is a Hindu religious system and is not compatible with Christianity. It denies the central doctrines of the Christian faith and asserts the futile Hindu system of monism and maya.

THE DOCTRINE OF GOD

ISKCON

As we discussed in our review of Hinduism, the Hindu deity is essential pantheistic. ISKCON teaches this, with the explanation that the one God which is all is Krishna.

> ALL the lists of the incarnations of Godhead are either plenary expansions or parts of the plenary expansions of the Lord, but Lord Sri Krsna is the original Personality of Godhead Himself.[39]

TM

The God of TM is also one and pantheistic, in much the same way as ISKCON's deity, but more emphasis is laid on this God's pantheistic nature.

> Being is the living presence of God, the reality of life. It is eternal truth. It is the absolute in eternal freedom.[40]

> The one eternal unmanifested absolute Being manifests itself in many forms of lives and existences in creation.[41]

By contrast, the God of the Bible is distinct from His creation and is personal. He is the only One who is eternal, omniscient, omnipotent, and omnipresent. Throughout the Bible we find consistently that God and His creation are two distinct entities. The first verse in the Bible teaches that God created the heavens and the earth—they are not eternal. The Hebrew word for "create" implies the calling into existence of something that had not previously existed, the creating of something out of nothing.

It is true that God is omnipresent, but it is *not* true that God is of the same essence as His creation. When we say that God is present everywhere, we mean that there is nothing in all of existence that can ever escape His attention. Although God exists eternally outside our dimension, He operates within our dimension, and nothing in creation is removed from his presence in any degree.

Creation cannot be identified as God. The error of pantheism is condemned in Romans 1:20-25:

> For since the creation of the world God's invisible qualities—his eternal power and divine nature—have been clearly seen, being understood from what has been made, so that men are without excuse.
>
> For although they knew God, they neither glorified him as God nor gave thanks to him, but their thinking became futile and their foolish hearts were darkened. Although they claimed to be wise, they became fools and exchanged the glory of the immortal God for images made to look like mortal man and birds and animals and reptiles.
>
> Therefore God gave them over in the sinful desires of their hearts to sexual impurity for the degrading of their bodies with one another. They exchanged the truth of God for a lie, and worshiped and served created things rather than the Creator—who is forever praised. Amen.

Neither pantheism nor monism can be reconciled with the biblical doctrine of God. Both ISKCON and TM deny the biblical Jehovah.

THE DOCTRINE OF JESUS CHRIST

ISKCON

The Jesus Christ of ISKCON is not the Jesus Christ of the Bible. In ISKCON, Jesus is subordinate to Krishna. He is even called Krishna's son![42] In no way could he be considered equal with God.

TM

As is true with ISKCON and most other Eastern groups, very little is said or taught about Jesus. However, what is said is definitely not Christian. The Jesus of TM never suffered or died for our sins, and was, as all other people, merely one with the Ultimate Reality, the Creative Consciousness.[43]

We know from the Bible that Jesus is much more than any of us could ever hope to be. He is not subordinate to any finite, illusionary god of Hinduism. He is the God of the Bible, the one supreme Being over every so-called God. First Corinthians 8:4-6 shows the supremacy of Christ over the idols by saying that "an idol is nothing in the world," and that there is "no God but one." Jesus is that God incarnate (John 1:1; 8:58; 20:28; Titus 2:13; etc.).

Jesus is not merely an enlightened man. He is the unique Son of God, the only One who has ever shared the nature of God and man (Philippians 2:1-11). John 1:14 informs us, "The Word became flesh and lived for a while among us. We have seen his glory, the glory of the one and only Son, who came from the Father, full of grace and truth." He is called "God the only Son" in verse 18.

Contrary to TM's denial of the suffering of Christ, 1 Peter 3:18 affirms, "For Christ died for sins once for all, the righteous for the unrighteous, to bring you to God."

THE DOCTRINE OF SALVATION

ISKCON

Salvation in ISKCON is consistent with Hindu salvation in general. That is, it is inconsistent as Hindu salvation is inconsistent. IKSCON teaches that in reality all are perfect and part of the one eternal Being, Krishna. There is no sin and therefore no salvation from sin. But in this illusory world (maya) there are both sin and the effects of that sin, which is karma. Salvation is obtained by repeated incarnations, during which the soul expiates his sin by devotion to Krishna and right acting.

Only one whose heart is washed with tears of love for God is purified of sinful reaction.[44]

The devotees of the Lord are released from all sins because they eat food which is offered first for sacrifice.[45]

All these performers who know the meaning of sacrifice become cleansed of sinful reactions, and, having tasted the nectar of the remnants of such sacrifices, they go to the supreme eternal atmosphere.[46]

From the body of any person who claps and dances before the Deity, showing manifestations of ecstasy, all the birds of sinful activities fly away upwards.[47]

TM

TM's salvation is realizing that one is in union with the Creative Intelligence. Of course, this can only take place through the practice of TM. There is no room in TM for atonement by Christ.

This meditation makes us content. It brings us more ability for achieving something through right means, and very easily a sinner comes out of the field of sin and becomes a virtuous man.[48]

>The answer to every problem is that there is no problem. Let a man perceive this truth and then he is without problems.[49]

>If a man has not gained consciousness in Being through the practice of transcendental meditation, he continues to live in ignorance and bondage.[50]

>...a huge mountain of sins extending for miles is destroyed by Union brought about through transcendental meditation, without which there is no way out.[51]

In the Bible, sin is not merely a state of mind that can be removed by altering the consciousness, but it is a state of the spirit and heart, and it is only through identification with Christ that we become free of sin. Romans 6:6 tells us, "For we know that our old self was crucified with him so that the body of sin might be rendered powerless, that we should no longer be slaves to sin." This salvation comes only through Jesus Christ, the only One by whom we can be saved (Acts 4:12). True spiritual regeneration comes only through the renewing work of the Holy Spirit, operating through the sacrifice of Jesus Christ (Titus 3:5,6).

Romans 3 discusses the role of Christ in man's salvation. "This righteousness from God comes through faith in Jesus Christ to all who believe. There is no difference, for all have sinned and fall short of the glory of God, and are justified freely by his grace through the redemption that came by Christ Jesus" (3:22-24). We cannot help Jesus obtain our salvation. Hebrews 7:25 tells us that "he is able to save completely those who come to God through him, because he always lives to intercede for them." Ephesians 2:8-10 reminds us that salvation is by grace—not by meditation or chanting, or eating the food of the gods.

When one has salvation in Christ, he has peace with God. He does not have to endure endless feelings of guilt. He does not learn to accept his own deity. We have a way through Jesus Christ to rid us of all the stains of sin. We have sinned:

we are not God. First John 1:8,9 assures the Christian, "If we claim to be without sin, we deceive ourselves and the truth is not in us. If we confess our sins, he is faithful and just and will forgive us our sins and purify us from all unrighteousness."

We can have comfort and peace with God. He is our Maker, our Master, our Lord, our loving Father. Hebrews 9:14 shows us the eternal peace available to the Christian who has been saved from sin by the blood of Jesus Christ: "How much more, then, will the blood of Christ, who through the eternal Spirit offered Himself unblemished to God, cleanse our consciences from acts that lead to death, so that we may serve the living God!"

We do not serve an adulterer and killer, as the ISKCON devotees do. We do not realize our oneness with an impersonal, static force, as TM devotees do. Instead, we worship and serve the living and personal Creator of all things.

CONCLUSION

The religion of Hinduism, for all of its diversity, cannot expand to include Christianity as one of its sects. There is no harmony between Christianity and Hinduism/ISKCON/TM. Hinduism denies the biblical Trinity, the biblical Jesus Christ, the biblical salvation. While the Hindu works out his own salvation and has no future other than becoming one with impersonal mind, the Christian looks forward to eternity with the Creator of the universe, to a time when "No longer will there be any curse. The throne of God and of the Lamb will be in the city, and his servants will serve him. They will see his face, and his name will be on their foreheads. There will be no more night. They will not need the light of a lamp or the light of the sun, for the Lord God will give them light. And they will reign for ever and ever" (Revelation 22:3-5).

CHAPTER NOTES

1. Bruce J. Nicholls, "Hinduism," in *The World's Religions,* by Sir Norman Anderson, ed. (Grand Rapids: Eerdman's, 1974), p. 136. (Internal quote by Nicholls from K.M. Sen, *Hinduism* (Baltimore: Penguin, 1962), p. 7).

2. Yogi Ramacharaka, *The Philosophies and Religions of India* (Chicago: The Yogi Publication Society, 1930), pp. 271-72.

3. Nicholls, op. cit., pp. 154-55.

4. Radhakrishnan, *Indian Philosophy, Vol. I* (London: George Allen and Unwin Ltd., 1923), pp. 236-37.

5. Swami Prabhavananda and Frederick Manchest, transs., *The Upanishads: Breath of the Eternal* (New York and Toronto: New American Library, 1948), p. 27.

6. Nicholls, op. cit., pp. 143-44.

7. Nicholls, op. cit., pp. 144-45.

8. Radhakrishnan, op. cit., Vol. I, pp. 495-96.

9. Ibid., pp. 85-86.

10. Os Guinness, *The East No Exit* (Downers Grove, IL: InterVarsity Press, 1974), pp. 11-12.

11. Ainslie T. Embree, ed., *The Hindu Tradition* (New York: The Modern Library, 1966), pp. 197-98.

12. Radhakrishnan, op. cit., Vol II, p. 539.

13. *The Philosophies and Religions of India* (Chicago: The Yogi Publication Society, 1930), p. 97.

14. Ibid., pp. 105-06.

15. Radhakrishnan, op. cit., Vol. II, pp. 614-16.

16. Ibid., p. 614.

17. Embree, op. cit., pp. 255-56.

18. *Back To Godhead,* Vol. 12, No. 9, 1977, inside cover.

19. Prabhupada, *On Chanting the Hare Krsna Mantra* (Boston: ISKCON Press, n.d.), p.8.

20. Ibid., p. 9.

21. Ibid., p. 8.

22. Ibid., p. 10.

23. *Back to Godhead,* Vol. 12, No. 6, 1977, p. 16.

24. Ibid., p. 16.

25. Hans Conrad Zander, "My Brief Life as a Hare Krishna," in *Atlas World Press Review,* Vol. 21, No. 8, Sept. 1974, pp. 26-27.

26. Gordon R. Lewis, *What Everyone Should Know About Transcendental Meditation* (New York: Pillar Books/Gospel Light, 1975), p. 29.

27. Maharishi Mahesh Yogi, *The Science of Being and Art of Living* (New York: The New American Library, 1968), p. xv.

28. Jack Forem, *Transcendental Meditation, Maharishi Mahesh Yogi and the Science of Creative Intelligence* (New York: E. P. Dutton and Co., 1974), p. 204.

29. United States District Court, District of New Jersey, Civil Action No. 76-341.

30. David Haddon and Vail Hamilton, *TM Wants You! A Christian Response to Transcendental Meditation* (Grand Rapids: Baker, 1976), pp. 68-69.

31. "The Impact of Transcendental Meditation on Cognitive Flexibility, Field Dependence, and Directional Priorities in Attention Deployment," by Jeanette Towery, reviewed in *Dissertation Abstracts,* July 1976, pp. 475-76.

32. Pat Means, *The Mystical Maze* (San Bernardino, CA: Campus Crusade for Christ, Inc., 1976), p. 24.

33. George Domino, "Transcendental Meditation and Creativity: An Empirical Investigation," in *Journal of Applied Psychology,* June 1977, pp. 358-62.

34. *Time* magazine, October 13, 1975, p. 71.

35. *An English Translation of Transcendental Meditation's Initiatory Puja* (Berkeley, CA: Spiritual Counterfeits Project, n.d.) p. 1.

36. Maharishi Mahesh Yogi, *Maharishi Mahesh Yogi on the Bhagavad-Gita* (New York: Penguin, 1967), p. 257.

37. Mahesh Yogi, *Meditations of Mararishi Mahesh Yogi,* pp. 17-18.

38. Ibid., pp. 59, 60, 95.

39. Siddha Swarup Ananda Goswami, *Jesus Loves KRSNA* (Vedic Christian Committee and Life Force, Krsan Yoga Viewpoint, n.d., 1975), p. 14.

40. *The Science of Being and the Art of Living,* op. cit., p. 22.

41. Ibid., p. 23.

42. *Jesus Loves Krsna,* op. cit., p. 26.

43. *Meditations of Maharishi Mahesh Yogi,* op. cit., pp. 123-24.

44. *Jesus Loves KRSNA,* op. cit., p. 51.

45. A.C. Bhaktivedanta Swami Prabhupada, *Bhagavad-Gita As It is* (New York: The Bhaktivedanta Book Trust, 1968), p. 50.

46. Ibid., p. 81.

47. A.C. Bhaktivedanta Swami Prabhupada, *The Nectar of Devotion* (New York: The Bhaktivedanta Book Trust, 1970), p. 75.

48. *Meditations of Maharishi Mahesh Yogi,* op. cit., p. 119.

49. *Maharishi Mahesh Yogi on the Bhagavad-Gita,* op. cit., p. 66.

50. Ibid., p. 14.

51. Ibid., p. 299.

CHAPTER

4

EST: ERHARD SEMINARS TRAINING★

HISTORY

Werner Erhard, founder and director of Erhard Seminars Training (referred to by most people, including members, as *est*), promotes his own brand of "salvation"—one's peace with God—through an organization of men and women dedicated to advancing the sovereignty of self.

Est cannot be considered primarily a religious cult, since its origin, main tenets, and most important objectives are not wholly religious. However, structurally and sociologically it fits the definition of a cult, and the characteristics of cult followers are found in *est* supporters.* In addition, when Erhard does speak from a religious context, he denies the essentials of the Christian faith and embraces some occultic teachings, all the while claiming that *est* is compatible with Christianity. Since *est* is gaining thousands of new members continually, we felt the necessity of including it in this study. Since *est* does not fit the same mold as the wholly religious cults we have also included, we will depart at times from the established format of the other chapters.

Werner Erhard was born Jack Rosenberg in 1935. After

★ Researched by John Weldon and Gretchen Passantino.

* See Chapter 1 for detailed information on the characteristics of cults and cultists.

abandoning his wife and four children in 1960, he changed his name. He was known as Jack Frost during the time he ran an auto dealership. He supervised the salesmen of Grolier Society, Inc., an encyclopedia sales organization which was later convicted by the State of California for using lies and trickery to persuade prospective customers.[1]

In 1963 Erhard claimed to have an "enlightenment experience" which prompted him to search for religious/existential disciplines for permanent enlightenment. The best from all of these sources were combined with Erhard's own mystical experiences to produce today's Erhard Seminars Training. During Erhard's search he tried Scientology, Mind Dynamics, Zen Buddhism, Hinduism, hypnosis, Subud, Yoga, Silva Mind Control, psychocybernetics, Gestalt and encounter therapy, transpersonal psychology, and others.[2] Finally, in 1971, he reached permanent enlightenment by realizing "What is, is, and what isn't, isn't."[3] He also repaired the relationship with his wife and children, abandoned 11 years earlier. As a Jewish person, Erhard "had long acknowledged Nietzsche as one of his intellectual mentors and the creation of a super race as his greatest ambition."[4]

Est is a conglomeration of mystical and pseudopsychological techniques designed to master and then rebuild individuals into the molds prescribed by Erhard as human fulfillment. Over 250,000 people have paid more than 50 million dollars for the experience. Dr. Herbert Hansher, professor of psychology at Temple University, says that est is "one of the most powerful therapeutic experiences yet devised."[5] Est is an intensive, 60-hour seminar of psychological manipulation designed to restructure a person's world view, to bring it in line with Erhard's world view. The seminars were started in 1971 by Erhard, after his "permanent enlightenment." The seminars consist of three basics: lectures, mind exercises (attempting to achieve altered states of consciousness), and group sharing of feelings and experiences. One of *est's* trainers conducts the seminar in a rigid, authoritarian manner, holding absolute control over all participants. The first three days of the seminar prepare or condition the initiates for the fourth day, when each new member is expected to "get it."[6] (No one ever explains what "it" is.) *Est* staffer Dr. William Bartley stated, "The training provides a very highly controlled content which opens people to certain kinds of experiences."[7]

The growth of Erhard's seminars is phenomenal, and the publicity generated by the organization and its graduates is tremendous. In 1975 over 193 articles were written on *est*. Over 200 more articles were written in 1976, in addition to nine books, which had sold well over a million copies by May of 1977.[8] Graduates number in the hundreds of thousands, and many are public figures from the arts, theater, movies, government, and business.

Singer John Denver wrote a song about *est,* dedicated one of his albums to Werner Erhard, donated 10,000 dollars to the organization, and sits on *est's* advisory board. Actress Valerie Harper praised Erhard's teachings before a national audience during the Emmy Awards. John Denver declared in *Newsweek,* "It's the single most important experience of my life. . . .I can do anything. One of these days, I'll be so complete I won't be a human, I'll be a god."[9] Valerie Harper reported on her proselytizing efforts in *est's Graduate Review,* "Any talk show I'm ever on, or any magazine interview I do, I speak about *est* because it does come up. People are interested."[10]

Other celebrity graduates include Yoko Ono, Carly Simon, Anthony Zerbe, George Maharis, Richard Roundtree, Joanne Woodward, Cloris Leachman, Cher, Polly Bergen, John Davidson, Norman Lear, Judy Collins, Carl Wilson, and Diana Ross. Jerry Rubin, after his graduation from the training, stated,

Est will spread like wildfire throughout America. It addresses itself to basic human needs, and does work by giving people a greater sense of themselves. In many ways, it was the most powerful growth experience I had.[11]

Business and political ties through *est* graduates are also numerous. On the organization's advisory board are Roger Sand, former Assistant Administrator of the Federal Energy Administration; Phil Lee, former Chancellor of the University of California's Medical School; Frank Berger, M.D., Consultant to the Surgeon General and to the U.S. Army; Jack Thayer, President of NBC Radio; Eugene Stevens, Mayor of Lompoc, California, and former UPI correspondent; and Peter Lenn, President of American Analysis Corporation, a firm developing educational training materials.

Est has its own public relations firm, Daniel J. Edleman, Inc., of New York. The separate *est* Foundation was established to advance research on the transformation of society and the self. Many of its grants have gone to Eastern religious movements like the Naropa Institute (Tibetan Buddhist) and Tibetan Buddhist Gyalwa Karmapa. *Est* sponsored the American tour of Hindu guru Swami Muktananda.

The University of California at Berkeley Extension offers three units of credit for taking the *est* training (along with a few other requirements). Nearly 10 percent of the educators in the San Francisco Unified School District are *est* graduates. Erhard candidly states, "The real thrust and goal of *est* is to put it in education."[12] The organization has special programs for children, teenagers, parents, college students, professors, blacks, prisoners, clergy, scientists, lawyers, psychiatrists, and homosexuals. There are offices in 17 cities. The first European training program was started in London in May of 1977. In 1976 there were 170 paid staff members and 13,000 volunteer staff members.

With an income of about a million dollars per month, *est* has still greater expansion plans. "If the Buddha could reach 400 million people without television, then we can certainly get 40 million,'' he has told his staff.[13] In 1976, *est* graduates brought over 83,000 people to Guest Seminars.[14]

The first children's training was in September 1971. Since then over 2000 children have been trained in California, Colorado, Hawaii, and New York. *Est* graduate Carl Frederick, author of *est: Playing the Game the New Way,* believes that schools should be created with one purpose: teaching children to follow whatever their natural inclinations are.[15] He instructs parents to ''set up very few rules with kids,'' and to ''get yourself out of the right/wrong game with your kids.''[16] Phyllis Allen, who conducts Children's Trainings, states, ''In the training, children discover. . .they are limitless, they are infinite.''[17]

One eight-year-old child who completed the training was asked by his mother to explain what he had gotten from the training. His reply: ''He just looked at me calmly and said, 'I don't really need you.' ''[18]

Erhard is a charismatic personality, described by some people as almost hypnotically fascinating. He commands respect from many prominent people. He has solicited thousands and thousands of people to pay his organization 200 to 300 dollars to learn that ''what is, is, and what isn't, isn't.'' An ex-trainer expressed the confusion he felt concerning Erhard: ''I don't know who Werner Erhard is, I don't know what his intentions are, and I don't know what his purpose is ultimately.''[19] One graduate said, ''My feeling is that *est* was the most valuable 60 hours of my life, and that Werner's a crook.''[20]

STRUCTURE AND AUTHORITY

Erhard demands complete submission from his workers. Adelaide Bry, *est* graduate and author of *est: 60 Hours that Transform Your Life,* recounted that she heard graduates and staff quote Erhard ''as though he were God.'' '' 'Werner says. . .' is the final word at *est,* from the trainers down to the pre-trainers.''[21] Bry herself says, ''I see him as totally powerful.''[22]

Stuart Emery, who was Erhard's first trainer, later left the organization, stating:

> You see, I've been in other meetings where Werner openly told people that if they were working for him, they had no rights, no privileges. They were not to have any desires or intentions of their own; they were not to foster any relationships for their own purposes. They were only to do what served Werner. So I left.[23]

Some graduates have at least some reservations about Erhard and his motives. Pat Marks recorded some of those reservations in her book *est: The Movement and the Man.*

> Freddy: I don't think he really cares whether he helps anyone or not.

> Arnold: The only thing that scares me about *est* is the Manchurian Candidate aspect. That is, that some day Werner's going to call us all up to vote for him.

> Earl: I don't know about Werner. . . .I think he's probably a con man.

> Jo: How do I feel about Werner? I hate him. I can't stand him. He is what he says, and I don't like those things. I don't like Werner. . .and thank God he's there. . . .There's just something about Werner that I don't like.

> Bobby: I mean, I don't care if he's a fraud, I think he's doing a lot of good for people.

Marks concluded, ''It amazed me that so many of them had reservations about either Werner or *est*.''[24]

Erhard defends himself against such suspicions, not by denying specific allegations, but by saying he's not afraid to admit his faults.

> How dare you attack my integrity with guilt by association. . . .Look, if you're trying to make me Wrong, I know how to make me Wrong much better than you could ever hope to do it. And I'm totally willing to do it: I have done evil things. Leaving a wife and four children is one hell

of a lot more evil than any of the bull---- that comes up in any
of the articles.[25]

Longtime friend Bill Thaw remembered that during the fifties he and Erhard were both interested in conning people,[26] and James Kettle notes, "Werner has said that he sees one of the great evils is our resistance to being conned."[27]

Some of Erhard's erratic demeanor is perhaps explained by his strange view of truth. He states, "The truth believed is a lie. If you go around telling the truth, you are lying."[28]

Erhard's techniques for answering media challenges sometimes appear dishonest. An *est* publication, *The Graduate Review,* gave the following, perhaps tongue-in-cheek (perhaps serious) account:

Lewis: Speaking of the old days, do you remember back to the time when *est* was getting all the attention from the media?

Trainer: Oh, yes. All those articles and stories about how *est* was fascistic, neo-Nazi brainwashing, and how *est* was dangerous and wanted to control everything?

Lewis: Yes, how was that all handled?

Trainer: Well, we gave them space, expanded to include them in our purpose, took total responsibility for them, and then we beat the sh-- out of them.

Lewis: How did Werner finally calm all that furor over what he did with the money?

Trainer: He bought the media.[29]

In the final analysis, however, Erhard, with all of his inconsistency, is the absolute master of the organization, his staff, and his graduates. Ex-trainer Stuart Emery recalled a confrontation between him and Don Cox, *est*'s President, when Cox upheld Erhard's supremacy. Cox was chastising Emery for visiting Peter Wagner, former Chief Executive Officer of *est,* with another staff person, Carol Augustus. Emery quoted Cox:

Stuart, I understand that you saw Peter Wagner. . . .Well, I consider that your presence there and Carol's presence there to be a disservice to Werner. It indicates to me that we can't trust you. And that's also true of Carol. So my response is that I have terminated Carol and asked her to leave the premises and she has done that. Now, what we have to discuss is the continuation of your relationship at *est*. I would only be willing for you to be at *est* if I were absolutely certain that you had given up all of your own intentions, purposes, desires and objectives in life and only had those purposes, desires, objectives, and intentions that Werner agreed for you to have.[30]

In addition to the dictatorship imposed by Erhard, the structure of the organization itself and of the all-important training sessions work together to produce a graduate who has completely "bought" the system.

The training consists of two weekends totaling 60 to 70 hours of lectures, confrontation sessions, "mind expansion meditation" exercises, and group interaction. *Est*'s primary form of proselytizing is by word of mouth, from graduates who promote it on a personal level. These graduates almost "testify" of how the training has changed their lives radically. Graduates are put under pressure to recruit new converts. Prospective trainees are brought to special Guest Seminars which introduce *est*. After the lecture, guests are strongly urged to sign up for the actual training.

A midweek evening seminar is sandwiched between the two weekend seminars to make up the complete training. There are eight optional graduate seminars which solidify the changes initiated at the original training. *Est* trainers have been personally selected by Erhard and trained by him for two years in the special techniques of passing *it* on. Through this personal work by Erhard, the format and content of each training is exactly the same. One training is a carbon copy of each other training.

Graduates' testimonies and potential converts' expectations often reflect desires to "improve oneself." However, *est* carefully distinguishes between *transforming* oneself and *improving* oneself. The goal of *est* is transformation, not betterment. Erhard said, "Sometimes people get the notion that the purpose of *est* is to make you better. It is not. I happen to think you are perfect exactly the way you are."[31] Transformation is its primary focus: "We want nothing short of a total transformation—an alteration of substance, not a change in form."[32] We will discuss Erhard's concept of transformation in the following discussion of his world view and semantics, perhaps the two most important concepts in *est* philosophy.

THE ESTIAN WORLD VIEW

Before we can discuss and see the impact of the actual *est* training we must understand the world view held by Erhard and promoted through *est*. One's world view may be determined by answering questions such as What is truth? What is reality? What is man? What is the world? Who is God? † and How does man reach his potential? We will explore *est*'s world view from these points.

The *est*ian world view is relativistic, subjective, and self-centered. There is no objective reality or truth; all ethics (issues of right and wrong) are personal and are not submitted to some independent criterion of right and truth; the self becomes the ultimate creator, experiencer, and judge of reality.

This shift in world view (which is radical for the usual person with a naive or critical-realistic world view) is accomplished in the training by manipulating words so that the initiates become confused and eventually agree that words may have no objective meaning. Once one believes in the futility of rational thinking and communicating, it is simple to also believe in the futility of a rational, objective world view.

---

† Discussed in depth in the section on the *est* doctrine of God.

Est staffer Dr. William Bartley states:

> Various altered states of consciousness play an important role in the training. . . .Certainly one can enter an altered state of consciousness through a number of the *est* processes. This will frequently produce solutions which would be beyond the reach of the so-called rational mind or normal state of consciousness.[33]

The importance of redefining and confusing words was stated by Erhard when he declared, "There are only two things in this world, semantics and nothing."[34] Ordinary language means nothing in Erhard's system. The prerequisites of all verbal communication are destroyed in his system. As William Greene declared, "Ordinary, commonplace words, with which everyone is familiar, take on a different meaning with *est*."[35]

Rather than trying to explain the difficult redefinition of terms in *est* and its own complicated and contradictory semantics, we will simply reproduce some representative quotes to show the verbal confusion which fights against the trainee's rationality.

> Perfection is a state in which things are the way they are, and are not the way they are not.[36]

> Understanding means a lie...the opposite of the truth. Understanding prevents an individual from experiencing.[37]

> Wrong is actually a version of right. If you're always wrong—you're right.[38]

> Although people are told not to believe anything the trainer says, under the circumstances in which the training is delivered (which uses some of the best technology to get people to hear information), they'll go away believing some of the stuff that they absolutely shouldn't believe.[39]

> The truth believed is a lie. If you go around telling the truth, you are lying.[40]

> Obviously the truth is what's so. Not so obviously, it's also

so what.[41]

Truth is not something of the mind. When the mind is no more, truth is. . . .And you become enlightened when you have found that there are no meanings in life. In fact, when you have found that there is nothing to be achieved, you have become enlightened. When you have come to realize that there is nowhere to go, you have arrived.[42]

Once one's critical thinking apparatus has become dismantled by the training's semantical barrage of nonsense, the trainee is in a state of limbo, unable to critically analyze what he is being told and how he is being manipulated. As soon as one is convinced that contradictions can be simultaneously true, he cannot test anything he experiences, thinks, feels, or is told.

Now that the stage is set on which *est*'s world view is presented, we can examine the organization's relativism, subjectivism, and self-centeredness.

Est views reality as completely created, controlled, experienced, and determined by the individual. There is no such thing as external objective reality. Whatever is perceived to exist by the individual has been created by that individual. What Oceania's Party said of the collective mind in George Orwell's *1984* is affirmed on an individual level in Erhard's world view. The folly of belief in objective reality was scorned by Orwell's Party character, O'Brien, when he declared to Winston, who believed in objective reality:

You believe that reality is something objective, external, existing in its own right. You also believe that the nature of reality is self-evident. When you delude yourself into thinking you see something, you assume that everyone else sees the same thing as you. But I tell you, Winston, that reality is not external. Reality exists in the human mind, and nowhere else. . . .[43]

Erhard confirms, ''Now what you and I normally call experience is that stuff that comes in from the outside, but that is part of the experience which I call non-experience.''[44]

The subjectivism promoted by the training denies any objective ethics or sense of right and wrong. In *est,* right and wrong are determined by the individual and depend on how things affect the individual.

> As long as a person is coming from his experience, whatever he says is perfect. It's just a question of accuracy.[45]

> And I found out in the training that success and failure are the same thing.[46]

> To master life, you simply need to know what you want. There's nothing you SHOULD want. Whatever you want's fine. There's no intrinsically valuable importance. . . .Wake up in the morning and make up a goal. It doesn't make any difference.[47]

Since all reality is subjective and relative to the individual, the individual becomes the creator of the reality he experiences, according to *est.* The individual is the God of his own universe. Nothing is real unless the individual chooses to make it real by experiencing it in his own subjective world. Consequently, whatever the individual experiences is a product of his creation. Erhard presupposes that one would not create what he does not want to exist. If this presupposition is correct, then whatever one experiences (and thus has created) is what one wants or desires.

The extreme self-centeredness of the *est*ian world view becomes plain. This world view is *monistic,* since the *est*ian world proceeds from, is shaped by, unfolds before, culminates in, and is real in only the *individual.* All of existence is summed up in one underlying principle or substance.‡ This world view is *narcissistic,* since all of existence is purely for the pleasure and edification of the *self.* There is no room for altruism or charity. The self is the only good, the only beautiful, the only significant one. Self is

---

‡ For further information on the idea of monism in theology and philosophy, see Warren Young's *A Christian Approach to Philosophy* (Grand Rapids: Baker, 1954), pp. 69, 74, 83, 170.

God! The *estian* self continually preens himself in the mirror of his private universe.

My notion is that what happens in the training is that the individual is given the opportunity to. . .re-experience the fact that he created himself.[48]

Efforting and struggling to get life to work is. . .[useless]. No matter what you do life only turns out the way it turns out. If you look back over your life you will see life has always turned out the way it did and never any other way—no matter what you did.

When I found out that nothing I had ever done had made a difference in my life, I was sad for a week. And on the other side of the realization that there was nothing I could do to force life to work, came the realization that it worked perfectly. A thing is perfect when it is the way it is. When it is not the way it is then it is flawed.[49]

The emotionally shattering implications of this world view are apparent when one is forced to agree that he has desired and created every experience he has ever had. This is one of the chief goals of the training. The following is a dialogue with a trainee who is being convinced by her trainer that she liked having her apartment robbed.

Trainer: Do you take responsibility for not having created friends who might have stayed in the apartment most of the time?

Trainee: Maybe, but—

Trainer: Whose idea is it that because you come home and find things missing from your apartment that you were robbed?

Trainee: My idea!

Trainer: Precisely.

Trainee: Damn it! [says Barbara irritably]. Precisely what!?

Trainer: Precisely you created the idea that you were robbed.

Trainee: But I didn't cause the robbery.

Trainer: There was no robbery unless you created it. If your stereo was stolen you did it.

Trainee: You're out of your mind!

Trainer: That's what *est* is all about. . .GET OUT OF YOUR MIND, BARBARA! YOU'RE THINKING IN CLICHES AND LETTING OTHER PEOPLE DICTATE REALITY when you actually create it yourself![50]

A graduate who later came to Christ and renounced *est* recalled how the implications of this world view affected those she knew in the organization.

She [the *est* staffer] wouldn't allow herself to be pinned down by saying that Sharon Tate DID choose to be murdered—only that if SHE was murdered, she would know that she had chosen it! You can only experience your OWN experience, never someone else's. With *est,* you have to keep getting that no one else really exists. Outside of yourself and your own experience NOTHING is even real, except that YOU are creating it, or THEM, to be real FOR YOU! To either love you or hate you.

Many people think they have FULL control over their bodies. There was a guy in our group who had to sit in the front row, all during the training, because he said he had a hearing problem. At the post-grad seminar, he was sitting in the back row and shared that he had no trouble hearing and wasn't wearing his hearing aid. He "got" that it was OK to have normal hearing.

After that a young girl shared that she no longer felt the need for contraceptives since she now knew she was in control of her body, and could simply "choose" not to get pregnant.[51]

We see that the *est*ian world view is completely relativistic, subjective, and self-centered. It is diametrically opposed to the Christian world view, which is rooted and founded in objective, absolute reality and truth and is Christ-centered. We will discuss this further.

Before we criticize the *est*ian world view, we need to briefly examine Erhard's "appendix" to his system. In an effort
to account for some of the problems with his world view and
to justify actions reminiscent of one's pre-*est* world, Erhard
invented "Games." Erhard's theory of Games is basically
that we gods (masters of our own subjective universes) got
bored being gods, so we decided to play games as if we were
men (Erhard does not define these men, who, before games,
wouldn't even have existed to be imitated by gods).

What nongraduates would consider reality, and what
graduates consider illusion, is the world of games. People's
problems come from their forgetting which is the game and
which is the reality. The majority of the world is in the sorry
state of constantly playing the games, since they have
forgotten that they are actually gods. Erhard's aim is to
eventually bring all individuals back to the point where they
remember that they are gods and are supreme in their own
subjective universe, and they play games for entertainment
rather than because they mistake the games for reality. For
now, those gods who have been enlightened must try to
bridge the gap between the two perceptions of reality.

I mean you start going around telling people that physicists
spend all their time playing with illusions and they'll lock you
up. A physicist won't be bothered, he knows that his whole
profession is based on the intelligent playing with agreed-
upon unrealities, but everybody else will cancel your vote.

And try telling people that the only real thing is your experience. Lots of luck. No, we'll have to stick to the code
words society accepts. When we talk about the unreal
physical universe we'll have to call it by its code word: 'reality.'[52]

Just to be on the safe side, trainees are warned that illusions can have serious collisions with inhabitants of *est*ian
reality. "The unreal physical universe is solid, it can kill."[53]

To escape the boredom of eternal existence in blinding
light (the state of pure reality, according to Erhard), we

gods have decided to make games. Since Erhard's world view is essentially monistic (there is only one underlying substance to all reality), all is one, all is sameness; there is no variety, no importance, no good, no bad—just Being. Therefore, "To have a game, you have to agree that something is more important than something else"[54]—even though all of us gods know that nothing is more important than anything else.

> THE POINT IS THAT YOU LOSE YOUR ABILITY TO PLAY THE GAME, TO MASTER THE GAME, WHEN YOU FORGET THAT A GAME IS A GAME. In order to master life, we need to recover the realization that life is truly a game.[55]

> But when all is said and done, life is a game. Some of the games have enormous consequences. However, if you get stuck in the importance of it, then you no longer see that it's a game. Even when the consequences are enormous, you need to realize it's a game. EVERYTHING in life is a game, EXCEPT LIVING.
> Living is not a game. Living is simply what is.[56]

Despite Erhard's attempt to make his system less fanciful by acknowledging some idea of the external world through his "Games" theory, the *est*ian world view is solipsistic—totally self-centered. Self is the only reality. This effectively isolates individuals from each other, the external world, reason, and, ultimately, the infinite God, who is outside of man and on whom all of us depend for all things. The *est* graduate, having bought Erhard's warped picture of reality, is now immune from everything outside himself.

The graduate has now been transformed. Transformation is the key in the *est* system. Transformation is not change. Once one is transformed, and recognizes that he is God and that he is the master and maker of reality, anything he does is good. It is *his* game. The individual makes all the rules and all the players, and he *always* wins.

I want to be clear with you that *est* and transformation are NOT a matter of getting better. I support things that make people better; I support things that contribute to the content of people's lives. But *est* is not about getting better. *est* is about transformation.[57]

Living is just what's happening right now, right this instant, and that's all perfect. Perfect means what is—is, and what isn't—isn't, and that's flawless.[58]

The goal of the training is summed up by Erhard in his ambivalent statement that, however irrational it may seem, the graduate enthusiastically doesn't care:

WHAT is, IS, and what ain't, AIN'T. So what! That's precisely what people say when they find out. Enthusiastically—So what! There's an enormous freedom in experiencing that. When you can really observe and experience that, it transforms your ability to experience living.[59]

All the techniques of the training are designed to transform the individual so that he adopts the world view presented here. All of Erhard's disjointed doctrine and religious belief stems from this illogical world view. To refute Erhard's world view is to refute his training, his doctrine, and his religious belief. All depends on his world view. No wonder the training is oriented solely to producing this world view in all participants!

No matter how hard Erhard may try to assert the validity of his view, he is defeated logically and scripturally. We shall first examine the logical inconsistency of his system and then the biblical answer to the *est*ian world view.

If reality is truly solipsistic (wholly within the self), then nothing exists outside the self. How, then, does nonexistent Werner Erhard communicate to me, the only existence in reality? Am I really alone, as he says? Then how can he be there to say I am alone? If Erhard grants himself enough objective reality to enable him to communicate his beliefs to others, then he has granted enough objective reality to *refute* his own beliefs. This makes as much sense as the man who asserts that he is absolutely sure there are no absolutes! §

The Bible refutes Erhard in that it affirms the existence of objective reality—one God who is independent of any created thing, who is the Maker of all human personalities, and who is eternal, omnipotent, omniscient, and transcendent. ☆ Isaiah 5:20,21 speaks directly to vain philosophies like Erhard's:

> Woe to those who call evil good and good evil, who put darkness for light and light for darkness, who put bitter for sweet and sweet for bitter. Woe to those who are wise in their own eyes and clever in their own sight.

THE TRAINING

Many of the techniques used in the actual training sessions are similar enough to other occultic, Eastern, metaphysical, and/or mind-control disciplines as to be almost identical. Of the many activities in the four-day seminars, the "Truth Process" and the "Danger Process" are perhaps the most important and the most emotional. We will discuss them separately.

In the Truth Process exercise, trainees are told to lapse into a meditative state and to start locating "spaces" in their bodies for 20 or 30 minutes. This relaxation and conditioning prepares them to follow the trainer into the core of the exercise. During the meditation time they are told that they are perfect and good.

With implicit trust in the trainer, they are told to directly ("realistically") experience a particularly painful or distasteful situation. With prompting from the trainer, they are led to imagine a situation as being so real that they can, in the training, experience every emotion that would accom-

---

§ In philosophy, this is known as a self-stultifying statement.
☆ For further information, see the section on *est's* doctrines (later in this chapter).

pany the actual situation. Graduate William Greene remarks, "Taking everyone through specific situations, the trainer skillfully manages to reach the inner emotional depths of practically everyone present."[60]

Participants are encouraged to openly express all the emotions that now rush in rapidly on them. A torrent of emotion and inner turmoil burst from the participants, sending the entire room into vocal and visual upheaval, indicating the emotional upheavel erupting within the trainees.

It seems now that almost the entire roomful of people are crying, moaning, groaning, sobbing, screaming, shouting, writhing. 'Stop it! Stop it!' 'No! No! No!' 'I didn't do it! I didn't do it!' 'Please. . .' 'Help!' 'Daddy, daddy, daddy. . .' The groans, the crying, the shouts reinforce each other; the emotion pours out of the trainees. For some, the uninhibited hysterics of others becomes a barrier: they freeze and lose contact with their own experience.[61]

A trainee reviewed:

Soon the room was filled with moans, sobs, whimpers, and cries. Then there was an earsplitting scream. A man cried out, "It's on my chest—get it off!" I felt I was the only normal person in the place. I sat up and saw hundreds of people writhing and flailing the air. I was in a snake pit and I wanted out—to hell with the money! I never might get it, but I had had it.[62]

Greene reported:

More people join the screaming and the crying. The rustle of vomit bags is heard as they are passed among the sick. As the Process continues, more people begin to get sick. After what seems an endless period of time to most people—about an hour—the room begins to quiet. The screams fade to moans. The wailing and crying become soft weeping and moaning. . . .People pick themselves up and wander out of the room. (During my training, we all meandered around a girl who was lying unconscious on the floor as a result of the Process.)[63]

Some say the Truth Process is emotionless compared to the wrenching emotional torture of the Danger Process. Groups of trainees are marched onto the stage and stand in a straight line in front of the audience. They are instructed to make eye contact with the audience. They are then mercilessly harrassed, criticized, and badgered by the *est* staff. The verbal assault emotionally rapes the trainees, leaving them with torn and mutilated emotions. Greene described it:

> Like a scene from a horror movie, people began to fall apart right before your eyes. The man who had never been able to tell his wife that he really needed her went into a catatonic state. The woman who confessed to never having an orgasm cried until she collapsed. A young man, who had come with his married sister, cried hysterically. A tall, thin man swayed like a willow in the wind. Finally, he fainted on the floor. The trainer ran over and started screaming at him. "Cut the act, Michael. That's just a big ----- game you're playing."[64]

Next the trainees are told to lie on the floor and are told to "go into their spaces." Their "spaces" are mentally constructed fantasy environments where they can supposedly experience anything "safely." They are told to pretend they are filled with fear and terror of the person lying next to them. Progressively they are told to fear the others in the room, the city, and then the whole world. The trainees are to experience the feeling that the whole world is trying to murder them.

> A lot of people take the instructions to heart and scream and throw up and curl into the fetal position. Some black out and finally faint. The hotel room has become a madhouse. Many people are obviously not pretending. It is as if they are in a deep hypnotic trance and living out their fears.[65]

> The screams started coming. By the time the trainer had everyone frightened of the entire universe, the room was alive with screaming. Once again, I could hear people retching all about me. For a fleeting moment I opened my eyes and look-

ed out onto mass hysteria. That was enough to bring me back.[66]

Soon I could hear people having eerie, unreal, almost animal moanings—then yelling—screaming at the top of their lungs! I heard noises like bodies were slamming down on the floor—hitting the floor, I guess (I was too afraid to open my eyes, so this may not be the case, but it sounded like it). I was truly scared half to death! How many of those people were unstable enough to start believing the process was real?

That's all I could think of, was that someone would start beating me to death because they thought I was trying to kill them. I wasn't doing the process! I was scared half to death because of what others were doing. How could even the *est* people know who was pretending and who really believe it?

I wouldn't recommend *est* to anyone—if for no other reason than that one process! One girl did flip out, but I'm not sure it wasn't permanent. I guess *est* would say she chose to flip out or at best they would say that she would have sooner or later anyway. Our particular trainer wouldn't talk about it. He just said to forget it and worry about our self.[67]

There are many other processes and techniques used by the trainers to manipulate and "transform" the trainees. These include exercises in switching male and female roles; imagining oneself climbing in or on imaginary giant fruits and flowers; and literally making fools of themselves. Women are asked to play the roles of loud, stupid drunks, men are asked to play precocious little girls, etc.[68] Trainees are taught that "every heterosexual has a homosexual element in him someplace, and every homosexual has a repressed heterosexual inside."[69]

Based on Erhard's world view (discussed previously), the battered trainees are taught that now that they have abandoned all previous self-concept and self-worth, they are ready to accept the truth: they are each their own gods, the masters of their own universes, engaged in only those mortal games in which they choose to engage themselves. Everything we experience, trainees are told, we have created and desired.

Snapping back to the present, 1 heard Werner screaming that we create everything that happens to us in our lives. . . .He said that Vietnamese babies created the napalm that fell on their heads, the Jews constructed Auschwitz, that rape victims desired to be raped. The audience went crazy, screaming, turning off, throwing up their hands in outrage. Werner ran around the room arguing his theory of self-responsibility with each person, obviously trying to offend, shock, scare, create a mood.[70]

However, Erhard is doing more than just trying to offend and create a mood. Because of his world view, he actually believes what he is screaming, and he instills that belief into his followers. All good *est* graduates are completely self-centered. After all, the self is the only reality, the only God, the only good, the creator of all experiences. These are the lasting effects of the trainings on graduates.#

Graduate therapists echoed Erhard's callous treatment of others to Peter Marin, writer of "The New Narcissism," in *Harper's* magazine (October 1975):

I listen for two hours in a graduate seminar to two women therapists explaining to me how we are all entirely responsible for our destinies, and how the Jews must have wanted to be burned by the Germans, and that those who starve in the Sahel must want it to happen, and when I ask them whether there is anything we owe to others, say, to a child starving in the desert, one of them snaps at me angrily: "What can I do if a child is determined to starve?"

Marin also interviewed a dozen *est* graduates, and each of them displayed the same self-centered world view that Erhard propagates. Referring to one woman graduate, he recorded her beliefs:

. . .that because of the training she now understood: (1) that the individual will is all-powerful and totally determines

---

Est sources promote nebulous positive effects from the training. We have chosen to let the graduates speak for themselves as to the results.

one's fate; (2) that she felt neither guilt nor shame about anyone's fate and that those who were poor and hungry must have wished it on themselves; (3) that the North Vietnamese must have wanted to be bombed, or else it could not have happened to them; (4) that a friend of hers who had been raped and murdered in San Francisco was to be pitied for having willed it to occur; (5) that in her weekend at *est* she had attained full enlightenment; (6) that she was God; (7) that whatever one thought to be true was true beyond all argument; (8) that I was also God, and that my ideas were also true, but not as true as hers because I had not had the training; and (9) that my use of logic to criticize her beliefs was unfair, because reason was 'irrational,' though she could not tell me why.[71]

A typical graduate's response to charges that Erhard manipulates people is likely to be, "I take responsibility for the people that let me step on them, and I don't feel guilty."[72]

Suzanne Gordon in her *Lonely in America* summarized the self-centered, nihilistic pessimism of *est*.

If I do something bad to someone, it's because the other person asked for it. A convenient side effect is that anything that happens to a person inside an *est* training is the individual's fault, not *est*. One man who had gone to *est* with his girlfriend said that she had tried to commit suicide the week after the training, and having failed, she joined the army. It was perfectly all right, the man said, that that had happened. It was neither his responsibility nor *est*'s because she must have wanted it to happen.[73]

How this contrasts with the attitude of the Christian following the example of his Lord and Master, Jesus Christ! *Est* is self-centered; Christianity is other-centered. *Est* condones selfishness; Jesus' command was, "Love each other as I have loved you. Greater love has no one than this, that one lay down his life for his friends" (John 15:12,13). The two greatest commandments of all time were declared by Jesus: to love God and to "love your neighbor as yourself"

(Matthew 22:37-39). Paul summarized the Christian attitude by saying, "Whatever other commandments there may be are summed up in this one rule: 'Love your neighbor as yourself' " (Romans 13:9).

DOCTRINE

The greater portion of this chapter has dealt with the structure, authority, and world view of *est*. Since *est* is primarily a personality-manipulating process, neither Erhard nor *est* spends a great deal of time discussing religious concepts. However, all world views encompass one's religious stance. This may be as simple as the atheist's world view, which actively denies the existence of any God and the validity of any religious system, or as complicated as the constantly evolving polypantheism which is intricately woven into the Hindu world view. We have already seen that *est* denies the God-centered and other-centered world view of Christianity. We will now examine *est*'s assertions concerning God, man, Jesus Christ, and salvation.

God and Man

Since *est* teaches that God is man and man is God, we shall treat the doctrines of God and man together here. When a religious system asserts that man is God or God is man, it may mean one of several things. Mormonism believes that to say that man is God is to say that obedient male Mormons may eventually become individual gods. Mormonism teaches both the deification of man and polytheism, or the belief in many gods.**

Armstrongism would define the statement to mean that man becomes part of the one God, who will eventually consume all of existence within himself. Armstrongism teaches the deification of man and a monotheism that borders on

---

** See Walter Martin's *The Maze of Mormonism* for further information on Mormonism.

pantheism.†† Hinduism contradictorily combines both ideas, teaching that individual men can become individual gods but that the ultimate goal of existence is for all to become part of the one impersonal god, which is all existence. Hinduism teaches polytheism and pantheism in its definition of the deification of man.‡‡

When *est* says that man is God, it means something different from all of the above ideas. The deification of man within Erhard's theology means that the individual becomes (or realizes that he is) an individual, personal god. However, in addition, Erhard asserts the presupposition that this individual God is the only substance in existence in all of reality. This would appear to be a form of pantheism. However—and this complicates *est*ian theology—Erhard must at least tacitly admit the existence of a multiplicity of individuals (or gods) to whom he can communicate these wonderful truths. This is contradictory. The least problematical way of understanding this would be to say that there must be a multiplicity of realities which are at the same time self-contained and yet interrelating. In other words, Erhard seems to be asserting that within reality there is one substance: the god-self that is experiencing that reality. However, since there are a multiplicity of god-selves, there must be a multiplicity of realities.

The important element to remember about *est* theology is its claim that man is God and God is man. When one has mastered the training and the belief system of *est*, then he can ridicule the untransformed as the trainer ridicules the new trainees:

> You can't win in here. Nobody wins in here except me. Unless I decide to LET you win. It ought to be perfectly clear to everyone now that you're all ----holes and I'm God. Only an ----hole would argue with God. I may let you be Gods too, but that'll come later.[74]

††See Walter Martin's *The Rise of the Cults.*
‡‡See Chapter 3 for information on Hinduism and Eastern thought.

In actuality, each of us, as the sole creator of our universe, is a God, and because we have created all, everything is as important as everything else. When we're fully in touch with what already is and accept what is as more important than what isn't, then all games are over. There's nothing to do, nowhere to go, everything is perfect.[75]

Your're God in your universe. You caused it. You pretended not to cause it so that you could play in it, and you can remember you caused it any time you want to.[76]

But we Gods get bored with this perfection, and so we always end up pretending that something which ISN'T is more important than what is, and that's a game. . . .As long as we're sitting here feeling perfect, being fully aware of our being Creator, then all is equally important. There's nothing to do, no game to play, we can sit for a while in bliss examining our navels. But we get bored. We decide to begin playing again.[77]

And now I'm going to step down from the platform and return to playing the game of Michael, God pretending He's a human, interacting with you other Gods, also pretending you're humans.[78]

You see, it's O.K. with Werner that Jesus called Himself God, and claimed pre-existence and eternal life. But what Werner *(est)* wants to do, and is doing, is telling us that we too are God—pre-existed and can have eternal life, in the form of reincarnation.[79]

My notion is that what happens in the training is that the individual is given the opportunity to. . .re-experience the fact that he created himself.[80]

'In your universe you're God,' Rod said, 'you caused it, and pretended not to cause it so you could play in it. And there are at least as many universes as there are people on this planet. It all comes out of your point of view.[81]

Transformation is THE SELF AS THE SELF, the self as the context of all contexts, everything/nothing. The self itself is the ground of all being, that from which everything arises.[82]

The Scriptures categorically deny that God is man or that man is God. According to the truths of the Bible, there is an infinite gap between Creator and created. The one divine Being, who eternally exists in three distinct Persons—Father, Son, and Holy Spirit—is that Creator.

The eternal, unchanging God is not like finite, fickle humanity. Numbers 23:19 declares, "God is not a man, that he should lie, nor a son of man, that he should change his mind. Does he speak and then not act? Does he promise and not fulfill?" The distinction between God and man is emphasized in Job 37:23,24: "The Almighty is beyond our reach and exalted in power; in his justice and great righteousness, he does not oppress. Therefore, men revere him, for does he not have regard for all the wise in heart?"

Far from God being man, God created man. "It is I who made the earth and created mankind upon it. My own hands stretched out the heavens; I marshaled their starry hosts" (Isaiah 45:12).

Man is not God and can never become or realize deity. One cannot be transformed into God. Self-centered pride is at the heart of such boasts (Genesis 3:5; Isaiah 14:14). Ezekiel 28:2b clearly affirms, "In the pride of your heart you say, 'I am a god; I sit on the throne of a god in the heart of the seas.' But you are a man and not a god, though you think you are as wise as a god." As Paul reminds us, we are totally dependent upon God for our existence: "He himself gives all men life and breath and everything else" (Acts 17:25b).

The pagans in Lystra held the mistaken belief that men like Paul and Barnabas could be gods (Acts 14). Paul rebuked them, saying, "Men, why are you doing this? we too are only men, human like you" (v. 15). Romans 1:21-23 speaks to those who substitute worship of the true, infinite God with futile worship of man:

For although they knew God, they neither glorified him as

God nor gave thanks to him, but their thinking became futile and their foolish hearts were darkened. Although they claimed to be wise, they became fools and exchanged the glory of the immortal God for images made to look like mortal man and birds and animals and reptiles.

Christ

Erhard does not present a systematic Christology, or study of his beliefs concerning Jesus Christ. However, the random comments he makes concerning Christ make it evident that the Jesus of *est* is not the Jesus of the Bible.

Erhard denies the unique deity of Christ, as do all non-Christian cultic leaders. Although he would say that Jesus is God, he means it in the same sense in which each of us is God of our own realities. The deity of Christ for *est* is not different from the deity of every human being.

You see, it's O.K. with Werner that Jesus called Himself God, and claimed pre-existence and eternal life. But what Werner *(est)* wants to do, and is doing, is telling us that we too are God—pre-existed and can have eternal life, in the form of reincarnation.§§

Technically he's not denying the Divinity of Jesus—only His uniqueness. That boils down to Jesus being an enlightened guy who knew he was God, but was on too much of an ego trip to tell others that they were also God.[83]

Werner Erhard: How do I know I'm not the reincarnation of Jesus Christ? You wouldn't believe the feelings I have inside me.[84]

All belief is the least reliable form of knowing. Belief represents UN certainty. People believe in God because they have no real certainty about Her [sic]. . . .A belief is a statement that does NOT COME OUT OF EXPERIENCE. 'Christ died and on the third day rose from the dead.'. . .It's a belief.[85]

___

§§ See Chapter 11, on reincarnation, for information on that subject.

I've read the Bible a lot, and now I see that the church totally misinterpreted what Jesus said. He kept telling everyone over and over that everybody was like he was: perfect. He was experiencing life, like Werner. He knew he was total source, living moment to moment, and was spontaneous.

Jesus is just another guru who happens to be popular here in Western civilization. I can't go into a church and praise Jesus. But I really got where he is coming from. He wants to let everybody know "I'm you." So my whole point of view about religion has been totally altered.[86]

Est teaches a Jesus who is just like each one of us—his own god in his own private universe. This Jesus could be reincarnated as Werner Erhard—who is, if not the reincarnation of Jesus, at least said to be the most transformed individual in history. A Christian's beliefs concerning Jesus cannot be trusted—what the Bible asserts as historical fact (that Jesus rose bodily from the grave) is said by *est* to be the product of "the least reliable form of knowing." Jesus is not Lord and Savior to the *est* graduate: he is "just another guru who happens to be popular."

According to the Bible, the Jesus of Werner Erhard is a false Jesus (2 Corinthians 11:4) and is nothing like the historical Jesus (1 John 2:22). The Jesus Christ of history is the second Person of the Trinity, fully God, the unique Son of the Father, eternal. He became man (while not relinquishing His deity) as the ultimate selfless act to redeem fallen mankind. As an objective fact of history He died and rose again immortal, with a glorified body, triumphant over death, assuring us of salvation and ultimate resurrection like Him if we belong to Him.

That Jesus is God the Son is asserted many times in the Bible (John 1:1; 5:18; 8:58; Colossians 2:9; Philippians 2:1-11; Titus 2:13; etc.). In Person He is distinct from the Father (John 17:3-5) and the Holy Spirit (John 14:26), although each of these three shares fully in the nature of the one God (Luke 3:21,22; Matthew 28:19). ☆ ☆

Jesus is the unique Son of God. There is no man like Him today, there never has been at any time in the past, and there never will be at any time in the future. First Peter 1:20 tells us, "he was chosen before the creation of the world, but was revealed in these last times for your sake." The first chapters of Hebrews show clearly the uniqueness of Jesus Christ. He is no ordinary man, the same as all around Him. He alone can claim perfect humanity and perfect deity subsisting in one divine Person. "The Son is the radiance of God's glory and the exact representation of his being, sustaining all things by his powerful word" (Hebrews 1:3). Unlike sinful mankind, Jesus Christ "is holy, blameless, pure, set apart from sinners, exalted above the heavens" (Hebrews 7:26).

The uniqueness of Christ is seen in the Apostle John's description of Him in the first chapter of his Gospel. Jesus is described as Deity, Creator of all things (John 1:1-3), who "became flesh and lived for a while among us" (John 1:14). However, He is not just like us: "We have seen his glory, the glory of the one and only Son, who came from the Father, full of grace and truth" (John 1:14b). Verse 18 calls him literally "God the only Son."

The resurrection of Jesus cannot be dismissed as lightly as *est* attempts to dismiss it. Although it is true that Christians believe that Jesus rose immortal from the grave, our belief does not rest on a lie which contradicts reality. The resurrection of Christ is a historical event. Peter, who had been with Jesus since the beginning of His ministry, declared, "We did not follow cleverly invented stories when we told you about the power and coming of our Lord Jesus Christ, but we were eyewitnesses of his majesty" (2 Peter 1:16). The disciples empirically verified the glorified body of Jesus after the resurrection (Luke 24:39; John 20:27,28).

☆ ☆ See Appendix "The Local Church of Witness Lee," and its section on the doctrine of the Trinity for a more thorough analysis of the biblical doctrine.

Peter preached to Jews shortly after the resurrection and appealed to the evidence to convince them of Christ's resurrection. He said, "Jesus of Nazareth was a man accredited by God to you by miracles, wonders and signs, which God did among you through him, as you yourselves know. This man was handed over to you by God's set purpose and foreknowledge; and you, with the help of wicked men, put him to death by nailing him to the cross. But God raised him from the dead, freeing him from the agony of death, because it was impossible for death to keep its hold on him" (Acts 2:22-24).

When Paul asserted the resurrection of Christ before Governor Festus, this exchange took place.

I am saying nothing beyond what the prophets and Moses said would happen—that the Christ would suffer and, as the first to rise from the dead, would proclaim light to his own people and to the Gentiles.

At this point Festus interrupted Paul's defense. "You are out of your mind, Paul!" he shouted. "Your great learning is driving you insane."

"I am not insane, most excellent Festus," Paul replied. "What I am saying is true and reasonable. The king is familiar with these things, and I can speak freely to him. I am convinced that none of this has escaped his notice, because it was not done in a corner" (Acts 26:22-26).

Finally, "if Christ has not been raised, our preaching is useless and so is your faith. More than that, we are then found to be false witnesses about God, for we have testified about God that he raised Christ from the dead" (1 Corinthians 15:14,15). Christ's resurrection has assured us a resurrection like His if we belong to Him. At that time "the perishable must clothe itself with the imperishable, and the mortal with immortality. When the perishable has been clothed with the imperishable, and the mortal with immortality, then the saying that is written will come true: 'Death has been swallowed up in victory'" (1 Corinthians

15:53,54).

Salvation

Salvation in the world of *est* is static. One is not saved at all: one merely realizes that he is already perfect and divine. There is no room in this world view for a savior, sin, or judgment. In this respect *est* resembles Christian Science and Science of Mind.

In actuality, each of us, as the sole creator of our universe, is a God, and because we have created all, everything is as important as everything else. When we're fully in touch with what already is and accept what is as more important than what isn't, then all games are over. There's nothing to do, nowhere to go, everything is perfect.[87]

After I graduated and after becoming a Christian, I asked four *est* staff members if I was correct in getting from the training that I didn't need Jesus for salvation or anything else. They all told me that I should be clear that no one needs salvation or Jesus![88]

The difference between the enlightened man and the unenlightened man is nothing. . . .The enlightened man does nothing. The fully enlightened man ALWAYS does nothing. Doing nothing is simply doing what you're doing when you're doing it. Doing nothing is simply accepting what is.[89]

My self is absolute.[90]

Once you know that you're totally all right (and you can call that God, or anything you want to call it), you can encompass anything within your alrightness.[91]

. . .in the *est* training YOU are God. . . .Therefore, you cannot look to any supreme being for special treatment, goodness, or award.[92]

We've been conditioned to look for answers outside ourselves. But that's not what people get from us. What they get is an experience of enlightenment, which is different from the belief system called salvation. If I get the idea that God is going to save me, therefore I'm all right, that's salvation; if I get the idea that nothing's going to save me, therefore I'm all right, that's enlightenment.[93]

Life is always perfect just the way it is. When you realize that, then no matter how strongly it may appear to be otherwise, you know that whatever is happening right now will turn out all right. Knowing this, you are in a position to begin mastering life.[94]

Realize you're all right the way you are and you'll get better naturally.[95]

Est is not going to save mankind; mankind is going to have to save itself. I got this point so clearly that I won't forget it ever again.[96]

The "salvation" of *est* is not salvation at all, but transformation. And transformation itself is nothing other than thinking that one is *already* perfect, the master of his own destiny, and, in fact, God. We have already seen that man is not God. We can also see that by substituting reincarnation for the cross of Christ and His resurrection, Erhard attacks the core of the Christian gospel. Christ purged our sins by Himself (Hebrews 1:3); not by cycles of rebirth, but once-for-all. The Bible repeatedly reminds us that we are sinful, imperfect, corruptible, and in need of a Savior. We cannot save ourselves by reincarnation or by our own works, as Erhard would have it. God alone has provided salvation through His Son.

Even apart from the Bible we know that mankind is sinful. All around us we see things that we realize are evil, wicked, wrong—evidences of the depravity of mankind. Romans 3:10-12 tells us that all men are sinful: "there is no one who does good, not even one." Verse 23 of the same chapter declares that "all have sinned and fall short of the glory of God." No matter how much good we think we may do, no matter how righteous we think ourselves to be, God reminds us that "all our righteous acts are like filthy rags" (Isaiah 64:6).

Salvation is God's way of restoring us to right fellowship with Him and forgiving us of our sins. This salvation is only possible through God's action toward us: there is nothing we can do to achieve it on our own. God accomplished our salvation through the gift of His own Son, Jesus Christ, a ransom for many, the propitiation for our sins. John the Baptist declared of Jesus, "The Lamb of God, who takes away the sin of the world!" (John 1:29). The only "work" anyone can do to obtain salvation is what Jesus declared: "The work of God is this: to believe in the one he has sent" (John 6:29). Those of us who are saved have been purchased with Jesus Christ's blood shed on the cross.

Romans 3:24 gives us the good news that we "are justified freely by his grace through the redemption that came by Christ Jesus." It is by the atonement accomplished by Christ that we are saved. "Therefore, since we have been justified through faith, we have peace with God through our Lord Jesus Christ, through whom we have gained access by faith into this grace in which we now stand. And we rejoice in the hope of the glory of God" (Romans 5:1,2).

Contrasting the sacrifices of the Old Testament with the supreme sacrifice of Christ on behalf of all the believers throughout all time, the writer of Hebrews exclaims, "How much more, then, will the blood of Christ, who through the eternal Spirit offered himself unblemished to God, cleanse our consciences from acts that lead to death, so that we may serve the living God!" (Hebrews 9:14).

Salvation is not the result of our own works or the works of anyone other than Jesus Christ, the Savior of our souls. "Salvation is found in no one else, for there is no other name under heaven given to men by which we must be saved" (Acts 4:12).

CONCLUSION

The maze of intermingled religious, pseudopsychological, and mystical ideas which constitute Werner Erhard's *est* leads away from the living God of the Bible, and to destruction. It is impossible to serve the selfish ego god of *est* (the unrepentant self) and also the true God, the God of the Bible. Erhard's theories are not in harmony with the Bible and cannot be reconciled with historic Christianity. *Est*ian love is impotent and emaciated compared to the all-encompassing, vital, multiplying, and altruistic love described in the Bible and given to all Christians.

This is how we know what love is: Jesus Christ laid down his life for us. And we ought to lay down our lives for our brothers. If anyone has material possessions and sees his brother in need but has no pity on him, how can the love of God be in him? Dear children, let us not love with words or tongue but with actions and in truth. This then is how we know that we belong to the truth, and how we set our hearts at rest in his presence whenever our hearts condemn us. For God is greater than our hearts, and he knows everything.

. . .And this is his command: to believe in the name of his Son, Jesus Christ, and to love one another as he commanded us (1 John 3:16-20,23).

CHAPTER NOTES

1. R.C. Heck and J.L. Thompson, "EST: Salvation or Swindle," in *San Francisco Magazine,* Jan. 1976, p. 70.

2. "Werner Erhard—An Interview with the Source of EST", Part 1, *The New Age Journal,* No. 7, Sept. 15, 1975, pp. 18-20.

3. Werner Erhard, "The Transformation of EST," in *The Graduate Review,* Nov. 1976, p. 2.

4. Jesse Kornbluth, "The Führer Over EST," in *New Times,* Mar. 19, 1976, p. 41.

5. Adelaide Bry, *EST: 60 Hours That Transform Your Life* (New York: Avon, 1976), p. 200.

6. Marcia Seligson, "EST," in *New Times Magazine,* Oct. 18, 1974.

7. Donald Porter and Diane Taxson, *The EST Experience* (New York: Award Books, 1976), p. 180.

8. *The Graduate Review,* Mar. 1977, p. 10.

9. Maureen Orth, "The Sunshine Boy," in *Newsweek,* Dec. 20, 1976.

10. Gary Clarke, "The Struggle to Share It," in *The Graduate Review,* Feb. 1977, p. 4.

11. Jerry Rubin, "The *est* Things in Life Aren't Free," in *Crawdaddy,* Feb. 1976.

12. "Werner Erhard: All I Can Do is Lie," in *The East-West Journal,* Sept. 1974.

13. Kornbluth, "The Führer Over Est," op. cit., p. 40.

14. Ibid., p. 50; *The Graduate Review,* June 1977, p. 14.

15. Carl Frederick, *est: Playing the Game the New Way* (New York: Delta, 1976), p. 63.

16. Ibid., pp. 118-19.

17. Neil Rogin, "A Trainer Is a Graduate Who Does the Training, Part 1," in *The Graduate Review,* May 1977, p. 4.

18. Bry, op. cit., pp. 140-41.

19. Robert Hargrove, *est: Making Life Work* (New York: Dell, 1976), p. 212.

20. Pat Marks, *est: The Movement and the Man* (Chicago: Playboy Press, 1976), pp. 156-58.

21. Bry, op. cit., p. 66.

22. Ibid., p. 135.

23. "Forum: *est,* Who Got What?" (Interview with Stewart Emery, Carl Fredericks, Peter Marin, Robert Hargrove), in *The East-West Journal,* Dec. 15, 1975, vol. 5, no. 12, p. 12.

24. Marks, op. cit., pp. 156-58.

25. Kornbluth, op. cit., pp. 40, 43, 45, 50.

26. Ibid., p. 41.

27. James Kettle, *The est Experience* (New York: Kensington Corp, Zebra Books Edition, 1976), p. 78.

28. "Werner Erhard: All I Can Do Is Lie," op. cit.

29. *The Graduate Review,* Aug. 1976, p. 11.

30. "Forum: *est,* Who Got What?" (Interview with Stewart Emery, Carl Fredericks, Peter Marin, Robert Hargrove), op. cit., p. 12.

31. "What Is the Purpose of the *est* Training?" *est* brochure, 1976, p. 1.

32. Erhard, "The Transformation of *est,*" in *The Graduate Review,* Nov. 1976.

33. Porter and Taxson, op. cit., p. 175.

34. Bry, op. cit., p. 198.

35. William Greene, *est: 4 Days to Make Your Life Work* (New York: Simon and Schuster, Pocket Books Edition, 1976, p. 27.

36. "Werner's Aphorisms," *est* publication, no city, no date (leaflet).

37. Greene, op. cit., p. 35.

38. Bry, op. cit., p. 192.

39. "Forum: *est,* Who Got What?" op. cit., p. 12.

40. *East West Journal,* Sept. 1974, op. cit.

41. *est* Graduation booklet.

42. Bhagwan Shree Rajneesh explaining Werner Erhard's Aphorisms, in *The Graduate Review,* July 1977, p. 12.

43. George Orwell, *Nineteen Eighty-four* (New York: The New American Library, Signet Classics, 1949, 1961), p. 205.

44. "Werner Erhard: All I Can Do Is Lie," op. cit.

45. Hargrove, op. cit., p. 158.

46. Marks, op. cit., p. 55.

47. Erhard, "Life, Living, and Winning the Game," in *The Graduate Review,* July 1976, p. 3.

48. "Werner Erhard: All I Can Do Is Lie," op. cit.

49. Erhard, *The Graduate Review,* June 1976, p. 12.

50. Luke Rhinehart, *The Book of est* (New York: Holt, Rinehart, and Winston, 1976), pp. 139-40.

51. Private correspondence from a former *est* devotee to researcher John Weldon (name of correspondent withheld for privacy). Documentation on file with researcher Weldon.

52. Rhinehart, op. cit., p. 133.

53. Ibid., p. 134.

54. *The Graduate Review,* July 1976, p. 5.

55. Ibid., p. 5.

56. Ibid., p. 3.

57. Erhard, "The Transformation of *est,*" op. cit., p. 3.

58. Erhard, "Life, Living, and Winning the Game," op. cit., p. 2.

59. Ibid.

60. Greene, op. cit., p. 67.

61. Rhinehart, op. cit., p. 101.

62. Private interview with researcher John Weldon. Trainee's name withheld by request. Interview on file with researcher.

63. Greene, op. cit., p. 67.

64. Greene, op. cit., pp. 68-69.

65. Lande, op. cit., p. 139.

66. Greene, op. cit., p. 73.

67. Private interview with researcher John Weldon. Interviewee's name withheld by request. Interview on file with researcher Weldon.

68. Rhinehart, op. cit., p. 150.

69. Ibid., p. 153.

70. *Crawdaddy*, Feb. 1976, op. cit.

71. Peter Marin, "The New Narcissism," in *Harper's*, Oct. 1975, p. 46.

72. R.C. Heck and J.L. Thompson, "*est:* Salvation or Swindle," in *San Francisco Magazine*, Jan. 1976, p. 22.

73. Suzanne Gordon, *Lonely in America* (New York: Simon and Schuster, 1976), p. 103.

74. Rhinehart, op. cit., p. 47.

75. Rhinehart, op. cit., p. 217.

76. "W90. "The Transformation of *est*," op. cit., p. 10.

77. Rhinehart, op. cit., p. 47.

78. Ibid., p. 220.

79. Private interview with researcher John Weldon. Interviewee's name withheld by request. Interview on file with researcher Weldon.

80. "Werner Erhard: All I Can Do Is Lie," op. cit.

81. Hargrove, op. cit., pp. 101-02.

82. "The Transformation of *est*," op. cit., p. 3.

83. Private interview with researcher John Weldon. Interviewee's name withheld by request. Interview on file with researcher Weldon.

84. Kornbluth, op. cit., p. 42.

85. Rhinehart, op. cit., pp. 38, 46.

86. Bry, op. cit., p. 182.

87. Rhinehart, op. cit., p. 217.

88. Private interview with researcher John Weldon. Interviewee's name withheld by request. Interview on file with researcher Weldon.

89. Rhinehart, op. cit., p. 209.

90. "The Transformation of *est*," op. cit., p. 10.

91. "Werner Erhard Live!" Part II, in *The New Age Journal*, No. 8, Oct. 15, 1975, p. 50.

92. Greene, op. cit., p. 131.

93. Seligson, op. cit.

94. "What's So," Jan. 1975, *est* publication, no data (leaflet).

95. "Werner's Aphorisms," op. cit.

96. "Werner Erhard—An Interview with the Source of *est*," op. cit., p. 46.

CHAPTER 5

THE CHILDREN OF GOD
(THE FAMILY OF LOVE)★

HISTORY

The Children of God, also known as the Family of Love, is an international organization claiming to promote liberty in Christ under the dictatorial power of its leader and founder, "Moses" David Berg. This liberty includes gross sexual license, heavy drinking, and other moral indiscretions. The growth of the group from a small handful of ex-hippies at a California coffeehouse in the midsixties to several million followers throughout the world spurs Christians to examine their doctrines, compare them with the Bible, and then declare to the world that the Children of God have twisted the message of God's Word.

David Brandt Berg (also known as Moses, Mo, Moses David, or Father David) was born on February 18, 1919, in Oakland, California. Berg was the son of a Christian evangelist couple, Hjalmer Emmanuel Berg and Virginia Lee Brandt-Berg. Hjalmer was a pastor for many years and then taught at Westmont College, a Christian college in Santa Barbara, California. Virginia was a Christian and Missionary Alliance radio evangelist whose life profoundly affected her son, David.

★ Researched by Carole Hausmann and Gretchen Passantino.

After Berg's medical discharge from the U.S. Army in 1941, he began full-time evangelistic work with the Christian and Missionary Alliance. Jane Berg (later renamed Mother Eve) became David's first wife in 1944 and bore four children, all of whom later served in leadership positions in the Children of God organization. All members take new, biblical-type names upon joining the group. David's children were renamed Deborah, Faith, Aaron, and Hosea.[1]

Between 1949 (when Berg built a church in Arizona and was then asked by the congregation to leave) and 1968, Berg was engaged in a variety of ministry-related activities. He claims that he was asked to leave the church in Arizona because of his "integration policies and radical preaching that they should share more of their wealth with the poor, beginning with my little family, whom they failed to support!"*[2] It was this encounter with rigidity within the church that Berg says led him to reject organized religion and resign from "the whole hypocritical Church System."[3]

He enrolled in college and took a three-month course, the "Soul Clinic Personal Witnessing Course," in association with evangelist and television religious personality Fred Jordan. The two began a long but turbulent association, each one helping the other in many projects. For 13 years Berg was Jordan's booking agent, booking Jordan's television show on over 300 TV stations and his radio messages on over 1100 radio stations.

In 1968 Berg's mother (in Huntington Beach, California) asked Berg to join her in a ministry at the Teen Challenge Coffee House there. Berg began teaching at the coffeehouse, and here was formed the first nucleus of what was to become the Children of God.[4]

The coffeehouse ministry was to the hippies, who swarmed the Huntington beaches, pier, and downtown area in the

---

* Berg's writings are filled with italics, capitalized words and underlinings. To enable the reader to accurately read the material quoted from COG literature, we have eliminated these extraneous markings. All quotations are word-for-word.

late sixties and early seventies. The ministers dressed like hippies, and their simple gospel messages were couched in the hippie vocabulary and style, bringing salvation to a unique crowd. Berg combined his gospel preaching with his own denouncement of the present American social, economic, educational, religious, and political systems.[5] Berg quickly took over the coffeehouse himself, breaking with Teen Challenge, and renaming it "Teens for Christ." He advocated a communal life pattern, a habit readily endorsed by the hippie community to which he ministered. It was at this time that he installed his own family members as leaders in the fledgling movement. Today Berg claims that his group was the first of the "Jesus People," or "Jesus Freaks."[6]

However, Berg's radical movement departed from the majority of the youthful converts to Christ at that time. Many of the young people who joined the "Jesus Movement" tended to worship together, forming homogeneous fellowships of predominantly young, life-minded believers. At the same time, most of these young converts readily accepted the established evangelical church, although they often did not feel comfortable in a formal setting, as is found in most established congregations. Berg did not agree. He not only met in youthful fellowships with his converts, but he openly denounced established churches and even went so far as to say that God would eventually abandon those who had forsaken the evangelism he promoted. In addition, he even had his followers disrupt school activities with their radical preaching.[7]

The school disruptions were the last straw. The coffeehouse was forced to vacate in 1969, and Berg took his 50 to 75 followers to Tucson, Arizona. Later the group split into four teams, which were sent to other areas of the country to establish new coffeehouses. All of these efforts failed. Meanwhile, Maria, a local church secretary in Tucson, joined the movement and traveled with Berg to Texas. Berg and

Maria were soon living together.

On a visit to an area near Montreal, Canada, Berg first organized his followers into a religious body. He organized the group into 12 tribes, each with different duties (mirroring the 12 apostles and the 12 tribes of Israel). The followers abandoned their given names and assumed biblical names to represent their new life in Christ.

The first of the famous "Mo Letters" from Berg to his group was shortly published. Entitled *Old Love, New Love, or The Old Church and the New Church,* the pamphlet justified his new relationship with Maria by using her as the symbol of the new church (COG), approved by God, and the old church (established Christianity), represented by his first wife, Jane. Berg did not entirely abandon Jane. According to the letter, she was still allowed to sleep with him every other night.[8] The name "Children of God" was coined by a newsman in Camden, New Jersey, and was quickly picked up and used by Berg.[9]

Berg's relationship to Fred Jordan surfaced again in 1970, when the Children of God moved (at Jordan's invitation) to his ranch in Texas, called the Soul Clinic Missionary Ranch. The 120 members moved in, and in 18 months grew to 250 members.

In 1971 Jordan invited some COG members to rejuvenate his Skid Row mission in Los Angeles, and Berg sent them, commissioning them to start a new colony in Southern California. This became the established COG pattern for starting new colonies. Jordan gave heavy support to the COG at this time, using them on his television program and raising money for them to buy the "Children of God Ranch" in Coachella, California.

Controversy accompanied the COG members to Southern California. Charges of kidnapping, holding members against their will, brainwashing, and fraud were lodged against COG. Groups of concerned parents were formed, such as the "Parents' Committee to Save Our Sons and

Daughters from the Children of God Organization,'' in San Diego.

Jordan looked for a way to disassociate himself from the movement, and in September of 1971 he banned all COG members from all of his property (the Texas and California ranches and the Skid Row mission). The 2100 members scattered to the 40 other colonies, which were by then in strong operation.

Converts to the COG were predominantly young people, and they included some of the early leaders of the Jesus Movement. Jeremy Spencer, from the rock group Fleetwood Mac, joined COG and moved from England to the U.S.[10]

The controversy concerning COG caused Berg to become more and more inaccessible to the public and his followers, although he exerted enormous power over all COG members through his letters, which soon attained the status of Scripture to his devoted followers.

1973 marked Berg's first public false prophecy,† as well as the in-depth investigation of COG activities by the New York Charity Frauds Bureau for the State Attorney General.

Berg prophesied that the coming of the comet Kahoutek would signal the destruction of America unless America repented before the end of January.

> . . .I believe God means what he says in this shocking revelation above! You in the U.S. have only until January to get out of the States before some kind of disaster, destruction or judgment of God is to fall because of America's wickedness![11]

Berg's followers are still waiting to see the fulfillment of their leader's dubious prophecy.

The investigation into COG activities was conducted in

---

† Earlier, Berg had prophesied to his close followers that California would be destroyed by earthquakes. See Moses David, *Mountainslide* (Dallas: Children of God, Oct. 21, 1971, GP No. 120).

1973 and presented to the New York State Attorney General on September 30, 1974. This invaluable study documented some of the many charges against the COG. The report documented draft evasion, dishonest tax practices, kidnaping and indoctrination practices, assault on members' parents, and sexual perversion, with which we will deal later. The report is still available to the public by writing to the New York State Attorney General's office in Albany, New York. Those interested will be billed and should request the *Final Report on the Activities of the Children of God to Hon. Louis J. Lefkowitz, Attorney General of the State of New York,* submitted by Charity Frauds Bureau, Herbert J. Wallenstein, Assistant Attorney General in Charge; dated September 30, 1974.

The impending doom on America from Kahoutek and the bad publicity from the New York Attorney General prompted a mass exodus of the COG to points around the world. Berg had already left the country, directing operations from Europe. He felt that the large colonies were unwieldy, so he commanded that they be broken up into smaller ones. His tight hold was further strengthened by rearranging the leadership in order to keep any one leader from attracting too large a following.

The leadership structure was set up as a pyramid—the structure that Berg declared God had ordained, even for the New Jerusalem. Berg's "Royal Family" was at the pinnacle of the pyramid, and lesser leaders ranged down from that, all the way to the "babes," the new converts in the local colonies.‡¹²

But the structure was short-lived, since only four years later, in February of 1978, Berg abolished the pyramid system in what he called the "Reorganization—Nationalization—Revolution." Regardless of Berg's stated reasons for the shuffling of leadership, its result is the complete dependence of all members on Berg and the Royal Family.

‡ We will discuss more concerning COG structure in the following pages.

The 1978 reorganization backfired to some extent, since the lack of consistent local leadership allowed the members to become lax in their activities, especially fund-raising. Now the threat from Berg is for all groups to produce monetarily or be excommunicated.[13]

It is almost impossible to find accurate outside statistics on the movement, since the members are so frequently moved, and since most of the leadership stays undercover. However, recent activities tend to affirm that the group is growing steadily and that literature distribution has become voluminous throughout the world, except in the United States, which has been figuratively abandoned by the COG as far as any serious evangelism efforts are concerned.

COG sources report that in 1974 the COG witnessed to 2½ billion persons in 1973-74. 1975 literature output topped five million pieces a month in 28 languages. In 1972 COG counted 140 colonies in 40 countries with 2400 full-time workers. Berg claims that in 1975 the group had 400 full-time couples with over 500 children in 200 colonies of 3000 members.[14] In 1977 he claimed that COG had two million members in over 100 countries, with 8000 workers in 800 homes in 80 countries on all six continents. Literature distribution is said to be over 60 million pieces per year.[15]

David Berg is now 61 years old, with a heart condition and what appears to the outsider to be a drinking problem. (One recent tract shows him sitting, with face on the table, in front of a bottle, with a glass in his hands. He also makes frequent references to his drinking in his letters and encourages it among his disciples.) References in several of his letters indicate that he doesn't think he will live much longer. Recently he officially relinquished control of the movement, turning it over to his Royal Family, although he still dictates every movement of all the members through his authoritative letters and his organizational structures. He is trying to avoid the bad publicity that has surrounded the Children of God through the years, urging members to call themselves the Family of Love rather than the Children of God.

> . . .Speaking of registration, in all areas where we're not already officially or legally registered in the name of the Children of God, whenever any new registration or any new legal matters take place they should be handled in the name of the Family of Love, if you have to have an organization name at all, and begin to get away from the Children of God and its image.
>
> . . .Now, some places it may be advantageous to retain the Children of God name where we've got good relations and good legal status and good PR. But if the Children of God are dead ducks and their name is mud in that area, then they ought to forget all about that and call themselves the Family of Love.[16]

Berg is not ready, however, to relinquish actual control of his "family." He is the absolute dictator of the entire worldwide organization.

> God has so seen fit and chosen for you a Voice and a Man through whom he speaks to give you the message, which gives you the vision, which creates the faith, that gives you the courage. . .to take the initiative.
>
> I didn't choose to be your leader: God chose me! –I merely obeyed! I said, "Lord, I'll follow—show me the way!" —And he did, and it led straight into your hearts and you took me in! You opened your hearts and you took me in and received me as your Friend, and more, as your own beloved Father in the Lord, your Shepherd, whose voice you suddenly knew was yours, and followed, for it was the Lord's voice through me! —They that love me most, follow closest![17]

Even though Berg is closer to death now than when he wrote the above, he is still confident that he will continue to rule the Children of God. He is even hoping to "haunt" his followers after his death!

> He'll be here to the end. He says "I will never leave thee nor forsake thee. Lo, I am with you always, even unto the end

of the world." (Heb. 13:5, Mt. 28:20.) Amen? Praise God!

So I'm never going to leave you nor forsake you either, if I can help it, even if I have to haunt you afterwards! I hope the Lord will let me stick around and see what you're doing and see if you're still obeying and doing what He wants you to do, telling folks about the Lord, about Jesus, and showing them God's love, amen? Praise the Lord![18]

AUTHORITY AND STRUCTURE

The Children of God have metamorphosed from a small group of hippie Christians to an international sex cult since their beginning in the late sixties. In order to understand such changes, it is necessary to understand the force behind the changes: David Berg.

David Berg has declared himself to be God's prophet today. He demands unquestioning obedience from his followers and even calls himself a dictator. His self-image is so exalted that sometimes it is hard to distinguish in his writings between himself and Jesus. His followers adore him as their King, brother, father, and protector.

> Forget not thy King, for He doth unlock thy bracelets and hath dropped the chains off thee. Forsake not His ways, for He hath the key, even the key of David! I have used the spirit of my David to unlock the prisons that have them bound. —we enter a new world of freedom from the shackles of the flesh, into the vast and boundless universe of the Spirit![19]

> Therefore, thou shalt kiss the mouth of David. Therefore hast thou loved the heart of David. For thou art enamoured of My words and thou art in love with Me, thy Savior! Therefore dost thou love him! Therefore dost thou cherish the words of My David. Behold, the man whom the Lord hath chosen! Hear ye him!

> Kiss the mouth of David that hath spoken to thee. For truly there are many Davids but this one have I chosen! —And this one have I annointed that it might fulfill all of that which was written of him, and which thou shalt write of him, and which

shall yet be written of him. And all these words shall be in-
scribed in a book, that it may be said of thee that this the
Lord thy God loveth thee, as it was written in the Book of
David.[20]

. . .Now I'll tell you one thing right now, that God won't
bless if they have had doubts about me or the Letters and
some troublemaker has instilled some of his doubts into
them. I know God wouldn't bless that.

. . .If they had the slightest doubt about the letters and
obeying them, there is no such thing as half-way
obedience.—You know what I mean? There is no such thing
as half obeying.

. . .See, if you have even the slightest reservation in your
mind as to whether this is true: . . .that is really dangerous
because that can lead you all the way back.

. . .If they agree that I'm wrong about one thing, then they
believe that I could be wrong about it all. That's why in court
if a witness lies about one thing, they throw his whole
testimony out, all of it. —No matter even if all the rest is true,
they bar it from the case if he has perjured himself in only one
thing. If they start doubting me about one thing, where do
they stop?[21]

Berg's arrogance extends to the world outside his group.
He believes that his prayers are so powerful that even large
disasters are seen to be God's answers to his prayers.

So we ask together right now in Jesus name that thou shalt
defeat the enemy! Vindicate Thy servant and Thy children,
show the people who is right. You really vindicated us in the
United States by the downfall of Nixon. People didn't believe
us, but You embarrassed our accusers and humiliated them
and humbled them when they found out we were right, so that
they even wrote to us and said they were sorry. . . .

And you cursed that city of New York that harboured the
charges against us, and the people behind them, and now it is
bankrupt with all kinds of problems! Thank You Lord!
Thank You Lord! Thank You Jesus! . . .[22]

In his role as God's dictator over the "Family," Berg sees

himself in a godlike role. He is the one to mete out judgment and punishment on wayward followers. He often proclaims divine curses on those who disobey him, and his anger seems even hotter toward backslidden members than it does toward nonmember antagonists. The following is excerpted from a "spirit communication" done through Berg under the direction of his "wife," Maria. It concerns the rebellion exhibited by Berg's daughter (Deborah) and her husband.§

Now you tell Rachel she is the executioner to obey the Word of God and the King [Berg] and to sock it to them [Deborah and her husband], and it's either going to kill them or drive them stark raving mad or insane, or it's going to deliver them, one or the other! . . .

So whatever God's will be done! If the truth kills them or drives them insane, that's what's supposed to happen to them!—The end of their troubles then—they'll go to be with the Lord if they're His. There's lots worse things than killing people!

My God, then let him commit suicide! It would be good enough for him! Then that would prove exactly what the Lord has said! If he commits suicide that just shows you exactly what he is, a devil! . . .

You tell her to get busy and kill them! Kill them! The quicker the better! I mean if they can't stand the truth they ought to die and be dead! Let's hope maybe they'll go to Heaven and not to Hell! Even Jethro's got better sense!—Even Jethro knows he's a sinner![23]

Berg teaches that his letters to the COG members are God's proclamations for today, as fully inspired as the Old and New Testaments, and more valuable because they are more relevant for today. Members must faithfully read and memorize, as well as unquestioningly obey, all "Mo Letters." Berg's evolution from a Bible-believing conservative to God's prophet for today was chronicled by Berg himself in one of his Mo Letters.

---

§ We will discuss the occultic/spiritistic involvement of Berg and the Children of God later.

I was so crazy about the Bible when I was a young man that I said, "Everybody and every cult has always gone astray on somebody's writings! God forbid that I should ever write a book!" I was fanatical about that right up to Huntington Beach.

But I found there that they needed something to hold in their hands to help them grasp the truth that was in the Bible but they couldn't understand.

So I wrote a little two page leaflet with a map to try to summarize the whole Bible. When I felt a little tract was needed, I printed up solid Scripture because I was so afraid to put down any words of my own.

But God finally had to do it supernaturally by almost forcing prophecy through me to give me the true living water for today. he almost forced me to write what needed to be written and to show me the Bible was not enough. . . .[24]

One of the characteristics of the cults ☆ is that a cult usually emphasizes its own teachings and/or scripture to such an extent that followers must spend a disproportionate amount of time learning those teachings. This is also the case with the Children of God. Berg commands his followers to spend at least 1½ to 2 hours each day studying the Mo letters—without fail. He warns that to neglect this study opens the follower up to falling away from the faith:

You'd better read and study them and share them or you, too, are going to miss the original pattern that God has given from the very beginning and fall by the way like the rest of the Jesus People. . . .[25]

The exalted position of the Mo Letters is evident in Berg's letters, where he refers to them as "God's Word." Remarkably candid about his purpose in urging the memorization of his letters, Berg actually tells his followers to brainwash themselves with the Mo Letters.

. . .I hope you are brainwashing yourselves with it constantly and absorbing it into the very fiber of your being, for

---

☆ See Chapter 1 for the major characteristics of the cults.

it is His Spirit in his Love that makes you strong! Please do not neglect it, for it is food for your soul and gives you strength for the battle! Even getting out lit[erature] is not as important as getting into the lit yourself first! We need to get the Words in as well as out! You'll never have the spiritual strength and stamina nor even the spirit that will sustain your bodily strength—unless you yourself are drinking in the Word and being spiritually nourished and strengthened by it yourself first.[26]

Berg's daughter, Faith, sometimes writes under her father's authority and urges the same blind obedience to his words in the Mo Letters.

. . .What has shown you the way? It's been the MO Letters, right? They've really opened up your eyes and shown you some of the most important things you've ever seen! You see the truth, because it's the living Word. It's flowing today! It's God's communication to us for right now![27]

. . .It doesn't matter how great you have been at any point, when you cease to obey the words of David you're going to fall. If it comes to the point that you don't believe and continue to obey the words of David, then you'll be a systemite, because the only thing that makes you revolutionary is obeying the words of David![28]

Berg's letters are considered to be God's words to his only true followers—the Children of God.

. . .Do you want to know what the real avant-garde of this movement is? It's the MO Letters! That's what is leading us all! All the general on the battlefield does is carry out the orders that come from higher up, from the Lord through MO![29]

Since many of Berg's teachings contradict the Bible, it is no wonder that he rejects many portions of the Old and New Testaments. His letters are claimed to be the only sure guide.

Now there's plenty that's good for you to study and

memorize of what the writers of the Bible have said, but much is old hat and out of date—except for what Jesus said.

. . .So, I want to frankly tell you, you had better read what God said today in preference to what he said 2,000 or 4,000 years ago! . . .[30]

. . .Well, I'm sorry to say, I don't agree with all that Paul said, and I'm sure, dear Paul, you understand. I think right now he is probably sorry for some of the things he said and certainly for some of the things he did. I've had to back down on some of my stands, he ought to be willing to back down on some of his.[31]

So you have to believe in the Lord and in me, that I am a new prophet of a new day of a whole lot of new things that Paul never even thought about!

. . .I wouldn't be a bit surprised if some of this new wine has driven them back to the old to check it out. Well, I'll tell you, it certainly doesn't check with some of Paul's wine. And if they consider Paul infallible, then I've got to be wrong in quite a few things. . . .[32]

In almost the same breath with which Berg denies the infallibility of the Bible, he also asserts that the Bible is our test for modern revelations. One wonders why Berg and/or his followers have not followed these words from Berg and discovered that since Berg contradicts the Bible, he cannot be God's prophet for today!

We know what is true or false by the standards of God's Word. The Word is our foundation, our guide, our standard, and the rod of measurement whereby we measure all things, even the words that God gives us today. It's the Bureau of Standards by which we measure all truth and all error!

. . .In God's Word, you can find the answer to every question, every problem you will ever have in life.—There's nothing like the Word![33]

Contrary to Berg's assertions, he is not God's prophet for today. He has promulgated false prophecies (like California's great earthquake and the coming of the comet

Kahoutek) and therefore stands condemned by Deuteronomy 18:22: "If what a prophet proclaims in the name of the Lord does not take place or come true, that is a message the Lord has not spoken. That prophet has spoken presumptuously. Do not be afraid of him." Since Berg also teaches false doctrine about God, Jesus, and salvation, Deuteronomy 18:20 condemns him with the Lord's words: "A prophet who presumes to speak in my name anything I have not commanded him to say, or a prophet who speaks in the name of other gods, must be put to death."

The Bible instructs us to test the words of all men. We are not to believe them just because they claim to speak for God. Even the Bereans tested Paul's words with Scripture (Acts 17:11). First Thessalonians 5:21,22 warns Christians to "test everything. Hold on to the good. Avoid every kind of evil."

Christ's words to the Jews of the first century seem to be said to those who would exalt David Berg to the high position he commands for himself. We are not to submit blindly to David Berg as our "father" any more than the Jews were to submit to the false religious leaders in the first century. Jesus said:

> But you are not to be called 'Rabbi,' for you have only one Master and you are all brothers. And do not call anyone on earth 'father,' for you have one Father, and he is in heaven. Nor are you to be called 'teacher,' for you have one Teacher, the Christ. The greatest among you will be your servant. For whoever exalts himself will be humbled, and whoever humbles himself will be exalted.[34]

There is only one Savior, Jesus Christ, and David Berg has no part in anyone's salvation or standing with God (Acts 4:12). First Timothy 2:5,6 says, "There is one God and one mediator between God and men, the man Christ Jesus, who gave himself as a ransom for all men—the testimony given in its proper time." David Berg is not our mediator.

Although God commands us to pray, and He answers prayer (Matthew 6:6-13; James 5:16), it is His right to comply with our requests or not. A nation is not destroyed because we pray for it to be destroyed. It stands or is destroyed on the basis of God's omniscience and justice (Jeremiah 18:7-10). Berg's hatred toward others is evidence that he does not have the love of God ruling in his heart. Matthew 6:14,15 carries this warning for those who pray curses upon their enemies rather than forgiving them: "For if you forgive men when they sin against you, your heavenly Father will also forgive you. But if you do not forgive men their sins, your Father will not forgive your sins." This follows the same train of thought expressed by Jesus in Matthew 5:43-48:

> You have heard that it was said, 'Love your neighbor and hate your enemy.' But I tell you: Love your enemies and pray for those who persecute you, that you may be sons of your Father in heaven. He causes his sun to rise on the evil and the good, and sends rain on the righteous and the unrighteous. If you love those who love you, what reward will you get? Are not even the tax collectors doing that? And if you greet only your brothers, what are you doing more than others? Do not even pagans do that? Be perfect, therefore, as your heavenly Father is perfect.

Berg's hatred toward others puts him at odds with Christ, who prayed as He was dying at the hands of others, "Father, forgive them" (Luke 23:34). Berg's attitude toward those he admits may be Christians (like his daughter, Deborah) is contrary to the picture of a Christian presented in 1 John 4:20,21:

> If anyone says, "I love God," yet hates his brother, he is a liar. For anyone who does not love his brother, whom he has seen, cannot love God, whom he has not seen. And he has given us this command: Whoever loves God must also love his brother.

The contradictory and antibiblical words of David Berg

contrast with the godly words of the Bible. Anyone who attempts to add to God's Word should take into account the Bible's own warning against claiming one's own fallible words as God's words:

> Every word of God is flawless; he is a shield to those who take refuge in him. Do not add to his words, or he will rebuke you and prove you a liar.[35]

Before we discuss the three largest nondoctrinal aberrations of the Children of God, we must mention two other areas dealing with the general structure of the Children of God organization.

The Mo Letters are divided into several categories, not all of which are equally publicized. Each letter is assigned a lettered category, referring to its intended audience. The General Public (GP) letters are handed out on the streets for donations; the Disciples Only (DO) and Disciples and Friends Only (DFO) letters are reserved for firm COG members and staunch supporters of the group. It is in the DO and DFO letters that we first find explicit sexual language and illustrations, which are also included in the remaining categories of letters. Leader or Leader Training (L or LTO) letters, which usually concern leadership and administrative matters, are carefully restricted to leaders in COG or their apprentices. Finally, RFO letters are for Berg's Royal Family Only—those who immediately surround Berg.

In addition to the Mo Letters, COG publishes the *New Nation News* newsletter, which is classified as Disciples Only. In 1976 the COG published a 1519-page book entitled *The Basic Mo Letters*. A sort of super training manual (complete with exams on the letters' contents in the back), the book contains many DFO letters which have now been classified as open to the public.

However, the more recent DFO letters, which contain blatant immorality and sexual perversion, are absent from the book and are extremely difficult to obtain because of

COG's tight security system. We will discuss the contents of these letters when we discuss the sexual deviations of the COG.

David Berg has the final word on the significance of all Mo Letters to his followers:

> We have heard of quite a few instances where leaders have changed the meaning of my letters by their actions or verbal interpretations. My Letters mean exactly what they say, literally, and they don't need explaining away, spiritualizing or reinterpreting by anyone![36]

We shall take David Berg at his word and thus be able to see clearly his aberrant doctrines and morals.

A word also needs to be said about the finances of COG. Although vast sums are raised through literature distribution, wealthy supporters, and what we could loosely term prostitution,# recently COG has been suffering financially. In part this financial setback was caused by the confusion resulting from his "Re-Organization—Nationalization—Revolution," the organizational upheaval instituted by Berg in February of 1978 to consolidate his control on COG. The Mo Letters from January through March of 1978 repeatedly express Berg's concern at the dwindling revenues of COG.

The recent emancipation of colony members from rigid surveillance and tight leadership has spawned a discipline problem. Berg has now decided to crack down on his followers and force them to once more submit blindly to authority—his authority. He has demanded that the colonies return to the profit-making practices which were the mainstay of the organization in the past, such as obtaining sizable donations for COG literature from the public (called "litnessing"); actively evangelizing converts who will "forsake all," giving all of their possessions and assets to the organization; and mass writing of appeals for funds to pro-

---

we will discuss this practice shortly, when we discuss the COG sexual practices.

spective donors. Berg has even urged members to obtain full-time jobs to help support the local colonies.

The COG mainstay, "FFing" (Berg's synonym for free sex), is now to be engaged in only when it will produce a material reward for the organization. Because the solicitation practices of the COG are so blatantly exploitative, we are reproducing here the substance of Berg's unorthodox fund-raising beliefs.

If FF-ing's** costing you money and not paying besides, and then you're losing time in the morning sleeping, then you're losing three ways! Terrible! Some apparently have really FFed all right, but they sure didn't know how to make it pay. Why are the boys still going with them? Let the girls go together and the fish will pay!

Make everybody sit down for at least 1-2 hours and write letters home.—One letter to the parents, one letter to their self-supporting brothers and sisters, or relatives they know could help them. Tell them we are in desperate need and having a hard time meeting our needs, could you please help us? Don't stop and wait for a prayer letter, write your own—TONIGHT![37]

I'm getting fed up with people who don't show their gratitude by something material. It's nice to say "thanks" or "I love you," but it doesn't pay the bills! They better start putting works to their faith!—"Faith without works is dead" (Ja. 2:17), and love without some material manifestation is doubly dead!

If you can't do any one of the first 6 things you should get a job! And if you can't get a good job here, I suggest you go someplace where you can.[38]

We took away their tyrants so now they're doing less for Thee and us than they did for them! Now Lord, we're going to have to be their tyrants—You and me!

We are going to get on their case and herd these sheep and ride herd on them until they produce and they get out and work for that grass themselves and produce the wool to sup-

---

** Casual sex.

port Thy work!

...It's time to go back to work and work better than we ever did before! I want to see you kids produce better now than you did under the tyrants!—Not produce less but more! I'm going to be harder on you than the tyrants you had!

If you can't produce more for God and for me, then you don't deserve the job! If you would produce more for some pipsqueak of a little local tyrant than you will for God and for love and for me, you don't belong in God's army!—And I mean it!

Last but not least, there are degrees of punishment and degrees of reward. The Homes that prove by the 1st of May that they can make it or look like they may be able to make it, we'll leave them alone.

But the homes that do not prove they can make it by the end of April we are going to close down. Is that clear? The hard workers are going to be rewarded and the others are going to be closed down.

Well, we're going to weed out the under-workers and ship them someplace else or hit the road with them or send them home! We're going to totally excommunicate unproductive Homes, period![39]

Berg has completely turned around the priorities Jesus gave Christians. According to Jesus, the spiritual was of much more importance than the material, and His disciples were told not to worry or concern themselves needlessly with the material things in life, but to concentrate on their spiritual lives and to share the gospel with others. With the spiritual first, God steps in and takes care of the material. Berg has become materialistic, ignoring the supreme value of the spiritual. Paul reminds us that "the kingdom of God is not a matter of eating and drinking, but of righteousness, peace and joy in the Holy Spirit" (Romans 14:17). Jesus' simple words stand in stark contrast to the materialism of Berg's self-centered desires.

> Therefore I tell you, do not worry about your life, what you will eat or drink; or about your body, what you will wear.

Is not life more important than food, and the body more important than clothes? Look at the birds of the air; they do not sow or reap or store away in barns, and yet your heavenly Father feeds them. Are you not much more valuable than they? Who of you by worrying can add a single hour to his life?

And why do you worry about clothes? See how the lilies of the field grow. They do not labor or spin. Yet I tell you that not even Solomon in all his splendor was dressed like one of these. If that is how God clothes the grass of the field, which is here today and tomorrow is thrown into the fire, will he not much more clothe you, O you of little faith? So do not worry, saying, "What shall we eat?" or "What shall we drink?" or "What shall we wear?" For the pagans run after all these things, and your heavenly Father knows that you need them. But seek first his kingdom and his righteousness, and all these things will be given to you as well. Therefore do not worry about tomorrow, for tomorrow will worry about itself. Each day has enough trouble of its own.[40]

REVOLUTION, SEX, AND THE JEWS

The three predominant teachings in the COG involve worldwide revolution, sex, and anti-Semitism. We shall discuss each of these three areas, since they form the core of COG belief and practice. COG's sexual beliefs and practices are its most debased and immoral characteristics. We shall first discuss Berg's concepts of revolution, then the COG and sex, and finally Berg's rampant anti-Semitism.

Revolution

As we mentioned earlier, the basic message of the Children of God has been for its new converts to "forsake all" and "drop out" of the "system" for Jesus' sake. However, even the watchword of COG, "revolution," has succumbed somewhat to the rise of sex into COG prominence. COG is still against the system, is still the "Jesus

164 / THE NEW CULTS

revolution," and is still God's "New Church," but COG members will temporarily join the system and reap the benefits of the system for their own (or ultimately, Berg's own) profit. COG has become a system in itself.

Berg preached against the established church†† and condemned it with the words of Jesus against the Pharisees.

> That's the difference between the churches and us! Jesus said to the common people, "The scribes and pharisees (the church leaders) sit in Moses' seat." All therefore they bid you observe, that observe and do; but do not ye after their works: for they say and do not." And that goes for today's churches too![41]

In addition, Berg taught that the whole economic and political system throughout the world was corrupt, and that those who wanted to follow Jesus must disavow the system. (In part, this holds true today, although Berg is now actively promoting COG members' manipulative use of the system.)

> Our main witness (which includes both our way of life and our sermon) is that we are against the system; that is 95% of our witness. It is a damning witness against them. By the System, I'm not talking about the legal laws—I'm talking about the damnable Satanic principles on which the damned System is built, its laws of selfishness and do your own thing and keep on living just as you did, refusing any change. . . .
> The old religious and economic systems cannot be patched up, for they are tattered, threadbare, and rotten and must be cast upon the fires of His Judgment that He may create "a new Heaven and a new earth" in which "old things are passed away and all things are become new."
> So, it is always necessary to root out, pull down, destroy and throw down the old in order to build and to plant the new; there just isn't room for both.[42]

An early publication, *The Revolutionary Rules*,[43] is a handbook of basic guidelines for COG members and colo-

---

††See the history section of this chapter for some of the actions taken by COG members against the established churches.

nies. It outlines the commitment demanded of members and the daily routines of colonies. (Except for some small changes and the new sexual practices, these rules still represent the commitment of today's COG member.) The converts have been characterized by a lifestyle of disciplined work and study, long hours, unquestioning obedience to leaders, and relinquishing of all material possessions to the "family." The colony sun rises and sets on the divine pronouncements of "Father" David Berg.

Berg has also taught his followers to hate their parents, often directing a convert to cease all contact with his parents after staging an emotional and heated exchange between them, culminating in the convert's loud vow to "forsake all for Jesus." (With today's emphasis on increased COG financial backing, one is requested to disavow his family only if they refuse to contribute to the convert's support or if all possible monetary return has been realized from them over a period of time.)

> You, my dear parents, are the greatest rebels against God and his ways—not us, and unto you will be the greater condemnation; for how can we rebel against a God whom we know not, whose ways you never showed us, and you denied Him. You heard His Word, but heeded it not. You were shown His Ways, but followed them not. . . .
>
> To hell with your devilish system. May God damn your unbelieving hearts. It were better that a millstone be hung around your neck and you be cast into the midst of the sea than to have caused one of these little ones to stumble. You were the real rebels, my dear parents, and the worst of all time. God is going to destroy you and save us, as we rebel against your wickedness, deny your ungodliness, break your unscriptural traditions and destroy your idolatrous System in the name of God Almighty."

Sex

The one word which best describes Berg's supreme preoccupation is sex. Although some of his early materials seemed sexually conservative, his morals over the years have degenerated to depths deplored by almost every church, no matter how liberal. Berg places a great deal of emphasis on sex and sexual imagery in his writings. He seems fascinated with his own sexual conquests (whether of his consort/wife Maria, COG members [both male and female], non-COG members, or even angel/demons), and describes them in great detail in his letters. He carefully and explicitly controls and develops the sexual attitudes and activities of his followers, and requires regular reports in detail from all members on their own sexual activities.

Sexual language abounds in many COG materials amid what would often be termed pornographic drawings and photographs. The most important doctrine to Berg and the COG is called "flirty fishing," or "FFing." Plainly stated, this means fornication with any and all who are willing, male or female, whether the COG member is married or single. The only restriction seems to be that, since the COG has been experiencing financial difficulties, the FFers are now urged to find partners who can reward them for their actions materially.

Because of the exalted, holy view of married love and physical union presented in the Bible, Christians treat any discussion of it with great seriousness and reverence. Paul presented the ideal picture of Christian union in Ephesians 5:31,32, which reminds us, "For this reason a man will leave his father and mother and be united to his wife, and the two will become one flesh. This is a profound mystery—but I am talking about Christ and the church. However, each one of you also must love his wife as he loves himself, and the wife must respect her husband."

There is nothing shameful or secret about the sanctified sex that God honors in marriage. However, the act which makes a husband and wife "one flesh" is a private, spiritual union between the spouses, expressing their love for each other in the Lord, and is not to be considered lightly or to be exploited. It is not the desire of this section to do so. However, in order to even briefly and circumspectly present some of the COG views on sex, it is necessary to present some of the vocabulary and imagery used by the COG. We will endeavor to discuss only what is absolutely necessary to accurately present COG's ideas to the reader.

Berg's sexual tendencies were beginning to surface even in the early days of COG, and Berg's own admission of his early sexual experiences[45] shows that he had unbiblical sexual attitudes since childhood.

In 1977 two former members of the COG exposed some of the inner workings of the group through an interview with Joseph M. Hopkins in the February 18 issue of *Christianity Today.* Jack Wasson left the COG in 1973 with his wife, who had been in the group since its beginnings in Huntington Beach. David Jacks, a member for over five years, and a COG archbishop, left the group in 1975. Wasson and Jacks discussed the sexual practices in the early years of the COG:

Hopkins: What about sex in the COG? There have been rumors of immorality and hanky-panky in the higher echelons. Are they true?

Jacks: Extramarital relationships, definitely. Berg cites Abraham, Solomon, David, and so on, as examples for his having concubines. The top leaders have sexual affairs with girls in the group. But the disciples are practically eunuchs for a year or so until they get married in the COG.

Wasson: This fooling around with sex goes way back. Married couples were encouraged as a group to participate in "skinny-dipping"—swimming in the nude. It was considered unrevolutionary not to participate. And COG members will do almost anything to avoid being called unrevolutionary. It was also policy for all married couples to attend evening "leadership training" sessions at the TSC (Texas Soul Clinic) Ranch in west Texas in the early days of the COG. These sessions would be led by David Berg, and no matter what subject they started out about, they always ended up on the subject of sex, with David Berg frequently leading the couples into a mass love-making session while he looked on. Then this doctrine came up that was taught only among the top leadership: "all things common," based on Acts 2:44. They applied the "all things" even to wives and husbands. The wife-and-husband-swapping was not explicitly condoned in a MO letter, but it was allowed and participated in by the top leadership.[46]

Berg's earlier letters to the public (GP) reflected some of his preoccupation with sex, although recently he has tried to limit the explicitly sexual materials to the COG membership. The four best-known GP Mo Letters discussing sex were *Mountin' Maid* (GP No. 240, December 27, 1970); *Revolutionary Sex* (GP No. 258, March 27, 1973); *Revolutionary Women* (GP No. 250, June 20, 1973); and *Come On Ma!—Burn Your Bra!* (GP No. 286, December 22, 1973).

In *Revolutionary Sex,* Berg condones polygamy and homosexual acts between women, and tries to show that adultery, fornication, and incest were sometimes permitted in the Bible. He describes in detail his earliest sexual activities (beginning at the age of seven), and encourages COG colonies to promote playing and sleeping together nude among their children, allowing full sexual exploration and activity. He concludes that Jesus had sex, and that God had intercourse with Mary to produce Jesus.

In the tract *Come On Ma!—Burn Your Bra!* Berg states that if one is not sexually liberated, he is not fully saved!

We have a sexy God and a sexy religion with a very sexy leader with an extremely sexy young following! So if you don't like sex, you'd better get out while you can still save your bra! Salvation sets us free from the curse of clothing and the shame of nakedness! We're as free as Adam and Eve in the Garden before they ever sinned! If you're not, you're not the fully saved! Come on Ma! Burn your bra! Be liberated tonight! Halleluja![47]

Berg's belief about God's attitude toward marriage is completely contradictory to the Bible's record of God's attitude. Berg openly advocates divorce as a good way to solve problems.

Is breaking up families anything new with God?—God is in the business of breaking up families—little private families! If you have not forsaken your husband or wife for the Lord at some time or other, you have not forsaken all![48]

The *Final Report on the Activities of the Children of God* from the New York Attorney General's office reports promiscuity and sexual and physical abuse in COG colonies. This is based on testimonies and case histories of former members. COG betrothals consisted of male disciples picking females with whom they wanted to have intercourse that night, and then receiving simple permission from the colony leaders. The testimony of a Dr. Blackburn's daughter, an ex-COG member, is revealing.

In July of 1972, COG made the decision to dismiss Dr. Blackburn's daughter because she would not ask her parents for any more money; she would not agree to kill her parents for the revolution, and she refused to marry the person whom they chose for her (marriage in this sense is sleeping with another person). Sometime prior to this decision, she had been transferred to the commune in Philadelphia. Before her release from COG, she was placed in solitary confinement in the "cage" for refusing to obey the above directives. They said that she was "of the devil" and played tapes continuously during her confinement in an attempt to program her mind in the desired direction. Upon leaving solitary confinement, she was directed to take a shower and then masturbate in front of the men, or she would be condemned to Hell. She refused and was kicked out of the Philadelphia commune on July 6, 1972.[49]

Even the members of the "Royal Family," Berg's close relatives, could not escape the immorality pressed upon COG members. The following is excerpted from testimony given by Sarah Berg, former wife of the late Paul Berg, David's oldest son.

> . . .Frightened, she was forced to have intercourse with Paul in the presence of David Berg. Similar incidents occurred thereafter, until her spirit was broken. She then was compelled to obtain her mother's permission to marry Paul because she was terrified and believed, mistakenly, that she was pregnant.
>
> A year later, after the birth of her first child, Nathan, David Berg wanted to have intercourse with her stating: "I see you with Paul's son. Why can't you have my son?"...
>
> She...gave birth in a "system's doctor's" office, over the objections of the family who follow Berg's admonition that the cult is to have nothing to do with "system doctors."
>
> As punishment her son was taken away from her and she and the new child were kept prisoner in a trailer. On the second night she slipped past the guard who had walked away without permission. She walked six miles carrying her newborn daughter and escaped.
>
> She later returned, with others to the COG Thurber commune to get her infant son, she was refused by Paul Berg and John Treadwell to obtain the child.
>
> . . .After her husband's death, she wrote the attorneys for the COG asking their help in locating her missing son, (then age 2½). She was advised that they "had determined through appropriate inquiry that at the time she and her husband separated, her son was left in the custody of her husband;" and that the COG was unaware of her son's whereabouts.
>
> . . .Sarah Berg has been unable to locate her infant son from the time she escaped from the COG commune to the present.[50]

Part of Berg's preoccupation with sex is expressed in his repeated use of a sex vocabulary to describe all kinds of things, even God and His actions toward man! One of the worst aspects of the sexual obsession is Berg's employment of sexual terminology in his descriptions of the Lord, the Bible, and our relationship to God.

. . .Experience a spiritual orgasm by being filled with the Spirit! It far surpasses the fleshly orgasms of sex, which, however, is a type and symbol of it—the ecstasy of the unity of body with body. . .all a type and glorious picture of the spiritual realities of the unity of Christ with His Bride—You, His Body, His Wife, His Lover, His Spiritual Sex Partner, in whom he revels with delight, and with whom you can experience orgasm after orgasm of spiritual ecstasy, unending and eternal![51]

Berg even blasphemes to the point of calling God a pimp who makes the church His prostitute.

The Lord showed me how he literally shares his wife, the Church with the world to prove His Love....

God is a Pimp! How about that! —Boom! He's the biggest one there is—He uses His Church all the time to win souls and win hearts to Him to attract them to Him.[53]

The above quote can serve to introduce the predominant doctrine of the COG: Flirty-Fishing (FFing). Berg's sexual perversion is expressed in his demands that COG women (and recently, COG men) use sex to "win souls." This has become Berg's favorite subject in his Mo Letters, and is the major practice in the group, replacing "litnessing" (passing out literature for donations) as the major fund-raising and evangelism tool of the group. Litnessing early replaced the general street preaching of the Jesus Movement from which COG emerged.[54]

Berg sees FFing as the ultimate evangelism tool from which no one can escape. A side effect of FFing is that it degrades the participants and binds them even more closely to the Jesus that Berg has manufactured.

Help her, O God, to catch men! Help her to catch men, be bold, unashamed and brazen, to use anything she has, O God, to catch men for Thee!—Even if it be through the flesh, the attractive lure, delicious flesh on a steel hook of Thy reality, the steel of Thy Spirit!

. . .List Thou, and heed Thou these warning words of thy

Father that thou stray not, neither flee thou from the sacrifice to which I have ordained thee! Thou shalt be pierced and impaled with the power of My love, that thou shalt tempt others that would feast of thee to be caught by the same![55]

Berg tries to explain that FFing is only a means to an end, and that therefore those who engage in it are not completely promiscuous. He says that FFing is a way of witnessing God's love, the first step in conversion. ("They should fall in love with you first, and then with the Lord! Now you and your flesh and your spirit and your love and real affection are the bait. But particularly your flesh is the bait"—Moses David, *FFer's Handbook!—Condensed Selected Quotes from More than 50 FF Letters!* [Justus Ashtree, ed.], Children of God, Rome, January 1977, p.3.)

He does allow the COG members to be somewhat selective with those they "love."

For God's sake—and yours—use a little wisdom and try to be Spirit-led! Not every guy who wants to lay you necessarily deserves to be laid!

Frankly, the bed is a last resort when all else has failed to fully convince him that you and God love him, and he just won't believe it till he sees it!

When it's hard from dancing, it's hard for him to believe you love him if you won't love him all the way and help his hard state of desperate and almost incontainable physical need![56]

Ultimately, however, almost any sex act for any reason is condoned by Berg, who says:

Remember sex is God-created so it's no sin, unless it hurts or offends somebody. God's going to put so much love in your heart for them that you're going to want to take them to bed to show them how much you love them.[57]

This introduces us to Berg's FF doctrine. Berg claims that having sex with others shows one's love for God and mankind. He claims that members who participate in FFing are truly serving God and doing His will. He has confused sexual love with divine love.

Are you willing to go that far?—If not, don't even start, or you may not be able to stop until you land in a permanent predicament! How far are you willing to go? Well, in Flirty Fishing the answer has got to be "All the way!" from the very beginning if necessary, even if God never requires it of you, because He may, and you must be prepared for it.

The time will come when you love God so much and love these men so much you're willing to send your own wife to bed with them. You can't go to bed with them, you can't supply what they need, but you're willing to send your own wife! God has given me the grace where I've wanted to give Maria to them because I love them so much![58]

Blasphemy in the highest degree is reached when Berg equates FFing with intercourse with Jesus.

Berg declares that the reason the early church did not indulge in FFing and the other sexual practices seen in the COG is that the early church was mistakenly still bound to the Mosaic Law, not realizing their "freedom" in Christ, as Berg and his followers have done.[60] Essentially, the COG has adopted antinomianism, or freedom from all rules, as its lifestyle. Anything is permissible "if it's done in Love and all parties concerned are agreed because they love each other, then there is no sin.—It is love!"[61] Antinomianism is self-serving—not selfless, as Jesus taught us to be. Antinomianism follows the idea of hedonism—right equals what benefits the self. Berg says:

God created pleasure, He created the very nerves that give these pleasurable sensations we enjoy. He created all this pleasure. . . .
If it feels good, it is good! Right? That's how the whole discussion began. . . .[62]

The technique: Berg encourages his followers to frequent bars and other such places to entice desirable "fishes" (converts). He also encourages them to drink in order to relax and enjoy their important work for the Lord.[63] He warns his female followers to be prepared to be raped, since they will soon gain a reputation for free sex.[64]

The allegedly altruistic motives of COG FFing have been clouded recently as FFing has permeated other areas of COG conduct and has been used to solve other problems within the group. FFing is now seen as a way to increase a colony's standing in a community, if the "fish" has the COG member live with him and represent the colony's interests to the community from without.[65] Berg advises American COG members living in foreign countries to take additional mates from among the national members in order to be more accepted among the nationals.

> So a capable American woman can marry a native husband and train him, or a capable American husband can marry a native wife and train her. My God, if a married man's got to take on another wife and have one American and one native, that's the way it'll have to be! A woman who is an American and has an American husband, well, maybe she can interest her fish in being another husband, so at least one of the team will be native.[66]

Another change in the FFing doctrine is that, although it was originally to be considered as an evangelism technique, it has now become one of the main sources of revenue for the COG. As the COG financial problems increased, Berg more adamantly stressed the profit-making aspects of FFing.

> Fishing can be fun, but fun doesn't pay the bills! You've got to catch a few to make the fun pay for itself! So don't do it for nothing! We're not in it for the money but we are in it for the men! If we don't catch some pretty good fish as a result, including what they've got and can do for us, you're just wasting your time and your tail![67]

> . . .We may not accept money for sexual service or get paid on the spot, but we'll sure accept the money if they want to

give it to us!

If you don't know how to let these guys know that you need money you ought to get out of the FFing business! It's nice to win souls, but it's got to pay for itself.[68]

As well as using FFing to raise money, Berg uses it himself to solidify his power over his followers and the followers use it to bind new members to the group.[69] Berg's tight grasp on his followers extends to his requiring that the homes (colonies) submit monthly "FF Witnessing Reports" in which individual members must report their month's sexual activities. At the beginning of 1978, all COG members were required to submit to Berg a lengthy "Confidential Questionnaire," which contained eight pages of personal questions, two pages of which were questions asking for explicit information on the person's past and present sexual activities. These questions dealt with incestuous relationships in the family, present sexual partner, number of present sexual partners, number of sexual encounters (past and present), childhood sexual experimentation, masturbation habits, homosexual or lesbian experiences, and one's sexual feelings toward Berg.‡‡

Berg even encourages licentious behavior with COG children. Children are taught to memorize Mo Letters, even those which deal with FFing and other such subjects. The COG even uses nude pictures to teach children to read.

They should be encouraged in nude mixed bathing and nude mixed play where socially, legally, and climatically permissible, acceptable, and advisable. They should also not be prohibited from mutual and self-sexual examination, experimentation or interplay when playing or sleeping together where legally possible and social and housing conditions permit. . . ."[70]

FFing is also used to COG's advantage with political and economic leaders of the countries in which colonies reside.

---

‡‡ Copies are on file with the author. These were never openly published by COG.

Berg advocates FFing to get to the top leaders of each country.

> This is a totally new different ministry and its top priority is to the system and the leaders of the System. Believe it or not, for the first time in our lives we're beginning to reach the System!—so here I don't want girls who just want to dance with cotton pickers, hippies, teenagers, weirdy beardies, communists and whatnot!
>
> Here we're reaching the city fathers, the leaders, the important men who are influential and essential to our stay here, is that clear? This is our PR outreach. We may not get all of them saved, but at least we can make friends out of them—and if nothing else, at least make them tolerate us, and that's very important to our security and stay here.[71]

For anyone who knows the Bible, Berg's sexual aberrations are clearly anti-Christian. The Bible absolutely condemns such behavior. Contrast Berg's debauchery with the Bible's spiritually pure picture of marriage:

> Wives, submit to your husbands as to the Lord. For the husband is the head of the wife as Christ is the head of the church, his body, of which he is the Savior. Now as the church submits to Christ, so also wives should submit to their husbands in everything.
>
> Husbands, love your wives, just as Christ loved the church and gave himself up for her to make her holy, cleansing her by the washing with water through the word, and to present her to himself as a radiant church, without stain or wrinkle or any other blemish, but holy and blameless. In this same way, husbands ought to love their wives as their own bodies. He who loves his wife loves himself. After all, no one ever hated his own body, but he feeds and cares for it, just as Christ does the church—for we are members of his body. "For this reason a man will leave his father and mother and be united to his wife, and the two will become one flesh." This is a profound mystery—but I am talking about Christ and the church. However, each one of you must also love his wife as he loves himself, and the wife must respect her husband.[72]

Biblical marriage has been instituted by God (Genesis 2:18-24) and is a permanent bond between a man and a woman whom God has called together (Matthew 19:5,6). Sexual love should be with one's own, sole partner in marriage. One should always be satisfied with his own sole spouse, not many women (Proverbs 5:1-18). The Bible condemns Berg and uplifts Jesus' view of marriage in Hebrews 13:4: "Marriage should be honored by all, and the marriage bed kept pure, for God will judge the adulterer and all the sexually immoral."

The Bible condemns incest (Leviticus 18:6-18), adultery (Matthew 5:32), and polygamy (Leviticus 18:18), and instead teaches that marriage promotes man's happiness (Genesis 2:18) and the complete satisfaction of both man and wife (Proverbs 5:19; 1 Timothy 2:15; 5:14).

Since marriage is figurative of Christ's union with the church (Ephesians 5:22-33), Christians are challenged to follow all of God's directives concerning it. Marriage is not to be self-centered and physically controlled, as Berg's system is. Biblical union involves selfless sacrificing of one partner to the other, even as Christ sacrificed Himself for the church.

Anti-Semitism

Before we discuss the COG beliefs concerning God, Jesus, and salvation, we should briefly discuss Berg's rabid anti-Semitism. In addition to despising the governments of the United States and the Soviet Union, Berg has nourished a deep hatred for the Jews. Berg's hatred for the Jews surfaced shortly after his trip to Israel in 1970. He claims that since the Jews were told God's truth when Jesus came and yet rejected it, they are reprobates and unworthy of any grace from God. Berg even goes so far as to label the Old Testament as anti-Semitic!

A recent Mo Letter shows Berg's hatred for the Jews.

So I asked the Lord to really curse those God-damned Jews and to do something to teach them a lesson. I think maybe Sadat and his Arabs. My God, help him!

May God damn the God-damned Jews! My God, I think if I could get over there and had a gun I think I'd shoot 'em myself! My Lord, help us to help them somehow, Lord, in Jesus' name! My Lord help us!

How can God tolerate those God-damned Jews!—Those God-damned Americans! The Americans are just as guilty of the whole thing. The Jews probably apprised them of the whole thing before they even started and told them what they were going to do.

God damn the Jews! Those Anti-Christ, Christ-hating Jews, God damn them! O God, if I had a gun I'd shoot them myself! My God, why don't You do something, Lord, why don't You do something! In Jesus name why don't you do something?

Stop this God-damned devil Begin! Kill him, Lord, as he has killed the poor, kill him! Slaughter him!

God damn those rich U.S. Jews, those anti-Christ God-hating Jews who hate us, Thy children, and are trying to destroy us. God damn them everywhere, Lord!

I don't want you for my God if you're on the side of the Israelis and the Americans, those God-damned Christ-hating Jews! If You're on their side, Lord, I don't want to be on Your side!—Deliver me, slay me also!

May God damn every Israeli! They are all robbers!—All terrorists! And all thieves! All oppressors! They're all guilty! There's no such thing as an innocent Israeli civilian!

There's nothing but those God-damned anti-Christ horrible hateful awful Jews, the devils incarnate, the devils themselves! That's all there is left without God!—No God, no Saviour, no Jesus, no Christ, no nothing! I'm through. I'm fed up![73]

Contrary to Berg's pronouncements, God has mightily blessed the nation of Israel, as is seen in the Old Testament. Many of the great leaders of our faith were Jews (Hebrews 11:8-40). God inspired Israeli prophets to proclaim His

Word (1 Peter 1:10-12). The messianic promises came to the Jews (Acts 3:18-26). God used Israel as His example to the world of His grace in working with mankind. Jews are no better and no worse than any other people. All citizens of all nations need to call on Christ as their Savior, thereby freely receiving God's grace (Romans 3:24). In Romans 9:4,5, the Apostle Paul described some of the blessings that God has bestowed on the nation Israel:

> Theirs is the adoption as sons; theirs the divine glory, the covenants, the receiving of the law, the temple worship and the promises. Theirs are the patriarchs, and from them is traced the human ancestry of Christ, who is God over all, forever praised! Amen.

DOCTRINE

The Children of God is a revolutionary organization dedicated to supporting and propagating itself through fund-raising and evangelism. The supreme preoccupation of its members and its leader is unbiblical sex. Because of this, the COG and David Berg have very little to say directly about the nature of God.

Berg's writings about God are haphazard and confused. It is difficult to determine his theology from his literature, which is devoted almost exclusively to himself and sex. Berg is also vague and contradictory concerning the Person of Jesus Christ and the Person and deity of the Holy Spirit. Because his writings are so disjointed on these three subjects, we will depart from our normal format and discuss all three doctrines—God, Christ, and the Holy Spirit—in one section.

In a recent publication, Berg stated that he does not believe in the Trinity, although this might be taken to mean only that he refuses to use the word "trinity" because it is not found in the Bible. He shows a definite confusion concerning the nature of Christ: he calls him "partly God" in one place and then goes on to explain that Christ is actually a created being (though this does not take away from Christ's divinity, he says).

Berg's views on the Holy Spirit are also confused. Sometimes he seems to imply that the Holy Spirit is an impersonal substance which is poured out as the "love" of God, while in other places the Holy Spirit is lumped together with "the seven spirits of God" and other spirits of the heavenly realm (see the later section in this chapter).

> Well, if they believe in the virgin birth then they have got to believe in the divinity of Jesus, that He was partly God, even though according to some of their advocates they claim they don't. See they're contradicting their own Bible, because if he was virgin-born then He was the Son of God!
>
> "Even so God createth what he willeth"—In other words He, Jesus, was a creation of God. Oh, this is exactly according to the Scriptures! Can you think of a verse on it? What does God's Word say about Jesus? It says that He was "the beginning of the creation of God!" (Rev. 3:14)
>
> Now you know the Catholics and some are so strong on the so-called Trinity, but I don't even believe in the Trinity. You can't find that word in the Bible, so why should I believe it? But I believe in the Father and I believe in the Son, Jesus, and I believe in the Holy Ghost.
>
> If you want to call it Trinity, all right, but I don't believe in it in some ways, the way some over emphasize and stress it, you know. You would think that Jesus just always was, just like God, but in a sense he was not until He was made man, although He was in the beginning and He was a part of God. But God's Word also says that He was the beginning of the creation of God—you know where that's found? I recall it's in Revelation in the first two or three chapters there.[74]

If Berg is to have a consistent theology, he will have to decide whether Jesus was created or is the Creator. If Jesus is God in human flesh, the second Person of the Godhead, then He cannot have been created. There is an infinite gap between the created and the Creator. Only the Creator deserves worship (Romans 1:25). Jesus is deserving of our worship because He is our Creator (John 20:28; Colossians 1:15-17).

Berg has confused the two natures of Christ. As God, the divine Person, Jesus possesses all the attributes and nature of God. He is God, the second Person of the Godhead. When He became incarnate, He could not stop being God, the eternal One. Instead of discarding one nature and adopting a new one, Jesus took on an *additional* nature—that of a perfect man. His human nature did not exist eternally, but the *divine* Person (the Logos—John 1:1) is eternal. That one Person now possesses two natures, one human and one divine.

This is clearly expressed in Philippians 2:1-11. There Paul talks of Jesus, the supreme Example to the Christian of true humility. Paul urges us to be humble, and, although we are all equal because of Christ, to consider others' benefits before our own. He uplifts Christ as our Example, who, although He was equal to the Father in every way, and was God, was willing to submit Himself to the Father's initiative. God became flesh (John 1:14), and as a man He humbled himself even further by submitting to the actions of man, knowing that His willing sacrifice at the hands of others was the means of redemption for the world. As God He was humble before the Father. As man He was humble before other men. Philippians 2:1-11 expresses the two natures in Christ: He was fully God (Malachi 3:6; Hebrews 13:8) and He was also truly man (Philippians 2:7).

In addition, Berg does not understand the meaning of Revelation 3:14, where Christ is called the "beginning of the creation of God." Far from asserting that Jesus is created, as Berg asserts, this declares his supremacy as *Creator*. Berg has made the same misunderstanding of the word "beginning" as do the Jehovah's Witnesses, who also try to use this verse to show that Jesus was created.

The Greek word for beginning here is *arche,* and it is the

same root word from which we get such English words as "architect" or "archeology." In this passage, the best Greek scholarship has determined that the word signifies that Jesus is the *Origin* or *Source* or *Designer* of creation—not a product of it!

Berg imitates another well-known cult by asserting that Jesus was the product of sexual intercourse between Berg's god and Mary. This belief is shared by historic Mormonism, whose resurrected god (Adam or Elohim, depending on the Mormon source), was said to have had intercourse with Mary to produce Jesus.[75] Berg declares:

> Of course God is not our natural Father, but he's like a father to us in a spiritual sense....God didn't f--- my mother and produce me in the utmost literal sense, of course not.
>
> In the literal sense regarding Jesus, yes, we do believe that and that's where we differ, one of the doctrines on which Islam differs—at least so they say....[76]

Berg has contradicted those Scriptures which firmly declare that Mary was a virgin until after the birth of Jesus. Matthew 1:18 says that "she was found to be with child through the Holy Spirit"—not through intercourse with God! Luke 1:35 answers Mary's question (as to how she could be with child, since she was a virgin) by declaring the supernatural means by which she would become pregnant: "The Holy Spirit will come upon you, and the power of the Most High will overshadow you. So the holy one to be born will be called the Son of God." Matthew 1:25 confirms that Mary remained a virgin until the birth of Jesus: "But he [Joseph] had no union with her until she gave birth to a son." God did not have sexual relations with Mary; the power of the Holy Spirit overshadowed her, and the conception which took place within her was miraculous.

Berg sometimes refers to the Holy Spirit as though He were God's impersonal force, or a synonym for love:

> It must mean you can pour the spirit of God on the bumpers by prayer. People used to pray: Cover us with Thy

blood, Lord. But I never could see how they could pray that. But this makes more sense—being covered by His Spirit.

I'm sure the Lord has prevented a lot of accidents. That coming down like rain is like an outpouring of His Spirit. That's all the things that His Spirit does or can do. The Spirit is love! It's God, and God is love! Do you have His Elixier of Love?!—It can do miracles! Would you like some?—There's lots more where this came from!—Write to us![77]

Although Berg identifies the Holy Spirit with God in the above quote, his imagery is still of the Holy Spirit as the impersonal love force of God. Calling the Holy Spirit the "elixir of love" even makes it sound like a love potion!

The Bible declares that the Holy Spirit is God (Acts 5:3,4; Hebrews 9:14), is a Person (Acts 13:2; John 14:26), and is the Person of the Trinity whose ministry is to be a Counselor, sent to advise the Christian and to "convict the world of guilt in regard to sin and righteousness and judgment" (John 16:8).

Berg seems to see a dichotomy between the character of the God of the Old Testament and the character of Jesus Christ. Berg prefers to be like his Old Testament God.

I'm sorry, I guess I'm not so loving as Jesus—I'm more like King David. (I Sam. 26:19.) Jesus could forgive His enemies, but I curse my enemies. But God said David was a man after His own heart, so maybe I'm more like God, 'cause I want to curse them for hurting my little ones! They love us so much, like sheep having no shepherd. They look for a liberator.[78]

However, there is no dichotomy between the God of the Old Testament and Jesus, who is that God. The picture of God in the Old Testament shows that He can be merciful, as merciful as Jesus was. God reminds us in Ezekiel 18:32, "For I take no pleasure in the death of anyone, declares the Sovereign Lord. Repent and live!" This thought is echoed in Psalm 32:10: "Many are the woes of the wicked, but the Lord's unfailing love surrounds the man who trusts in him."

Jesus in the New Testament could use the same judgment displayed by God in the Old Testament. He drove the money-changers from the temple (John 2:13-16). Jesus' condemnation of the hypocrites of the first century are memorialized for us in Matthew 23:37-39, and the delicate balance between God's justice and mercy is sharply demonstrated in Jesus' concluding remarks there:

O Jerusalem, Jerusalem, you who kill the prophets and stone those sent to you, how often I have longed to gather your children together, as a hen gathers her chicks under her wings, but you were not willing. Look, your house is left to you desolate. For I tell you, you will not see me again until you say, "Blessed is he who comes in the name of the Lord."

One of the final pictures we are given of Jesus in the New Testament, in Revelation 19:11-16, shows Him as the Judge of the universe, the righteous Ruler exacting payment for sin after He has showered His mercy on His bride, the believers who have turned to Him and His grace.

I saw heaven standing open and there before me was a white horse, whose rider is called Faithful and True. With justice he judges and makes war. His eyes are like blazing fire, and on his head are many crowns. He has a name written on him that no one but he himself knows. He is dressed in a robe dipped in blood, and his name is the Word of God. The armies of heaven were following him, riding on white horses and dressed in fine linen, white and clean. Out of his mouth comes a sharp sword with which to strike down the nations. "He will rule them with an iron scepter." He treads the winepress of the fury of the wrath of God Almighty. On his robe and on his thigh he has this name written: King of Kings and Lord of Lords.

Berg even tries to attribute to God the proliferation and nourishment of all false religions:

God therefore both originates and controls even all false religions!—And if you want to say they're of the Devil, that's merely because he's God's instrument.[79]

However, the Bible tells us that the Lord is not the source of false religion; disobedient people are. Deuteronomy 18:22 denies that God speaks through false religions: "If what a prophet proclaims in the name of the Lord does not take place or come true, that is a message the Lord has not spoken. That prophet has spoken presumptuously. Do not be afraid of him." Galatians 1:6 delcares that those who follow false teachings are "deserting the one who called you by the grace of Christ and are turning to a different gospel."

Berg's involvement with spiritism, which we shall discuss shortly, has even affected his beliefs concerning the work of Jesus Christ. To the COG, Jesus is not the only mediator. Instead, Berg states that one of the COG leaders, Abner, who died, is now COG's personal representative in heaven. In the same way that Christ was sent to earth and then taken up to heaven for further purposes, so was Abner!

> He has for a long time been our Chief of Security, concern-ed with our defenses, so how fitting of the Lord to take this one who was most concerned and promote him to an even higher position amongst God's Heavenly Security Forces to watch over us from an even better vantage point— Hallelujah!...How foolish and selfish we are to want to keep him, when he is serving us and the Lord much better over there as our own Personal Representative before the Lord. Who could know us better than he and plead our cause more effectively!...If God had to send Jesus, and then take Him for this purpose, how fitting it was that our own dear Abner was given, and then taken for us also!

> ...Abner can appear through its spiritual windows and see us, watch us, and even watch over us, as he was wont to do when here with us in the flesh—only now he can do it even better!...He is now the Personal Representative of the Children of God in the Counsels and Courts of Heaven! He stands in the Gap![80]

The Bible absolutely contradicts this assertion by Berg.

Neither Abner nor anyone else is involved in our spiritual communion with God. It is the ministry of the Holy Spirit, not Abner, to make our needs known to God (Romans 8:26,27). It is the ministry of Jesus, not Abner, to be our mediator before God (1 Timothy 2:5). Hebrews 7:25 reminds us, "Therefore he is able to save completely those who come to God through him, because he always lives to intercede for them."

What Berg attributes to the Father he sometimes also attributes to Jesus, as when he says that Jesus had sexual intercourse with the Marys. He has stated that he believes that Jesus was the product of sex between God and Mary.§§ Jesus Himself, in COG theology, seems to have a relativistic ethic, since Berg declares that nothing was wrong for Jesus, since he showed love to the Marys in having intercourse with them!

> I even believe that he [Jesus] lived with her and Mary and Martha later, which was no sin for Him, because He couldn't commit sin. Everything that He did He did in love, He probably did it for their sakes as much as His own—He had physical needs just like they did.[81]

Berg's sacrilege does not stop here. After asserting in several publications that Jesus had sexual intercourse with several women, he states that Jesus also had venereal disease!

> He may have even contracted a disease from Mary Magdalene, who had been a known prostitute, and several other women that were prostitutes that followed Him, or Mary and Martha. If so, then He was certainly tempted in all points like as we are, and He bore it for their sakes because they needed His love!
> Well, if He'd never suffered their sexual diseases, He could never really have full compassion on their sufferings, could He?—to be willing to even contract their dieseases!—That seemed to me too much. Isn't that something?[82]

§§ See preceding section on Berg's doctrine concerning this.

The illogical argumentation of Berg here is only surpassed by his blasphemy. So Christ had to experience VD in order to have full compassion on those who do? Then why didn't He sin so that He could have full compassion on those who sinned? Why didn't He have leprosy? Why wasn't He blind? Jesus became a man, and it was that incarnation itself which allowed Him to empathize with our sufferings. Hebrews 2:14 shows us how Jesus identified with us: "Since the children have flesh and blood, he too shared in their humanity so that by his death he might destroy him who holds the power of death—that is, the devil." Hebrews 4:15 declares, "For we do not have a high priest who is unable to sympathize with our weaknesses, but we have one who has been tempted in every way, just as we are—yet was without sin." Temptation has nothing to do with sexual diseases!

The love that Christ showed for the two Marys and for Martha was the same kind of love He showed for all of us when He died for our sins. He did not have sex with them to show His love—He *died* for them to show His love. Jesus declared that the greatest love was a sacrificial love: "My command is this: Love each other as I have loved you. Greater love has no one than this, that one lay down his life for his friends" (John 15:12,13). The love of God for mankind was expressed in the sacrifice of His Son: "But God demonstrates his own love for us in this: While we were still sinners, Christ died for us" (Romans 5:8).

The COG is so enamored of its own power and importance in God's plan that one can find many quotes where COG compares itself or its members to Jesus. Nowhere is this more explicit or more offensive to the biblical Christian than in the COG quotes linking sexual immorality with the atonement of Christ.

> Every one of you boys here who has a mate who does FFing is "playing God"! Did you know that? You know what I mean? You are doing the same for these lost souls that God did for your soul! He gave you His only Son to save your

188 / *THE NEW CULTS*

soul.—Just as some of you men are giving your only one to save other's souls!

They know God is love because you loved them that much! For you so loved the world that you gave your only begotten wife, that whosoever believeth on her shall not perish but have everlasting life! Is it worth it?[83]

We have been comparing this ministry to the ministry of Christ, the sacrifices and the crucifixion of Christ. It is the most difficult and the most dangerous ministry I think we have ever entered into and costs the most in sacrifice, in crucifixion and suffering—for the boys as well.

You are not the ones who did evil—they're the ones who did evil and contracted those diseases! You're simply bearing them because of their sins in order to try to save them!

But he allowed Christ to bear our sins and our iniquities. If we are to be vicarious with others the same way He was with us, then we sometimes have to suffer for their sins too!...

When you girls feel their "nails" pounding into you, maybe you can think about the nails pounding into Jesus on the cross—even when it hurts! What a comparison![84]

The Bible denies that anyone but Jesus can save people's souls. Salvation is accomplished through Christ's death on the cross, not through prostitution! VD is not the sacrifice that must be made in order to save sinners. "Since we have now been justified by his blood, how much more shall we be saved from God's wrath through him!" (Romans 5:9). Our reconciliation to God is accomplished wholly by Jesus Christ, and it is Jesus "through whom we have now received reconciliation" (Romans 5:11). Hebrews 7:25 reminds us that Jesus needs no help in saving us, since "he is able to save completely those who come to God through him, because he always lives to intercede for them." Peter's declaration in Acts 4:12 denies a multiplicity of saviors: "Salvation is found in no one else, for there is no other name under heaven given to men by which we must be saved."

No one can share fully in the sufferings of Christ. He is

the only One who was able to resist sin to the point of shedding blood. Our affiliations are inconsequential in comparison. Hebrews 12:3,4 reminds us, "Consider him who endured such opposition from sinful men, so that you will not grow weary and lose heart. In your struggle against sin, you have not yet resisted to the point of shedding your blood."

David Berg and the theology of the Children of God do not embrace the God of the Bible. The God of the Bible is holy, pure, just, and loving. He exists eternally as the one God in three distinct Persons—Father, Son, and Holy Spirit. The Holy Spirit is not some love potion. The Father is not some oversexed god, as is Krishna and the god of Mormonism. The Son is not a promiscuous bachelor with VD. We worship "God, the blessed and only Ruler, the King of kings and Lord of lords, who alone is immortal and who lives in unapproachable light, whom no one has seen or can see" (1 Timothy 6:15b,16a).

Salvation

Because the Children of God movement was born of the Jesus Revolution of the sixties, it still mingles a large amount of evangelical terminology and belief with Berg's heretical doctrines. This is evident in the COG doctrine of salvation. In its early years, COG promoted an evangelical gospel message of salvation by grace alone through the sacrifice of Jesus Christ for our sins. Although some of their methods were unorthodox, and the commitment to the organization they required as evidence of salvation was inappropriate, they still preached what most Christians would accept as the true gospel. Many people came to a saving knowledge of Jesus Christ through the street witnessing of the Children of God.

However, very quickly Berg's aberrant doctrines neutralized what good his group's street witnessing was doing, and then these doctrines contaminated the group's view of salvation as well. The FFing doctrine thrust its way into the forefront of COG doctrine and practice and quickly eclipsed all other doctrines and practices, including the salvation preaching done on the streets by COG members. Today it is very hard to find mention of the biblical way to salvation in COG literature.

In addition, the exclusiveness of the COG has changed its attitude toward salvation. Since the group believes that it alone is fully following Jesus, and since it damns any church system, its assumptions concerning salvation reflect this. COG members will admit that there are Christians outside the group, but consider that these are not really obeying Jesus, and will be judged accordingly. Berg even goes so far as to assert that one is "of God" if he admits that God has come in the flesh of the Children of God![85]

Berg also asserts the error of universal salvation—that all people, or nearly all, will eventually be saved. This declares that there is a second chance to be approved by God after death.

> Only the most wicked of all, Satan, the Antichrist, his False Prophet and his most ardent followers who received the Mark of the Beast and worshipped him and his Image will remain in the Lake of Fire to be punished and purged of their diabolical rebelliousness as long as God sees fit, even until such time as they, too, may have learned their lesson sufficiently for God to forgive them and restore His entire creation to its original perfection where all is well![86]

> I'm looking forward to the day when—this may be another shocking thing for some people—when everybody or almost everybody will be saved—at least there won't be many left in Hell, if any.[87]

Berg here contradicts the Bible, which declares clearly that salvation is only for those who come to Christ on His terms. All others have chosen eternal separation from God (and hell) instead of eternal fellowship with God in Jesus Christ. The Bible clearly teaches that salvation is offered freely to all men, but that many people refuse that offer.

Matthew 25:11-46 describes the two classes of people whom Jesus will judge in the last day. The righteous are those who have followed Jesus, and the unrighteous are those who have rejected Jesus. Jesus acknowledges that the eternal fire of hell was prepared for the devil and his angels (Matthew 25:41), but He also asserts that it will become the eternal habitation of those who have rejected Him. Matthew 25:46 declares the destinies of the unrighteous and the righteous: "Then they will go away to eternal punishment, but the righteous to eternal life."

Berg also believes that those who are living can "pray people out of hell." In harmony with common universalist thought, hell is described by Berg as a place of reforming punishment, a temporary prison in which the sinner is incarcerated until he repents.

> ...I've been praying him out of hell so he can go to Heaven.—isn't that beautiful? (Maria: Yes. Did he go to hell?) Well, for a little while he had to go, because he didn't know Jesus, but now I've prayed him out. You know? (Maria: And he's out now?) Yes, I prayed him out.[88]

This contradicts John 3:36, which clearly says, "Whoever believes in the Son has eternal life, but whoever does not obey the Son will not see life, for God's wrath remains on him." The man Berg says he prayed out of hell does not have an excuse by saying that he didn't know Jesus, for the Bible says that all have the opportunity to come to God through Christ (Romans 1:20; Acts 4:12). Revelation 20:11-15 unequivocally teaches eternal punishment for the unrighteous. Those who are not Christians will be thrown in the lake of fire, along with the devil, the beast, and the false prophet, who "will be tormented day and night for ever and ever" (v. 10b).

David Berg and Spiritism

Our final discussion of the Children of God will concern

Berg's deep involvement with spiritism. Many of the heretical teachings of the Children of God are a result of alleged communications from disembodied spirits who speak to Berg and appear to him. This violates the many biblical admonitions against spiritistic activities.

Berg's closest and initial spirit guide is named Abrahim the Gypsy King. Berg first encountered him during one of the group's early dispersions. Berg encourages occultic involvement on the part of his followers, and emphasizes complete submission to such spirits as imperative for true "spiritual" growth. Becoming spiritual becomes synonymous with becoming more occultically involved.

> ...Another shocker which I think you will enjoy and be receiving soon is *'God's Witches!'* In there you'll hear all about God's wizards and witches and enchantresses and enchantments and spells and hypnotisms and all kinds of things, very, very interesting, about things in the spirit world![89]
> ...Thanks be unto God for all the good spirits of God and his saints! Seven of them stand about David at this very moment as the personal Honour Guard of God's King! All I have to do is close my eyes in the spirit to seem [sic] them at anytime! One would be enough, considering the mighty power each one has; so when I asked the Lord why seven, He replied very clearly that this was a special honour becoming the position of His King! Hallelujah![90]

When I first remember seeing Abrahim in vision he was a very old man, the Gypsy King of Bulgaria. But apparently I was seeing his past through his eyes, the way he used to look in those days.

I can remember my mother being very old when she died. But from the first time I saw her after she was back in the spirit world, she looked young and beautiful again—totally mature in the prime of life—like about 40, I'd say.

That's the way Abrahim looks now: about 40, in the prime of life....

Abrahim's superviser [sic] is definitely an angelic spirit. Abrahim was a human being, but this other spirit was never a human being. He is Abrahim's angelic overseer.

...Why should the Lord want us to get into all these spirits and how they operate? Is it to prepare the kids for what is coming? These are things they even need to know here and now....[91]

These spiritual contacts have also included such amazing characters as my own Mother, Father, Grandfather, William Jennings Bryan, Martin Luther, Tyndale, Peter the Hermit, the Pied Piper, Eric the Norseman, Ivan the Terrible, Czar Nicolas, Rasputin, Anne Boleyn, a Czarina named Katrina, another Russian girl named Karenina, Ivan Invanovich of Moscow, Alexis of Kharkov and others, as well as now the legendary Snowman![92]

It is small wonder that with his deep involvement with spiritism, Berg would compare his own experiences with those of other cult leaders who were involved with spiritism.

The prophet William Branham was about the only one I ever heard come out and flatly declare that his guiding spirit was an angel through which he got his messages and all of his information, and a lot of people thought he was a heretic because he kept seeing this angel. He said his angel was very dark-skinned and looked like an Oriental Indian!

Maybe some of those spiritualistic churches are not so bad after all! They sing hymns and talk about Jesus and preach the Gospel. When I was at that spiritualistic church in Miami they sang beautiful hymns. It seemed very sweet, but I was scared to death because I thought it was all of the Devil!—That's what I'd always been taught....

The divining spirit the girl had that followed the apostles around kept saying, "These men are the servants of the Most High God which show unto us the way of salvation." (Acts 16:16.) Apparently the only reason Paul rebuked the spirit was because it got to be a nuisance, a bother to them, a distraction.[93]

The prophet William Branham told us his angel always appeared in a circle of light. Joseph Smith accepted Christ but he didn't like the church. He had an angel who came and appeared to him in a circle of light and materialised out of this circle of light.—A flying saucer?[94]

The spiritism practiced by David Berg is categorically condemned by Scripture. However, there is one more area of spiritism that Berg is heavily involved in: he says he has frequent sex with spirits. The two most dangerous doctrines of the COG, FFing and spiritism, are thus united.

Berg frequently speaks of having violent sex with "goddesses," spirits from the various countries who supposedly come to him because they want the COG in their countries. These "goddesses" even show jealousy toward Maria, thereby divulging their fallen nature.

> While making love this morning . . . I had a very strange experience: A very beautiful woman covered with green scales like a wetsuit but no clothes, appeared to me to make love to me!
>
> Could this be the goddess or angel of the Canaries? She suddenly gave me such a terrific surge of power that I absolutely exploded! . . . That evening I was thinking about what had happened this morning and I had the question on my heart,
>
> Who is she? All of a sudden I saw her swimming in the water out here above what is supposed to be the sunken remains of Atlantis, that she was like the Goddess of Atlantis, and that in a way she is bound to the remains of Atlantis. . . .

> People just don't realise that the spirits in the spirit world are still very much like us in their feelings and their emotions and their desires and their choices and opinions and preferences and all these things. For example, the goddesses I make love to are jealous of Maria.[96]

Any form of spiritism is condemned in the Bible, both Old and New Testaments. ☆ ☆ There are no witches who are approved by God. There are no wizards who are approved

---

☆ ☆ See Chapter 6, "The 'I AM' Ascended Masters," for further refutation of spiritistic practices.

by God. Those who cast spells and enchantments, as the spirits who visit Berg claim to do, are condemned by God. It is forbidden by God in the Bible to have anything to do with someone who consults the dead.

Deuteronomy 18:10-13 warns all believers:

> Let no one be found among you who sacrifices his son or daughter in the fire, who practices divination or sorcery, interprets omens, engages in witchcraft, or casts spells, or who is a medium or spiritist or who consults the dead. Anyone who does these things is detestable to the Lord, and because of these detestable practices the Lord your God will drive out those nations before you. You must be blameless before the Lord your God.

King Saul rightly suppressed witchcraft in Israel (1 Samuel 28:3,9), until he backslid and consulted a witch (1 Samuel 28:7-25). For this God condemned him, as 1 Chronicles 10:13,14 reminds us: "Saul died because he was unfaithful to the Lord; he did not keep the word of the Lord and even consulted a medium for guidance, and did not inquire of the Lord. So the Lord put him to death and turned the kingdom over to David son of Jesse."

God promised through the prophet Micah to destroy the witches there when He said, "I will destroy your witchcraft and you will no longer cast spells. I will destroy your carved images and your sacred stones from among you; you will no longer bow down to the work of your hands" (Micah 5:12,13).

We know from our study of Berg and the COG that they do not teach the truths of the Bible. We can echo with Ezekiel, "Their visions are false and their divinations a lie. They say, 'The Lord declares,' when the Lord has not sent them; yet they expect their words to be fulfilled. Have you not seen false visions and uttered lying divinations when you say, 'The Lord declares,' though I have not spoken?" (Ezekiel 13:6,7). With false visions pouring forth from Berg, we are reminded of others who claimed to prophesy in the Lord's name in Jeremiah's day. The Lord condemned them by saying, "The prophets are prophesying lies in my name. I have not sent them or appointed them or spoken to them. They are prophesying to you false visions, divinations, idolatries and the delusions of their own minds" (Jeremiah 14:14).

We can judge Berg's practices of spiritism on the basis of God's Word. On that basis, they are false and cannot be trusted. Whoever trusts in them cannot trust in God's Word. We can judge the Children of God on the basis of God's Word in Isaiah 8:19,20:

> When men tell you to consult mediums and spiritists, who whisper and mutter, should not a people inquire of their God? Why consult the dead on behalf of the living? To the law and the testimony! If they do not speak according to this word, they have no light of dawn.

CONCLUSION

We have examined the Children of God and their leader, David Berg, systematically and in the light of God's Word, and have found them to be spiritually erroneous and corrupt. Beginning with divisiveness, the COG has moved farther and farther into heresy. While there are many in the COG who may have been Christians when they joined the group but were misled by the false teachings of Berg, the cult itself cannot in any way be considered Christian.

David Berg is a false prophet: his prophecies do not come to pass, and he preaches doctrine contrary to the Bible. Berg claims to be God's prophet and the chosen dictator over the Children of God. He has held his own writings above the authority of the Bible. He rejects those portions of the Old and New Testaments which contradict his own beliefs and practices. The sexual aberrations of the COG completely divorce its followers from the ranks of obedient Christians. God is not a pimp and the church is not His prostitute, no matter how much COG may assert it. Although Berg condemns Jews completely, God has decreed that members of the Jewish nation and race can come to Christ just as all others: through faith and God's grace (Galatians 3:28). Berg perverts the biblical doctrines of God, the Holy Spirit, and Christ. His assertion that Jesus had sexual relations with many women and even contracted VD denies everything the Scriptures declare about the purity of Christ. Contrary to COG beliefs, salvation is by faith in the Son of God—not by periods of punishment or penance in hell or by having Berg pray someone out of hell.

By practicing and promoting spiritism, Berg and the Children of God have aligned themselves with the forces of darkness rather than with the living God. For the sake of Christ we must pray for their deliverance from error, for the alternative is God's judgment.

CHAPTER NOTES

1. This portion of COG history is from the *Final Report on the Activities of the Children of God to Hon. Louis J. Lefkowitz, Attorney General of the State of New York,* submitted by: Charity Frauds, Herbert J. Wallenstein, Assistant Attorney General in Charge, 9-30-74.

2. Moses David, "Survival," in *The Basic Mo Letters,* #70-73 (Hong Kong: Children of God (COG), 1976), pp. 126-27.

3. Loc. cit.

4. Ibid., pp. 130-33.

5. Ibid., pp. 131-34.

6. Ibid., p. 134.

7. Charity Frauds Bureau, op. cit., p. 3, referring to a Huntington Beach Police Department report dated May 21, 1973.

8. James Knoblock, *The Children of David: A Biblical Examination of Moses David and the Children of God,* unpublished, 1977-78, P.O. Box 711, Escondido, CA 92025.

9. "Survival," op. cit. p. 138.

10. Ronal M. Enroth, Edward E. Erickson, and C. Breckinridge Peters, *The Jesus People* (Grand Rapids: Eerdmans, 1972), pp. 26-29.

11. Moses David, *40 DAYS! AND NINEVAH SHALL BE DESTROYED!* (London: Children of God, Nov. 12, 1973, GP No. 280).

12. Moses David, *The Crystal Pyramid* (Dallas: Children of God, Mar. 1973, No. 214), pp. 1, 2.

13. Moses David, (aka. Father David), *Excommunication!* (Rome: Family of Love, Mar. 13, 1978, DO No. 683), pp. 2, 3, 5, 7.

14. Moses David, *The Lit Revolution! — But Where Is the Harvest?* (London: Children of God, Feb. 17, 1975, DFO No. 328A), pp. 2-4.

15. Moses David, *More Truth!* (Rome: Children of God, Aug. 23, 1977, GP No. 598), p. 12.

16. Moses David, (aka. Father David), *Nationalisation!—Indigenuity at Last!* (Lima, Peru: Children of God, Jan. 1978, DO No. 659), p. 7.

17. Moses David, *Daily Might: Readings from the Mo Letters, Compiled by Justus Pound & Adar David* (Hong Kong: Family of Love, 1977), pp. 2, 11.

18. Moses David, *Death in Your Arms!* (Rome: Family of Love, Dec. 24, 1976, GP No. 680), pp. 1-8.

19. Moses David, *Daily Might,* op. cit., p. 2.

20. Moses David, *The Kingdom: A Prophecy* (Children of God, Aug. 20, 1971, LO No. 94), p. 1.

21. Moses David, *Grace vs. Law* (Rome: Children of God, Nov. 1977, DFO No. 635), pp. 2, 4, 5.

22. Moses David, *The Wrath of God!* (Rome: Children of God, Mar. 5, 1977, DFO No. 577), pp. 3-9.

23. Moses David, *Alexander the Evil Magician!* (Rome: Family of Love, Feb. 7, 1978, DO No. 666), pp. 3-6.

24. Moses David, *The Word—New and Old (Mt. 13:52)* (London: Children of God, Sept. 1974, GP No. 329), pp. 1-4.

25. Loc. cit.

26. Moses David, *Daily Might,* op. cit., p. 1.

27. Faith David, *Talk to the Translators* (London: Children of God, Nov. 1972, DFO No. 16), p. 1

28. Faith David, *Pioneering, Popularity, and Persecution* (London: Children of God Trust, Oct. 25, 1973, DO No. 20), p. 3.

29. Ibid. p. 5.

30. Moses David, *The Word—New and Old (Mt. 13:52),* op. cit., p. 3.

31. Moses David, *Grace vs. Law* (Rome: Children of God, Nov. 1977), pp. 7-8.

32. Ibid, pp. 8-9.

33. Moses David, *Daily Might,* op. cit., p. 13.

34. Matthew 23:8-12.

35. Proverbs 30:5,6.

36. Moses David, *Re-Organization Nationalization Revolution!* (Rome: Children of God, Jan. 1978, DO No. 650).

37. Moses David, *The Shepherd's Rod!* (Rome: Family of Love, Mar. 13, 1978, DO No. 682), p. 3.

38. Ibid., p. 4.

39. Ibid., pp. 6-8.

40. Matthew 6:25-34.

41. Moses David, *Our Message* (London: Children of God, Sept. 1974, GP No. 330), pp. 1-3.

42. Loc. cit.

43. Moses David, *The Revolutionary Rules* (London: Children of God, Mar. 1972, GP No. S-RV).

44. Ibid., p. 1.

45. Moses David, *Revolutionary Sex* (London: Children of God, Mar. 27, 1973, GP No. 258).

46. Joseph M. Hopkins, "The Children of God: Disciples of Deception," in *Christianity Today,* Feb. 18, 1977, p. 20.

47. Moses David, *Come On Ma!—Burn Your Bra!* (Children of God, Dec. 22, 1973, GP No. 286), p. 2.

48. Moses David, "One Wife," in *Leader's Book* (London: Children of God, 1974), p. 32.

49. Charity Frauds Bureau, op. cit., p. 40.

50. Ibid., pp. 52-54.

51. Moses David, *He Stands in the Gap* (London: Children of God, May 20, 1971, GP No. 73A), pp. 4, 5.

52. Moses David, *Do You Want a Penis?—Or a Sword?* (Rome: Children of God, July 19, 1976, DO No. 545), pp. 1-4.

53. Moses David, *God's Whores?* (Rome: Children of God, Apr. 26, 1976, DO No. 560), p. 3.

54. Moses David, *Shiners—or Shamers!* (Children of God, June 26, 1973, DO

No. 214).

55. Moses David, "The Flirty Little Fish," in *The Basic Mo Letters,* op. cit., p. 528.

56. Moses David, *God's Love Slave!* (Children of God, Apr. 21, 1974), p. 7.

57. Moses David, *FF-er's Handbook!,* op. cit., p. 19.

58. Moses David, *FF-er's Handbook!,* op. cit., pp. 1, 5.

59. Moses David, *The FF Revolution!* (Rome: Children of God, Aug. 7, 1976, DO No. 575), p. 10.

60. Moses David, *Married to Jesus* (London: Children of God, Dec. 1973, DFO No. 25), p. 1; Moses David, *Grace vs. Law,* op. cit., p. 9.

61. Moses David, *Love vs. Law* (Rome: Children of God, July 23, 1977, GP No. 647), pp. 1-4.

62. Moses David, *Spaceship!* (Rome: Children of God, Dec. 17, 1976, GP No. 624), p. 7.

63. Moses David, *Teamwork!—The Gaffers!—Mo 'FF Tips!* (Rome: Children of God, May 1976, DO No. 553), pp. 1,2.

64. Moses David, *FF-er's Handbook!,* op. cit., p. 22.

65. Ibid., p. 30.

66. Moses David, *Nationalisation!—Indigenuity at Last!* (Lima, Peru: Children of God, 1978, DO No. 659), pp. 4-7.

67. Moses David, *FF-er's Handbook!,* op. cit., p. 26.

68. Moses David, *7 Supporters!* (Rome: Children of God, Feb. 1978, DFO No. 673), pp. 1, 2, 5, 7.

69. Moses David, *FF-er's Handbook!,* op. cit., p. 25.

70. Moses David, *Revolutionary Sex,* op. cit., p. 10.

71. Moses David, *Winning the System* (Rome: Children of God, Nov. 25, 1976), p. 2.

72. Ephesians 5:22-23.

73. Moses David, *A Prayer for the Poor!* (Rome: Family of Love, Mar. 19, 1978, DO No. 681), pp. 1, 3, 4, 5, 8, 9, 10.

74. Moses David, *Islam! (Chapter One)* (Rome: Children of God, May 18, 1975, DFO No. 631), p. 14.

75. See Walter Martin, *The Maze of Mormonism,* for further information on Mormon doctrine and the virgin birth of Christ.

76. Moses David, *Islam!,* op. cit., p. 10. See also Moses David, *Revolutionary Sex,* op. cit., p. 11: "God Himself had to have intercourse with Mother Mary in order to have Jesus!"

77. Moses David, *The Elixir of Love!* (Rome: Family of Love, Jan. 20, 1976, GP No. 677), p. 3.

78. Moses David, *The Wrath of God!* (Rome: Children of God, Mar. 5, 1977, DFO No. 577), pp. 1,2.

79. Moses David, *The Fan* (Rome: Children of God, May 22, 1975, GP No. 626), pp. 2, 3.

80. Moses David, *He Stands in the Gap* (London: Children of God, May 20, 1971, GP No. 73A), pp. 1, 5.

81. Moses David, *Love vs. Law!,* op. cit., p. 4.

82. Moses David, *Afflictions* (Children of God, Nov. 25, 1976, DO No. 569), pp. 2-5, 7.

83. Moses David, *FF-er's Handbook!*, op. cit., pp. 6, 8.

84. Moses David, *Afflictions*, op. cit., pp. 3-4, 8-9, 11.

85. Moses David, *The Spirit World* (Rome: Children of God, Nov. 1977), p. 6.

86. Moses David, *Heavenly Homes!* (London: Children of God, Oct. 21, 1974, GP No. 316), p. 3.

87. Moses David, *Revolutionary New Life!* (London: Children of God, June 1974), p. 1.

88. Moses David, *Taurig!* (Rome: Children of God, Oct. 5, 1977, GP No. 616), p. 1.

89. Moses David, *Communicate!* (Rome: Children of God, Apr. 25, 1977, DFO No. 580), p. 2.

90. Moses David, *Snowman* (Rome: Children of God, Dec. 26, 1972, DO No. 195), pp. 1179, 1180.

91. Moses David, *The Spirit World!*, op. cit., pp. 1-4.

92. Moses David, *Snowman*, op. cit., p. 1180.

93. Moses David, *The Spirit World!*, op. cit., pp. 4, 5.

94. Moses David, *Flying Saucers! UFO's! Spiritual Vehicles?* (Rome: Children of God, Sept. 30, 1973, GP No. 623), p. 2.

95. Moses David, *Atlanta!—Goddess of Atlantis!* (Rome: Children of God, Oct. 2, 1974, GP No. 615), pp. 1,2.

96. Moses David, *The Spirit World!*, op. cit., p. 6.

CHAPTER

6

THE "I AM"
ASCENDED MASTERS★

HISTORY

Among the many "new age" cults, the I AM or Ascended Masters movement is one of the most bizzare and baffling. When we speak of the I AM movements, or those who adhere to the teachings of the "Ascended Masters," we are referring to several groups or cults, both large and small, all of whom claim the same basic teachings. Other than common teachings, there are no ties between the groups, and, as we shall see below, some groups even rival each other for supremacy.

The movement consists of many metaphysical "churches" and "secret societies" or "mystery schools" which are not in any form of cohesive organization. The frontrunner today among the I AM groups is the Church Universal and Triumphant, while one of the earlier prominent groups was the mighty I AM group, led by Guy and Edna Ballard. The various roots of the belief system of these different groups reach to nineteenth-century Theosophy, and much earlier, to ancient gnosticism.

★ Researched by Elliot Miller.

The beliefs which distinguish the I AM groups from other cults include the conviction that since the latter half of the nineteenth century a progressive revelation has been coming forth from the spiritual realm with the distinct purpose of preparing the world for the coming of the Aquarian Age, an age where Christ Consciousness will reign supreme. The beginning of this "revelation" is commonly attributed to the emergence of Theosophy under Helena Petrovna Blavatsky.[1]

E.R. McNeile, a Theosophist who was converted to Christ in the late nineteenth century, provides a good background to the Theosophical movement and its relationship to the "Ascended Masters" doctrine:

> It is claimed that there exists, and has existed for untold ages, a body of supermen, adepts, initiates, the Brotherhood of the Great White Lodge (they are known by various names), who are possessed of all knowledge on every subject. Such knowledge includes cosmology, ethnology, the physical sciences, and all that range of subjects commonly associated with the term religion. From time to time, some parts of this knowledge have been revealed to such men as were found developed enough to receive it. . . .
>
> Some forty years ago, the Great Brotherhood decided that the time had come for a fresh and fuller revelation, and certain of their members were entrusted with this task. These members selected Mme. Blavatsky for their first disciple, and through her and Col. Olcott they founded the Theosophical Society. They are known to Theosophists as 'the Masters.' The teaching of Theosophy, therefore, consists of information either directly imparted by them, or acquired with their help, or by the methods indicated by them. A belief in the Masters is fundamental to Theosophy.[2]

For Theosophists and other "Ascended Masters" followers, these masters are deceased persons who communicate from beyond the grave!

As Christians, we know that we are to look to Jesus alone for help in all of our concerns. Jesus is committed to caring about our every problem and circumstance (see Matthew 18:6; 25:40; etc.). However, the early Theosophists rejected that idea, asserting that Jesus was only one of many "Masters" and that none of the masters was concerned with individuals' problems or concerns. According to Blavatsky:

. . . the Masters would not stoop for one moment to give a thought to *individual*, private matters relating to one or even ten persons, their welfare, woes and blisses in this world of Maya* to nothing except questions of really universal importance. . . . *You who* have unconsciously and with the best of intentions and full sincerity of good purpose, *desecrated* Them, by thinking for one moment, and believing that *They* would trouble Themselves with your business matters, sons to be born, daughters to be married, houses to be built, etc. etc.[3]

However, in some I AM cults, the Masters appear to take some interest in the individual, thereby pointing to the inconsistent nature of the doctrines and practices of the I AM cults.

The ascended (dead) masters consistently reject orthodox Christian theology. A supposedly ascended Buddhist once declared: "Nay more, those who read our Buddhist scriptures, written for the superstitious masses, will fail to find in them a demon so vindictive, unjust, so cruel and so stupid, as the celestial tyrant upon whom the Christians prodigally lavish their servile worship. . . ."[4] He also says, "Our chief aim is to deliver humanity from this nightmare. . . ."[5]

In the early days of Theosophy, the Masters would often communicate to their disciples in writing "precipitated"–upon letters—that is, not written by pen or pencil (supposedly letters would just materialize on paper). The truthfulness of these events is in serious question, especially since Mme. Blavatsky admitted that she sometimes claimed that something she had written herself was written by masters when she thought people would be more apt to

---

* "Maya" is an Eastern term for "illusion" and is often synonymous with this world, which is said to be illusionary.

believe her message if they thought it was coming from the other world.[6]

GNOSTICISM

The idea that one receives communication from God through lesser intermediaries is much older than the Theosophical Society. Gnosticism was an early religiophilosophical idea that was especially popular shortly after New Testament times. Those of us who believe the Bible believe that God has communicated to us directly and clearly in many ways throughout history (see, for example, Hebrews 1:1). However, the fundamental tenet of gnosticism (common to ascended masters groups today) declares that God is unknowable by man and can only communicate to him indirectly, through intermediaries.

Pantheistic (everything-is-God) religious systems teach that because of His infinite nature, God can only communicate to finite man through descending emanations, which become more and more personal and finite as they approach humanity more closely. McNeil observes:

Associated with the unknowable Brahman of the Upanishads is the almost unlimited pantheon of Hindu gods and goddesses; and associated with the Abyss of Gnosticism is the hierarchy of intermediary beings, known as aeons. Theosophy, as has been seen, follows the way of Gnosticism.[7]

Basically, gnosticism teaches that God is so far removed from man, so spiritual, so utterly good, that He cannot condescend to relate directly to man, who is material and evil, and that God must instead communicate through a series of messengers who act as buffers, thereby preventing God from being contaminated with the evil material world.

THE LIFE AND TEACHINGS

Another key influence of the development of the I AM

movement was a series of books published between the years 1924 and 1955 by Baird T. Spalding. The five volumes, entitled *Life and Teachings of the Masters of the Far East,* contain many of the beliefs central to modern I AM cults. With no substantiation, the volumes purport to tell of amazing events experienced by Spalding and ten others while the group was on a research trip in the Far East in 1894. Although Spalding asserted that he and his fellow researchers confirmed everything they saw,[8] he made "no attempt to authenticate these experiences. . ."[9] in his books. In fact, he even omitted names and places because "I feel that I am at liberty to withhold names of places and locations, according the reader the privilege of accepting as fact or fiction, as he deems expedient, the accounts set forth herein, remarking only that facts are at times more astonishing than fiction."[10]

In his books, Spalding developed the concept of the Ascended Masters in much the same way as they are viewed in modern ascended masters cults. Ascended masters are leaders from past times who have died and have become one with God, and then are appointed from the spiritual world to communicate "eternal truths" to those still living through practices we think of as mediumship.

> They have all lived a certain time here in visible form, then passed on and taken their bodies with them, to a place in consciousness where they are not visible to mortal eyes; and we must raise our consciousness to the Christ Consciousness to converse with them. But those that have so perfected the body that they can take it to this Celestial Realm can return to us and go away at will. They are able to come and instruct all who are receptive to their teaching, and appear and disappear at will. It is these that come and teach us when we are ready to receive instruction, sometimes intuitively and at times by personal contact.[11]

Spalding even described these beings as "Masters," the name now associated with almost all of the cults which hold these types of beliefs.[12]

Spalding was also instrumental in asserting the concept of the "I AM presence." This is the idea that God is within each man, and that the man who realizes this can experience divinity in this life. This extreme self-centeredness is common to most Eastern thought and is one of the effective attractions of the ascended masters cults.

> The failure of outer things to satisfy, leads the soul to seek the power within. Then the individual may discover that I AM, he may know that within him lies all power to satisfy the soul, to fulfill its every need and desire. This knowledge may not come until the individual is driven by the buffetings of the world to seek this inner plane of peace and calm. When he knows I AM is the fulfillment of his desire, the desire is filled. To look outside the God self for the fulfillment of his desire is folly. To unfold, the self must do the unfolding.[13]

Spalding's books were popular among occultists and Theosophists during the 1920s. One of the two great I AM cults, founded in 1930[14] by Guy and Edna Ballard, holds to most of the beliefs set forth in Spalding's books.

The Ballards had been Theosophists when Mr. Ballard was reputedly contacted in 1930 by the Ascended Master Saint Germain in a visible, tangible body on Mount Shasta, California. These experiences are recorded in the first two books of what is known as the Saint Germain series: *Unveiled Mysteries and the Magic Presence.*

Saint Germain was said to have taught Ballard about the "Great Creative Word" (I AM) and the use of the Law of Life (akin to the Eastern concept of karma).

Spurred on by a belief that he and his family were appointed to spread the message of the Ascended Masters, Ballard began a movement which as early as 1936 was holding large meetings across the United States. It was also in 1936 that Ballard began to publish his monthly magazine, *Voice of the I AM,* which contained the teachings and messages of the Ascended Masters. In 1939 Guy Ballard unexpectedly died. The cause of his death was unknown, according to former members of the group, and they waited vainly for him to rise again the third day. Edna Ballard assumed leadership and helped the cult to grow, until in 1942 they claimed a membership of between three and five million people. The main headquarters is in Chicago, with additional facilities in Mount Shasta and Santa Fe, New Mexico.

The dictations from the masters to Guy Ballard came to him visibly as "liquid light." The masters would project writing in front of him in golden light in the atmosphere, and with his eyes closed he could read it and would then repeat the message to his faithful followers.

For a number of years after Ballard's death no new messages from the masters were received in the group. Eventually Mrs. Ballard began receiving what she called "the word on the light ray." She would hear the words in the same manner as a psychic medium, although she vehemently criticized traditional mediums.

No one else in the movement was allowed to claim that they received any communications from those who had passed on and "ascended." The mantle of prophecy was passed after Mrs. Ballard's death to Jerry and Ann Craig, who rule the movement along with Frederick Landwehr, who was formerly Mrs. Ballard's organist and is now the president of the cult. The Craigs are the only authorized lecturers in the group, whose membership has been dwindling steadily over the last two decades. Today there is very little youth recruitment, and even the children of members rarely join the group.

The Ballards' interpretation of the I AM presence is well-summarized in the following quotation:

When Moses was told to go forward and lead the children of Israel out of the wilderness,—hesitating he asked: "Who shall I say has sent me unto them?" He was told: "Say unto them: 'I AM' that 'I AM' hath sent me unto you.'' Who in the teachings in the outer world today, knows what that statement means yet, within that statement, lies the whole of the law. ''I AM'' is the individualized God presence of every human being on earth, which in the ''I AM'' Instruction is known as the ''Mighty I AM Presence''.

From out of the Heart Center of Infinity, which we know as the Great Central Sun, comes forth the individualized Presence of God—The ''Mighty I AM''—clothed in a Body of Pure Light Substance. This Electronic Body abides immediately above every human being on earth and pours down into the human form, the Life, the Light, the Substance and Energy that enables the physical body to move, breath and have Self conscious Life. This Individualized Focus of the Great Supreme Source of all Life, is what was referred to in the statement made by Moses; which means he had been sent forth by the Divine Power of Life—his own ''Mighty I AM Presence''.[15]

As with all gnostic cults, the I AM Movement believes that Christ is an impersonal force or principle: ''They had *real inner understanding,* and acknowledged the *fulness* of the power from this Great Central Son which today we call the 'Christ,' for it is the Heart of the Christ Activity in the Universe.''[16] Typical of occultic beliefs, Guy Ballard (under the pen name of Godfre Ray King) identified the Holy Ghost with a feminine gender, ''the Mother Expression of Deity.''[17]

Although Theosophy tried to appeal to those who were philosophically inclined, the Ballards' movement appealed more to those who were emotionally naive. Of course, the ultimate appeal of the movement is its offer of self-deification:

These great Wondrous Ascended Masters, are Those who have lived in human forms, but thru Their attention to Their God Presence have perfected Their bodies and raised them into the Ascension, where They now dwell in Perfection. They stand ready and willing to assist those of earth who will give attention, make the call, give the obedience necessary thru Self-control and Harmony, to enable the "Mighty I AM Presence" and the Great Ascended Beings to pour thru that which will purify their physical structures and bring them back to Perfection—back into their own "Mighty I AM Presence," where they too become Ascended Masters.

Today, thru the Teaching of Those Great, Wondrous God-Beings, the Ascended Masters, Who are our Elder Brothers, we have come to know the Truth of our Being and how we may turn to the "Mighty I AM Presence" and thru our attention to It, again find our way back to Perfection and free ourselves from the maze of human beliefs, thoughts, feelings and discord.[18]

The key recipient of praise and adoration in the I AM Movement is not Jesus Christ. Rather, it is Saint Germain, an occultist who lived in France in the eighteenth century. According to a former member, the I AM Movement focuses 80 percent of its worship toward Saint Germain, and dispenses the remaining 20 percent among the other Ascended Masters, including Jesus. Mrs. Ballard wrote:

The Great Ascended Master, Saint Germain, is One of those Powerful Cosmic Beings from the Great Spiritual Hierarchy of Ascended Masters Who govern this Planet. He is the same Great Masterful One who worked at the Court of France previous to and during the French Revolution and Whose Advice, if it had been heeded, would have prevented the Revolution and saved great suffering. It was because of His Transendent Divine Power, that He was referred to at the time as "The Wonderman" of Europe.

...Saint Germain has brought This Light of the "Mighty I AM Presence" forth to the people of America since 1932—to again give the Instruction which it is imperative for the people of America to understand and apply if they are to avoid the perils which are destroying Europe at the present time.[19]

It is very clear from I AM Movement material that Jesus Christ is not considered as important as Saint Germain. Jesus Christ is supposedly quoted in the *Voice of the I AM* magazine as follows:

> ...Never for one moment think or have such a feeling, as Saint Germain replacing Me or interfering with My Work. He is the Greatest Blessing that has ever come to mankind; because He operates under the Ray which is the purifying Power to the earth. Without this Purifying Power, nothing on the earth would be accomplished and mankind would be destroyed in spite of My Ministry.[20]

The reason for the emphasis placed on Saint Germain is that he has brought the "Violet Consuming Flame"—as important to the I AM Movement as Christ's shed blood is to the Christian. This flame is supposed to purify a person, so that the person can get rid of his sins and "negative influences," which are like the Eastern concepts of karma. The activity of the flame presupposes the truth of reincarnation, the belief that souls live multiple lives throughout a long timespan.

> The conscious use of the Violet Consuming Flame is the only means by which any human being can free himself or herself from his or her own human discord and imperfection....
> Thus he can dissolve and purify all unnecessary discordantly qualified substance and energy which he has used in all lives....[21]

The Violet Consuming Flame tries to replace all that the Christian gospel offers to the members of the ascended masters movement. As with most gnostic cults, the ascended masters cults redefine Christian terminology to fit their own doctrinal systems. According to the I AM Movement, grace is not God's unmerited favor, bestowed through the sacrifice of Christ on the cross. Instead, the term "grace" is redefined to mean something totally foreign to its biblical usage.

> ...Grace means the bringing of all into Divine Order, thru Divine Love and this is done by the use of the Violet Consuming Flame—the ONLY WAY in heaven or earth it ever was or ever will be done; because that is the way the Divine Law

maintains order permanently.

FEEL yourselves always surrounded by a Great Pillar of Violet Consuming Flame the shade of the violet Neon signs, with the Flame flowing from the feet upward thru the body to the top of the head and up into your own 'Mighty I AM Presence.'[22]

The I AM followers are encouraged to practice this presence for 15 minutes, three times each day, to keep all of their current "bad karma" consumed. At the same time they will be burning bad karma from their previous lives, so that by the time they die they will be completely cleansed, and through the power of their own supposed deity they will become ascended masters themselves, working for change in this world as masters before them have done.

Followers in the I AM Movement believe that they too can work for good changes in this world by a chanting they call "decreeing." As Mrs. Ballard stated,

> When you say and feel 'I AM,' you release the spring of Eternal, Everlasting Life, to flow on its way unmolested. In other words you open wide the door to Its natural flow.[23]

The I AM Movement claims to be the only perfect representative of the ascended masters on the earth today. Mrs. Ballard criticized all other religious systems, including other similar movements, by saying:

> There have been many channels thruout the centuries which have had some phase of the Great Law of Life—the Law of the Truth of the Universe; but they certainly have not had enough of the understanding—or the complete understandding—required to free themselves from the discord of this earth, or humanity would not be in almost total destruction today.
>
> Something has been missing in every channel which has tried to help mankind in the past.[24]

For all of the decreeing done by the Ballards' movement, society today has seen a steady decline in human and societal values, and the world seems closer to destruction rather than closer to some mythical utopia envisioned by the Ballards.

THE CHURCH UNIVERSAL AND TRIUMPHANT

Although the Ballards' cult is declining in membership, the I AM Movement as a whole is growing rapidly. Elizabeth Clare Prophet and her Church Universal and Triumphant have emerged as the front-runners of the movement as a whole. The group is the strongest force within the ascended masters movement. Mrs. Prophet adheres to most of the doctrines taught by the Ballards, but presents them in an appealing manner, especially designed to attract young people to the movement. Because of defections from the Ballards to the Church Universal and Triumphant, and a belief by Ballard followers that Mrs. Prophet has plagiarized the Ballards, there is intense antagonism between the two groups. Mrs. Prophet has been successful in recruiting large numbers of young people through offering more freedom and a smorgasbord of current popular Eastern and occultic practices. This is in direct contrast to the Ballards' harsh moral and dietary laws which are enforced among their followers.

While there is no doubt that Mrs. Prophet and her late husband, Mark, were greatly influenced by the Ballards, another figure also played a prominent role in the development of the mystical dogma of the Church Universal and Triumphant. Stanley Petrowski, former aide to Mrs. Prophet, states that Mark Prophet received much of his information on the ascended masters from the Ascended Master called El Morya, and took many of the doctrines of his movement from a book by Nicolas Roerich titled *Leaves of Morya's Garden*. Roerich was a leading political and social figure, the founder of the Roerich Museum Foundation, and a strong devotee of the teachings of the masters as they were dispensed during the early days of Theosophy.[25]

The Church Universal and Triumphant published a work that was said to be written by El Morya, in which he explained the history of the I AM cults from the ascended masters' point of view.

In 1876, Helena Petrovna Blavatsky was ordered by the Master Kuthumi and me, then known as the Masters K.H. and M., to write *Isis Unveiled*....Commissioned by Jesus the Christ, the Ascended Master Hilarion, and Mother Mary, Mary Baker Eddy† was given certain revelations which she set forth in *Science and Health with Key to the Scriptures*. Though at times beset with their own preconceptions and the burden of the mass consciousness, these witnesses codified the truth and the law of East and West as the culmination of thousands of years of their souls' distillations of the Spirit....

In the 1930's came the twin flames Guy W. Ballard and Edna Ballard imparting the sacred mystery of the law of the I AM, further knowledge of hierarchy, the invocation of the sacred fire, and the path of the ascension. Representatives tried and true of Saint Germain, they were commissioned to remain the only messengers of the hierarchy of the Aquarian age until mankind should redeem a certain portion of their karma.

When that cycle was fulfilled, Saint Germain, together with the Darjeeling Council, sponsored Mark and Elizabeth Prophet to carry on the work not only of the Ballards and the I AM movement, but also of Nicholas and Helna Roerich....And so the Mother flame of Russia and the Mother flame of America converge in the spirals of freedom and victory for the sons and daughters of God in both nations and in every nation upon earth.[26]

The Church Universal and Triumphant was founded as the Summit Lighthouse in 1958 in Washington, D.C.

Elizabeth Wolf met Mark Prophet on April 22, 1961, in Boston, where he was used as the medium for the Archangel Michael. She said that she and Mark shared a mystical experience that night, confirming to her that Mark

---

† Founder of the Christian Science cult.

was to be her teacher. This experience was furthering her journey into the psychic world, since she had already receiv-ed several messages from Saint Germain. Mark Prophet was born on December 24, 1918, in Wisconsin. He was an only child. He died in Colorado Springs, Colorado, on February 26, 1973. From that time forward, Elizabeth Clare Prophet has reigned as the living master.[27] Stanley Petrowski briefly summarized the Prophets' work together in the *Spiritual Counterfeits Project Newsletter* (previously cited).

> Their mutual mediumship expanded beyond the somewhat limited access to El Morya and St. Germain, and they were soon communicating with a virtual pantheon of spirits, demi-gods and "Ascended Masters." Eventually, Mark and Elizabeth began to proclaim themselves the divinely ap-pointed messengers of the "Great White Brotherhood" and sought international outlets for their teachings....
>
> Mark Prophet's sudden death in 1973, the result of a stroke, left the burden of responsibility for the expanding psycho-spiritual empire on the shoulders of Elizabeth, who by that time had already been proclaimed the incarnation of the "Divine Mother."...Mark himself is now esteemed as an Ascended Master with the spiritual name of "Lanello." On occasion Lanello transmits dictations through the mediumistic powers of Elizabeth who has fully assumed the role of amanuensis‡ to the spiritual realm.

The stated purpose of the organization (originally called the Summit Lighthouse, but changed in 1976 to the Church Universal and Triumphant) is to "publish the teachings of the Ascended Masters, to shed light on the lost or distorted teachings of Christ, and to provide humanity...with the knowledge of cosmic law which, when applied, will lead him to freedom, to self-mastery, to the fulfilling of his divine plan, and to the reunion of his soul with God...."[28]

---

‡ Amanuensis—a secretary or scribe.

CHURCH UNIVERSAL
AND TRIUMPHANT TODAY

Church Universal and Triumphant is one of the fastest-growing "new age" cults in the world. It advertises zealously and utilizes high-level technology in its promotional productions. Membership is growing so rapidly that officials in the organization are not even sure how many thousands of members there actually are. Representatives of the church have conducted major promotional tours through the country, and the church mailing list numbers in the hundreds of thousands. Church Universal and Triumphant is represented in over 50 foreign countries, with heavy membership in Sweden and Ghana. In 1978 there were ten teaching centers in the United States, five of which are in California. Additional study groups operate in 100 American cities. Of the 16 books published through the church, many are supposedly from "ascended masters" who have dictated messages through Mrs. Prophet. Central to the discipleship program of the cult is *Pearls of Wisdom,* a weekly publication which serves as a voice for the latest teachings of the Ascended Masters.

Membership is available on several levels, each level of which provides the initiate with closer contact with the ascended masters. The lowest level is called the Keepers of the Flame Fraternity. Membership dues are ten dollars the first month and three dollars each following month. These dues entitle members to receive teachings from the *Masters and Keepers of the Flame Lessons* and to attend classes at quarterly and weekend conferences. Intense training in many areas of occultic practice is offered through Summit University, which offers 12-week quarters of classes in which about 150 students receive instruction from the "Masters" themselves. International retreats are held quarterly at the University, where "Guru Ma," as Mrs. Prophet's "chelas" (disciples) call her, presents the newest teachings from the ascended masters.

Church Universal and Triumphant appears to be one of the most syncretistic cults today, trying to cull the best from all religions, including such dissimilar faiths as Christianity and Hinduism. The cultist's vocabulary is liberally sprinkled with orthodox terminology from a variety of faiths, although every religious word has been redefined in harmony with the cult's own world view.

This religious mixture is deceptive, since all religions are *not* considered equal in quality. Mrs. Prophet is the *only* legitimate messenger to bring the message from beyond to mankind. Her word is the final authority in all matters for church devotees. As we have seen from the church's publications, Elizabeth and Mark are the only two people in these days who have a comprehensive understanding of God and truth.

As in most cults, the Church Universal and Triumphant world view, or systematic theology, appears almost ludicrous to the outsider, but has a magnetic appeal to the cultist. Once one is drawn into the system, and once one or two of the main tenets of the cult are accepted, then one is usually persuaded to accept all that is taught—even what the Bible describes as satanic mediumship.

CHURCH UNIVERSAL
AND TRIUMPHANT DOCTRINE

The major authoritative text of the Church Universal and Triumphant is Mark and Elizabeth's *Climb the Highest Mountain,* published in 1972. The book, almost 500 pages long, expounds all of the cult's basic tenets. We shall refer to it as the major representative work of the Prophets' theology.

The Bible

The Bible is seen as less accurate and authoritative than

the newer revelations from the ascended masters, especially as represented in *Climb the Highest Mountain*. That book makes the following reference to the Bible:

> We may well ask as we look at the world around us, Has Christianity failed or have men failed the Christ? Our answer would be that men have failed because the complete teachings of the Master of Galilee, of John the Baptist, and of the prophets who preceded them have not been made available to the multitudes. These we must make plain.[29]

In contrast, they make this statement concerning *Climb the Highest Mountain:*

> ...No work has ever contained the practical and scientific explanations on the workings of your self and your universe....
>
> You will be shown mysteries that will no longer be mysteries, a linking-together of the whole tapestry of Truth in each multiform part....
>
> Please recognize that we, as Messengers for the spiritual Hierarchy, have been commissioned to speak the unspeakable, to utter the unutterable, and to set forth in writing what no man has written.[30]

PRELIMINARY CONSIDERATIONS

Before we discuss the cult's beliefs about God, the Trinity, Jesus Christ, and man, we should briefly highlight some of the cult's teachings on related subjects which will not fit precisely within any of the succeeding sections, but which help to illuminate our current discussion of the major doctrines.

As we noted before, members of the Church Universal and Triumphant are living under a counterfeit system of reality. Bearing in mind that the teachings of previous ascended masters groups, notably the Ballards, are generally accepted by this cult, let us examine the following statements by the Church Universal and Triumphant on several key aspects of its belief system.

Gnosticism and pantheism are evident throughout the group's writings. Both beliefs are asserted in this quote:

> HIERARCHY. The chain of individualized beings fulfilling aspects of God's infinite selfhood. Hierarchy is the means whereby God in the *Great Central Sun* steps down the energies of his consciousness, that succeeding evolutions in time and space might come to know the wonder of his love.[31]

We see that the group teaches that God is impersonal, being composed of many individuals, and that God is detached from His creation, communicating only through successions of messengers.

The Church Universal and Triumphant teaches, as does the Ballards' movement, the validity of "decrees," or chanting to produce the wished-for results in the chela's world.[32]

Also typical of the occult philosophy from which the church borrows is the belief that the servants of God and the servants of Lucifer (they call Lucifer the ranking evil one and Satan a different individual, a lieutenant of Lucifer)[33] draw their power from the same source, one using it for good and the other misusing it. This is also akin to Eastern philosophy, which sees the entire cosmos as a unified whole, with good and bad as different sides of the same coin.[34]

In addition to believing in life on other planets, including Venus, the Prophets have also returned to the animistic beliefs that were prevalent in primitive societies. Animism includes a belief that inanimate natural objects are inhabited by spirit beings.

> Our sun, giant hub of activity, aggregate focus of the Creator's Self-expression in all planes of Spirit and Matter, is governed and ensouled by Helios and Vesta, the highest representatives of the Godhead in this system of worlds.
>
> Let not the mind prevent the assimilation of this concept by the heart; for if we can admit that God is in nature in the universal sense, then we must also admit that He is in nature in the individual sense....

Might He not also have seen fit to create a God-man, a god-ly manifestation of Himself, and to place him in the sun? Indeed, this is precisely what He has done—over and over again in suns and stars through galaxies without number....[35]

Having briefly touched on some miscellaneous teachings in the foundation of the Church Universal and Triumphant, we will now turn our attention to the essential areas of faith concerning God, Christ, and man.

God

As we have stated before, the God of the I AM movement is an impersonal God, a God devoid of self-cognizance and not distinct from His creation. In fact, *Climb the Highest Mountain* declares on page 318: "The Creator dwells in his creation; His Presence endows it with innate immortality...." In addition to an impersonal God, the Church Universal and Triumphant (representative of the I AM movement) teaches that God has both male and female aspects, and refers to God as "Father-Mother."[36]

We find throughout the Bible the consistent teaching that God and His creation are two distinct entities. The first verse in the Bible teaches that God *created* the heavens and the earth. The Hebrew word for create implies the calling into existence of something that had previously not existed: the creating of something out of nothing. This is what we believe as Christians and what is taught in the Bible. The pantheistic God of the I AM movement is nowhere to be found in the Bible.

It is true that God is omnipresent, but it is not true that God is the same as His creation. When we say that God is present everywhere, we mean that everything that exists is immediately in God's presence, not that God is the same as His creation. Although He exists eternally outside our dimension, He operates within our dimension, and nothing in creation is removed from His presence.

Creation does not find its identity in God. The error of equating God with His creation is condemned in Romans 1:20-25:

> For since the creation of the world God's invisible qualities—his eternal power and divine nature—have been clearly seen, being understood from what has been made, so that men are without excuse.
>
> For although they knew God, they neither glorified him as God nor gave thanks to him, but their thinking became futile and their foolish hearts were darkened. Although they claimed to be wise, they became fools and exchanged the glory of the immortal God for images made to look like mortal man and birds and animals and reptiles.
>
> Therefore God gave them over in the sinful desires of their hearts to sexual impurity for the degrading of their bodies with one another. They exchanged the truth of God for a lie, and worshiped and served created things rather than the Creator—who is forever praised. Amen.

The idea of God being male and female will be answered in the following section.

The Trinity

Although the I AM movement calls the members of the Trinity by such names as Father, Mother, and Son, the movement actually denies the Persons of the Godhead.

> If God is Father-Mother, what, then, is the Trinity? When we refer to God as Father, God as Son, and God as Holy Spirit, we are actually referring to God as He is found in Spirit and in Matter, thus recognizing that His Being and Consciousness appears in the Persons of the Trinity according to the level or plane of individual awareness.
>
> ...Thus, in Spirit God the Father is the Wisdom-Power that plans the creation and God the Mother is the Power-Love that gives it birth. In Matter God the Father is the Power-Love that provides the energy for its manifestation, while God the Mother is the Wisdom-Power that executes the plan. In Spirit the Christos is the focal point for the Power Love-Wisdom of

the Word that went forth giving Light to all creation. In Matter Christ, as the epitome of Wisdom, is the culmination of the Love-Power of the Father-Mother.[37]

The Prophets' trinity is consistent with the classical occultic interpretation of the trinity. In a pantheistic system, which asserts that God is everything and everything is God, a correct understanding of the Trinity cannot exist.

The historic and biblical teaching on the Trinity is that three eternal Persons exist within the nature of the one God. In pantheism, however, the one God is impersonal and is made up of all that exists, whether personal or impersonal, animate or inanimate.

A pantheist who wishes to use the term "trinity" must redefine the term to fit his concept of God. In occultism as well as in the I AM movement we find that the Father is defined as the power of God, the Mother as the wisdom of God, and the Son as the love of God.

The most obvious problem with the occultic definition of the Trinity is that it is nowhere taught in the Bible. We have already seen that the Bible condemns a pantheistic God. The Bible also clearly presents the Father, Son, and Holy Spirit as distinct, sexless Persons who share the nature of the one God. Nowhere in the Bible is God referred to as actually being female or a mother.

We do not believe in a plurality of gods, nor do we believe that God is His own creation. The Bible informs us that there is only one God, has always been only one God, and will always be only one God, and that this one God is distinct from His creation (Isaiah 43:10).

However, the Scriptures also clearly teach that this one God exists eternally in three distinct Persons, called the Father, the Son, and the Holy Spirit. We cannot confound or confuse the Persons. The Father is not the Son, the Son is not the Holy Spirit, and the Holy Spirit is not the Father. However, each of the Persons shares equally in the one divine essence. We find from 2 Peter 1:17 that the Father is called God and is distinct in person from the Son. The Son is shown to be God but to also be distinct from the Father, in John 1:1,14. Acts 5:3,4 shows that the Holy Spirit is God, and John 14:16 shows that the Spirit is distinct from the Father and the Son in person. Finally, Matthew 28:19 and Luke 3:21 show us the unity of nature and the distinctness among the three Persons. We will discuss the Son and the Holy Spirit below.

Jesus Christ

To the I AM movement, "Christ" is a term referring to a principle or consciousness rather than to a historical Person in whom two natures, human and divine, reside.

Consistent with the movement's gnostic tendencies, we find a division between "the Christ" and "Jesus." The Christ is said to represent the divinity in every man (not unique to Jesus), while Jesus refers to the ordinary human who was essentially no different from anyone else.

> CHRIST SELF—The individualized focus of "the only begotten of the Father full of grace and truth" (John 1:14); the universal Christ individualized as the true identity of the soul; the *Real Self* of every man, woman, and child to which the soul must rise. The Christ Self is the mediator between a man and his God; it is a man's own personal mentor, priest and prophet, master and teacher. Total identification with the Christ Self defines the Christed one, the Christed being, or the *Christ consciousness*.[38]

> ...The Master's greatest desire was that they should not mistake the son of man (Jesus) for the Son of God (the Christ). Should confusion arise regarding the source of his humanity (in Christ) and the source of his divinity (in God), the Savior knew that generations to come would not worship the Christ, but the man Jesus....[39]

> The Universal Christ is the universal Consciousness of God that went forth as the Word, the Logos that God used to fire the pattern of His Divine Identity in His sons and daughters

and to write His laws in their inward parts. The individual Christ is the fulfillment of this Word, this Logos, in the undivided duality. Each individualization of the Universal Christ is unique, because each individual was ordained by God to reflect in all of its glory a particular facet of the Universal Christ. This is the meaning of the divine blueprint that God created for every manifestation of Himself as the individual fulfillment of the Universal Christ.[40]

The I AM movement asserts a distinct difference between Jesus and the Christ, and also asserts that every man can manifest the Christ in the same way that Jesus did.

Sometimes Christians are tempted to accept the popular belief that deep within our souls there is a spark of God that is our true identity. But if one accepts the concept that one's true self is God, he is forced to deny the uniqueness of Jesus' deity. In the gnostic Christology, Christ is qualitatively no different from the rest of humanity. In line with this, the Church Universal and Triumphant teaches that Jesus was a man who purified himself to a level where he was able to become a Christ, something which every man is ultimately capable of achieving. The Church Universal and Triumphant goes so far as to say that it was fallen angels who fostered the heretical practice of worshiping Jesus.

> Not at all content in having caused the rape of a planet, the fallen angels had as their goal the thorough indoctrination of the people...so that when the Christ should come to save their souls from perdition, they would no longer recognize him as the archetype of their own God-identity and the exemplar of that mission which they had failed to fulfill. They would either reject him totally or worship his personality as one who could do for them that which they had no right to do for themselves.[41]

Contrary to such false assertions, Christ, being God in human flesh, is to be worshiped as the Father is worshiped (Hebrews 1:6). The Apostle Paul, borrowing from an Old

Testament reference to Jehovah (Isaiah 45:23), declares that ultimately all intelligent beings will worship Christ: "Therefore God exalted him to the highest place and gave him the name that is above every name, that at the name of Jesus every knee should bow, in heaven and on earth and under the earth, and every tongue confess that Jesus Christ is Lord, to the glory of God the Father" (Philippians 2:9-11).

The faith which embraces Christ as everyone's true self is antithetical to the historical Judeo-Christian faith. All Jewish culture before the time of Jesus looked forward to the coming of one individual who would be the Christ of God. Many of the events of this individual's life were prophesied hundreds of years before He came. The Old Testament prophesied His birth (Micah 5:2), His triumphal entry into Jerusalem (Zechariah 9:9), and even the exact year of His death (Daniel 9:26). The entire New Testament testifies that Jesus was the fulfillment of the messianic prophecies of the Old Testament (John 20:31).

Nowhere does Scripture state that we can become Christ. "Christ" is the title of Jesus alone (Matthew 16:17,18), the only One who is eternal God manifest in the flesh (Colossians 2:9; Philippians 2:6,7). The I AM movement attempts to evade all the biblical passages which exalt Christ by saying that these passages are only applicable to the Universal Christ which is manifest in all of us, and not to the personal Jesus.

However, Scripture teaches that it was *Jesus Christ* who created the universe, and not just some impersonal Christ principle (1 Corinthians 8:6; Ephesians 3:9). First Timothy 2:5 tells us that the one Mediator between God and man is "the man Christ Jesus," not our Christ-self. Acts 4:10-12 declares that it is the name of Jesus which alone can save. Despite the sure testimony of the Bible, the cultic prophets still declare that "the Master's greatest desire was that they should not mistake the Son of man (Jesus) for the Son of

God (the Christ).''[42] Scripture denounces such statements, declaring, "Who is the liar? It is the man who denies that Jesus is the Christ. Such a man is the antichrist—he denies the Father and the Son. No one who denies the Son has the Father; whoever acknowledges the Son has the Father also'' (1 John 2:22,23).

The Holy Spirit

Despite scattered references to the Holy Spirit's personality, in practice the I AM movement regards the Holy Spirit as impersonal.

> The Holy Spirit...is the ingredient of Life which is the Fire of Cosmos, the germinal power in nature; it is the power that beats the heart and infuses every form of Life with the essence of the Father-Mother God.[43]

> The Holy Spirit is the energy man uses either to expand Good or to expand an energy veil.§[44]

Remember that, to these cultists, "energy veil" is another name for evil, and thus the teaching is that the power of the Holy Spirit can be used for good or evil. However, the Bible warns against such blasphemy against the Holy Spirit (Matthew 12:31,32), and shows us that the Holy Spirit, the third Person of the holy Trinity, is completely good, and that His actions are always in harmony with the other two Persons of the Godhead.

Throughout the Bible the Holy Spirit is depicted as a distinct, divine Person. In Acts 13:2,4 we see the Holy Spirit referred to as a Person and even directly quoted, something that can only be done of a person. Several verses in the Bible assert the deity of the Holy Spirit. Words attributed to Jehovah in the Old Testament are in Hebrews 3:7-11 attributed to the Holy Spirit. The Holy Spirit has always been truly God, and He exists eternally (Hebrews 9:14).

The doctrine of the Trinity is biblical, but this is definitely

---

§ In I AM theology, "energy veil" equals "evil."

not the God of the I AM movement, represented by the Church Universal and Triumphant. As Christians, we believe that within the nature of the one true God (Isaiah 43:10) there are three eternal, distinct Persons (Luke 3:21): the Father (2 Peter 1:17), the Son (John 1:1,14), and the Holy Spirit (Acts 5:3,4). These three Persons are the one God (Matthew 28:19).

Mankind

The primary difference between the orthodox view of man and the I AM movement's view of man is the difference between created and Creator, finite and infinite. To the ascended masters, man is basically God. Some men, hindered by past karma, have stifled their divinity and need to progress over an extended period of time to realize their ultimate oneness with God.

Hand in hand with this deification of man is the ascended masters' teaching that man is basically good (in harmony with their belief that evil does not actually exist—a semi-gnostic belief).

Self-deification is a heresy which has been embraced since the beginning of man. It is the promise given by the serpent to Eve in the Garden of Eden (Genesis 3:5). Yet the promise is today, as then, empty.

> Men find it is not at all difficult to believe that the fulness of the Godhead bodily dwelleth in Jesus...but they do find it difficult to believe that it also dwelleth in themselves. Yet this God has done....[45]

> ...man is truly blessed with immortal opportunity. One with his Creator, he is omnipresent, omniscient, and omnipotent. Ever in contact at inner levels of his being with all others who were also made in the image of immortal Spirit, he is yet involved in the ritual of becoming, through his mastery over the cycles of time and space in matter.[46]

Jehovah's response to such claims is summed up in Ezekiel

28:2-9:

In the pride of your heart you say, "I am a god; I sit on the throne of a god in the heart of the seas." But you are a man and not a god, though you think you are as wise as a god. Are you wiser than Daniel? Is no secret hidden from you? By your wisdom and understanding you have gained wealth for yourself and amassed gold and silver in your treasuries. By your great skill in trading you have increased your wealth, and because of your wealth your heart has grown proud....Because you think you are wise, as wise as a god, I am going to bring foreigners against you, the most ruthless of nations; they will draw their swords against your beauty and wisdom and pierce your shining splendor. They will bring you down to the pit, and you will die a violent death in the heart of the seas. Will you then say, "I am a god," in the presence of those who kill you? You will be but a man, not a god, in the hands of those who slay you.

The beliefs and practices of ancient Babylon bear some resemblance to modern-day cultic beliefs and practices. Central to Babylonian belief was the idea that God is in everything and that man can become divine. The divine name of Jehovah in the Old Testament, I AM, connoted the eternity of God, and God condemned anyone who would dare to arrogate the right to such a title for himself. He condemned the Babylonian attitude in Isaiah 47:8-11:

Now then, listen, you wanton creature, lounging in your security and saying to yourself, "I am, and there is none besides me. I will never be a widow or suffer the loss of children." Both of these will overtake you in a moment, on a single day: loss of children and widowhood. They will come upon you in full measure, in spite of your many sorceries and all your potent spells. You have trusted in your wickedness and have said, "No one sees me." Your wisdom and knowledge mislead you when you say to yourself, "I am, and there is none besides me." Disaster will come upon you, and you will not know how to conjure it away. A calamity will fall upon you that you cannot ward off with a ransom; a catastrophe you cannot foresee will suddenly come upon you.

As we mentioned before, the Church Universal and Triumphant, representative of the I AM movement, also believes that man is basically good. This stems in part from its belief that evil does not exist, declared in *Climb the Highest Mountain,* page 323: "...Good and evil can never be in polarity. They are diametrically opposed and will forever so remain; for the former is real and the latter is unreal." That the Church Universal and Triumphant believes that man is basically good is shown by several quotes from its literature.

Contrary to the lie that man is a sinner and gravitates to the baser elements of his nature, man is inherently Good; he polarizes to Good and to the highest representatives of God-Good.[47]

Unfortunately, feelings of personal guilt for wrongs real or imagined, for sins committed or contemplated, interfere with the beautiful and harmonious state of the soul fresh from God's own hand. In this frame of mind man becomes unduly uncomfortable; his emotions become unstable, his thoughts confused, until finally his whole being is guilt-ridden. In the name of the beauty that the Lord has placed in the souls of all men as well as the mercy He has extended to all, let me warn those who aspire to do His will that just as it is dangerous to be without conscience, so it is dangerous to be possessed with an unwieldly one....[48]

From the Bible, we know that all men are sinful, and that no man can be reconciled to God or satisfy his conscience except through the sacrifice of Jesus Christ. Romans 3:23 and 1 John 1:8 are just two of the many verses in the Bible which tell us that man is not basically good, but basically evil. Romans 3:10-18 tells us that there is not so much as one person who is without sin.

However, rather than neurotically repressing our guilt feelings, we know that in Jesus Christ we can have forgiveness of sin and peace with God. We will discuss this further under the next section.

Salvation

Salvation in I AM theology is not biblical salvation. To the members of the Church Universal and Triumphant, salvation is realizing that self is God. This realization does not come from the grace of God shown in his unique Son, Jesus Christ. The I AM movement deprecates Jesus' role in salvation and asserts nonbiblical salvation through other intermediaries.

Now you who are living in the advancing decades of the century are the beneficiaries of this legacy of Saint Germain bought with a price—the overwhelming love of the Master Saint Germain, whose love for you even before you took embodiment was such that he was willing to lay down a portion of his life that you might live in the fulness of your individual God Self-awareness.[49]

Avatars—souls of great Light and spiritual attainment, such as Jesus the Christ and Gautama Buddha—were sent to take upon themselves a certain portion of mankind's planetary karma.[50]

Only the right use of the power of the spoken Word, the Divine Logos, can atone for mankind's sins.[51]

...the erroneous doctrine concerning the blood sacrifice of Jesus—which he himself never taught—has been perpetuated to the present hour, a remnant of pagan rite long refuted by the word of the Lord. God the Father did not require the sacrifice of His son Christ Jesus, or of any other incarnation of the Christ, as an atonement for the sins of the world....[52]

Man attains his immortality by grace *and* by works.[53]

In the Bible we find that only Jesus Christ, God's Son, could make any atonement for our sin. We cannot be saved by anything but His gift to us on the cross.

Romans chapter 3 discusses the role of Christ in man's salvation: "But now a righteousness from God, apart from law, has been made known, to which the Law and the Prophets testify. This righteousness from God comes through faith in Jesus Christ to all who believe. There is no difference, for all have sinned and fall short of the glory of God, and are justified freely by his grace through the redemption that came by Christ Jesus'' (Romans 3:21-24).

Jesus is the only One through whom salvation can come (John 14:6), and this salvation does not include the deification of man. Salvation is described by Paul in 2 Corinthians 5:16,17 as a change in attitude, a change in allegiance. Salvation means moving from sin's dominion to God's dominion (Romans 6:6,7). Jesus needs no help from Saint Germain, Buddha, or anyone else to effect our salvation. Hebrews 7:25 tells us that "he is able to save completely those who come to God through him, because he always lives to intercede for them."

Salvation is not by works but is entirely by God's freely given grace. There is nothing that we can do to earn any part of our salvation. Romans 6:23 declares that "the wages of sin is death, but the gift of God is eternal life in Christ Jesus our Lord." Ephesians 2:8-10 emphatically states the biblical teaching of salvation by grace:

> For it is by grace you have been saved, through faith—and this not from yourselves, it is the gift of God—not by works, so that no one can boast. For we are God's workmanship, created in Christ Jesus to do good works, which God prepared in advance for us to do.

When one has salvation in Christ, he has peace with God. He does not have to endure endless feelings of guilt. He need not learn to "live with" his guilty conscience, as the I AM movement counsels. We have a way through Jesus Christ to rid us of all the stains of sin. First John 1:8,9 assures the Christian, "If we claim to be without sin, we deceive ourselves and the truth is not in us. If we confess our sins, he is faithful and just and will forgive us our sins and purify us from all unrighteousness."

We can have comfort and peace with God. Hebrews 9:14 shows us the eternal peace available to the Christian who has been saved by the blood of Jesus Christ: "How much more, then, will the blood of Christ, who through the eternal Spirit offered himself unblemished to God, cleanse our consciences from acts that lead to death, so that we may serve the living God!"

CONCLUSION

In examining the long history of the ascended masters groups, we have seen that they are cults in every sense of the word. Although the Bible clearly condemns all the beliefs of these cults, the Bible also offers the cults' followers freedom in Christ. While we cannot condone the practices of the cults, we love the members of the I AM movement as souls for whom Christ has died. They too can come to Christ freely and accept His sacrifice for their sins and become new creatures in Christ (2 Corinthians 5:17).

At the root of the diseased tree of the Church Universal and Triumphant is the cult's refusal to submit to biblical authority. The cult would do well to heed its own warning:

> And so there is abroad in the land an enticing spirit, beguiling as the serpent, that is not the true spirit of prophecy. Nor is it come as the gift of the Holy Spirit; it is the voice of rebellion and of witchcraft, of vain talkers and deceivers.[54]

The Bible clearly identifies these false spirits in verses like 1 John 4:1-3:

> Dear friends, do not believe every spirit, but test the spirits to see whether they are from God, because many false prophets have gone out into the world. This is how you can recognize the Spirit of God: Every spirit that acknowledges that Jesus Christ has come in the flesh is from God, but every spirit that does not acknowledge Jesus is not from God. This is the spirit of the antichrist, which you have heard is coming and even now is already in the world.

It is the spirits of the I AM movement which are telling lies. They are denying the cardinal doctrines of the Christian faith, the teachings so clear in the Bible—teachings which alone bring eternal life.

We can leave our discussion of the Ascended Masters with the warning against such practices contained in Deuteronomy 18:9-12:

> When you enter the land the Lord your God is giving you, do not learn to imitate the detestable ways of the nations there. Let no one be found among you who sacrifices his son or daughter in the fire, who practices divination or sorcery, interprets omens, engages in witchcraft, or casts spells, or who is a medium or spiritist or who consults the dead. Anyone who does these things is detestable to the Lord, and because of these detestable practices the Lord your God will drive out those nations before you.

CHAPTER NOTES

1. See, for example (by the anonymous author of the *Story of Atlantis) Man's Place in the Universe* (London: Theosophical Publishing Society, 1902), p. 1.

2. E.R. McNeil, *From Theosophy to Christian Faith* (Longmonds, Green and Company, 1919), pp. 1-2.

3. Jinarajadas, C.M.A. edition, *The Early Teachings of the Masters* (Chicago: The Theosophical Press, 1881 and 1923), intro.

4. Ibid., p. 192.

5. Ibid., p. 189.

6. Ibid., intro.

7. McNeil, op. cit., p. 59.

8. Baird T. Spalding, *Life and Teachings of the Masters of the Far East, Vol. 1* (Santa Monica, CA: De Vorss and Company, 1924), p. 9.

9. Loc. cit.

10. Ibid., vol. 2, p. 1.

11. Ibid., vol. 1, p. 151.

12. Ibid., vol. 1, p. 157.

13. Ibid., vol. 1, p. 143.

14. Mrs. G.W. and Donald Ballard, *Purpose of the Ascended Masters "I AM" Activity* (Chicago: Saint Germain Press, Inc., 1942).

15. Ibid., p. 14.

16. Godfre Ray King, *Unveiled Mysteries* (Chicago: Saint Germain Press, 1939), p. 7.

17. Ibid., p. 8.

18. Ballard, op. cit., p. 40.

19. Ibid., p. 9.

20. Ibid., p. 11.

21. Ibid., p. 35.

22. Ibid., pp. 35, 36, 37.

23. Ibid., p. 24.

24. Mrs. G.W. and Donald Ballard, *'I AM Decrees for Ascended Masters Supply of All Good Things—Including Money* (Chicago: St. Germain Press, n.d.), p. 18.

25. *Spiritual Counterfeits Project Newsletter,* Dec./Jan. 1977, vol. 2, no. 9, Berkeley, CA, p. 3.

26. El Morya, *The Chela and the Path* (Colorado Springs, CO: The Summit Lighthouse, Inc., 1975), pp. 121, 122.

27. "Lanaello," Dictated to the Messenger Elizabeth Clare Prophet, in *Cosmic Consciousness, the Putting On of the Garment of the Lord* (Colorado Springs, CO: Summit University Press, 1974), pp. 2-4.

28. Mark and Elizabeth Prophet, *Climb the Highest Mountain* (Los Angeles: Summit Lighthouse, Inc., 1975), pp. xxvi, xxii.

29. Ibid., p. xvi.

30. Ibid., pp. xvi, xvii, xviii.

31. Kuthumi, *Studies of the Human Aura* (Summit University Press, 1971), p. 109.
32. Ibid., p. 105; and Mark and Elizabeth Prophet, *Climb Every Mountain,* op. cit., p. 34.
33. Kuthumi, op. cit., pp. 11, 116.
34. Ibid., pp. 114-15.
35. *Climb the Highest Mountain,* op. cit., pp. 332, 333.
36. Ibid., pp. 321, 322.
37. Ibid., p. 322.
38. Kuthumi, op. cit., p. 103.
39. *Climb the Highest Mountain,* op. cit., pp. 301, 302.
40. Ibid., p. 125.
41. Ibid., p. 71.
42. Ibid., p. 301.
43. Ibid., p. 346.
44. Ibid., p. 132.
45. Ibid., p. 228.
46. Ibid., p. 22.
47. Ibid., p. 59.
48. Ibid., pp. 95, 96.
49. Morya, op. cit., pp. 45, 46.
50. *Climb the Highest Mountain,* op. cit., p. 443.
51. Ibid., p. 280.
52. Ibid., pp. 279, 280.
53. Ibid., p. 161.
54. Morya, op. cit., pp. 115, 116.

CHAPTER 7

SILVA MIND CONTROL *

HISTORY

Silva Mind Control is a psychoreligio technique developed by Texas hypnotist Jose Silva. As is true of Roy Masters'* pseudopsychological system, Silva Mind Control originated as a meditation technique, and only in development did it acquire religious dogma. Consequently, the theology of Silva Mind Control is incomplete and sometimes inconsistent. For example, Silva does not comment at all on the Holy Spirit, and he both asserts the supremacy of the individual and contradictorily asserts pantheism.

Jose Silva, SMC's founder, began teaching his system in 1966 in his native town of Laredo, Texas. Silva was born on August 11, 1914. He worked during most of his childhood at odd jobs to help support his poor family. He received no formal education, was taught to read and write by his brother and sister, and at age 15 passed a correspondence course on radio repair. He began a small radio repair business, which became so successful that it eventually was capable of financing his 20 years of research which culminated in his "discovery" of Silva Mind Control.

It was during his time in the Signal Corps (beginning in 1944), while he was being trained in electronics, that he

---

★ Researched by Carole Hausmann and Gretchen Passantino.
* See Chapter 9.

became interested in the mind and its functions. He read extensively in psychology, studying the writings of Freud, Jung, Adler, and other pioneers in psychotherapy. At the same time Silva studied metaphysical writings and works on parapsychology. Silva left the Signal Corps, returned to his radio repair business, and concentrated on the use of hypnosis and related techniques on his own children, attempting to aid their learning capabilities. After successfully helping his children, he conducted similar experiments with other children and gained a reputation as a researcher and lecturer on hypnotic regression.

Silva theorized from his studies that the brain can work more effectively at lower brain-wave frequencies, a state which is commonly associated with the hypnotic state. His main goal was to keep the mind alert and the subject in conscious control during more–relaxed subjective states of consciousness, instead of being under the control of the hypnotist. He began developing exercises which included vivid mental visualization and relaxed concentration in order to maintain control of one's mental faculties while at the same time producing levels of consciousness even more relaxed than that associated with the hypnotic state, levels normally associated with daydreaming and sleep. From these exercises evolved the Silva Mind Control Method. The proof, he said, of the effectiveness of his early experiments was the children's markedly improved school grades over a three-year experimentation time.

Silva's interest in parapsychology was stimulated when his daughter, practicing the mind-control exercises, showed mind-reading abilities. Over the next ten years he experimented with training 39 Laredo children in "practicing ESP," and Silva claims today that his was the first method which actually trained people in ESP. In correspondence with Duke University parapsychologist Dr. J.B. Rhine, Silva reported that he had trained his daughter to practice ESP, but Dr. Rhine assumed that the girl was probably just developing latent psychic abilities.

In 1966 formal SMC classes were started in Mexico, where Juan Silva, Jose's brother, now serves as national director. With the advent of the formal SMC classes came both acclaim and criticism from the academic psychology community. Since its formal inception, SMC has continued to stir controversy among both professionals and nonprofessionals. We shall discuss the structure, authority, and methods of SMC, and then show why, from a biblical and doctrinal stance, Christians cannot accept the validity of SMC's claims.

Today Silva Mind Control is promoted as a technique which teaches a person how to gain conscious control of subjective levels of mind normally associated with the subconscious. This technique is offered in a 40-hour beginning course consisting of 30 hours of lecture and ten hours of mental exercises (costing around 200 dollars). The method borrows freely from hypnosis, biofeedback principles, and yoga. Transcendental Meditation and Zen meditation resemble SMC, and psychic phenomena and terminology are prominent.

SMC promises to help a person perform a wide variety of feats, such as solving problems, being more loving, reading other people's minds, and even healing psychological and physical problems. The ultimate goal of SMC, as with most Eastern religions, is to reach oneness with Reality—the pantheistic deity of which all creation is believed to be composed.

Through 1976 over 600,000 people had graduated from the SMC courses, which are offered in 50 states and 31 foreign countries. Projecting SMC's previous growth rate into the future, this year's graduates should bring the total to well over two million. Many types of people are attracted to SMC, although those who are interested in parapsychology and psychic phenomena, as well as those who are oriented to a belief that the self can resolve all problems, are especially drawn to it. SMC combines the allure of self-help techniques, supernatural occurrences, self-deification, and pseudo-psychotherapy. As Christians we have the obligation to share our faith intelligently with those who are deluded by the false hopes of Silva Mind Control.

STRUCTURE

Silva Mind Control representatives are quick to emphasize that SMC is different from what seem to be similar techniques in that it teaches one not only how to reach a certain level of consciousness, but also how to function actively at that level.

The human brain is constantly emitting brain waves of different types, usually called by scientists "alpha," "beta," "delta," "theta," etc. SMC claims that the conscious person can learn, through SMC courses, how to manipulate those brain waves to make the mind reach particular beneficial states of consciousness. Once one is able to manipulate his mental states, he can use his mind to perform a variety of tasks, some of which were listed above.

Although Jose Silva is quick to point out the harmony between certain aspects of SMC and other techniques and religious systems, he is also adamant in asserting that SMC is the only method that is complete. SMC is admittedly not necessarily logical,[1] but SMC instructors and Silva are quick to point out that, as far as they are concerned, it works. That is all that counts.[2]

We've always thought heaven was a place. But Christ said the kingdom is within you. The question was, how do you get there? The answer was, you have to be as a little child....In four days, you'll be more childlike. You'll be skeptical up to the last day—we can never believe we can do it. But as long as you're physically in this room, you'll get it all. The interesting thing about Mind Control is that whatever you feel, it's the right thing. In 48 hours you're there.[3]

When we can control even Delta through practice we have

attained Level 7—Cosmic Consciousness, Enlightenment, Self-Actualization—all that Christ Awareness has come to mean. Then we can do whatever needs to be done—we then will have arrived at the end of this earth plane mission.[4]

...the Mind Control graduates eventually will have so balanced all the proper levels and frequencies that they will have awakened control even of Delta. At that moment they will have mastered earth and become the Masters they are called to be.[5]

We shall discuss further the exclusive claims of SMC in our treatment of the doctrine of salvation.

The goal of SMC is to control one's brain waves to the extent that the graduate of SMC can be the master of the universe. This is accomplished through the initial four-day course, the graduate courses, and regular meditation (called "getting at level"). Silva Mind Control has invented a whole new vocabulary to describe the training meditation exercises introduced in the elementary courses. †

In the normal person, beta brain waves are the ones which predominate during waking, functioning periods. The alpha state is associated with relaxation and meditation, and delta and theta are lower or deeper levels yet. The elementary courses strive to bring the subject from beta level to the point where he can put himself into alpha, delta, and theta states. This is accomplished with lectures and meditations utilizing some of Silva's unique techniques as well as more traditional psychotherapy and hypnosis techniques. As is true with the majority of cultic indoctrinations, SMC conducts its sessions from early morning (9 A.M.) until late at night (10:30 P.M.). This tends to overwhelm the subject and effectively eliminate any time for critical reflection on what

---

† Pertinent vocabulary terms will be defined as they are used in our text. A sample of SMC vocabulary includes "Building Blocks of Matter," "Dynamic Meditation," "Mental Screen," "Memory Pegs," "Three Fingers Technique," "Mirror of the Mind," "Hand Levitation," "Glove Anesthesia," "Glass of Water Technique," "Effective Sensory Projection (ESP)," "Laboratory," "Counselors," etc.

he has been taught, and it can fatigue him to the point that he is likely to lose most restraint.

When this session is completed, the first important step has been taken to put the logical mind in the back seat and the imaginative mind up in front where the controls are. In the kind of exercises I am describing now, the logical mind tells the student, 'No, don't tell me you're inside a wall or some other outlandish place.‡ You *know* that can't be; you're sitting here.'

But the imaginative mind, now strengthened by a series of visualization exercises, is able to ignore this. As the imagination grows even stronger, so do our psychic powers. It is the imaginative mind which holds them.[6]

SMC student Sam Merrill described what happened to him as he relinquished his self-control to the SMC instructor:

At this point there definitely *was* a feeling of relaxation and well-being. Also, I seemed to have lost my kinesthetic sense—I couldn't feel my arms and legs and had forgotten in what position I'd left them. I settled back and immediately became aware of a strange sensation: disjointed, dream-like images over which I had no control flickered through my mind while my eyeballs careened wildly under their lids.

...Again, I had lost touch with my extremities. I shuffled my feet, scratched my head in a half-hearted reality test, but kept my eyes closed for fear of losing this extraordinary inner landscape.[7]

Another observer/participant reported:

Very clever, I think. He is allowing us our skepticism. He will repeat again and again that our doubting won't interfere with the process that is happening to us. Passivity. His confidence is a river we will drift on. And since our skepticism can't protect us from the process, we loosen our hold on it. Very clever....[8]

After each lecture in the four-day beginning course, the new students are helped in developing the proper meditative

---

‡ Reference to the exercise billed as "projecting oneself into inanimate objects."

techniques which will enable them to achieve their "level" (of meditation or brain-wave pattern) and at that level to engage in "problem solving."

On the evening of the second day the spiritual dimensions of SMC are introduced, including a discussion of psychic phenomena and reincarnation.§ The third and fourth days of the indoctrination are clearly oriented around psychic phenomena. Practices usually termed by non-SMC devotees as synonymous with hypnotism, ESP, and clairvoyance are encouraged and produced in the various meditation exercises during these two days.

The meditation for which SMC is best known, and the one which most clearly displays the occultic entanglements of SMC, is the meditation which utilizes the student's "laboratory" and his "spirit guides" or "counselors."

Simply, the students are taken to "level" and asked to visualize (with their newly developed psychic perception) a room in which they can "work" at "solving cases," where they can psychically project themselves and subsequently perform acts of healing, clairvoyance, ESP, mind reading, etc. Once the room or laboratory is completely furnished,⁹ the student is then told about his new "counselors."

> Before the big day to come, the soon-to-be psychics will need their counselors for consultation in the laboratory. The lecturer explains how to evoke or create them, then answers students' questions.
>
> The seventeenth meditation is a memorable one: Two counselors appear in the laboratory, where they will be available whenever the student needs them....Many are surprised at who turned up as their counselors; others will have had genuine psychic experiences.[16]

Who are these counselors? Are they merely the products of fertile imaginations? Are they the spirits of those who have died, as in spiritism's claims? Or is their origin more

---

§ See Chapter 11, on reincarnation, for complete information on and refutation of reincarnation.

sinister—are they demons? Let us examine these spiritual counselors more closely.

> As the student works with these tools [from his laboratory], he may have need of some wise counsel to help in perplexing moments—an inner "still small voice." For the Mind Control student, though, it is not a small voice but a strong one, and not one but two.
>
> In his laboratory he evokes two counselors, a man and a woman. He is told before he begins this meditative session that he will do this and, if he is like most other students, he will have a pretty firm idea of whom he wants as counselors. Rarely does he get his wish; almost never is he disappointed....
>
> Counselors can be very real to Mind Control graduates. What are they? We are not sure—perhaps some figment of an archetypal imagination, perhaps an embodiment of the inner voice, perhaps something more. What we do know is that, once we meet our counselors and learn to work with them, the association is respectful and priceless.[11]

> The concept of the counselors, I gathered, was reassurance. They were more or less guardian angels. Mind Control is acutely aware of the prankish note the counselors often provide, but these add, it seemed to me, a liberating human oddity. Frank, an erstwhile gambler and diamond in the rough, said, "I never told nobody this before, but one night I pictured that Mario Lanza came in and sang a few songs for me. Could he be my counselor?" Afterward, furnishing our labs, Frank said he'd gone into his setup and all he'd found was a page of sheet music....Surely, Mario was en route. Alas, no, Frank's counselors were philistines.
>
> I had had trouble visualizing the lab....I had willed Bernard Shaw (very high beta gent, he) and Isak Dinesen, on the grounds that delectable conversation would suffice if nothing worked. Surprisingly enough, they complied. A fusillade of wit? Nary a vocable. Which flustered me, until I realized they had another purpose.[12]

Other testimonies concerning the counselors are similar.

One SMC student reported that his counselors, William Shakespeare and Sophia Loren, met each other, "shook hands, exchanged pleasantries, then fell to the sand, began thrashing, throbbing, grunting, squealing—making the most passionate, vulgar, bestial and voluptuous love I'd ever seen."[13]

What are the counselors? Most of those who have published their personal accounts about the counselors have attributed their existence to imagination, and it is probable that most of such counselors are imaginary. However, not all of the appearances of counselors in SMC can be attributed to fertile imaginations. The world of spiritism is dangerously close to that of SMC.

Someone asks when we're going to get our counselors. We've been promised spiritual guides. They will help us with our mental work. "Every major religion has them—we shall not be outdone." The first day they were explained as a trigger mechanism—"being human we can't accept our being all-knowing." The second day the story is that they're real spirits who've been with us all our lives....Gerry [the SMC instructor] says there are people standing behind him in the corner. "How many, Lana?" Lana sees spirits. "Seven yesterday, five today."

...We design our labs and come up for beta air. We're told we'll have two counselors, one male, one female. "One uptight woman got a naked Viking who refused to put on his clothes...."

"Christ walked into one guy's lab, then walked out. The guy was a Moslem. Another guy, a Christian, said he got Christ, but a little bit late. He described him and the Moslem said that was the guy who came in and left. He'd obviously gone to the wrong room first...."

One woman was visited by "Marlon Brando in a Napoleon suit, and my grandmother who just died. She was wearing a housecoat." Gerry asks, "Was it quilted? Was it pale blue?" Yes, why? No answer. Jay the schoolteacher got a psychic, a woman who died a year ago. Gerry: "Is she stocky? Does she have a matronly figure?" Yes, why? "Because she's standing behind you."

David, who's been meditating for five years, belongs to Luke and Golda Meir. "I've had Luke for about five years." Gerry says if we come back for graduation seminars, he'll show us how to see the counselors with our eyes open.[14]

The appearances of the counselors to more than one person at a time, their immoral actions, and their function in recognized psychic phenomena show parallels to classical spiritism which cannot be ignored. ☆

Spiritism is not biblical. Of the three options we discussed as the source of these counselors, we said that it is possible that many of the counselors are merely imaginative characters, with no objective existence outside the mind of the SMC practitioner. What of the other two options—demons, and the spirits of dead people? SMC does believe in reincarnation, and communication supposedly from departed spirits is common among reincarnationists. However, in SMC we see that often the counselors take on the identities of people who are still very much alive. In addition, we know from the Bible that it is impossible for the dead to communicate with the living. Reincarnation is not possible. Just as surely as the fact that Jesus died only once for our sins, so "man is destined to die once, and after that to face judgment" (Hebrews 9:27).

Since we know that these counselors (the ones that are not a product of one's imagination) are not dead spirits, then we are left with the conclusion, according to the Bible, that they are demonic in origin. Since the counselors condone and promote unbiblical teachings (as shown later in this chapter), we know they cannot be good angels or from God. They must be demonic in origin. Leviticus 19:31 declares, "Do not turn to mediums or seek out spiritists, for you will be defiled by them. I am the Lord your God." Deuteronomy 18:9-13 categorizes "familiar spirits" and

---

☆ See Walter Martin, *The Rise of the Cults,* Chapter 7, "Spiritism: Faith in the Dead."

"spiritism" as detestable acts of the heathen. The antithesis between Christianity and spiritism (including the counselors of SMC) is clearly seen in Acts 19:18-20:

> Many of those who believed now came and openly confessed their evil deeds. A number who had practiced sorcery brought their scrolls together and burned them publicly. When they calculated the value of the scrolls, the total came to fifty thousand drachmas. In this way the word of the Lord spread widely and grew in power.

Not only is consultation with demons forbidden by God, but it is dangerous. Isaiah 8:19-22 describes the folly of consulting such "psychic counselors."

> When men tell you to consult mediums and spiritists, who whisper and mutter, should not a people inquire of their God? Why consult the dead on behalf of the living? To the law and the testimony! If they do not speak according to this word, they have no light of dawn. Distressed and hungry, they will roam through the land; when they are famished, they will become enraged and, looking upward, will curse their king and their God. Then they will look toward the earth and see only distress and darkness and fearful gloom, and they will be thrust into utter darkness.

HYPNOSIS

In some ways SMC could be considered the errant child of hypnosis. Many of the SMC meditation techniques borrow openly from hypnosis. To these hypnosis technques Silva has added what he considers the best from Yoga and other Eastern thought. However, according to SMC, its methods are far superior to anything promised by Yoga or hypnotism.

> ...The mental exercises not only teach persons how to relax the mind and body, as do other approaches such as biofeedback and Transcendental Meditation, but they go one step beyond. They teach persons how to function mentally when

they are at the relaxed level.[15]

Because of these outstanding differences, Mind Control Method is far superior [to hypnosis]. In addition, Mind Control students cooperate immediately, whereas in hypnotic research, it has been repeatedly reported that results are inconsistent because not all subjects cooperate. Sometimes the poor quality of the hypnotic operator is the causal factor, however....

And the end-result that seems to be most distinctive as far as students are concerned seems to be that Mind Control Method helps people help themselves. It may well be that this is a popular accomplishment among Mind Control students because the human mind does not like to be pushed around.[16]

Although SMC claims to differ in some ways from hypnotism,# there are many similarities between the two disciplines. The meditation exercises are accomplished with the use of a tape-recorded steady "clacking" or other rhythmic sound, while the students are instructed, as hypnosis subjects would be, to breathe deeply, relax, and listen to the soothing voice of the instructor as he repeats certain phrases. Graduates of SMC testify to the time distortion which accompanies these "mental exercises," a phenomenon which is familiar in hypnosis. Information on these hypnotic effects is available in *Encyclopaedia Britannica,* Macropaedia, vol. 9, p. 134, "Hypnosis." SMC participants report similar phenomena.

"You think we were hypnotized?"

"Could be. One characteristic of hypnosis is the distortion of time. How long do you think that took?"

"Ten minutes. Maybe 15. How about you?"

"Fifteen. It could have been 20."

I checked my watch. Over 50 minutes had passed. Where

Such differences are passivity in hypnotism; active involvement in SMC; the ability in SMC to initiate as well as to respond to conversation; SMC's increased memory statistics in contrast to hypnosis' usual loss of memory; etc.

did they go?

And was it *only* a distortion of time—events we perceived as taking ten to 20 minutes actually taking much longer—or was it something more? Is there now half an hour missing from Laraine's and my life? And could we have done something or learned something during that time, something that was deliberately erased from our memory?

Where did those minutes go?[17]

The repetition of "positive beneficial phrases"** during SMC lectures and meditations corresponds to the use of suggestion in hypnosis. Of this practice in hypnosis, the *Encyclopaedia Britannica* says:

...of special therapeutic potential is the effect of hypnotically suggesting altered attitudes. It may be suggested to someone who feels unattractive, for instance, that he will find that people like him and are drawn to his company. When used judiciously, suggestions such as these may result in enduring therapeutic changes by modifying the person's behaviour toward others. To the degree that his new optimism leads to friendlier, more confident approaches to people, their typically reciprocal responses will reinforce the changes initiated by hypnotic suggestion.[18]

That Silva Mind Control practices the same technique is obvious to those who are familiar with the SMC courses.

An inordinate amount of time is being spent selling the course, making promises, backing them up with wild stories. We're here. We've bought it. It becomes apparent the talk is more than salesmanship. It is seeding possibilities, burying them deeper and deeper. Repetition will condition us to believe we have these powers. We *will* do these things. We will *do* these things. The fourth day, we will do physical readings. Given the name of a stranger we will diagnose him or her.[19]

Many of the results obtained through SMC are also obtained through hypnosis. The parallels between the two are clear. Some of the claims of SMC in improving memory are

---

** This positivism will be discussed under the doctrine of salvation.

also made by hypnosis, although such claims have been seriously called into question.[20]

It is not our purpose here to discuss the validity of hypnotherapy as such, or its relationship to Christianity. However, one warning concerning hypnosis is equally valid concerning SMC. In improperly administered hypnotherapy, as well as in SMC, one faces risks when he uses such techniques to remove the symptoms of problems (sleeplessness, drinking, etc.)†† without taking care of the problems themselves.

> ...While little skill is required to induce hypnosis, considerable training is needed to evaluate whether it is the appropriate treatment technique and, if so, how it should properly be employed. When used in the treatment context, hypnosis should never be employed by individuals who do not have the competence and skill to treat such problems *without the use of hypnosis*....Improperly used, hypnosis may add to the patient's psychiatric or medical difficulties.[21]

SILVA MIND CONTROL DOCTRINE

As we mentioned previously, like Roy Masters' Foundation of Human Understanding, Silva Mind Control was developed as a technique before it assumed religious trappings. For this reason, the doctrinal structure of SMC is incomplete and at times contradictory. Most of the SMC materials mention God and religion only in passing. However, from the scant references in SMC literature and from its non-Christian world view, we can determine that the doctrines held by SMC are not biblical.

God

Jose Silva and Silva Mind Control promote a pantheistic God. This means that they believe that God is all and is in all

---

††See *The Silva Mind Control Method* for the many habits that SMC claims to be able to control.

that exists. God is in the trees, in animals, in man; the entire universe is ultimately composed of God. SMC even believes that all thoughts are part of God.

These views are based on the assumption that everything is, ultimately, "energy," or "mind," and that therefore an individual can get in touch with this "energy" within him, and have access to all knowledge:

Everything is energy....there is nothing that is not energy, including you and me and everything we think. Thinking both consumes and creates energy, or to be more accurate, it converts energy.[22]

We've never found the kingdom [of heaven] in beta. It's such a restricting way of operating. How far can you see? How acute is your hearing? Silva says mind can project itself anywhere to get the information it needs. Intelligence is awareness.[23]

Throughout the course, the role of imagination is stressed: Again, on the presupposition that our thoughts control reality, since reality is basically mind....[24]

Throughout the basic series, you have cultivated your inner senses that we discussed in Chapter 3, and you have awakened your imagination, thereby opening the doorway into the psychic or spiritual realms. In MC303ESP you begin to use that doorway, and you enter the subjective world of reality. Reality? That's right, REALITY! Reality is all that is, and the subjective levels at which you learn to function are real....[25]

Pantheism is not biblical; the Bible teaches a permanent distinction between God and His creation. In Genesis 1 we read of the creation of all things by God, who was already existing before anything else. Deuteronomy 33:27 calls God eternal, as does 1 Timothy 1:17. That the universe and everything in it (including man) is finite and created is clear not only from Genesis 1 but also from such Scriptures as Genesis 2:4; Psalm 148:5 ("Let them praise the name of the Lord, for he commanded and they were created"); Isaiah

42:5 ("This is what God the Lord says—he who created the heavens and stretched them out, who spread out the earth and all that comes out of it, who gives breath to its people, and life to those who walk on it"); Isaiah 44:24; Isaiah 45:18; Malachi 2:10; Mark 13:19; Ephesians 3:9 ("...God, who created all things"); Colossians 1:16; and Revelation 10:6. Revelation 4:11 declares the distinction between God and the creation by saying: "You are worthy, our Lord and God, to receive glory and honor and power, for you created all things, and by your will they were created and have their being." Romans 1:21-23 condemns pantheists who "exchanged the glory of the immortal God for images made to look like mortal man and birds and animals and reptiles."

Pantheism presupposes an impersonal deity, since all is God. Such a deity is foreign to the Bible. Scripture declares that God is personal, loving, just—the perfect Personality. Only a personal God could or would declare Himself as "I AM"—the Eternal One, the Person (self-cognizance) who has no beginning and no ending (Exodus 3:14; Isaiah 43:10). All human personalities are created in God's likeness (Genesis 1:26). One cannot, therefore, deny God's personality without denying his own personality.‡‡

God is not some impersonal mass of energy operating mechanistically. Such a God cannot show mercy—one of the greatest attributes of God in relation to its saving effect on sinful man. The God of SMC cannot show mercy; the God of the Bible is merciful. Psalm 100:5 assures us, "For the Lord is good; his mercy is everlasting; and his truth endureth to all generations" (King James Version).

Christ

Silva Mind Control hardly discusses the Person of Jesus Christ. This alone indicates a questionable position regard-

---

‡‡ SMC teaches that all is energy in one form or another. Therefore, by implication SMC denies the personhood of man.

ing our Lord. There is a great contrast between the incidental mention of Jesus in SMC literature and in the biblical writings, where Jesus is the focal point of both Old and New Testaments (Luke 24:25-27; John 14:26; 20:31). The Apostle Paul considered Jesus Christ so important as the Author and Sustainer of our faith, as well as our Savior, that he told the Corinthians, "...I resolved to know nothing while I was with you except Jesus Christ and him crucified" (1 Corinthians 2:2).

When SMC does mention Jesus, He appears to be relegated to a position far below that of God incarnate, the Savior of men.

> Christ walked into one guy's lab, then walked out. The guy was a Moslem. Another guy, a Christian, said he got Christ, but a little bit late. He described him and the Moslem said that was the guy who came in and left. He'd obviously gone to the wrong room first.[26]

> Blending Level 1 as they do with their levels of functioning, the Mind Control graduates eventually will have so balanced all the proper levels and frequencies that they will have awakened control even of Delta. At that moment they will have mastered earth and become the Masters they are called to be. They then have attained what might be called *Supra-Consciousness*. Such consciousness is oftentimes referred to as illumination and enlightenment, but in such a way that it is a permanent state, perfectly self-controlled. In other words, the Mind Control graduates will then have attained what is called *Christ Awareness*. And the experience is open to all alike—Christian, Jew, Moslem, Hindu, Atheist—after all, we are from the same Ultimate Source and we all live within the same system of law. We all call only One our Father. And the Father is within each of us.[27]

Silva Mind Control appears to deny that Jesus Christ is the only true way to salvation for any man, of any nation. By maintaining that Christ did not appear as a counselor to a Moslem, but did to a Christian, SMC is implying that

Christ is a valid manifestation of God for Christianity only. This is a common Eastern thought. In Eastern thought we find the idea that there are many manifestations or incarnations of God—different ones for different times and different groups of people.

The Bible teaches the opposite. Jesus Christ Himself declared that He was the only way to the Father when He said, "I am the way and the truth and the life. No one comes to the Father except through me" (John 14:6). The Apostle John called Jesus "the one and only Son, who came from the Father, full of grace and truth" (John 1:14b). The Apostle Peter declared that "Salvation is found in no one else, for there is no other name under heaven given to men by which we must be saved" (Acts 4:12). The Apostle Paul criticized pagan religion and asserted the universal need of man to come to Christ alone for salvation.

> Therefore since we are God's offspring, we should not think that the divine being is like gold or silver or stone—an image made by man's design and skill. In the past God overlooked such ignorance, but now he commands all people everywhere to repent. For he has set a day when he will judge the world with justice by the man he has appointed. He has given proof of this to all men by raising him from the dead.[28]

Paul also instructed Timothy to remember that "there is one God and one mediator between God and men, the man Christ Jesus, who gave himself as a ransom for all men" (1 Timothy 2:5,6a).

Since Jose Silva teaches that all is God, it follows that each SMC student is part of God. From this Silva Mind Control argues that Jesus Christ is not the unique God-man, but is instead one who had the "Christ-consciousness," as any of us can obtain through SMC.

Scripture declares Jesus to be the unique Son of God, the Only-begotten, one with the Father (John 1:14; John 1:18; John 10:30). He is and always has been eternal God (John

1:1), and He became a man (John 1:14) to bring us salvation (Acts 17:31).

Since we know that God is distinct from His creation, we need only show that Jesus is the one true God to show that "Christ-consciousness" is not possible for any other man.§§ Prophesying of the coming Messiah, Isaiah 9:6 declares, "For to us a child is born, to us a son is given, and the government will be on his shoulders. And he will be called Wonderful Counselor, Mighty God, Everlasting Father, Prince of Peace." Matthew 1:23 foretold that the Son of God would be called "Immanuel—which means, 'God with us.'"

When Jesus attempted to loose the man-made Sabbath restrictions, "the Jews tried all the harder to kill him; not only was he breaking the Sabbath, but he was even calling God his own Father, making himself equal with God" (John 5:18). Jesus asserted His own deity in John 8:58 by ascribing to Himself the eternal name of God from Exodus 3:14 (see also Isaiah 43:10): "I AM." The Apostle Thomas recognized the unique deity of Christ after His resurrection, when the risen Christ appeared to Thomas and prompted his exclamation, "My Lord and my God!" (John 20:28).

The two natures of Christ, human and divine, are mentioned in Romans 9:5, which relates part of the legacy of the Jews: "From them is traced the human ancestry of Christ, who is God over all, forever praised!" The mystery of the incarnation is discussed in Philippians 2:5-8, where the two natures of Christ are given as examples of Christ's willingness to humble himself both before the Father and before men:

> Your attitude should be the same as that of Christ Jesus: Who, being in very nature God, did not consider equality with God something to be grasped, but made himself nothing, taking the very nature of a servant, being made in human

---

§§ "Christ-consciousness" is usually considered a gnostic term and is discussed further in Chapter 6, "The 'I AM' Ascended Masters."

likeness. And being found in appearance as a man, he humbled himself and became obedient to death—even death on a cross!

That Christ is truly God is clear from Colossians 2:9, which states, "in Christ all the fullness of Deity lives in bodily form." Our hope is based on the deity, death, resurrection, and coming again of Jesus Christ, the God-man. We seek to serve Christ "while we wait for the blessed hope—the glorious appearing of our great God and Savior, Jesus Christ" (Titus 2:13). Even the Father called Jesus God in Hebrews 1:8. "Through the righteousness of our God and Savior Jesus Christ" we have received the faith to serve God, confident in the sacrifice of His Son (2 Peter 1:1). First John 5:20 calls Jesus "the true God and eternal life."

The last words we have of Jesus are recorded in the Book of Revelation. These are words which strongly affirm Christ's deity and give Christians confidence in His love and mercy.

Behold I am coming soon! My reward is with me, and I will give to everyone according to what he has done. I am the Alpha and the Omega, the First and the Last, the Beginning and the End....I am the Root and the Offspring of David, and the bright Morning Star.[29]

Truly we believe that Christ is the Source of our creation (Colossians 1:15) and the Judge of our souls, the One with the power of deity to determine our eternal destiny (Revelation 1:18).

The Jesus of SMC is insignificant compared to the majestic KING OF KINGS AND LORD OF LORDS of the Bible.

Mankind

In line with its pantheistic presuppositions, SMC teaches that man is basically divine, good, and incapable of sin. As with most gnostic or Eastern systems, ☆ ☆ SMC contradicts

---

☆ ☆ See Chapters 3, 6, 10, and 11 for other information on gnostic and Eastern ideas.

itself by denying sin and yet teaching that one must over-come his own sin (sometimes by reincarnation).

You are in control of your life. Not your mother or your spouse but you. Moreover, you are entitled to what you need from life. There is nothing wrong with being selfish.

We have to learn that we are all created equal in energy. Basically, we all know everything. But we don't use our powers. You have to be tuned to the proper channel in your mind. *Anything* you can conceive of you can do.[30]

We've always thought heaven was a place. But Christ said the kingdom is within you. The question was, how do you get there? The answer was, you have to be as a little child. A child doesn't get hung up with ego. A child is in Alpha about 50% of the time. In four days, you'll be more childlike. You'll be skeptical up to the last day—we can never believe we can do it. But as long as you're physically in this room, you'll get it all. The interesting thing about Mind Control is that whatever you feel, it's the right thing. In 48 hours you're there.[31]

In fact, Mind Control is eminently applicable to all sorts of theoretical inquiry. In the field of parapsychological and metaphysical research, for example, many Psychorien-tologists are researching life before (reincarnation theory) and life after (survival theory) this present one we are given. Lec-turers usually counsel, however, whenever the topics arise in class, that this present life that we are given should be our primary focus....[32]

More and more individuals are now uplifting themselves as this planet moves into its second phase of human evolution. As the individual units of the human race uplift themselves, then all of humanity will be swept into the vortex spiralling toward fulfillment. Whether you call the New Age an Omega Point, the Aquarian Age, the Age of Cosmic Consciousness, or the Age of Love, Light, and Life, it still is the cultural uplift that each person has a rightful heritage.[33]

The doctrine of man held by SMC is not the doctrine of man described in the Bible. According to the Bible, man was created perfect but distinct from his divine Creator (Genesis

1:26). However, the first man, as our representative, chose to disobey God, and consequently sin and death have fallen on all men (Romans 5:12 ff.). Without Christ, all men are sinful. Romans 3:9-12 pronounces the whole world under sin:

> What shall we conclude then? Are we any better? Not at all! We have already made the charge that Jews and Gentiles alike are all under sin. As it is written: "There is no one righteous, not even one; there is no one who understands, no one who seeks God. All have turned away, they have together become worthless; there is no one who does good, not even one."

Romans 5:12 affirms that all men are basically sinful. Neither SMC graduates nor anyone else can escape the guilt of sin. As Galatians 3:22 declares, "the whole world is a prisoner of sin." The Word of God declares that those who deny sin (like SMC) are liars: "If we claim to be without sin, we deceive ourselves and the truth is not in us....If we claim we have not sinned, we make him out to be a liar and his word has no place in our lives" (1 John 1:8,10).

Man is not God or a part of God. God is eternal, uncreated, and the Creator of all things. Man is finite, in the image of God, created at a point in time, and destined to spend eternity either with God in fellowship or in complete isolation from God. Satan propagated the same falsehood when he promised Eve that she could become like God (Genesis 3:5). Numbers 23:19 distinguishes between man and God. Isaiah 31:3,4 denies that man is God: "But the Egyptians are men and not God...." Pagans think that men can be God, as we see from Acts 14:15. God condemns those who would exchange "the glory of the immortal God for images made to look like mortal man and birds and animals and reptiles" (Romans 1:23). Psalm 90:2-6 denies that man is God or that God is man. God emphatically declared His uniqueness in Hosea 11:9b when He said, "For I am God, and not man—the Holy One among you."

One of the dominant but less essential SMC beliefs concerning man is its belief that positive and negative thoughts can change reality. This "positive thinking" parallels some of the gnostic thought, especially that of Christian Science.[34]

Nothing exists without a thought. If you think you're going to get a headache, you'll get it. Even cancer is mind-made and mind-developed. We have had people in class who have had cancer and who have used Mind Control's methods and have gotten enormous results. We know it works.[35]

'Can't' is one of the verboten words of Mind Control, along with 'kill,' 'burn,' 'hate,' and any destructive term. The brain is a highly sophisticated computer, and when we employ phrases negatively, 'I'm sick of that,' 'He's a pain in the neck,' 'That burns me up,' 'I'm dying to do that,' we are in effect programming ourselves into sickness, pain, burning out, and death. Mind Control is very concerned with the impact of language on the psyche.[36]

...The difference between a genius mentality and a lay person's mentality is that a genius uses more of his mind and uses it in a special manner. You are now able to use more of your mind and use it in a special manner.

Beneficial phrases for your benefit: My increasing mental faculties are for serving humanity better. Everyday in every way, I am getting better and better and better....[37]

...If you have an unhappy thought, replace it with a happy thought. When you hear yourself—or someone else—saying something negative, say 'Cancel. Cancel.' Quick. Cancel out the words. We don't say we have problems, but projects. We stress positive talking.

How to implement this change? By 'programming'. Once we are 'at our levels', with our eyes closed, we picture a TV screen. On it we are to see the positive result of what we want to happen and we are to send energy to that desire or program. June explains that if we send out negative thoughts, we'll attract negative events. If we have desire, belief, and expectancy, if we are meeting our needs as well as the needs of others, we can learn to get into a 'positive channel' in our minds—and positive things will happen. 'Be careful what you program,' June says, 'because you *always* get what you ask for. *Always*. You can talk yourself out of anything, and that includes cancer.' Every day we learn to program ourselves; we practice positive thinking.[38]

At first glance, this "positive thinking" seems reasonable. However, careful reflection on such teachings shows their shallowness and their ultimate denial of reality. This positivism has replaced the biblical concept of reality and the biblical solution to man's problems.

The Bible does not deny the existence of sin, sickness, and death (Romans 5:12, etc.). The Bible does not remove the effects of sin, sickness, and death by ignoring them and asserting only positive thoughts. Sin is removed through the dynamic action of God in sending His own Son as a Ransom for sinful people (Matthew 20:28; Mark 10:45; 1 Timothy 2:6). Sickness is acknowledged and is ultimately done away with at the end of this age (Revelation 21:4). Jesus Christ could heal during His earthly ministry (for example, Matthew 4:23), and it is through His power that healing occurs today (Acts 3:6,7; James 5:13-16).

Death is very real, is the consequence of sin, and will claim the life of every person until the end of the age (Hebrews 9:27). Sin and death are not destroyed by positive thinking. It is triumphantly declared in Scripture that the second coming of the Risen Christ heralds the end of sin and death.

> ...then the saying that is written will come true: "Death has been swallowed up in victory." "Where, O death, is your victory? Where, O death, is your sting?" The sting of death is sin, and the power of sin is the law. But thanks be to God! He gives us the victory through our Lord Jesus Christ.[39]

Salvation

Jose Silva believes that all is God and God is good. He

believes that man is good. Still, he somehow contrarily teaches that man is sinful in that he has not realized his oneness with the Ultimate. What is the salvation of Silva Mind Control? As with all other cults, SMC teaches salvation by one's own works.

You are in control of your life. Not your mother or your spouse but you. Moreover, you are entitled to what you need from life. There is nothing wrong with being selfish.

We have to learn that we are all created equal in energy. Basically, we all know everything. But we don't use our powers. You have to be tuned to the proper channel in your mind. *Anything* you can conceive of you can do.[40]

If you only learn to meditate and stop there, you will be solving problems anyway. Something beautiful happens in meditation, and the beauty you find is calming. The more you meditate, the deeper you go within yourself, the firmer the grasp you will have of a kind of inner peace so strong that nothing in life will be able to shatter it.

Your body will benefit, too. At first you will find that worries and guilt feelings are absent while you are meditating. One of the beauties of meditation at the Alpha level is that you *cannot* bring your feelings of guilt and anger with you....Meditation is the first step in Mind Control; by itself it will go a long way toward setting free the body's healing powers and giving it back the energy once squandered on tension.[41]

We can't use Mind Control for evil purposes. We don't know why. When you function at these levels, you won't want to hurt anyone. We're not self-destructive here.[42]

...you probably reveal your persuasion about the perfectibility of humanity. We can effect changes through energy that we manage from an Inner Conscious Level. We can send help to people even though they be at a distance. We can even change our environment with our Mind Control Method....And until we realize what our power of thought is capable of we will be neglecting the crucial element in solving our planet's ecological upset; our controlled sense of awareness is the key to solving all our problems. It has always been.

Seek the Kingdom within you, and work according to the lawful relationships that prevail there, and everything you need comes.[43]

...the Silva Method helps individuals claim their own heritage of resourcefulness—that Kingdom within which Jesus spoke of and taught, and that Buddha and Mohammed intimated. Entering the Kingdom and working according to lawful relationships that prevail therein enables the student to get everything needed—even control of body functioning so widely written of in biofeedback training research.[44]

The Mind Control graduates eventually realize that they create their own destiny by responsibly making decisions for themselves....because of the Silva Method they have a new and reliable dimension of help for problem-solving and decision-making: Level 1. They have learned how to enter their Kingdom, and they are learning the laws that govern functioning there....they get everything they need. The more they are dependent on themselves...the more they accomplish what they program. They have tapped the Source of all good, the Fount of all energy. And they have found it all within themselves.[45]

Individuals in our planet's history seem to have attained such peak fulfillment that they managed all levels. Their lives and teachings remain in writings and traditions to spur us on and guide us to such fulfillment ourselves. As we desire and believe so, we, too, will achieve what they have before us, and more! We are called to nothing less....As the individual units of the human race uplift themselves, then all of humanity will be swept into the vortex spiralling toward fulfillment. Whether you call the New Age an Omega Point, the Aquarian Age, the Age of Cosmic Consciousness, or the Age of Love, Light, and Life, it still is the cultural uplift that each person has as rightful heritage. And our claiming our heritage will swing this whole planet toward fulfillment. For we are here to uplift, not tear down, and we will claim dominion over nature only when we establish our own control of ourselves. And that is what the Silva Method is all about.

...At that moment they will have mastered earth and become the Masters they are called to be. They then have attained what might be called *Supra-Consciousness*. Such consciousness is oftentimes referred to as illumination and enlightenment, but in such a way that it is a permanent state, perfectly self-controlled. In other words, the Mind Control graduates will then have attained what is called *Christ Awareness*. And the experience is open to all alike—Christian, Jew, Moslem, Hindu, Atheist—after all, we are from the same Ultimate Source and we all live within the same system of law.[46]

Silva Mind Control salvation is salvation by the self. One needs depend on no God, no grace, no savior other than himself. Each man has within himself the means for achieving deificiation, SMC salvation.

However, the Bible tells us that salvation is not possible on a purely human level. We have not just sinned against some mute natural law or "Ultimate Source." We have sinned against our personal, loving, omnipotent, and righteous Creator. His justice must be met. The late theologian James Oliver Buswell, Jr., commented:

The guilt of one individual's sin against another *can* morally be borne *either by the sinner* (as in the case of justice without forgiveness...). *or by the one sinned against* (as in the case of forgiveness...). *Christ was not a third party in the affair at Calvary.* He was God *against Whom that sin* (and every sin in the last analysis) *was committed.*...No voluminous system of theology could comprehend the meaning of the death of Jesus Christ, but in the word 'forgiveness' it is more fully comprehended than in any other human formula. When the Son of God, being hanged on a gibbet of shame by the sons of men, said, "Father, forgive them," instead of saying, "Angelic hosts, destroy them," He did, in the clearest imaginable way, substitute Himself for the sinners, and bore their sin "in His own body on the tree." What a wonderful Saviour![47]

Man must either bear the burden of his own sin, or he

must trust fully and completely on the forgiveness of God for salvation. There is no middle ground. The man who trusts in himself for the payment to God of his sin will always be disappointed. Our best works cannot stand up against the perfect and immutable justice of God. Isaiah 64:6 observes, "All of us have become like one who is unclean, and all our righteous acts are like filthy rags; we all shrivel up like a leaf, and like the wind our sins sweep us away."

No, salvation does not come by the imperfect and sinful works of man. There is only one work that can possibly avail man. John recorded Jesus' answer to the question "What must we do to do the works God requires?" Jesus answered, "The work of God is this: to believe in the one he has sent" (John 6:29).

Salvation is completely by God's mercy and grace. We can do nothing to deserve it. Romans 4:5 promises us, "to the man who does not work but trusts God who justifies the wicked, his faith is credited as righteousness." Galatians 3 asserts that "those who believe are children of Abraham. The Scriptures foresaw that God would justify the Gentiles by faith, and announced the gospel in advance to Abraham..." (Galatians 3:7,8). Righteousness can only come through faith, and it does not come from following the Law, as explained in Romans 3:21-26. God "justifies the man who has faith in Jesus" (not in self).

Hebrews 10:1 says concerning the Law that it can never "make perfect those who draw near to worship." By contrast, "we have been made holy through the sacrifice of the body of Jesus Christ once for all" (Hebrews 10:10). Since Christ has come and died for our sins, there is forgiveness of sins, "And where these have been forgiven, there is no longer any sacrifice for sin" (Hebrews 10:18). We can trust Christ completely for our justification.

To the Christian, salvation means peace with God and new life in Christ. We can have the joy of our salvation by worshiping and serving our Creator. Before we were Christians, we viewed everything from a human, self-centered point of view. Now, as Christians, we view everything from the perspective of what God, our Lord and Savior, thinks. Everything has been made new.

So from now on we regard no one from a worldly point of view. Though we once regarded Christ in this way, we do so no longer. Therefore, if anyone is in Christ, he is a new creation; the old has gone, the new has come! All this is from God, who reconciled us to himself through Christ and gave us the ministry of reconciliation: that God was reconciling the world to himself in Christ, not counting men's sins against them. And he has committed to us the message of reconciliation. We are therefore Christ's ambassadors, as though God were making his appeal through us. We implore you on Christ's behalf: Be reconciled to God. God made him who had no sin to be sin for us, so that in him we might become the righteousness of God.[48]

CONCLUSION

When we survey the Silva Mind Control Method, we should keep in mind the above admonition from the Apostle Paul. Silva Mind Control graduates have been given a poor imitation of the new life promised by the Bible. Fulfillment with the God of the Bible is not to be found in positivism and imaginary or occultic "counselors." Fulfillment is found in the Person of our Lord and Savior, Jesus Christ. All who have met the Lord of the Universe can echo with the Apostle Paul:

But whatever was to my profit I now consider loss for the sake of Christ. What is more, I consider everything a loss compared to the surpassing greatness of knowing Christ Jesus my Lord, for whose sake I have lost all things. I consider them rubbish, that I may gain Christ and be found in him, not having a righteousness of my own that comes from the law, but that which is through faith in Christ—the righteousness that comes from God and is by faith.[49]

CHAPTER NOTES

1. Jose Silva and Philip Miele, *The Silva Mind Control Method* (New York: Simon and Schuster, 1977), p. 84.

2. Ibid., p. 172.

3. Amy Gross, "Mind Control: Four Days that Shook My Head," in *Mademoiselle* magazine, Mar. 1972, pp. 127-28.

4. Harry McKnight, *Silva Mind Control: Key to Inner Kingdoms through Psychorientology* (Laredo, TX: Institute of Psychorientology, Inc., 1972), p. 71.

5. Ibid., p. 77.

6. *The Silva Mind Control Method*, op. cit., p. 84.

7. Sam Merrill, "Under Control," in *New Times* magazine, May 2, 1975, pp. 43-44.

8. Gross, "Mind Control: Four Days that Shook My Head," op. cit., pp. 127-28.

9. "Students are urged to exercise freedom and imagination in creating their laboratory and its instruments. During the sixteenth meditation the laboratory is mentally created. In most cases, it remains basically unchanged years after the course, and becomes as familiar to the graduate as his own living room" *(The Silva Mind Control Method*, op. cit., pp. 85-88).

10. Ibid.

11. Ibid.

12. Robert Taylor, "The Descent into Alpha," in *The Boston Globe*, Aug. 20, 1972.

13. Merrill, "Under Control," op. cit., p. 48.

14. Gross, op. cit., pp. 191, 192.

15. *The Silva Mind Control Method*, op. cit., pp. 67-68.

16. McKingith, op. cit., pp. 67-68.

17. Merrill, op. cit., pp. 44-45.

18. *Encyclopaedia Britannica*, op. cit., vol. 9, p. 137.

19. Gross, op. cit., pp. 127-28.

20. *Encyclopaedia Britannica*, op. cit., vol. 9, pp. 137-38.

21. *Encyclopaedia Britannica*, op. cit., vol. 9, p. 139.

22. *The Silva Mind Control Method*, op. cit., pp. 106-07.

23. Gross, op. cit., p. 128.

24. *The Silva Mind Control Method*, op. cit., p. 84.

25. McKnight, op. cit., p. 44.

26. Gross, op. cit., pp. 191, 192.

27. McKnight, op. cit., pp. 77-78.

28. Acts 17:29-31.

29. Revelation 22:12,13,16b.

30. Victoria Y. Pellegrino, *Today's Health*, vol. 53, Nov. 1975, p. 37.

31. Gross, op. cit., pp. 127-28.

32. McKnight, op. cit., p. 63.

33. Ibid., p. 77.

34. See Walter Martin, *The Rise of the Cults*, op. cit., Chap. 5, "The Crux of Christian Science."

35. Pellegrino, op. cit., p. 37.

36. *The Boston Globe*, op. cit.

37. Pellegrino, op. cit., pp. 38-39.

38. Ibid.

39. 1 Corinthians 15:54b-57.

40. Pellegrino, op. cit., p. 37.

41. *The Silva Mind Control Method*, op. cit., pp. 27, 28.

42. Gross, op. cit., p. 128.

43. McKnight, p. 59.

44. Ibid., pp. 66-67.

45. Ibid., p. 73.

46. Ibid., pp. 77-78.

47. James Oliver Buswell, Jr., *A Systematic Theology of the Christian Religion*, vol. 2 (Grand Rapids: Zondervan, 1962), pp. 76-77.

48. 2 Corinthians 5:16-21.

49. Philippians 3:7-9.

THE CHURCH OF
THE LIVING WORD★

HISTORY

The Church of the Living Word, sometimes called The Walk, was founded by its present leader, John Robert Stevens. The church today embraces doctrines from orthodoxy, Assemblies of God and Foursquare denominations, occultism, Eastern religions, and gnosticism. Adherents of The Walk can supposedly experience deification, tongues, prophecy, healings, auras, and "transference of powers" in noisy and emotional meetings. Adherents can remain secure in the rigid, authoritarian group structure, obeying without having to think for themselves. Stevens presides as an apostle over the movement from its headquarters in Washington, Iowa.

Stevens was reared in Washington, Iowa, as the son of a Foursquare pastor. Born on August 7, 1919, Stevens was ordained by the Full Gospel Temple in Moline, Illinois, before that temple was affiliated with the Foursquare denomination. Ten years later his ordination was approved by the Foursquare denomination, although there is no record that he ever attended the ordination service or received his credentials. Stevens attended the Foursquare denomination's

★ Researched by Todd Ehrenborg.

Life Bible College, in Los Angeles, during 1939 and 1940, although he never graduated from that school. Life Bible College revoked his ordination certificate in 1949, claiming that Stevens' aberrant doctrine precluded them from recognizing his affiliation with them or with the Foursquare denomination.

At the same time Stevens applied for ordination from the Assemblies of God denomination, which did not reordain him, but recognized his previous ordination. Stevens bolstered his resume to both denominations by claiming attendance at the American Bible College in Chicago. However, there are no records to show that this school ever existed, and the denomination never received Stevens' transcripts from that elusive school.

Stevens became swept up in the William Branham movement, introducing those errant doctrines to his congregation, the Metropolitan Tabernacle in Lynwood, California. These activities forced the Assemblies of God denomination to write him in April 25, 1951, requesting him to disassociate himself from them.

The Church of the Living Word grew out of a nondenominational church that Stevens then started in South Gate, California. Steven puts the founding date of the Church of the Living Word movement in 1954, after having a vision which he said was comparable to Paul's conversion experience on the Damascus Road.

Since 1954, The Walk has grown to 26 churches in California, 51 throughout the rest of the country, and 22 in foreign countries. Stevens presides over the approximately 100 churches with complete control. The children of followers are educated in two special schools, one in Washington, Iowa, and the other in the San Fernando Valley, near Los Angeles.[1]

Shiloh is the site of the cult headquarters in Washington, Iowa. According to Stevens, God has chosen Shiloh as the most important spot on the face of the earth: "Shiloh is now the spiritual center of the world, the beginning of God's creation."[2]

In common with many other cults, the Church of the Living Word is funded through sacrificial offerings of members (many live with other members, pooling their resources and giving all that is left to the church) and through church-owned and -operated businesses, like the Impact Industries paint roller factory in California.

AUTHORITY AND STRUCTURE

Although the Church of the Living Word upholds the Bible as the written Word of God, it also believes that the Bible is outdated and must be supplemented by the revelations, writings, and sermons of John Robert Stevens, whose pronouncements are on an equal par with Scripture. They are considered the Living Word for today. In addition to the "Living Word for" each week, which is a weekly collection of Stevens' utterances, the cult takes its doctrines from Stevens' longer works, the most important of which are *To Every Man That Asketh* and *The First Principles*.

The Church of the Living Word is claimed to be the only church today which is in God's will. Members of The Walk are said to have come out from Babylon in leaving their denominational ties. Only in The Walk lies salvation.

> ...We are probably the children of many movements in one sense, but in another sense, because we have come out, and we have been born out of travail and come forth from the traditional Church, we are going to turn and become the savior of the Church.[3]

Like Witness Lee's Local Church,* the Church of the Living Word claims to be the only church which can be called "New Testament." God has rejected all other churches.

> ...What are the harlots of Babylon? Every organization

---

* See Appendix.

and system of Christianity which is not a New Testament church built upon the Holy Spirit's work according to the bible pattern for the church. "Come out of her, my people." Rev. 18:4. God wants His children to be delivered from the Babylonian denominations and to be a part of New Testament churches.[4]

It is another mark of the cults that the importance of the individual members is ignored and the unity of the body, to the exclusion of individuality, is stressed.

According to II Thess. 1:10, Christ is coming to be glorified in His saints, not that a lot of individuals will be running around with Christ glorified in them, but that they will lose their own identity as saints; and the glorifying of Christ will have the emphasis. This is the purpose of the Parousia, which is the manifestation of Christ's presence.[5]

Stevens asserts emphatically that his movement is superior to any other church on the face of the earth. No church is doing God's will as well as his church is.

People often try to pigeonhole us to determine what we believe. They ask, "Are you like the Catholics? Are you like the Protestants? Are you like the Fundamentalists? The Pentecostals? The Holiness group?" We could answer, "Actually, we start where they leave off. We believe that everything spoken in the Scriptures can happen again in our times and through us."[6]

A characteristic of cults in general, including the Church of the Living Word, is the belief that the cult is being persecuted for its beliefs and that God in turn will judge those who are in "Babylon" who are doing the persecuting of the "saints."

Babylon is against the restoration and the divine order God is bringing forth. Remember that, because we are not against God's people in any way. If they reject the Word that God is bringing forth, they reject us too, because we are bringing forth the Word of this hour. Once they begin to reject us, God takes exception to them. It is God who says, "Come out of her," and God's words are like bombs that begin to go after them. At this particular point there is going to be a great exodus out of these churches, no matter how far they have gone with God.[7]

Stevens claims to be God's apostle for today. His authority is unquestioned and is ranked right along with biblical authority. In fact, the Bible is said to be meaningless without Stevens' divinely inspired interpretation of it.

Actually, their doctrine was not even based upon the Scriptures, because the Scriptures are not truly the foundation without an apostolic revelation of what the Scriptures teach.[8]

Followers of the Church of the Living Word must follow the leading of Stevens as though he were God speaking to them.

God is moving for us to go in to conquer with the sharp two-edged sword ministry under the Captain of the Lord's hosts, spoken of in Joshua 5. He is saying to us, "I am the Captain. I have come to lead you. You shall not cease to meditate upon My Word. You shall listen to it until it is not only written on the tablets of your heart, but until you become God's mouthpiece to speak the Word of the Lord as did the early Church." His Word becomes a living thing in us and a living thing through us. †[9]

Although God has commanded us to use the minds he has given us, many cults advocate a mindless allegiance to the group's teachings. Often reason is derided and treated with suspicion. Stevens can easily manipulate the Scriptures without fear of detection if his followers refuse to think over what they have heard, content instead to trust him implicitly.

This means literally renouncing reason and the right of ourselves to sit on the throne. We cannot say we are in this Walk because we have weighed it and made a decision. We are in this Walk because Christ is sitting on the throne, and

---

† Remember that the Word of the Lord in this cult's terminology is not the Bible, but the Word for Today spoken through Stevens.

we wouldn't make a move without Him. A person ought to leave if all that holds him are his decisions, reasonings, and understanding of things.[10]

Why should we ever trust our senses? How much can we see, feel, hear or taste? How much can we reason out, anyway? The senses are a very unreliable basis of arriving at conclusions. Still, in the past, we enthroned the senses; we enthroned reason. Now let us follow revelation! "The Spirit will lead us into all truth," not reason (John 16:13).[11]

Stevens attempts to justify his office of apostle by taking Ephesians 4:11-16 out of context and by misinterpreting the word "apostles" in verse 11.[12] He literalizes the figurative speech of 2 Corinthians 3:2,3 in an attempt to justify the continuing "scripture," which he calls a "Bible that is increasing."[13] The church's submission doctrine goes far beyond biblical bounds: Stevens urges his followers to follow him and other church leaders even if they are wrong, as long as they are sincere.

Even Stevens admits one of the most serious consequences of deep involvement in his group: membership in the Church of the Living Word carries with it the probability of severe family problems.

One of the first things which happens when you come into this walk is that the Lord does something to your family. Mothers find they can hardly stand their children; the children are suddenly rebellious; everything in them suddenly starts coming out. Home is just the grounds where everything comes out. You are not even allowed to know one another after the flesh, so that sweet, intimate family circle is shaken.[14]

When we examine the authority and structure of the Church of the Living Word in the light of the Bible, we find that the cult is not in harmony with biblical standards for Christ's church. God will not appoint a leader who teaches contrary to what He has already revealed.

The Scriptures as we find them in the Old and New

Testaments are God's perfect words, and anything that purports to be from God must be in harmony with these words that He has already said. God has never commanded believers to follow a leader without testing him continually with God's already-revealed Word. Acts 17:11 gives the biblical pattern for testing authority: "Now the Bereans were of more noble character than the Thessalonians, for they received the message with great eagerness and examined the Scriptures every day to see if what Paul said was true." According to Proverbs 30:5,6 all revelation must agree with what has been said already, or else the one who exalts himself as God's spokesman will be shown to be a liar: "Every word of God is flawless; he is a shield to those who take refuge in him. Do not add to his words, or he will rebuke you and prove you a liar."

God has given us a test by which we can determine if someone who claims to speak with the authority of God is truly from God. In Deuteronomy 13:1-5 we are told that if a prophet claims to represent God, but teaches doctrines about God that are heresy, we are not to believe him.

If a prophet, or one who foretells by dreams, appears among you and announces to you a miraculous sign or wonder, and if the sign or wonder of which he has spoken takes place, and he says, "Let us follow other gods" (gods you have not known) "and let us worship them," you must not listen to the words of that prophet or dreamer. The Lord your God is testing you to find out whether you love him with all your heart and with all your soul. It is the Lord your God you must follow, and him you must revere. Keep his commands and obey him; serve him and hold fast to him. That prophet or dreamer must be put to death, because he preached rebellion against the Lord your God, who brought you out of Egypt and redeemed you from the land of slavery; he has tried to turn you from the way the Lord your God commanded you to follow. You must purge the evil from among you.

Since, as we shall see, Stevens teaches the wrong doctrine of God, we must label him a false prophet and a false apostle (see 2 Corinthians 11:13-15).

The true apostle of God would uplift and glorify Jesus Christ, and not his own work, his converts, his church, or himself. The true apostle of God would invite close scrutiny, and his followers would carefully examine his credentials in the light of Scripture (See 2 Corinthians 13:3-8).

First Corinthians 12 talks about individual church members and the gifts which the Holy Spirit works through them. However, we can extrapolate Paul's admonitions concerning individual Christians to pertain to individual churches or congregations. Just as one Christian should not despise another Christian's gifts, so one church should not despise another church's work. "As it is, there are many parts, but one body. The eye cannot say to the hand, 'I don't need you!' And the head cannot say to the feet, 'I don't need you!'" (1 Corinthians 12:20,21).

The disciples displayed some animosity toward other believers and were quickly rebuked in Mark 9:38,39:

"Teacher," said John, "we saw a man driving out demons in your name and we told him to stop, because he was not one of us." "Do not stop him," Jesus said. "No one who does a miracle in my name can in the next moment say anything bad about me, for whoever is not against us is for us. I tell you the truth, anyone who gives you a cup of water in my name because you belong to Christ will certainly not lose his reward."

Rather than despising other churches and other believers' works, Jesus taught His disciples to be tolerant of those who were in other bodies and yet were still of the faith. We see this reemphasized in Galatians 2:7, where Paul spoke of the unity between him and the other disciples, even at their first meetings together. Although we would reject the teachings of the Church of the Living Word because they err in the essential Bible doctrines of faith, we can still see the inconsistency exhibited by the followers of Stevens, who claim to follow the Bible as other churches follow the Bible but who reject all others as part of "Babylon," the biblical symbol for corruption.

As we just discussed, 1 Corinthians 12 emphasizes the different functions of different Christians in the body of Christ. Rather than destroying our individuality when we join the church, as Stevens' followers do, God the Holy Spirit uses our individuality to make a complete and functioning body, able to perform the many varied functions necessary to serve other Christians and to evangelize and serve the world.

When Stevens says that Scripture is incomprehensible without a modern apostolic revelation to interpret it, he is in effect saying that the language the Bible is written in is completely subjective. However, God, the Author of all thought and language, chose to communicate to man in rational, comprehensible speech. We are not to renounce reason and we are especially not to relegate all thinking to another fallible human being, like Stevens.

Jude 3 clearly asserts that the faith has been "once for all" delivered to the saints. Even the words of the Apostle Paul were checked with existing Scripture. Acts 17:17 shows us how Paul presented the good news about Jesus and the resurrection: "So he reasoned in the synagogue with the Jews and the God-fearing Greeks, as well as in the marketplace day by day with those who happened to be there."

Second Timothy 3:14-17 admonishes us to continually study the Scriptures as they logically and rationally stand, comprehensible by the believer's mind without the help of some self-appointed apostle.

> But as for you, continue in what you have learned and have become convinced of, because you know those from whom you learned it, and how from infancy you have known the holy Scriptures, which are able to make you wise for salvation through faith in Christ Jesus. All Scripture is God-breathed and is useful for teaching, rebuking, correcting and training

in righteousness, so that the man of God may be thoroughly equipped for every good work.

The Old Testament prophets are the subject of Peter's discourse in 2 Peter 1:19-21. This description of a true prophet of God is nothing like the prophets of the Church of the Living Word.

And we have the word of the prophets made more certain, and you will do well to pay attention to it, as to a light shining in a dark place, until the day dawns and the morning star rises in your hearts. Above all, you must understand that no prophecy of Scripture came about by the prophet's own interpretation. For prophecy never had its origin in the will of man, but men spoke from God as they were carried along by the Holy Spirit.

Contrary to Stevens' claim, Ephesians 4:11-16 does not support the idea of a continuing apostolic office like that of the original apostles of our Lord. We claim the *gifts* of the apostles today since the *products* of the apostles are with us—the church and the New Testament. The passage is *not* promoting the idea of "apostles throughout all ages." R.C.H. Lenski, noted Lutheran theologian and commentator, has said:

All these men are named according to their office and their work for the church. Not one of them is what he is just by or for himself. By "apostles" we understand the Twelve plus Paul, Matthias being the substitute for Judas. These were called immediately by Christ in person to serve in the specific way already indicated in 2:20. They constitute Christ's gift to every single one of us to this day. We continue steadfastly in the apostles' doctrine (Acts 2:42) as the foundation of the church and of our faith. While "apostle" is at times used in a wider sense so as to include Barnabas and other assistants of Paul, in a grouping like the present one the wider sense would only produce an indefinite term.[15]

The apostles are part of the foundation of the church, not its upper story. It is because of the work and teaching of the apostles that the early church grew so quickly and was so obedient to God's revealed will. How was the "faith once for all delivered to the saints" (Jude 3)? By the foundation stones of the church, the apostles. Ephesians 2:20,21 talks of the church "built on the foundation of the apostles and prophets, with Christ Jesus himself as the chief cornerstone. In him the whole building is joined together and rises to become a holy temple in the Lord." We do not have 20 incarnations of Christ, one for each century since the founding of the church; and neither do we have many apostles with functions identical to foundational apostles. We have one cornerstone and one foundation, and it is from this base of certainty that we stand confidently in the Lord's body today. The Church of the Living Word cannot stand on the foundation of the apostles since it does not hold the teachings of the apostles.

Galatians 1:8,9 warns of those who would try to bring another gospel to us, claiming to be representatives from God. Paul declares that if anyone, even an angel from heaven, brings another gospel or another teaching, different from what the first apostles brought concerning Jesus, he was to be accursed. Second Thessalonians admonishes all believers: "So then, brothers, stand firm and hold to the teachings we passed on to you, whether by word of mouth or by letter" (2:15).

We have seen that the claims of the Church of the Living Word are not in harmony with what the Bible has already shown to be true. We shall now see that the doctrines taught by Stevens and his cult on the essentials of the Christian faith are also unbiblical.

CHURCH OF THE LIVING WORD DOCTRINE

God

The Church of the Living Word asserts belief in the Trinity[16] while at the same time teaching that God is not unique, since it is the destiny of the church to become God also. The Walk teaches that human deification is possible.

> When you ask the Lord Jesus to come into your heart and make you a child of God, you do not see the physical manifestation immediately. Something must first be wrought in your nature so that you will want to be a child of God and not a human being. Therefore, the Lord puts you through a process that will bring you into sonship, into deity....Assume the deity that God wants his people to have. The Gospel and the Epistles of John follow a similar pattern in emphasizing not only the deity of Jesus Christ, but also the deity of those who accept Him....What is in Jesus Christ will also be in the members of the Body of Christ: the Word becoming flesh, full of grace and truth, the glory of the Father coming forth. God becoming man means nothing unless we become God, unless we become lost in Him.[17]

> Like the Corinthians, you have not only the right, but also the responsibility of accepting deity....You have a responsibility to participate in God, a responsibility to react and respond with deity.[18]

The erroneous teaching that men can become God is totally foreign to the Bible. Isaiah 31:3,4 shows the contrast between men and God, between the finite and the infinite, between flesh and spirit. In Acts 14:15 Paul denies such a belief as it was held by pagans in Lystra. Christians do not believe that they are God or can ever become God: there is an infinite gap between the Creator and the created, between God and man. God condemns those who would exchange "the glory of the immortal God for images made to look like mortal man and birds and animals and reptiles" (Romans 1:23).

The god of The Walk is changing and growing. The God of the Bible is eternal and separate from His creation (Malachi 3:6; Psalm 102:26,27; James 1:17). Satan was the first one recorded in the Bible who taught that a man could become like God (Genesis 3:5). In fact, the king of Tyre was guilty of the same sin that Satan committed when he presumptuously boasted, "I will ascend above the tops of the clouds; I will make myself like the Most High" (Isaiah 14:14).

God emphatically declared His uniqueness in Hosea 11:9b when He said, "For I am God, and not man—the Holy One among you." The gap between God and man was graphically illustrated by the psalmist in Psalm 90:2-6:

> Before the mountains were born or you brought forth the earth and the world, from everlasting to everlasting you are God. You turn men back to dust, saying, "Return to dust, O sons of men." For a thousand years in your sight are like a day that has just gone by, or like a watch in the night. You sweep men away in the sleep of death; they are like the new grass of morning—though in the morning it springs up new, by evening it is dry and withered.

God is alone in His position of majesty, power, and eternity. There is no one like Him and there will never be anyone like Him (Isaiah 43:10; 46:9).

The teaching that the church becomes God extends to The Walk's eschatology (doctrines of the last things). Stevens teaches that the second coming of Christ has two aspects: the literal and the spiritual. The spiritual second coming is not a coming at all but is instead the belief that Christ is present in the world through His church, the Church of the Living Word.

> The Lord promised to do many things during His "presence" in the last days. The word "presence" implies an extended period of time in which He is revealed and works His will....[19]

> It is true that Christ is going to come in the clouds just as He was seen going away (Acts 1:11); however, that will be just the sign. The principal coming is his coming forth in the persons of His saints, a corporate manifestation of God in a

many-membered Body.[20]

We believe that in these last days Christ Jesus will manifest Himself in a spiritual visitation to His elect...and after this visitation He will personally return to this earth as He went away....[21]

Although we will discuss this dogma further in our discussion of Stevens' beliefs concerning Jesus Christ and man, we can see from our biblical discussion of the nature of God that Stevens is wrong. God will not be manifested in and through His church, as Stevens claims. Christ does not become the church, and the church does not become Christ.

Christ

The Church of the Living Word would rob Jesus Christ of His unique title as God the Son, second Person of the Trinity. In the theology of the Church of the Living Word, Jesus Christ becomes the church, and we as believers become part of Christ. He is no longer the only–begotten Son of God but is instead some sort of impersonal realm of deity, in whose attributes and nature all Christians share.

Then all that God is, Father, Son, and Spirit, came to be realized when He said, "Let us make man in our image...Genesis 1:26." It is as though man, in some unique way, becomes the image of the fullness and completeness of God.[22]

...But in John's interpretation, Christ is not one individual any longer, but Christ is composed of a many-membered Body. The Lord Jesus Christ left His individuality to become the Head of this great corporate Body, the Body of Christ of many members....Christ is not one Man, one Person: Christ is a many-membered Body. The Head is in heaven and we are members of that Body on earth. We are the Manchild that has been brought forth to rule and reign. The future of Christ is our future because we are a part of the Christ. We are members of the Christ....We will reign with Him because we are identified and one with Him. Everything that He is, we are. Everything that He will be, we will be. Everything over which He has dominion and authority, throughout the ages, we share in, because we are a part of the Christ.[23]

Christ Himself is forever divorced from individuality. Even though we have known Christ after the flesh, yet we know Him so no longer (II Cor. 5:16). The Lord Jesus Christ is no longer an individual. Never again will He be known as one Man. When He comes, He will be revealed in His people. He is coming to be glorified in us, to be admired in us![24]

Jesus also said that He and the Father will make their abode in us (John 14:23). He was saying that after His crucifixion, resurrection, and ascension to the Father, His spirit would once again be universalized. Then He could dwell in each one of us as perfectly and completely as He was dwelling in the body of the Nazarene. This means that Christ is coming forth in us now. We see Christ in each other.[25]

John 1:14,18 are verses which clearly deny the Christology of John Robert Stevens. There are not many Christs: there is only one Christ (Matthew 16:16,17).

The Word became flesh and lived for a while among us. We have seen his glory, the glory of the one and only Son, who came from the Father, full of grace and truth....

...No one has ever seen God, but God the only Son, who is at the Father's side, has made him known.

In the original Greek text we find the word *monogenes* translated as "only" or "one and only," or in some translations as "only-begotten." In the Greek this word means "unique" or "one of a kind." We are not all Christs, since these verses show that Jesus Christ is the *unique* Son of God. Why then are Christians called sons of God? Romans 8:14-17 calls us sons of God and co-heirs with Christ, and verse 23 explains the way in which we are sons: we are *adopted* sons of God. Jesus Christ, sharing the nature of the Father, is the *natural* Son of God. What Christ had by divine *right* we obtain by divine *grace* through Him. The relationship between Jesus and believers is clearly defined in Hebrews 2:10,11,14-18:

> In bringing many sons to glory, it was fitting that God, for whom and through whom everything exists, should make the author of their salvation perfect through suffering. Both the one who makes men holy and those who are made holy are of the same family. So Jesus is not ashamed to call them brothers....
>
> Since the children have flesh and blood, he too shared in their humanity so that by his death he might destroy him who holds the power of death—that is, the devil—and free those who all their lives were held in slavery by their fear of death. For surely it is not angels he helps, but Abraham's descendants. For this reason he had to be made like his brothers in every way, in order that he might become a merciful and faithful high priest in service to God, and that he might make atonement for the sins of the people. Because he himself suffered when he was tempted, he is able to help those who are being tempted.

Romans 8:23-25 tells us that we do not yet have our entire inheritance as adopted sons of God. When that time comes (at the resurrection) we will be glorified and will have resurrection bodies like Jesus' body. However, we will still remain created beings; we will not become God. The Apostle John has given us a glimpse of what it will be like when we are glorified as the adopted sons of God. We believers will still be separate individuals from God and we will still be the creations of God, giving Him worship and honor and praise (Revelation 21:3). We will not be Christ; we will *worship* Christ, as prophesied in Revelation 22:3,4, which declares, "No longer will there be any curse. The throne of God and of the Lamb will be in the city, and his servants will serve him. They will see his face, and his name will be on their foreheads."

Finally, Ephesians 1:5 comforts the Christian with the following: "he predestined us to be adopted as his sons through Jesus Christ, in accordance with his pleasure and will.''

The Holy Spirit

The Church of the Living Word places great emphasis on the supernatural gifts of the Holy Spirit in operation in the church. While Stevens does not comment extensively on his theological beliefs concerning the Person and deity of the Holy Spirit, his writings are liberally sprinkled with assertions of the Holy Spirit's moment-by-moment direction of the Church of the Living Word. Stevens believes that all the supernatural manifestations of the power of the Holy Spirit in evidence at the time of the early church are being manifested today in Stevens' churches.[26] He teaches that one of the primary functions of the Holy Spirit in the church today is the bringing of the divine nature of God into Christians.[27]

Our discussion on the nature of God has shown us that the church will never become God. Since we will never become God or a part of God, the Holy Spirit cannot possibly impart deity to us. (The Apostle Peter's statement ''that ye might be partakers of the divine nature'' [2 Peter 1:4 KJV] does not mean that Christians become God, as Stevens teaches, but rather that Christians enjoy an intimate spiritual relationship with God as His adopted children [Romans 8:14-17; John 17:21-23].)

It is not the aim of this book to discuss the validity of the supernatural gifts of the Holy Spirit in the church today. However, it should be clear from our discussion of Deuteronomy 13 that, since the Church of the Living Word teaches false doctrine, neither the Holy Spirit nor any other member of the Trinity is going to bless Stevens' churches with gifts from God, of whatever kind. Although many members of the Church of the Living Word are Christians who have been born again but who have been confused by false doctrine, we know from the Scriptures that God will not bless false teachers and false teaching (Galatians 1:8,9).

Mankind

The three main heresies on the doctrine of man taught by John Robert Stevens are all related to the error that man can become God. The Church of the Living Word teaches that man can become divine, that he can become perfect, and that he can become Christ.

In saying that man is divine, Stevens means that Christians share exactly the same nature as God. They become part of God.

> You're not only going to inherit things, but you're going to inherit a nature. You're going to be robed with deity itself—God's very nature being reproduced in you.[28]

> Do you want to be divine, to take on the nature of God, to be His new creation? Follow hard after the Lord and let Him work these changes within you.[29]

Stevens also teaches that man can become perfect in this life. This is sometimes called "perfectionism." By this Stevens means that there can come a time in the Christian's life when he no longer commits any sins. He becomes perfect as he becomes God.

> We believe in separation from the world of sin, and in sanctification....And we believe in the goal of Christian perfection....[30]

Third, the Church of the Living Word teaches that man becomes Christ. This deification is accomplished through his becoming one in every way with what has become, in practice, an impersonal Christ.

> Be the word of the Lord to the people! Be Christ! For many that sounds blasphemous: God's people parading their lives independent of Him. There is nothing worse than to live and express your life as something independent from Christ.[31]

As we have already seen, man cannot become God. Satan

tempted Eve with such a false promise when he said, "For God knows that when you eat of it your eyes will be opened, and you will be like God, knowing good and evil" (Genesis 3:5).

Since man is finite and changing, he can never hope to become infinite and unchanging. What is finite cannot be eternal. What is changing can never be immutable. While it is true that man will exist into the future forever (either in hell or in heaven), man had a definite beginning. But God has always existed and will always exist, completely changeless. Numbers 23:19 delcares God's immutability (changelessness) and His distinction from man: "God is not a man, that he should lie, nor a son of man, that he should change his mind. Does he speak and then not act? Does he promise and not fulfill?"

This same thought is echoed more fully in Isaiah 31:3,4: "But the Egyptians are men and not God; their horses are flesh and not spirit. When the Lord stretches out his hand, he who helps will stumble, he who is helped will fall; both will perish together. This is what the Lord says to me: 'As a lion growls, a great lion over his prey—and though a whole band of shepherds is called together against him, he is not frightened by their shouts or disturbed by their clamor—so the Lord Almighty will come down to do battle on Mount Zion and on its heights.'"

God does not say that man will become perfect, or without sin, in this present life. On the contrary, the Bible teaches that as long as man is in his corruptible body on this earth, he will suffer some of the effects of human sin. First John 3:2 says that, even though we are the children of God (God's adopted sons), we have not yet reached perfection: "Dear friends, now we are children of God, and what we will be has not yet been made known. But we know that when he appears, we shall be like him, for we shall see him as he is."

We have the imputed righteousness of Christ, which

means that God does not condemn us for our sin, but forgives us because we have appropriated the sacrifice of Christ for our benefit (Romans 4:2-8; Galatians 2:16). However, even Christians commit sins (1 John 1:8), although we are no longer *compelled* to sin (Romans 6:22). The difference between a Christian who sins and a non-Christian who sins is that "there is now no condemnation for those who are in Christ Jesus, because through Christ Jesus the law of the Spirit of life set me free from the law of sin and death" (Romans 8:1,2).

We can look forward to absolute perfection, or sinlessness, when we become like Jesus at the time of the coming resurrection (Romans 8:11; 1 Corinthians 15:42-44).

Paul explains in 1 Corinthians 15, the great resurrection chapter, that resurrection glory is just that—resurrection *glory*. It is not possible for our sin-scarred bodies to be raised in their present form. They must be changed and glorified, to be made like Christ's resurrection body.

I declare to you, brothers, that flesh and blood cannot inherit the kingdom of God, nor does the perishable inherit the imperishable. Listen, I tell you a mystery: We will not all sleep, but we will all be changed—in a flash, in the twinkling of an eye, at the last trumpet. For the trumpet will sound, the dead will be raised imperishable, and we will be changed. For the perishable must clothe itself with the imperishable, and the mortal with immortality. When the perishable has been clothed with the imperishable, and the mortal with immortality, then the saying that is written will come true: "Death has been swallowed up in victory."[32]

Philippians 3:21 tells us that Christians still have corruptible bodies, and that we are waiting for the second coming of our Savior, Jesus Christ, to obtain our perfect, glorious bodies. Romans 8:22-25 concludes:

We know that the whole creation has been groaning as in the pains of childbirth right up to the present time. Not only so, but we ourselves, who have the firstfruits of the Spirit, groan inwardly as we wait eagerly for our adoption as sons, the redemption of our bodies. For in this hope we were saved. But hope that is seen is no hope at all. Who hopes for what he already has? But if we hope for what we do not yet have, we wait for it patiently.

There is an eternal distinction between Christ and His church. Although it is true that the church is sometimes called the "body of Christ" (Ephesians 4:12, etc.), this language is figurative. The spiritual unity among believers, and between Christ and the "body" of believers, enables the church to operate almost like a human body obeys the commands of its head. This unity is not a result of denying our individuality, but is instead the result of individual lives consecrated to Jesus Christ. When we become Christians, our attitudes change. Instead of viewing everything from a self-centered point of view, we now view things in the light of God's revelation in Jesus Christ (Hebrews 1:2).

Ephesians 4 goes on to describe the mind of the Christian: "You were taught, with regard to your former way of life, to put off your old self, which is being corrupted by its deceitful desires; to be made new in the attitude of your minds; and to put on the new self, created to be like God in true righteousness and holiness" (vv. 22-24). We are not like God in that we *become* God; instead, we are like God in "true righteousness and holiness."

When Philippians 2:5 tells us to have the mind of Christ, it does not mean that we become Christ. The context (vv. 1-11) shows us that Paul is admonishing us to be humble, even as Christ was our ultimate Example of humility. As He thought of others before He thought of Himself, so we should think.

Our goal as Christians is to worship and serve God—Father, Son, and Holy Spirit—forever in the new heavens and new earth. We must not deny the personality and individuality which make us "in God's image" (Genesis 1:26) and which God gave us at the beginning (Genesis

1:27). Our ultimate destiny is oneness of purpose and unity with God our Father, with the Lord Jesus Christ, and with our Teacher and Comforter, the Holy Spirit.

> As you come to him, the living Stone—rejected by men but chosen by God and precious to him—you also, like living stones, are being built into a spiritual house to be a holy priesthood, offering spiritual sacrifices acceptable to God through Jesus Christ....
> But you are a chosen people, a royal priesthood, a holy nation, a people belonging to God, that you may declare the praises of him who called you out of darkness into his wonderful light. Once you were not a people, but now you are the people of God; once you had not received mercy, but now you have received mercy.[33]

Salvation

John Robert Stevens teaches a salvation that is dependent on him and his church rather than on Jesus Christ alone. In his soteriology (teachings about salavation), salvation is a continuing process, administered by Stevens' church and resulting in deification of its members. Like most cults, the Church of the Living Word adds to the Bible's simple declaration that salvation is completely by grace, apart from any works, and is accomplished wholly through Christ's sacrifice on the cross (Ephesians 2:8-10; 1 Timothy 2:5).

> Believers have been conditioned to think that the Lord either accepts or rejects people; however, there are degrees of rejection, and there are degrees of acceptance. God accepts the believer on the level he determines to live on....How totally will you be committed to a walk with God? How deep will your dedication be? You determine the limitations of your relationship to God by what is within you. You determine how it will develop.[34]

> We do not walk into the Kingdom: we do not fight or preach our way into it; we simply become so full we start overflowing and float into the Kingdom. It all becomes a mat-

ter of spiritual overflow.[35]

Not only is salvation in the Church of the Living Word accomplished in stages, based on personal effort, but it is also accomplished through the offices of the church.

> The ministry of the prophet and the ministry of the priest will be combined and manifested as one in the ministry that God is bringing forth today....that which was separated in the Old Testament ministries is being united now in the Body of Christ to form one effective ministry. In the ministry of the prophets, brothers can speak to the congregation and create a people to move before the face of God. As priests, the brothers with their effective ministry of intercession can transfer the people's guilt to Christ, who is our sacrifice, and transfer the innocence of Christ to the guilty....
>
> Your shortcomings are of no significance at all, because you can reach up and touch Him through the ministry of the priesthood and be cleansed.[36]

As we have already mentioned, the final goal of Stevens' brand of salvation is deification. Rather than being saved to worship and serve our Creator (1 Peter 2:4,5,9,10), the Church of the Living Word believes that we will be saved from our human natures and changed into nonpersonal divine natures!

> When you ask the Lord Jesus to come into your heart and to make you a child of God, you do not see the physical manifestation immediately. Something must first be wrought in your nature so that you will want to be a child of God and not a human being. Therefore, the Lord puts you through a process that will bring you into sonship, into deity. Do not be passive in that process. Assume the deity that God wants His people to have.[37]

The Bible is emphatic in declaring that salvation is in no way connected to any efforts on our part. Ephesians 2:8-10 tells us:

> For it is by grace you have been saved, through faith—and this not from yourselves, it is the gift of God—not by works,

so that no one can boast. For we are God's workmanship, created in Christ Jesus to do good works, which God prepared in advance for us to do.

Romans 4:1-8 shows that Christian salvation has nothing to do with works. Before the Law of Moses came with its commandments, Abraham was saved apart from his works (Romans 4:1-3). After the Law of Moses, David was saved apart from his works (Romans 4:6-8). If *they* were saved apart from works, is it any wonder that such a salvation is guaranteed to all of us who are Abraham's children by faith (Romans 4:16)? After all, what was written about Abraham's salvation was not written for him alone, "But also for us, to whom God will credit righteousness—for us who believe in him who raised Jesus our Lord from the dead. He was delivered over to death for our sins and was raised to life for our justification" (Romans 4:24,25).

There are no degrees of salvation. One either belongs to Christ or he does not. There is no middle ground. Jesus said, "He who is not with me is against me, and he who does not gather with me scatters" (Matthew 12:30). In another place (Mark 9:40) Jesus declared the same thing in another way by saying that whoever was not against Him was for him. Very early in His revelation to man, God made it clear that He would accept no halfway commitments. In Joshua 24:14,15 we read Joshua's stern warnings to the people of Israel:

Now fear the Lord and serve him with all faithfulness. Throw away the gods your forefathers worshiped beyond the River and in Egypt, and serve the Lord. But if serving the Lord seems undesirable to you, then choose for yourselves this day whom you will serve, whether the gods your forefathers served beyond the River, or the gods of the Amorites, in whose land you are living. But as for me and my household, we will serve the Lord.

The Church of the Living Word is somewhat like the church of Laodicea, which Jesus warned in Revelation 3:15,16: "I know your deeds, that you are neither cold nor hot. I wish you were either one or the other! So, because you are lukewarm—neither hot nor cold—I am about to spit you out of my mouth."

There is no man on this earth, no church that has ever existed, that can participate in a person's salvation. Salvation is accomplished entirely by God through the sacrifice of His Son. First Timothy 2:5 is plain in saying "For there is one God and one mediator between God and men, the man Christ Jesus." We need no "brothers" acting as "prophets and priests" to bring us to God and to tell us God's will. We have perfect fellowship with God through the personal ministry of the Holy Spirit within us (Romans 8:9,27). We know God's will through His Word, summed up in Christ Jesus (Hebrews 1:1,2). Jesus needs no assistance in saving us: "he is able to save completely those who come to God through him, because he always lives to intercede for them" (Hebrews 7:25). We can be sure that God would never have an error-ridden cult take part in the salvation or the perfecting of His saints.

Finally, as we have extensively covered in the sections on the doctrines of God and Jesus Christ, the church is not becoming God. We will never be deified and we will never lose our individuality. Our goal is to be approved before God, to worship and serve Him in the kingdom. We are looking to Christ's second coming, at which time we will receive our resurrected bodies and will be with Him forever.

For the grace of God that brings salvation has appeared to all men. It teaches us to say "No" to ungodliness and worldly passions, and to live self-controlled, upright and godly lives in this present age, while we wait for the blessed hope—the glorious appearing of our great God and Savior, Jesus Christ, who gave himself for us to redeem us from all wickedness and to purify for himself a people that are his very own, eager to do what is good.[38]

CONCLUSION

The Church of the Living Word teaches error on almost all the essential doctrines of the Christian faith. The theology of its founder, John Robert Stevens, cannot meet the test of biblical truth. The promise first made by Satan to Eve, that of becoming God, is echoed thousands of years later in the promise of the Church of the Living Word that its members can become deity.

Christians cannot afford to be accused (as the ancient Israelites were) of turning to foreign gods, much less to themselves. Joshua commanded then, and the Lord commands now:

> "Now then," said Joshua, "throw away the foreign gods that are among you and yield your hearts to the Lord, the God of Israel."
>
> And the people said to Joshua, "We will serve the Lord our God and obey him."[39]

CHAPTER NOTES

1. John Robert Stevens, *Every Blow Has to Count* (North Hollywood, CA: Living Word Publications, Feb. 5, 1978), pp. 17-20.

2. Stevens, *Apostolic Directives* (Living Word, Aug. 6, 1976).

3. Stevens, *The Delightful Bride* (Living Word, July 6, 1975), pp. 2, 3.

4. Stevens, *First Principles* (Living Word, 1970), p. 74.

5. Stevens, *From Many Comes One* (Living Word, May 29, 1977), pp. 2, 3.

6. Stevens, *To Every Man That Asketh* (Living Word, 1975), p. 39.

7. Stevens, *Lord, What Do You Think About Babylon?* (Living Word, 1975), p. 1.

8. Stevens, *Continuing in the Apostles' Teaching* (Living Word, Dec. 26, 1976), p. 3.

9. Stevens, *Beyond Passover* (Living Word, 1977), p. 137.

10. *To Every Man That Asketh,* op. cit., p. 55.

11. Ibid., p. 58.

12. Stevens, *New Testament Church* (Living Word, 1968), p. 13.

13. Stevens, *Speak the Word of the Lord* (Living Word, 1971), pp. 7, 8.

14. Stevens, *As Though Some Strange Thing Were Happening* (Living Word, July 15, 1973), pp. 8, 9.

15. R.C.H. Lenski, *The Interpretation of St. Paul's Epistles to the Galatians, Ephesians and Philippians* (Minneapolis: Augsburg Publishing House, 1937, 1961), p. 526.

16. See, for example, *To Every Man That Asketh,* op. cit., p. 15.

17. Stevens, *Plumb Perfect* (Living Word, Jan. 16, 1977), p. 13.

18. Ibid., p. 14.

19. *First Principles,* op. cit., p. 52.

20. Stevens, *Whole and Complete—At His Presence* (Living Word, May 5, 1977), pp. 14, 15.

21. *To Every Man That Asketh,* op. cit., p. 17.

22. Stevens, *Beyond Passover* (Living Word, 1977), p. 136.

23. Stevens, *The ManChild* (Living Word, 1972), pp. 6-7.

24. Stevens, *Whole and Complete—At His Presence* (Living Word, May 22, 1977), p. 12.

25. Stevens, *Judgment: When We Do and When We Don't* (Living Word, Apr. 10, 1977), p. 21.

26. *To Every Man That Asketh,* op. cit., p. 16.

27. Stevens, *Very Legally Yours* (Living Word, 1974), p. 22.

28. *Very Legally Yours,* op. cit., p. 20.

29. *To Every Man That Asketh,* op. cit., p. 43.

30. Ibid., p. 15.

31. Ibid., p. 50.

32. 1 Corinthians 15:50-54.

33. 1 Peter 2:4,5,9,10.
34. Stevens, *Dedicated to Total Loss* (Living Word, Oct. 3, 1976), p. 5.
35. Stevens, *Lord, Make Me Overflow* (Living Word, June 15, 1975), p. 7.
36. Stevens, *The Prophet-Priest of the Kingdom* (Living Word, Dec. 11, 1977), pp. 6-8.
37. *The Right to Become,* op. cit., p. 13.
38. Titus 2:11-14.
39. Joshua 24:23,24.

CHAPTER
9

ROY MASTERS: FOUNDATION OF HUMAN UNDERSTANDING*

HISTORY

The Foundation of Human Understanding embodies its solution to man's problems in the person of its founder and director, Roy Masters. Masters, a self-described "Christian mystic," combines Eastern and gnostic beliefs, Christian terminology, yoga, hypnotism, and self-help principles in his homogeneous religious philosophy, which is aired over numerous radio stations throughout the United States on a daily basis.

Masters was born 53 years ago to a Jewish family in London. After his father's death (when Roy was 15), he worked at his uncle's diamond-cutting factory in Brighton, England. During his adolescence he became interested in hypnotism, a pursuit he follows even today in his meditation technique, although he likes to say he "dehypnotizes" people.

Masters added to his hypnotism techniques when he studied some of the rites of African witch doctors during a stay as an apprentice at South African diamond mines.

★ Researched by Todd Ehrenborg and Gretchen Passantino.

In 1949, at age 21, Masters came to the United States to lecture on diamonds, choosing Houston as his home after his marriage. Lecturing on hypnosis became more personally rewarding in the fifties in the wake of the Bridey Murphy hypnosis case,* and Masters gave up diamond lectures for his new Institute for Hypnosis.

Unfortunately for Masters, the American Medical Association pressed charges against him for his hypnosis and meditation teaching, claiming that he was practicing medicine without a license. He was sentenced to 30 days in jail, and he declares today that his jail time was spent "unhypnotizing" half of the jail population.

Today Masters is the founder and director of the 20-year-old Foundation of Human Understanding, headquartered in Los Angeles. He claims that over 100,000 people have taken his meditation courses, and he ministers to around one million persons daily through his radio programs. The Foundation of Human Understanding is a nondenominational foundation with tax-exempt status. There is no membership and there are no fees charged for its services, although donations are accepted and all of the Foundation's publications are for sale. Masters says that he will always send his materials free to those who request them but have no money to pay the cost. Masters considers himself ordained, although no recognized religious body ordained him.[1]

The Foundation of Human Understanding is dedicated to helping "a person to thread his way back to a state of consciousness—innocence—that existed before the shock, trauma, upset or corruption."[2] The meditation techniques taught through Masters' publications are designed by Masters to "keep the meditator's mind in the present so he can get in touch with himself."[3]

---

* Bridey Murphy was an American woman who, under hypnosis, appeared to reveal details of a previous life as a young Irish girl. Later investigation showed that it was much more likely that she derived her story from an Irish relative, although the public became infatuated with the phantom Irish girl, starting a craze for hypnosis and reincarnation.

The primary textbook of the Foundation is Masters' book and record *How Your Mind Can Keep You Well*. The other publications are mostly by Masters and contain expanded treatments of subjects summarized in the primary textbook. The Foundation publishes its own materials, which are made available to the public at prices competitive with normal retail sales of comparable books.

MASTERS' MEDITATION METHODS

Before we discuss the Foundation for Human Understanding's doctrines, we will briefly discuss the central purpose of the Foundation and the work of Roy Masters. All teachings of the Foundation revolve around Masters' meditation method. This meditation is the cornerstone of all Foundation beliefs. In fact, when one compares the amount of material concerning the meditations with the amount of material on doctrine, he finds that doctrine is secondary to meditation.

Rather than starting from a well-defined theology and moving to resulting religious practices, the Foundation has seemingly started with religious practices (meditation methods) and gradually evolved an inconsistent theology from the meditation. As we will discuss under the doctrine of salvation, Masters' meditation techniques become, in effect, the way of salvation to all meditators. Instead of relying on Jesus for our salvation, we are told to rely on Masters and his meditation techniques:

> The writer does not guarantee the seeker wealth, but rather he offers knowledge of the way to contentment, peace of mind, and purpose. The road to riches is not the road to real happiness. The road to correct response in each moment of Truth is the first step to everything.[4]

Instead of relying on the power of the Holy Spirit to guide us and help us in our times of need, we are told to rely on ourselves, made seemingly all-powerful by successful meditation:

> The primary objective of the concentration is to cause the emotions and the intellect to respond to the quiet consciousness. Then when difficult situations present themselves, our unclouded impartial understanding will see what is right.[5]

The Foundation meditation claims to be "counter hypnosis." However, the technique that Masters employs involves a type of self-hypnosis, and the results of the meditation exercises are almost exactly like the results of some forms of therapeutic hypnosis. As in hypnosis, the subject is directed to empty his mind of all thoughts:

> The object of the meditation exercise is to free you from your squirrel cage by bringing the unconscious into subjection of the consciousness. This is made possible only through desiring guidance of an invisible Divine Will that we may know, or come to know, only as Conscience. Hence, we must dissolve all mental chatter in our mind, and fast from the excitement of love and hate that propels our selfish pride in its striving toward selfish goals. We must wait, empty, for a new direction.[6]

Another aspect of Masters' meditation is also parallel to hypnotism. Masters asks his subjects to surrender all disbelief and to relinquish control to Masters, his publications, and the meditation itself.

> There will come a time when serious problems lose their place of importance. This may be quite puzzling, but remember what I said, 'Do not analyze it.' Just be grateful that it is so. Be patient; in time you will understand what is happening.[7]

> Remember, do not analyze. Ponder on it, within yourself. Do not worry, 'Will it work? Will it last?' Cast out doubt. Bring your mind back again and again to your objective. Don't discuss this with anyone yet. Just think and feel it secretly, and do it.[8]

> Let your mind remain empty—it's better that way.[9]

In his book *How Your Mind Can Keep You Well,* Masters declares that his meditation system is the ancient technique of meditation practiced by the early Jewish and Christian mystics. This special technique was supposedly lost long ago but has just been rediscovered by Masters. The goal of the meditation is to "refer the individual back to himself, to help him achieve an inner perspective on his problems and their causes."[10]

The meditation exercise itself is described in *How Your Mind Can Keep You Well* (pages 5-9). The exercise resembles self-hypnosis and is designed to keep the meditator's mind "in the present" so he can get in touch with himself.

The meditator blanks his mind through a conditioning process (described in *How Your Mind Can Keep You Well*) and then is ready to proceed to the second stage in Masters' system.

When a meditator blanks his mind, he can then observe his own thoughts, according to Masters, in a detached manner in order to determine if those thoughts are right or wrong, constructive or destructive. Masters considers it very important that the meditator observes all of his actions in a completely detached manner. One is not to respond emotionally to anything he observes in this second stage of meditation. Passive observation becomes the vehicle for Foundation "salvation."

> The second stage of meditation can become a thought-observing process....any attempt to deal with your old thoughts and feelings merely sickens you and duplicates the egocentric 'coping' that confused you in the first place....[11]

The last stage of Foundation meditation is the Foundation's brand of salvation. As one is involved in observing his own thoughts in a detached manner (stage two), he then determines to keep the constructive thoughts and to "overlook" the destructive thoughts. Masters instructs the meditator to see the destructive thoughts (from which proceed destructive acts) as error or lies, and to overlook them so that they are no longer harmful to the meditator. From Masters' instructions, we can see that he is not concerned with one's outward behavior as such or with the well-being of our fellowman (the Golden Rule). Rather, the self is all-important. Evidently the meditator's goal should be to satisfy himself and to be unconcerned with others.

The Bible does not teach this kind of meditation. We are to be concerned with the welfare of others. In fact, Jesus declared that the entire Old Testament Law could be summed up in two great commandments:

> ...Love the Lord your God with all your heart and with all your soul and with all your mind. This is the first and greatest commandment. And the second is like it: Love your neighbor as yourself. All the Law and the Prophets hang on these two commandments.[12]

God is our supreme Example of what our attitude should be toward others. God did not retreat into His own mind and ignore others, as Foundation meditators are taught. Paul explained, "Very rarely will anyone die for a righteous man, though for a good man someone might possibly dare to die. But God demonstrates his own love for us in this: While we were still sinners, Christ died for us" (Romans 5:7,8).

Christians do not void their minds when they meditate. Christians are taught by the Bible to "test everything. Hold on to the good. Avoid every kind of evil" (1 Thessalonians 5:21,22). The stark contrast between Christian meditation and other kinds of meditation is evident when one examines the two processes. In Foundation meditation, one is told to relinquish his intellect and critical thinking. He is merely to empty his mind and to observe dispassionately. Christian meditation has been precisely defined by Gordon R. Lewis in *What Everyone Should Know About Transcendental Meditation*:

> In Christianity, [meditation is] a discipline of the whole

person by which his mind is guided by biblical teaching as his emotions and will are yielded to the illumination of the Holy Spirit to receive the truth of God into his life and interact appropriately with the visible and invisible realities of which that truth speaks.[13]

According to the Bible, we are not renewed and strengthened by empty minds and passive reflection on our thoughts and actions. We have dynamic life in Christ which far transcends the indolence of Foundation meditation. We do not discard our minds as Christians. On the contrary, we "have put on the new self, which is being renewed in knowledge in the image of its Creator" (Colossians 3:10).

We do not seek to avoid encountering others, ourselves, and God. We seek to worship God as He asks—in spirit and in truth (John 4:24). The Foundation meditation is self-centered, seeking to improve the meditator with no thoughts toward God or others. Christian meditation seeks to please the loving Creator: "May the words of my mouth and the meditation of my heart be pleasing in your sight, O Lord, my Rock and my Redeemer" (Psalm 19:14). Rather than meditating on nothing or on our own thoughts, the Bible instructs us to meditate on God's Word: "Oh, how I love your law! I meditate on it all day long" (Psalm 119:97).

The Christian is instructed to learn God's will through His objective revelation in the Bible, and to pray intelligently for the Holy Spirit to conform his life to that of Christ. The Apostle Paul instructed Timothy:

Until I come, devote yourself to the public reading of Scripture, to preaching and to teaching. Do not neglect your gift, which was given you through a prophetic message when the body of elders laid their hands on you. Be diligent in these matters; give yourself wholly to them, so that everyone may see your progress. Watch your life and doctrine closely. Persevere in them, because if you do, you will save both yourself and your hearers.[14]

Finally, the Bible does not condone one's placing his trust

blindly in a man or a system or a technique in order to reach God. The Bible commends those who make intelligent choices concerning faith. Acts 17:11 records:

Now the Bereans were of more noble character than the Thessalonians, for they received the message with great eagerness and examined the Scriptures every day to see if what Paul said was true.

The meditation methods of Roy Masters and the Foundation of Human Understanding are not biblical meditation methods and should be avoided by those who want to meditate scripturally. False meditation cannot produce the assurance and peace which are available from God alone, on His terms through Jesus Christ. As we examine the doctrines of the Foundation, we will see that they deny the doctrines which are central to God's revelation in the Bible.

THE FOUNDATION OF HUMAN UNDERSTANDING DOCTRINE

In our discussion of the doctrines central to the teachings of Roy Masters and the Foundation of Human Understanding, we will note the parallels between these thoughts and the thoughts of several other religious movements. The Foundation's teachings are syncretistic, meaning that they combine seemingly diverse thoughts from different sources to present a homogeneous doctrinal structure. We will observe Masters' use of yoga,† hypnotism,‡ and belief in many Eastern concepts.§

Authority

As with the other cults we have studied, the Foundation of Human Understanding asserts its own value while denying that the historic Christian church has had the truth. In-

---

† See Chapter 3 for further information.
‡ See Chapter 7 for further information.
§ See Chapter 3 for further information.

stead of the orthodox church, which has represented the cardinal doctrines of the Bible throughout history, the Foundation promotes its own teachings, which are anything but orthodox. Masters vehemently denounced the validity of certain preachers by declaring, "Damn all the hellfire and damnation preachers."[15] In his tape *The Cross of Christ,* he declared, "The Church doesn't teach the truth about why Christ died on the cross." Referring to the methods of most churches in their services, he said, "Preaching and teaching is brainwashing."[16]

Having dismissed the authority of the church to represent spiritual truth, Masters additionally elevates his words to the level of spiritual truth in the church's stead. According to Masters' teachings, "there's an imprint in our soul that cannot be erased and cannot be taught. It's God-given. It's our potential salvation."[17] It is to this spiritual goal that Masters' meditations techniques are supposed to guide the meditator. However, one must surrender himself completely to Masters' techniques in order to derive the intended benefit. One is not allowed to question what he is told by Masters. In this sense, then, Masters does not hold the Bible to be the final authority in all matters, whether temporal or spiritual.

> Again, I must tell you that I am writing to you to leave a trail of clues, and again, I implore you not to study me. Scan these words. Scan the Scriptures for understanding. BUT NEVER STUDY OR BE ABSORBED IN MERE WORDS.[18]

Concerning one's growth in Masters' meditation techniques he says:

> The veil over understanding the very Bible you read will fall away, and there—you will begin to perceive Truth in all its glory and splendor.[19]

God

As is true with other Eastern–oriented cults, the Foundation teaches that God is both personal and impersonal. Roy Masters claims to offer a meditation technique rather than a complete religious system, and so it is not surprising that his theology is often sketchy. However, he does make some pronouncements on the major doctrines of the Christian faith, and it is those pronouncements which separate his movement from Christianity.

Masters often speaks of God in personal terms, talking of the help "he" can give people, and the love shown from God. However, at other times Masters seems to deny a personal God, advocating an almost pantheistic God.

> According to law, man enters into relationship with principle (God)—provoking His compassion—in order that He may extend His forgiveness to us. With the energy of this love, we, like a God, extend our forgiveness (patience) to those who tempt us.[20]

> Therefore, nothing is still. Everything is in motion. However, since we must admit there can be no motion at all without stillness, everything in motion must revolve about a central creative stillness. That is God, the Ultimate Stillness, the cause of all motion, cause and effect.[21]

> If you are troubled, it is because your ego has crossed that threshold, trying to be as free as a Reality (God) is supposed to be....[22]

Although we do not know everything that combines to make personality, there are some attributes of God that can be affirmed only of a personal God. The Bible demonstrates conclusively that God is personal. Masters has promoted a God that is impersonal, a God like the Eastern ideas of God.☆ When we say that God is personal, we mean that He exhibits Himself to be personal within His nature. God exhibits will, intellect, and emotion, to name three aspects of personality. We must state clearly that God is intrinsically personal. We do not consider God as personal merely

---

☆ See Chapter 6 for more information on the Eastern concept of God.

because of biblical anthropomorphisms or other figurative language. God is actually personal.

In addition to being personal, the Bible shows us that God is personally triune. By triune, we mean that although the Bible teaches that there is only one true God, it also teaches that within that one essential Being are three intrinsic Persons—the Father, the Son, and the Holy Spirit. Although each of the Persons shares in the one essential Being of God, each of the Members of the Trinity is distinct as to person. The Father is God, the Son is God, and the Holy Spirit is God. However, the Father's person is not the Son's person, and the Holy Spirit's person is neither the Father's nor the Son's.

We know that God is personal from many Bible passages. In Acts 17:24,25 we find that this personal God is the Sovereign over everything. He is the universe's Creator. Romans 11:33,34 asserts the personality of God as well as His greatness: "Oh, the depth of the riches of the wisdom and knowledge of God! How unsearchable his judgments, and his paths beyond tracing out! Who has known the mind of the Lord? Or who has been his counselor?" Only a personal God, the God of the Bible, can have emotions such as the love God expressed for us in the sacrifice of His Son (John 3:16).

The Trinity is revealed throughout the Bible, and is especially clear in the New Testament. We know that there is only one true God from verses like John 17:3; that the Father is called God and is distinct from the Son from such verses as 2 Peter 1:17; that the Son is personally distinct and is called God (John 10:30-33); and that the Holy Spirit is distinct from the Father and Son and yet is God (John 14:16 and Hebrews 9:14). We believe, as the Bible teaches, that within the nature of the one true God (Matthew 28:19) there are three eternal, distinct Persons (Luke 3:21,22). The God of the Foundation of Human Understanding and Roy Masters is not the God of the Bible.

Christ

Even a careful examination of the Foundation publications produces only a few references to Jesus Christ. This in itself invalidates Masters' claim to bring salvation through his ministry, since the Bible declares that salvation can only come through Jesus (Acts 3:16; 4:12). Masters certainly did not follow the example of the Apostle Paul, who said, "...I resolved to know nothing while I was with you except Jesus Christ and Him crucified" (1 Corinthians 2:2).

Masters claims to renew the mind of man through his meditation techniques. Masters seeks to empty the mind and then refill it with what he determines are constructive thoughts. What a contrast to the biblical injunctions about the mind of the Christian! True spiritual renewal comes through the power of the Holy Spirit working in the life consecrated to Jesus Christ. Ephesians 3:16-19 promises the believer more than Masters' meditation methods could ever hope to achieve.

I pray that out of his glorious riches he may strengthen you with power through his Spirit in your inner being, so that Christ may dwell in your hearts through faith. And I pray that you, being rooted and established in love, may have power, together with all the saints, to grasp how wide and long and high and deep is the love of Christ, and to know this love that surpasses knowledge—that you may be filled to the measure of all the fullness of God.

God wants us to have a mind that is not empty but in harmony with Christ (Philippians 2:5). Christians do not strive to satisfy themselves, or to know themselves. They strive to know Christ, the Source of all blessings. As Christians, we join with Paul in praying, "I want to know Christ and the power of his resurrection and the fellowship of sharing in his sufferings, becoming like him in his death, and so, somehow, to attain to the resurrection from the dead" (Philippians 3:10,11).

Jesus Christ is central to the Christian faith and yet is sadly neglected in the religious system of the Foundation of Human Understanding. When Masters does mention Christ, it is usually in a negative context.

So if I speak of Christ, of Moses and their philosophies, at best they just mix into your brain with all of the prejudices and knowledge you have gathered and become poisoned. Words scramble here in your mind and come out in rather strange combinations, usually excusing all that is wrong.[23]

...So be careful of the "Christ who loves you AS YOU ARE" and thus makes you forget guilt....That hypnotic trick of instantly accepting people is a trick of the devil, a misuse of the real meaning of Love.[24]

Masters' strange view of the love of Christ contradicts the Scriptures: "But God demonstrates his own love for us in this: While we were still sinners, Christ died for us" (Romans 5:8).

Moses and Christ spoke of the same God (Exodus 3:14; John 8:58), but Christ was much greater than Moses. Christ is the only One who has ever lived who can rightfully claim to be God manifest in the flesh (Colossians 2:9). When we say that Jesus Christ is the God-man, we are saying that the divine Person, with a divine nature, took on Himself an *additional* nature—that of humanity. Philippians 2:5-11 explains that although Christ was by very nature God, and never ceased being God, yet he humbled Himself and also became man. This is the mystery of the incarnation. Jesus Christ is more than a man with a confusing philosophy, as Masters would have us believe. He is the "image of the invisible God, the firstborn [preeminent one] over all creation" (Colossians 1:15).

We cannot, as Christians, relegate Christ to a position equal to that of many other "philosophers," and we cannot ignore the supreme sacrifice He made for us while we were sinners. The Christian's entire existence should be devoted to pleasing Him. The Christian is eagerly waiting "for the blessed hope—the glorious appearing of our great God and Savior, Jesus Christ, who gave himself for us to redeem us from all wickedness and to purify for himself a people that are his very own, eager to do what is good" (Titus 2:13,14).

The Holy Spirit

The Foundation of Human Understanding focuses most of its attention on Masters' meditation methods, and it largely ignores doctrine. After carefully researching the publications of the Foundation, we have been unable to find any conclusive material on either the Foundation or Masters' beliefs concerning the Holy Spirit. He simply is not mentioned.

A biblical view of the Holy Spirit sees him as the third Person of the Trinity, the One who, after Christ's ascension, was sent by the Father and the Son as the Christian's Teacher, Comforter, and Reprover. However, the ministry of the Holy Spirit is much older than the New Testament church. The Holy Spirit also operated actively in the Old Testament.

The Holy Spirit, as a member of the Godhead, appeared in the very opening moments of history as Creator (Genesis 1:2). The Holy Spirit filled Old Testament believers (Genesis 41:38; Exodus 31:3; 35:31; etc.). Men in the Old Testament were guided by the Holy Spirit (Judges 13:25; Isaiah 48:16; 63:14). The Holy Spirit was active in the creation of man (Job 33:4). Our Old Testament faithfully represents God's message because the Holy Spirit inspired its writers (2 Samuel 23:2). Finally, God's will is accomplished by the Holy Spirit (Micah 3:8; Zechariah 4:6).

The Holy Spirit bears witness to the truth regarding Jesus Christ. John 15:26,27 records Jesus' words concerning the ministry of the Holy Spirit:

> When the Counselor comes, whom I will send to you from the Father, the Spirit of truth who goes out from the Father, he will testify about me; but you also must testify, for you

have been with me from the beginning.

It is only through the testimony of the Holy Spirit that anyone can ever come to a saving knowledge of Jesus Christ (1 Corinthians 12:3). To the unbeliever, the Holy Spirit's ministry is one of judgment or conviction. John 16:8-11 says:

> When he [the Holy Spirit] comes, he will convict the world of guilt in regard to sin and righteousness and judgment: in regard to sin, because men do not believe in me; in regard to righteousness, because I am going to the Father, where you can see me no longer; and in regard to judgment, because the prince of this world now stands condemned.

The ministry of the Holy Spirit to the believer is very different. In addition to teaching us about Jesus, the Holy Spirit assures us that we belong to Christ (Romans 8:14; 8:16). The Holy Spirit dwells in each Christian (Romans 8:9), acts in our salvation (Titus 3:5; John 3:3-5), and empowers us to live the Christian life (Ephesians 3:16; Galatians 5:22,23; Romans 14:17).

Is the Holy Spirit a Person? Or is the Holy Spirit merely some sort of power or force, as many cults teach? Is the Holy Spirit a divine Person worthy to receive our faith, love, and worship, or is the Spirit simply an influence emanating from God? If the Holy Spirit is a divine Person but we do not worship Him, we are denying God the worship to which He is due. We need to appreciate the Holy Spirit for who He really is. R.A. Torrey posed the dilemma as follows:

> It is of the highest practical importance that we decide whether the Holy Spirit is a power that we in our weakness and ignorance are somehow to get hold of and use, or whether the Holy Spirit is a personal being infinitely wise, infinitely holy, infinitely tender, who is to get hold of and use us. The one conception is heathenish, the other Christian. The one conception leads to self-humiliation, self-emptying and self-renunciation; the other conception leads to self-exaltation.[25]

The personality of the Holy Spirit is implicit in many biblical passages. Personal pronouns are used of Him (John 15:26; John 16:7,8,13,14). Personal knowledge is ascribed to the Holy Spirit (1 Corinthians 2:10,11); He has a personal will (1 Corinthians 12:11) and a mind (Romans 8:27). (By mind we mean thought, feeling, and purpose—not a material brain.) In harmony with God's nature the Holy Spirit can love (Romans 15:30), is good, and instructs the righteous (Nehemiah 9:20). The Holy Spirit thinks, feels, wills, knows, and loves. Only a person can do these things.

Personal acts are done by the Holy Spirit. He knows the depths of God (1 Corinthians 2:10); He speaks (Acts 13:2); He makes intercession for (pleads the cause of) the saint (Romans 8:26); He testifies of Jesus Christ (John 15:26); and He teaches (John 14:26).

What does it mean to say that the Holy Spirit is of God and is personal? As Christians, our attitude toward the Holy Spirit should be like our attitude toward Jesus Christ and the Father. He is as loving, wise, and strong, and as deserving of our trust and faith, as Jesus. He is our Comforter and Counselor.

In addition to being personal, the Holy Spirit is also *God*. He is the third member of the Trinity, and as such He shares all the attributes of deity. He is eternal (Hebrews 9:14); omnipresent (Psalm 139:7-10); and omniscient (1 Corinthians 2:10.11). He is co-Creator with the Father and the Son (Job 33:4). As Jesus is the One who gives resurrection life, so the Holy Spirit also gives resurrection life (Romans 8:11). God's Word is also the Holy Spirit's Word (2 Peter 1:21; 2 Samuel 23:2,3). Passages ascribed to Jehovah in the Old Testament are ascribed to the Holy Spirit in the New Testament (Isaiah 6:8-10; cf. Acts 28:25-27; Exodus 16:7; cf. Hebrews 3:7-9). The Holy Spirit is equated with God in Acts 5:3,4.

From our perusal of the Scriptures concerning the Holy Spirit, we can see that He is the third Person of the Trinity, and that He is holy and worthy of the same accord and praise that we offer to the Father and the Son. Unlike Roy Masters and the Foundation of Human Understanding, we do not ignore the Holy Spirit. We "do not grieve the Holy Spirit of God, with whom [we] were sealed for the day of redemption" (Ephesians 4:30).

Mankind

Human nature in the Masters System is inherently good, is not guilty of sin, and has within itself the capability to perfect itself. Man is not considered a dependent, sinful being who achieves right standing with God through God's unmerited favor toward man through the sacrifice of Christ.

The secret lies in the Meditation Exercise, a principle similar to self-hypnosis. All of us have within a natural inclination toward right action, such as helping an injured person.[26]

At this point, the author has already given you the key to your inner Self....you may be looking for external balm rather than inner direction. Remember that it is your own meditation that will re-establish your connection with your true Self and provide you with your own insight. Seek the Kingdom of Heaven within your Self, for that is where you will find it.[27]

Extended through the meditation exercise, it gives our realization full power to change our behavior so that we need no longer be guilty before Truth (through being oversensitive to life experiences).[28]

Meditation establishes a new relationship. Energy becomes available from within, so that we no longer have to wait for fear, irritation, or temptation to move us. What we say, do, and think, is intuitively impelled and friction-free. We grow in a new way—to see more, and to respond more to what we perceive. Naturally, without effort, we are impelled to do what we realize is wise and to shrink from what is unwise. In this way we come to inherit our own bodies and escape from our old enslavement to pleasure and pain.[29]

...Through patience you will come to perfection....[30]

Man is not as the Foundation of Human Understanding has perceived him. Although it is true that man was originally created in God's likeness and without sin, man since his fall has been basically sinful, not basically good. Adam, the first man, sinned willfully, and each man since Adam has followed in his father's footsteps (Romans 3:10,23). The Bible goes so far as to say that any person who claims not to sin is a liar (1 John 1:8,10). Furthermore, it is impossible for man to change himself, to get rid of his own sin. Romans 3:12 declares, "All have turned away, they have together become worthless; there is no one who does good, not even one."

Jehovah warned others of the tendency to feel self-sufficient. Of particular interest is Isaiah 47:10,16.

> You have trusted in your wickedness and have said, "No one sees me." Your wisdom and knowledge mislead you when you say to yourself, "I am, and there is none beside me." Disaster will come upon you, and you will not know how to conjure it away. A calamity will fall upon you that you cannot ward off with a ransom; a catastrophe you cannot foresee will suddenly come upon you.

In bold contrast to this is the simple assurance of help that David expresses in Psalm 130:

> Out of the depths I cry to you, O Lord; O Lord, hear my voice. Let your ears be attentive to my cry for mercy. If you, O Lord, kept a record of sins, O Lord, who could stand? But with you there is forgiveness; therefore you are feared. I wait for the Lord, my soul waits, and in his word I put my hope. My soul waits for the Lord more than watchmen wait for the morning, more than watchmen wait for the morning. O Israel, put your hope in the Lord, for with the Lord is unfailing love and with him is full redemption. He himself will redeem Israel from all their sins.

Romans 5 is sometimes called the great atonement

chapter. In it is the basic outline of the fall and redemption of man. In Romans 5:12 we learn that sin came through our representative, Adam, and that subsequently all men have sinned and are in need of forgiveness by God. Man is not intrinsically good and he does not have the power within himself to save himself or, as Masters puts it, "to come to perfection." We must trust in the Lord for our forgiveness, just as David and Israel did (Psalm 130). The man of Roy Masters' teachings is not the man described in the Bible.

Salvation

Closely linked to the doctrine of man is the doctrine of salvation. Obviously, if man is intrinsically good, then he needs no savior. The Foundation of Human Understanding rejects the salvation offered by God in the Bible and instead offers a poor substitute of self-effort.

> For the time being don't call upon a name that you have been educated to accept, or else you may revive a conditioned reflex response to words that connect you to the outer world. The God, Jesus, and Buddha that you may have accepted via brainwashing is not the real one. Many of us have accepted a 'holy spirit' in a moment of excitement, but it turned out to be the unholy one instead, and by him you justified every sin while you got worse.[31]

> The pain you will feel is Repentance. Bear it for awhile without cursing it or dealing with it; just watch it, perhaps with tears of regret....This is all we can do for salvation—observe, know, repent, and wait for the next opportunity to do right what we once did wrong.[32]

> Love (do not respond to) your enemy and do kindness to those who hate you and turn the other cheek are simply ways of saying that non-response is our only true pain reliever (salvation).[33]

> ...One by one, our sins will emerge from the body as babble thoughts, to be observed and resolved in the light of

understanding.[34]

No form of outer assistance can substitute for inner direction. Direction must come always from within. Moved by the spirit of intuition, we move without excitement, effort or strain. The more we exercise our dependency upon the Within, the stronger this relationship becomes, and we know it to be Grace.[35]

Salvation is by our intent to do right.[36]

The message of Salvation is to find the truth in the heart.[37]

Since Masters teaches that man is basically good, it is natural that he would teach that whatever problems men have can be solved within the self. This is contrary to the Bible, which repeatedly declares that man can do nothing for his own salvation. In addtion, Masters' definition of salvation is far from the biblical definition of salvation. Salvation is not self-effort: it is God working in our behalf in spite of our evil.

Biblical salvation occurs only through the gift of Christ upon the cross, when God the Son shed His own blood to save us (Acts 20:28). God is the One against whom we have sinned, and He alone can dictate a just payment for that sin. He determined that through Christ He would "reconcile to himself all things, whether things on earth or things in heaven, by making peace through his blood, shed on the cross" (Colossians 1:20). "God was reconciling the world to himself in Christ, not counting men's sins against them" (2 Corinthians 5:19).

To receive the benefit of the work of Christ, one only needs to repent (turn away) from his sins and ask God to save him through His grace and the work on the cross done by Christ. Acts 16:31 assures the repentant sinner, "Believe in the Lord Jesus, and you will be saved...."

There is nothing that man can do for himself that Jesus has not already done for him (Hebrews 7:27). Salvation is wholly by grace, and not at all by works (Ephesians 2:8-10;

Titus 3:5).

Once a person is saved, he has a new perspective on life and a new relationship to Jesus Christ (2 Corinthians 5:16,17). He has the promise of God that "If we confess our sins, he is faithful and just and will forgive us our sins, and purify us from all unrighteousness" (1 John 1:9). From the time of our salvation onward, our only aim should be to please God through our lives—lives that are consecrated to God through Christ and the power of the Holy Spirit (Romans 12:1).

CONCLUSION

The basic doctrines and many of the practices of Roy Masters and the Foundation of Human Understanding are decidedly not Christian. They are certainly not in harmony with what God has revealed to us in the Bible. Since the Masters system is a system of man and not a system of God, it has no spiritually transforming power, no capacity to permanently change the lives of men.

Those who are involved with the Foundation of Human Understanding are in double jeopardy. Not only are they being robbed of the opportunity for true salvation in Christ, but they are also being robbed of the opportunity for abundant life in Christ.

The Bible provides a timely warning for the unbeliever and assurance for the believer:

> See to it that no one takes you captive through hollow and deceptive philosophy, which depends on human tradition and the basic principles of this world rather than on Christ. For in Christ all the fullness of the Deity lives in bodily form, and you have been given fullness in Christ, who is the head over every power and authority.[38]

CHAPTER NOTES

1. *The Los Angeles Times,* article by Russell Chandler, July 16, 1977.
2. Ibid.
3. Ibid. Most of the history of the Foundation and Roy Masters is taken from the *Los Angeles Times* article of July 16, 1977.
4. Roy Masters, *How Your Mind Can Keep You Well* (Los Angeles: Foundation Press, 1971), p. vi.
5. Ibid., p. 31.
6. *How Your Mind Can Keep You Well,* op. cit., p. 69.
7. Ibid., pp. 3, 4.
8. Ibid., pp. 17, 18.
9. *How Your Mind Can Keep You Well* (record album).
10. *Foundation of Human Understanding* (publicity pamphlet, no publisher or date).
11. *How Your Mind Can Keep You Well,* op. cit., pp. 32, 33.
12. Matthew 22:37-40.
13. Gordon R. Lewis, *What Everyone Should Know About Transcendental Meditation* (Ventura, CA: Gospel Light Publications, 1975), p. 87.
14. 1 Timothy 4:13-16.
15. Masters, *Be Still and Know* (Foundation Press, 1976), p. 9.
16. Masters, *Guilt* (cassette by Foundation Press, n.d.).
17. *Los Angeles Times,* op. cit.
18. Masters, *Hypnosis of Dying and Death* (Foundation Press, 1977), p. 16.
19. *How Your Mind Can Keep You Well,* op. cit. pp. 17, 18.
20. Masters, *The Secret of Life and Death* (Foundation Press, 1964), p. 79.
21. Masters, *The God Game* (Foundation Press, 1977), p. 17.
22. Masters, *Sex: The Substitute Love* (Foundation Press, 1976), pp. 14, 15.
23. Masters, *Hypno-Christianity* (Foundation Press, 1977), p. 10.
24. Ibid., pp. 13, 14.
25. R.A. Torrey, *What the Bible Teaches* (Old Tappan, NJ: Fleming H. Revell, 1898-1933), p. 225.
26. *How Your Mind Can Keep You Well,* op. cit., p. xvii.
27. Ibid., p. 47.
28. Ibid., p. 53.
29. Ibid., p. 75.
30. Ibid., p. 194.
31. Ibid., pp. 185-86.
32. Ibid., p. 80.
33. Ibid., p. 132.
34. Ibid., p. 67.
35. Ibid., p. 165.
36. Masters, *Guilt* (cassette by Foundation Press, n.d.).

37. Masters, *Principles of Salvation* (cassette by Foundation Press, n.d.).
38. Colossians 2:8-10.

CHAPTER
10

NICHIREN SHOSHU BUDDHISM★

HISTORY

"The Buddhism of Nichiren Daishonin...will become the heart of the faith of the people everywhere and will thus grow to be the true universal religion."[1] In an intensive proselytizing sweep, this Japanese mystical form of Buddhism is seeking to snatch new converts from any and all established churches in the United States. "The campaign to awaken every individual to the Gohonzon, to that basic law which allows one to fuse with the universe, is the perennial mission of Nichiren Shoshu."[2] While claiming to be compatible with Christianity, Nichiren Shoshu Buddhism (NSB) proclaims doctrines and practices antithetical to biblical Christianity. One cannot follow both NSB and the Jesus of the Bible at the same time.

The history of NSB is rooted in the vague and mysterious original teachings of the Buddha. Nichiren Daishonin, founder of Nichiren Shoshu, claimed to use the Buddha's thought as a base for NSB's teachings.[3] However, no one is certain what the Buddha actually taught. His life history is clouded by the myths and traditional beliefs which sprang

---

★ Researched by John Weldon.

up concerning him shortly after his life (563 B.C. to 480 B.C.).

> ...in the present state of our knowledge we cannot in any instance declare that Buddha said so and so....[4]

> ...the only firm ground from which we can start is not history, but the fact that a legend in definite form existed in the first and second centuries after Buddha's death.[5]

Despite this, Nichiren Daishonin fervently believed that he had found the Buddha's true teachings in the Lotus Sutra, and the entire structure of his interpretation of Buddhism is based upon this sutra.[6] The Lotus Sutra, a pseudo-Buddhistic writing, has been dated at between 200 B.C. and 200 A.D.,[7] at least 200 years after Buddha lived. Buddhism itself did not become systemized before the sixth century B.C.[8] In addition, the Lotus Sutra differs in at least seven major areas from earlier Buddhistic beliefs.[9] It is clear that even though we may not have the original teachings of Buddha, the earliest traditions regarding his teachings are inconsistent with the Lotus Sutra and Nichiren's beliefs. It is not likely that Nichiren Shoshu Buddhism is "true" Buddhism. Dr. Kenneth Scott Latourette remarked:

> He was mistaken in conviction that the *Lotus Sutra* contained the primitive Buddhism. As a matter of fact, it was a late production, an expression of a form of Buddhism that would scarcely have been recognized by Gautama, or if recognized would have been repudiated.[10]

Nichiren Shoshu is the religious group founded after the teachings of the Japanese reformer Nichiren Daishonin (1222-82 A.D.). He denounced all other Buddhist sects. During his lifetime he wrote 430 volumes, called collectively *Gosho*. He believed himself to be the fulfillment of a prophecy in the Lotus Sutra about the coming of a second Buddha. After Nichiren's death, in 1282, his immediate successor, Nikko Shonin, founded the religious system of Nichiren Shoshu.

Nichiren Shoshu continued as a small sect of Buddhism until the founding in Japan of the Soka Gakkai (Value Creation Society), by Tsunesaburo Makiguchi in 1930. Soka Gakkai is the Japanese lay organization of Nichiren Shoshu and has become the evangelistic arm of the religion. When the Japanese government attempted to unify all of Japan under Shinto Buddhism in 1940, only Nichiren Shoshu refused to obey. (NSB claims to be the only orthodox sect among the many sects claiming Nichiren Daishonin as their founders.) In 1940 there were only 21 members, all of whom were arrested. Nineteen of those members converted to Shintoism and were released. Leader Makiguchi died in prison, and the only remaining member, Josei Toda, was released from prison in 1945, shortly before the end of World War Two.

Under Toda's leadership, the movement began growing and elected Toda the second president of Soka Gakkai. In 1960 Daisaku Ikeda was inaugurated president over 1.3 million members.[11] Ikeda expanded NSB's evangelism in foreign countries, opening a branch in the United States in 1960. The quickly growing branch of the sect held its first convention in 1963 in Chicago, with representatives from ten chapters. By 1973, membership was put at more than 250,000. From 1960 to 1973, NSB in the United States increased three-hundredfold! Japanese growth was even faster. The number of practicing Japanese families grew from three thousand in 1951 to more than seven million in 1971![12]

This phenomenal growth is directly attributable to the group's aggressive proselytizing, called *Shakubuku* (literally "brow-beating"). The members are committed to *Kosen-Rufu*, the belief that world unity and peace will be obtained when Nichiren Shoshu has converted the world. NSB has its own Japanese political party, the Komeito, which is the third-largest political party in Japan. The Komeito supports the U.N. and is basically pacifistic, but it advocates the execution of those who make nuclear weapons. The NSB periodical, *The Seikyo Times,* reports that the ultimate goal of Nichiren Shoshu is "the realization of complete peace throughout the world" and the uniting of mankind.[13] Nichiren Shoshu Buddhism is dedicated to conquering the religious world, and its mushrooming membership lends seriousness to its objective.

STRUCTURE AND AUTHORITY

Nichiren Shoshu boasts of a 700-year unbroken tradition and lineage of priests who have kept their teachings inviolate since the time of Nichiren Daishonin.* The central teaching of NSB concerns the *Gohonzon,* a black wooden box used as a private altar. The talisman contains a sheet of paper on which are written the names of important individuals in the Lotus Sutra. To each member, the Gohonzon represents one's life, together with its good and bad karma. The Gohonzon's supernatural powers are closely bound with the member's life; what happens to one's Gohonzon is frequently reflected in one's life. One former NSB follower reported a meeting where testimonies were given by members who had suffered some of the same effects that had inadvertently happened to their Gohonzons. One member reported that after accidentally splashing water on her Gohonzon, she almost drowned in a swimming pool.[14]

The Gohonzon, owned by NSB but in the possession of the individual members on a "lifetime loan," is the center of NSB ritual worship. This daily ritual is called *Gongyo,* and consists of three separate activities. First the devotee kneels before the Gohonzon, and then he recites passages from the Lotus Sutra. While rubbing rosary-type beads he chants the *Daimoku—"Nam-myoho-renge-kyo".* The ceremony is concluded in silent prayer. The Lotus Sutra passages are recited eight times during the day—five times in

---

* This is contrary to the traditional teachings of Buddha, who was said to declare, "Do not accept...tradition, do not accept a statement because it is found in our books, nor because it is in accord with your belief, nor because it is the saying of your teacher" (Huston Smith, *Religions of Man,* page 105).

the morning and three times at night. Chanting of the Daimoku continues "until one feels satisfied" (some advanced members may spend hours in chanting).

The basic essence of the Lotus Sutra is contained in the invocation "Nam-myoho-renge-kyo." Practicing this chant regularly is part of unifying one's life with the life of Buddha.

The goal of personal worship by NSB members is oneness with the essence of Buddha—the underlying essence of the universe. As with other Eastern religious systems,† NSB is pantheistic. God is all and all is God. All existence is one. All creation is in some way a reflection of the divine, impersonal Source. The Gongyo is the path one must follow to realize his oneness with God:

> Man must transform his own self into a being capable of self-realization and enjoying happiness to the full. The only way to that inexhaustible oasis of humanity is to practice Gongyo constantly and thereby manifest the Buddha's vitality and wisdom inherent in man himself. Only with these resources can one confidently achieve that desirable self-transformation.[15]

> Nam-myoho-renge-kyo is the essence of all life and the rhythm of the universe itself. Life can never be apart from Nam-myoho-renge-kyo, and yet because we have forgotten this, we have become out of rhythm with life itself. When we chant, we enter back into that basic rhythm and once again have the potential for indestructible happiness.[16]

The Daimoku, or NSB chant, is not a meaningless phrase. Its syllables represent all the truth of the universe. *Nam* means the dedication of one's whole being to something (in this case, the Gohonzon). *Myoho* means the supreme law, the natural working principles of the divine, impersonal universe. *Renge* refers to the lotus flower, symbol of the Lotus Sutra, and represents *Karma* (in Eastern religions the simultaneous nature of cause and effect, good and bad).

---

† See Chapter 3 for further information on Eastern thought.

Kyo is said to be the underlying sound or vibration of the universe.[17]

By chanting the Daimoku, one dedicates his life to the Gohonzon and all it represents. This results in increased harmony with the laws of the universe, which function by cause and effect. Chanting the Daimoku is the highest cause that a person can initiate, and it results in the best natural effect—benefits in one's daily life. The sound or rhythm of the chant puts one's life back in tune with "the basic flow of life."

The *Dai-Gohonzon* is the supreme object of worship and is located inside Daisekiji, the temple of Nichiren Shoshu at the base of Mount Fuji, in Japan. Over 3.5 million members each year make pilgrimages to worship the Dai-Gohonzon. This shrine has effectively replaced any idea of a personal God who answers prayer out of His benevolence. According to Nikkan Shonin, the twenty-sixth high priest of NSB, the Dai Gohonzon is "the origin and essence of all Buddhas and all the sutras of Sakyamuni...so if one prays to Gohonzon in earnest, no prayer is unanswered, no sin unforgiven; all good fortune will be attained, all ideals realized."[18]

Biblical Christianity criticizes the NSB belief that chanting in itself will produce blessings. Jesus said, "When you pray, do not keep on babbling like pagans, for they think they will be heard because of their many words. Do not be like them, for your Father knows what you need before you ask him" (Matthew 6:7,8). Biblical prayer is not to some impersonal wooden idol, a symbol of karmic law. Biblical prayer is to the Lord of creation, the God who is eternal, personal, all-powerful, and all-good.‡ The believer can look expectantly toward God for answered prayer. Psalm 5:2,3,7,8 echoes the confidence of all believers:

Listen to my cry for help, my King and my God, for to you I pray. Morning by morning, O Lord, you hear my voice;

---

‡ We will discuss more fully the nature and attributes of God under the NSB doctrine of God.

morning by morning I lay my requests before you and wait in expectation.

But I, by your great mercy, will come into your house; in reverence will I bow down toward your holy temple. Lead me, O Lord, in your righteousness because of my enemies—make straight your way before me.

Contrary to the Eastern concept of karma, which asserts that one's station in life cannot be improved without ridding oneself of the bad karma accumulated in previous lives, the Bible declares, "He will respond to the prayer of the destitute; he will not despise their plea" (Psalm 102:17).

The prayers of NSB are self-centered. The Daimoku is designed to improve one's own station in life. As with most Eastern thought, NSB is not concerned with others; other people are believed to be in their present states because of the inexorable law of karma. The Bible, however, commands us to be other-centered in our prayer. We are to ask for God's blessings and intervention on behalf of others as well as for ourselves. James 5:16 admonishes Christians, "Therefore confess your sins to each other and pray for each other so that you may be healed. The prayer of a righteous man is powerful and effective."

The Bible also condemns prayer to idols (like the Gohonzon). The Apostle Paul contrasted the true God with idols in Acts 17:24,25,29:

The God who made the world and everything in it is the Lord of heaven and earth and does not live in temples built by hands. And he is not served by human hands, as if he needed anything, because he himself gives all men life and breath and everything else.

Therefore since we are God's offspring, we should not think that the divine being is like gold or silver or stone—an image made by man's design and skill.

Nichiren Shoshu Buddhism is like other cults in that it has its own vocabulary and makes reality and truth relative to itself. With confused semantics and relativism, NSB members have no way to test NSB objectively. The members become caught in the exclusive "reality" of NSB, cut off from the reality accepted by the rest of the world.

The flux of NSB is promoted through a cultic vocabulary that identifies opposite terms as synonymous with each other.

> [The Buddha's] entity is neither being nor non-being: Neither cause nor effect; neither itself nor another...neither this nor that, past or future...[19]

In one place the state of Buddhahood is described as being the only place of "absolute, indestructible happiness," "the state of immutable, permanent happiness," etc. Inconsistently, NSB also asserts that "even in the Buddhahood realm there may exist the possibility of retrogression to one of the other realms."[20]

This semantical problem is based on the presupposition that all is God. Because all is God, there can be no "opposites" as such. All is part of God. This is not just an interesting philosophical presupposition; it is a serious semantical problem which opens the door by which members leave the world of objectivity and enter a world of constant uncertainty. Nichiren Shoshu Buddhism perceives all of reality in the same subjective way it uses its vocabulary:

> The limitless, eternal perception arrived at by destroying the illusions of distinction and separation...the absolute, unbounded world of truth attained by transcending the relative, hypothetical, the conceptual, and all ideas of existence and nonexistence.[21]

> All aspects of reality are so closely interwoven that they are imminent in one thought or, more precisely, the essential life of one moment.[22]

In NSB (as in Eastern thought in general), good is bad, right is wrong, etc. The Eastern concept of "yin and yang"—the inseparable forces (good/bad, male/female, black/white, etc.)—can be seen reflected in the basics of

NSB.

However, if one accepts such a presupposition, he has essentially admitted that no language or thought is meaningful at all. But such an admission is impossible in NSB, since the thought "all thought is meaningless" is self-defeating. If that thought is meaningless, then thought has meaning after all! In the same way, to say that all is one, good is bad, black is white, etc. is to say everything and nothing. If good and bad, truth and error are reflections of the same God, then one cannot discern good or bad in anything. For a follower of NSB to assert that NSB is right is at the same time to assert that it is wrong. Who wants to embrace a religion that is wrong? As human beings endowed with rationality by our Creator, our daily lives show that we accept the presupposition of absolutes. Simply denying the existence of absolutes becomes an absolute itself, defeating one's irrational position. Even NSB cannot refrain from asserting absolutes:

> Even such a low religion as Christianity underwent terrible sufferings. It is only natural that we, who propagate the highest of all religions—Buddhism—should encounter formidable obstacles. Even Christians, despite their shallow doctrine, had the enthusiasm to spread their faith over the earth.[23]

> Buddhism is superior to Christianity and Islam because... it expounds the reality of life.[24]

From the above two quotes we see that not only does NSB assert some sort of objective truth, but it also claims to be superior to Christianity—a claim shared by almost all cults. NSB's misunderstanding of Chritianity is part of the reason for its rejection of Christianity.

> It seems that the impulse arising from a sort of hatred and hostility because of worshipping the crucifix is more dominant [among Christians] than the concept of love explained in the Bible. These dark emotions have not yet lost their devilish

influence upon Westerners or humanity as a whole.[25]

To our eyes, the Christian doctrine of love is much inferior and much shallower than the Buddhist teaching of Jiki [mercy]. This is the very reason why Christians, though fully aware of the evil of war, have not yet succeeded in completely eliminating war among themselves....Christians pay only lip service to absolute peace. They will never be able to fulfill that ideal.[26]

By attacking Christianity as inferior, Nichiren Shoshu Buddhism has challenged Christians everywhere to assert the truthfulness of Christianity. We must examine the doctrines of NSB and compare them to the doctrines of the Bible, which has been declared to be the Word of God by the One who rose from the dead to prove objectively His identity as the God of the universe (Luke 24:39; John 20:28; 1 Corinthians 15:14-20; Romans 1:3,4). First Peter 3:15 reminds us to "always be prepared to give an answer to everyone who asks you to give the reason for the hope that you have." We must obey the instruction of 2 Timothy 4:2 to "preach the Word; be prepared in season and out of season; correct, rebuke and encourage—with great patience and careful instruction."

NICHIREN SHOSHU BUDDHISM'S DOCTRINES

World View

In order to understand the principal doctrines of Nichiren Shoshu Buddhism, it is necessary to understand more of its world view. How does NSB believe that the world got here?

NSB has its own interpretation of Buddhism. This interpretation is extensively discussed in Chapter 1 of President Daisaku Ikeda's *Buddhism: The Living Philosophy*. Since Ikeda, as other NSB members, believes NSB to be a revival of original Buddhism, he traces Nichiren Shoshu from the Mahayana tradition of the first Buddha through T'ien-t'ai Buddhism to NSB founder Nichiren Daishonin. The sect's world view is basically a naive humanism, including evolutionism and a near-pantheism based upon certain selected principles of Buddhism. Since we have seen that NSB beliefs can contradict each other, we will see how NSB teaches belief in a pantheistic god, polytheism, and atheism all at the same time.

Atheistic (apart-from-God) evolution is taught in the following quotation:

> No one has ever advanced convincing evidence that life was at some time created in such a way as to break the laws of nature or to violate the processes of evolution. The ability of man to synthesize organic substances from inorganic substances and the success of artificial insemination prove that the will of a god is unnecessary.[27]

It is not our purpose in this book to discuss the scientific arguments for and against evolution.[28] However, using the Bible as our guide, we know that it *was* the will of God to create everything in the universe. Genesis chapters 1 and 2 tell us that "In the beginning God created the heavens and the earth" (verse 1); that "God created man in his own image" (verse 27); and that "God saw all that he had made, and it was very good" (verse 31a). The facts that we find order and design in the universe, that man has a moral conscience, and that man has intelligence point away from a random, nonintelligent source for the universe and point toward an intelligent, all-powerful Designer for the universe—God.

The universe is composed entirely of dependent things. The universe as a whole is contingent. The only satisfactory explanation for this contingent world is that it depends on a noncontingent Being for its existence. In fact, Paul tells us, "The God who made the world and everything in it is the Lord of heaven and earth and does not live in temples built by hands. And he is not served by human hands, as if he needed anything, because he himself gives all men life and breath and everything else'' (Acts 17:24,25).[29]

As part of the NSB view that all is one, NSB followers believe that life itself is so much a part of matter that neither can exist without the other.

> According to Buddhist thought, the idea of a completely in-animate—that is, lifeless—world is inconceivable. *Shoho* [the living organism] and *eho* [the environment] are two aspects of one thing...indivisible because they are both ways in which essential life manifests itself.[30]

> ...and *hijo* [inanimate objects] can manifest sentience; though their emotions and consciousness are dormant, given the right conditions, insentient beings can evolve into sentience.[31]

> ...the same essential life flows through beings in both categories. The sentient form represents life in action; the insentient form, life in a latent condition.[32]

Arguing from the NSB position, man is ultimately no different from the rocks and trees and stars. According to NSB, life pervades everything in the universe—only differing in form, not essence. This important NSB concept needs to be understood, since it forms the basis of the rituals of Nichiren Shoshu. It also defines the Nichiren Shoshu beliefs concerning life, death, heaven, and hell. We will discuss these beliefs in subsequent sections of this chapter. Ultimately, the NSB world view is completely selfish.

> Nichiren Daishonin is the True Buddha of Mappo [the current age], who perceived the ultimate law of the universe and life, and inscribed it as the Dai-Gohonzon. When a person believes in this and chants Nam-myoho-renge-kyo, his inner life-force and that of the universe fuse harmoniously and enable him to bring forth all his potentialities which otherwise would remain dormant.[33]

> When we fervently chant Nam-myoho-renge-kyo to the

Gohonzon, our life force will permeate the universe and the Buddha nature will emerge within ourselves, enabling us to fulfill our wishes.[34]

Whether a NSB member understands the world view of NSB or not, he still is likely to embrace NSB and chant the Daimoku to achieve self-gratification and self-satisfaction. One of the biggest advertising tools of NSB is its claim of large material returns accrued by members through chanting the Daimoku.

God

The monistic world view of Nichiren Shoshu Buddhism precludes its belief in a God separate from His creation. According to conflicting NSB writings, the God of NSB is pantheistic, polytheistic, and henotheistic.

By saying that God is pantheistic, NSB is saying that He is one with His creation; He *is* the creation. This denies the personality of God.

The power which this Buddha has is as great as that of the Universe; in other words he is the Universe itself. He possesses an eternal power—the force that can bring change to anything and everything.[35]

In Buddhism, however, it is "the Buddhist Law" which is absolute. Once you have mastered the "Law" you are equal to Buddha.[36]

Pantheism is not compatible with Christianity. God is not the creation. He has always existed and will always exist as distinct from His creation (Acts 17:24). Romans 1:22,23 shows the foolishness of pantheism: "Although they claimed to be wise, they became fools and exchanged the glory of the immortal God for images made to look like mortal man and birds and animals and reptiles." Psalm 33:6-9 clarifies the difference between God and His creation, and shows the supremacy of God over His creation:

By the word of the Lord were the heavens made, their starry host by the breath of his mouth. He gathers the waters of the sea into jars; he puts the deep into storehouses. Let all the earth fear the Lord; let all the people of the world revere him. For he spoke, and it came to be; he commanded, and it stood firm.

The polytheism of Nichiren Shoshu Buddhism is evident in many of its writings. The polytheism of NSB seems simplistic, since the many gods are usually identified with some force of nature or the universe that has been personified.

From an overall universal standpoint, the forces of nature are partial functions of the universe...the monotheistic God of the Judeo-Christian tradition, who is assumed to have created the universe, is no exception to this argument. [37]

The God of the Bible has no other gods with Him; there is only one supreme, all-powerful, eternal Creator. The Hebrew declaration of faith asserts the oneness of God: "Hear, O Israel: The Lord our God, the Lord is one" (Deuteronomy 6:4). We cannot please many gods, but only the one true God, our Father. He commands us to reject those who say " 'Let us follow other gods' (gods you have not known) 'and let us worship them'; you must not listen to the words of that prophet or dreamer. The Lord your God is testing you to find out whether you love him with all your heart and with all your soul. It is the Lord your God you must follow, and him you must revere" (Deuteronomy 13:2b-4a).

There are not many true gods, each a personification of some natural force. The true God is mightier than that—He receives praise from all creation (Psalm 148:1-4); He is the Author of creation (Psalm 148:5); His power is limitless (Psalm 147:5); and His wisdom is infinite (Psalm 147:5). The Jehovah of the Bible is the only true God. He declared, "Before me no god was formed, nor will there be one after me" (Isaiah 43:10b). Isaiah 44:6,8 records the words of God against polytheism: ''...I am the first and I am the last; apart from me there is no God....You are my witnesses. Is there any God besides me? No, there is no other Rock; I know not one.''

Nichiren Shoshu Buddhism is also henotheistic. This means that although NSB believes in the existence of many gods, there is one main god, or one god who is worshiped above all others. This is common among polytheistic religious systems.

The Dai Gohonzon (and its representations in the individual Gohonzons) is like the supreme God of NSB. It is the visible manifestation of the pantheistic NSB God. The attributes we ascribe to the God of the Bible are in NSB ascribed to the Gohonzon, of which it is said:

1. It is the savior of mankind.
2. It is the source of all divine help.
3. The believer has faith in the Gohonzon.
4. It is the only source of eternal good fortune.
5. One must render it full devotion.
6. It is the source of happiness.
7. It is the ultimate source of the universe.
8. It purifies believers.
9. It forgives sin and answers prayer.
10. It is omnipotent.
11. The Dai Gohonzon is said to anxiously await the world's worship, and holds the key to world peace and happiness.[38]

(At the time that Nichiren Daishonin was alive, he was said to be the highest incarnation of the Buddha, or life force of the universe. After his death, that power was attributed to the Dai Gohonzon.)[39]

Men and idols can never rise to the position of the true God. The God of the Bible is not limited to the finite world: He *created* the finite world. The Old and New Testaments contain many denouncements of such idol worship. Isaiah 44:9-20 contains one of God's most powerful denouncements of idol worship. A careful reading of the passage shows the futility of worshiping man or wooden idols.

> All who make idols are nothing, and the things they treasure are worthless. Those who would speak up for them are blind; they are ignorant, to their own shame. Who shapes a god and casts an idol, which can profit him nothing?...The carpenter...shapes it in the form of man, of man in all his glory, that it may dwell in a shrine. He cut down cedars...It is man's fuel for burning; some of it he takes and warms himself, he kindles a fire and bakes bread. But he also fashions a god and worships it; he makes an idol and bows down to it....He prays to it and says, 'Save me; you are my god.' They know nothing, they understand nothing; their eyes are plastered over so they cannot see, and their minds closed so they cannot understand. No one stops to think, no one has the knowledge or understanding to say, 'Half of it I used for fuel...shall I make a detestable thing from what is left? Shall I bow down to a block of wood?' He feeds on ashes, a deluded heart misleads him; he cannot save himself, or say, 'Is not this thing in my right hand a lie?'

In the New Testament we find that idols are nothing when compared with the Sustainer of the universe. First Corinthians 8:4-6 declares, "We know that an idol is nothing at all in the world and that there is no God but one. For even if there are so-called gods, whether in heaven or on earth (as indeed there are many "gods" and many "lords"), yet for us there is but one God, the Father, from whom all things came and for whom we live; and there is but one Lord, Jesus Christ, through whom all things came and through whom we live."

God cannot condone the idol worship of NSB. Paul warns us, "We should not think that the divine being is like gold or silver or stone—an image made by man's design and skill. In the past God overlooked such ignorance, but now he commands all people everywhere to repent" (Acts 17:29b,30).

Christ

The imitation Christ of Nichiren Shoshu Buddhism is not the Christ of the Bible. Although NSB practitioners are quick to affirm that a person can be a Christian and still practice the Gongyo and chant the Daimoku, the actual teachings of NSB on Christ are perversions. There is no room in NSB for the Christ of Holy Scripture. NSB is a new revolution without Jesus and by the power of Nichiren Buddhism;[40] Christ is replaced by Nichiren Daishonin. Of Nichiren Daishonin it is said, "In no other human being has the power and compassion of this faith been as vividly manifest...."[41] Denying Christ's self-revelation, President Ikeda said, "There is no place for absolutism or myths of omnipotent, anthropomorphic divinities...."[42] Christ's teachings are considered to be inferior to the teachings of NSB:

> To our eyes, the Christian doctrine of love is much inferior and much shallower than the Buddhist teaching of Jiki [mercy]. This is the very reason why Christians, though fully aware of the evil of war, have not yet succeeded in completely eliminating war among themselves...Christians pay only lip service to absolute peace. They will never be able to fulfill that ideal.[43]

The Jesus of Nichiren Shoshu Buddhism is not the Jesus of the Bible. The biblical Jesus is the only way to salvation (Acts 4:12); He is not merely one of many ways or truths, but is the *only* way, truth, and life (John 14:6). There are not many Christs, but only one—the unique Son of God (John 1:1,14,18; 1 John 5:1). Nichiren Daishonin is a man who died and ceased to directly affect this world we live in. Jesus Christ died for the sake of the whole world (1 John 2:2); was raised immortal and incorruptible from the grave (Luke 24:39; John 20:28; 1 Corinthians 15:3-55); and sustains the entire universe through His power (Colossians 1:17). Nichiren Daishonin called himself a priest, but he died and is here no more. In contrast, "because Jesus lives forever, he has a permanent priesthood. Therefore he is able to save completely those who come to God through him, because he always lives to intercede for them" (Hebrews 7:24,25).

Jesus Christ is God manifest in the flesh (John 1:1,14; Romans 9:5). Thomas called him "my Lord and my God" (John 20:28). We are not looking forward to absorption into the stuff of the universe through the power of the Dai Gohonzon, but instead we look forward to "the glorious appearing of our great God and Savior, Jesus Christ" (Titus 2:13).

Christ's teachings are not inferior to those of NSB. He did not come to bring us mystical and contradictory flashes of spiritual "wisdom." Instead, He came to save sinners, "to preach good news to the poor...to proclaim freedom for the prisoners and recovery of sight for the blind, to release the oppressed, to proclaim the year of the Lord's favor" (Luke 4:18,19).

Mankind

The Nichiren Shoshu doctrine about mankind comes from a monistic world view. Since NSB believes that all is God and God is all, it teaches that man is one with all existence and is in fact divine. NSB also teaches that man's experiences are part of the eternal cycle of flux prevalent in Eastern thought. In this system contradictions can be asserted, since what today is life may tomorrow be death, in an eternal cycle of repetition. Finally, NSB teaches that karma is the inviolable law of human existence, determining all of a person's good and bad fortunes.

Since all is God and God is all, the goal of human existence, according to NSB, is the realization of this oneness with the divine.

The campaign to awaken every individual to the Gohonzon, to that basic law which allows one to fuse with the universe, is the perennial mission of Nichiren Shoshu.[44]

No matter what obstacles we may encounter, I, Nichiren and my disciples can eventually attain Buddhahood unless we hold doubts about true Buddhism. You should never be sorry that you are not leading a peaceful life. Although I have taught this to my disciples day and night, many deserted the Lotus Sutra. At a crucial moment the foolish will often forget what they have promised.[45]

Nichiren Daishonin is the True Buddha of Mappo [the current age], who perceived the ultimate law of the universe and life, and inscribed it as the Dai-Gohonzon. When a person believes in this and chants Nam-myoho-renge-kyo, his inner life-force and that of the universe fuse harmoniously and enable him to bring forth all his potentialities which otherwise would remain dormant.[46]

...When we fervently chant Nam-myoho-renge-kyo to the Gohonzon, our life force will permeate the universe and the Buddha nature will emerge within ourselves, enabling us to fulfill our wishes.[47]

But more basic than anything else is our duty to guard the truth, the truth that we and the universe are one, and that a single ordinary human thought contains the entirety of universal life. This is the great rule of the Mystic Law, and protecting it will make us resolute and will enable us to find our own meaning in life and to create a society that has reason for existing.[48]

True, our life appears to be confined within a five or six foot body. But...man's inner life is interrelated and fused with the lives of other people, creatures and plant life...the ultimate purpose of Buddhism is to reveal the throbbing universal life within each individual. Only Buddhism can guide civilization because it casts light on the infinite dormant forces in man.[49]

As we saw in our discussion on the nature of God, man is not God. There is a distinction between God and His crea-

340 / *THE NEW CULTS*

tion. Man is created in God's image and thus is personal. The same cannot be said of the rest of creation (excepting angels). Since man is personal, he has conscious distinction from other men, God, and the rest of creation. We are distinct from the rest of creation in that we were created by God, in His image; as Christians we reflect that original image: "to be made new in the attitude of your minds; and to put on the new self, created to be like God in true righteousness and holiness" (Ephesians 4:23b,24).

Man is not one with the rest of creation. Although it is true that man is created (even as the rest of the universe is created), and that man and the universe are intimately interdependent, man is nevertheless distinct from the rest of creation, and exists in the unique image of God. Genesis 1:28 informs us that man was given dominion over the earth and everything in it. He was to subdue it. Man is distinct from the rest of creation and is individually personal.

God is not one with man in nature. Many places in Scripture deny that man is God or that God is man. Ezekiel 28:2 absolutely denies that man is God: "In the pride of your heart you say, 'I am a god; I sit on the throne of a god in the heart of the seas.' But you are a man and not a god, though you think you are as wise as a god." The corruptibility of man and the immutability of God are contrasted in Numbers 23:19: "God is not a man, that he should lie, nor a son of man, that he should change his mind. Does he speak and then not act? Does he promise and not fulfill?"

The pagans of Lystra also worshiped man as god. They assumed that the apostles Paul and Barnabas were gods, and they wanted to worship them. But Paul and Barbabas asserted the distinction between man and God by saying, "Men, why are you doing this? We too are only men, human like you. We are bringing you good news, telling you to turn from these worthless things to the living God, who made heaven and earth and sea and everything in them" (Acts 14:15).

Nichiren Shoshu Buddhism also believes that man's existence is unalterably bound to the cyclical flux which comprises the world. Man is believed to adhere to the NSB system of contradictions in which everything is the same and different, good is bad, man is alive and dead, etc. In NSB anthropology (study of man), man's eternal cycle goes through ten realms. When a soul passes from realm one through realm ten, he has passed through seemingly endless cycles of life and death to reach oneness with the life principles of the universe. If this does not seem logical, it is because NSB is illogical. Man is said to be locked into an eternal cycle, and yet at the same time NSB says that the cycles will end for souls that reach the tenth realm. (One feature of Eastern thought is that it does not follow the rules of logic with which we are familiar.) The Ten Realms are:

1. Hell (the realm of suffering via disease, poverty, despair, etc.)

2. Rapacity (the realm of desire, where one is controlled by desires for wealth, fame, etc.)

3. Animality (the realm of domination by the instincts)

4. Anger (the realm of domination by the competitive spirit)

5. Humanity or tranquility (the ordinary state of life)

6. Heaven or Rapture (the realm of joy)

7. Learning (the realm of appreciating the joy of knowledge)

8. Absorption (the realm of appreciating the joy of creative ability)

9. Bodhisittvu (the realm of desiring happiness for others)

10. Buddhahood (the realm of highest enlightenment attainable).

Man (or "talented animals," as Nichiren called men) generally functions in the first six realms. The next three are higher but still imperfect. Only Buddhahood is the realm of true happiness. In the confusing system of NSB, however, it must be remembered that each realm contains all the others. At any given moment a man may be dominated by one realm but partaking of all ten realms! The goal is to be able to control the condition of your life by chanting.[50]

> Those who chant Daimoku to the Gohonzon are able to display the purest and most powerful life in their daily activities, controlling the other nine conditions from *Jigoku* [hell] to *Bosatsu* [Bodhisattva].[51]

In the Nichiren view, death is only a return to a latent and different form of life. Life and death are one. This belief in the essential unity of all things, even life and death, is the justification for the NSB devotees' chanting for an abundance of material goods. NSB followers believe that the success of the chanting in providing them with all material wants proves the validity of the NSB system.

> ...When we fervently chant Nam-myoho-renge-kyo to the Gohonzon, our life force will permeate the universe and the Buddha nature will emerge within ourselves, enabling us to fulfill our wishes.[52]

We will further discuss these views on the realms of man's existence and the goal of man's experience in our discussion of the NSB doctrine of salvation.

Within the state of flux, man finds himself also believing that there is an element of man which is constant. The "essential life" is really man's true self. It is the only aspect of him that is not subject to *Jo-Ju-E-Ku,* the Buddhist law of constant flux.

> Buddhism squarely faces the transient, impermanent aspects of life and casts light upon that entity within life which is not governed by the principle of Jo-Jo-E-Ku...the "self" within your life—as it were, the essence of your life—will not change from the beginning to the end.[53]

The flux of NSB as it relates to human existence is described in the following quotations:

As sleep is a source of energy for daily living, so death might be described as a kind of rest period for the process of the birth of a new life. In other words, Buddhism is not a teaching designed to prepare men for death. It is instead an affirmation, an exaltation of life.

Nichiren Daishonin has described the nature of life as being and non-being, birth and death, disappearance and appearance, existence and extinction. All of these are essential and everlasting processes....Life-in-birth is appearance in this world; life-in-death is disappearance from this world and return to the essential life.[54]

Because there is no demarcation between any state of human existence in NSB, it is hard to determine if NSB believes that man is sinful. On the one hand are NSB quotes that assert the sinfulness of mankind.[55] On the other hand, since all is God and God is good, man is good and cannot sin.[56] In practice, it appears that NSB does believe that man is sinful, since karma, the Eastern law of cause and effect, is said to operate and since it appears to be man's mission to return to his perfect state of divinity. It seems unlikely that man would have to "return" to perfection if he had never left it.

Man in the doctrine of NSB is not the special creation of God, beloved of the Father and capable of personal interaction with his God and his world. In NSB man becomes just another insignificant quirk in the plane of divine existence which constitutes the entire universe.

By contrast, the Christian view of man asserts that man is created in the image of God, capable of personal interaction with both God and the world, and created to have fellowship with the one Lord and God (Genesis 1:26,28; 2:8; Deuteronomy 10:12). Man is sinful (Romans 3:23) and in need of a Savior. He cannot save himself (Romans 3:10-12).

Salvation

Salvation according to Nichiren Shoshu Buddhism is not

the salvation described in the Bible. Salvation in NSB is twofold, including one's ability to recognize his own divinity and one's own efforts to remove the penalty of his own bad karma through penance, chanting, and even reincarnation.

As with other cults that claim exclusivity, deliverance is possible only through NSB:

> The campaign to awaken every individual to the Gohonzon, to that basic law which allows one to fuse with the universe, is the perennial mission of Nichiren Shoshu.[57]

> In the light of the Daishonin's doctrine of Ichinen Sanzen, the most Christians can do is reach to the state of Rapture....I state with the utmost certainty that as long as a life, whether of an individual or of a nation, is confined to the world of Rapture, it will inevitably fall into darkness sooner or later....
> Salvation as promised by Christianity is limited in the sense that the most its followers can do it, as I have pointed out, is to enter the world of Rapture. Very few, if any, reach the state of Bodhisittva.[58]

Salvation does not come from Jesus Christ, but from NSB and NSB followers:

> There are many in society who are unhappy, distressed, weak and hard-hearted. To save each of these people with our whole heart is our mission and lifeblood. No other project is more difficult, no other mission is as important and noble as to save people.[59]

Nichiren Shoshu Buddhism is declared to be "the only salvation for man in these dark times,"[60] and salvation is declared to come only through the Gohonzon.

Salvation in Nichiren Shoshu Buddhism is attaining "enlightenment" of "Buddhahood." This is accomplished by one's faith, expressed through worship (chanting) to the Gohonzon and good deeds. NSB President Ikeda declared:

> If a person faithfully repeats this invocation, he will

become one with the essential universal life: that is, he will attain Buddhahood, the state of immutable, permanent happiness and of direct experience of the universal life....It must be remembered, however, that reciting Nam-myoho-renge-kyo is not mere recitation, it involves prayers and deeds as well.[61]

Buddhahood alone is a realm of absolute indestructible happiness: and all the other realms are, to varying degrees, delusion....Firm faith and practice of the Buddhist philosophy of life is the sole way to reach the Buddhahood realm.[62]

Salvation according to NSB is by works performed by the devotee. It is not by grace through faith in Jesus Christ.

If one accepts and believes in Gohonzon (My-oji-soku), one will be sure to attain enlightenment through sincere daily practice.[63]

To attain enlightenment requires continuing faith....There is no doubt, however, that they can attain supreme enlightenment quickly.[64]

Salvation is not possible without the Gohonzon, the focal point of NSB worship.

Needless to say, the ultimate goal of our practice of the Daishonin's Buddhism is to attain Buddhahood or enlightenment. Whether or not we can successfully achieve this objective depends on whether or not we can continue to embrace the Gohonzon.[65]

That salvation in NSB is completely self-centered and dependent on one's own efforts is clear from President Ikeda, who states:

The ultimate source of everything in the universe is the Gohonzon and yourself. Do not seek happiness outside of this relationship. You have the potential for the attainment of your ideal and dreams within yourself, so never doubt your ability to achieve them.[66]

NSB salvation is always open to nonhuman and even

346 / THE NEW CULTS

nonliving things!

This is the highest teaching of Buddhist philosophy that Buddhahood can be developed even in insentient or inanimate things under light of Nam-myoho-renge-kyo.[67]

The biblical doctrine of salvation is very different from the salvation of NSB. Biblical salvation is the hand of God reaching out to man, the one created in His image who willfully sinned and cannot now save himself. Salvation is offered freely to anyone who comes to God on God's terms. There is no organization which can save. The living God, who cannot be contained in anything material, is not like the god of the Gohonzon. The living God has Himself paid the punishment for sin because of His great love for sinful mankind. The result of salvation, according to the Bible, is peace with God and self and the promise of an eternity in the presence of God. Man is cleansed from the guilt of sin and will ultimately achieve the created perfection that God intended him to have. Christian salvation is completely by grace and has nothing to do with one's own works. Finally, Christian salvation does not depend on anything other than the grace and love of God, the Lord of the universe.

According to the Bible, God is the One who took the initiative and reached out to man, lifting him from the mire of his sins and placing him in right relationship to God through the sacrifice of His only Son. Sinful man does not want God (Romans 1:21,28,32). In fact, Romans 3:11 declares, "There is no one who understands, no one who seeks God." Romans 5:8 shows us that God took the initiative in saving us: "God demonstrates his own love for us in this: While we were still sinners, Christ died for us."

Man cannot save himself. Even the best of man's works are considered as filthy rags in God's perfect sight (Isaiah 64:6). The only "work" God approves is the one promoted by Jesus in John 6:29: "The work of God is this: to believe in the one he has sent."

Salvation comes freely to all who will avail themselves of

God's gift through Jesus Christ. Romans 3:24 says that we "are justified freely by his grace through the redemption that came by Christ Jesus." Christians are not under any law, even the imaginary law of karma. In fact, "Clearly no one is justified before God by the law, because 'The righteous will live by faith.'...Christ redeemed us from the curse of the law by becoming a curse for us...so that by faith we might receive the promise of the Spirit" (Galatians 3:11-14).

Acts 17:24 denies that God manifests in shrines like the Gohonzons: "The God who made the world and everything in it is the Lord of heaven and earth and does not live in temples built by hands." Thinking God is reached through a box like the Gohonzon is folly, according to Isaiah 66:1,2, where Jehovah declares His supremacy over all creation: "Heaven is my throne and the earth is my footstool. Where is the house you will build for me? Where will my resting place be? Has not my hand made all these things, and so they came into being?" The Lord goes on to say that the one who is righteous in his sight is the one "who is humble and contrite in spirit, and trembles at my word" (Isaiah 66:2b). In the New Testament we find that believers are called the temples of God (1 Corinthians 3:16; 6:19,20).

The result of biblical salvation is peace with God; it is not self-satisfied realization of one's own deity. Christ "came and preached peace to you who were far away and peace to those who were near. For through him we both have access to the Father by one Spirit" (Ephesians 2:17,18). The perfection we strive toward as Christians is not a perfection of deity or self-exaltation. It is the perfection of souls in obedient love to their Maker. "You may become blameless and pure, children of God without fault in a crooked and depraved generation, in which you shine like stars in the universe as you hold out the word of life" (Philippians 2:15,16a). The goal of Christian existence is described by the Apostle Paul in Philippians 3:12-14:

Not that I have already obtained all this, or have already been made perfect, but I press on to take hold of that for which Christ Jesus took hold of me. Brothers, I do not consider myself yet to have taken hold of it. But one thing I do: Foregetting what is behind and straining toward what is ahead, I press on toward the goal to win the prize for which God has called me heavenward in Christ Jesus.

Christian salvation does not depend on man's works, but on the grace and mercy of God. Romans 5:1,2 assures the believer, "Therefore, since we have been justified through faith, we have peace with God through our Lord Jesus Christ, through whom we have gained access by faith into this grace in which we now stand. And we rejoice in the hope of the glory of God."

The salvation of Nichiren Shoshu Buddhism is empty self-effort. It cannot produce genuine peace with God and the eternal life of personal fellowship with God so freely offered through the sacrifice of God's Son (Acts 20:28).

CONCLUSION

Nichiren Shoshu Buddhism attracts many followers because it is self-centered and it sometimes produces material benefits through chanting to the Gohonzon. However, the offerings of NSB are transient and insignificant compared to the eternal riches offered—and delivered—by the God of the Bible. The Bible tells us to seek the things of God before we seek material benefits. By coming to God first, we can be assured that He will take care of our material needs (Matthew 6:33,34) and will give us true spiritual joy for all eternity (Philippians 1:6).

CHAPTER NOTES

1. Daisaku Ikeda, *The Future Is Your Responsibility* (NSA, n.d.), p. 9.

2. Presidential Address by Daisaku Ikeda, 35th General Meeting of Nichiren Shoshu Soka Gakkai (Japan's Lay Organization), Nov. 2, 1975, in *NSA Quarterly*, Spring 1976, p. 24.

3. Ikeda, *Buddhism: The Living Philosophy* (Tokyo: The East Publications, Inc., 1974), p. 7.

4. Edward J. Thomas, *The Life of Buddha as Legend and History* (New York: Barnes and Noble, 1956), p. 2.

5. Ibid., p. 251.

6. Daisaku Ikeda, "Buddhism, the Living Philosophy," op. cit., p. 29, *NSA Quarterly*, Spring 1973, p. 37; etc.

7. James Hastings, ed., *Encyclopedia of Religion* (New York: Charles Scribner's Sons, 1916), vol. 8, p. 146.

8. *Encyclopedia Britannica*, 1978, vol. 2 (Micropaedia), p. 342.

9. Huston Smith, *Religions of Man* (New York: Harper & Row, 1958), pp. 99-108.

10. Kenneth Scott Latourette, *Introducing Buddhism* (New York: Friendship Press, 1963), p. 38.

11. Anonymous, *Nichiren Shoshu and Soka Gakkai* (NSA, no city, n.d.), pp. 138-39.

12. *Seikyo Times*, Oct. 1971, p. 51; K. Murata, *Japan's New Buddhism* (New York: Weatherhill, 1969), p. 114.

13. *Seikyo Times*, Oct. 1971, p. 51; March 1973, p. 62.

14. In conversation with a former follower of NSB and the author.

15. *Nichiren Shoshu and Soka Gakkai*, op. cit., p. 43.

16. *NSA Quarterly*, op. cit., Spring 1973, p. 59.

17. Ibid., pp. 59-60.

18. *Nichiren Shoshu and Soka Gakkai*, op. cit., p. 57.

19. *NSB Quarterly*, op. cit., Spring 1974, pp. 68-69; Fall 1973, p. 54.

20. Ikeda, *Buddhism: The Living Philosophy*, op. cit., pp. 39, 40, 56.

21. Ibid., pp. 33-34.

22. Ibid., p. 35.

23. *Seikyo Times*, November 1972, p. 45.

24. Ibid., March 1973, p. 27.

25. *NSA Quarterly*, Fall 1973, p. 127.

26. *Seikyo Times*, Nov. 1972, p. 45.

27. *Buddhism: The Living Philosophy*, op. cit., pp. 20, 23.

28. There are many fine books on evolution and Christian faith. See, for example, John W. Klotz, *Genes, Genesis, and Evolution* (St. Louis: Concordia, 1955), or A.E. Wilder-Smith, *Man's Origin, Man's Destiny* (Minneapolis: Bethany Fellowship, 1968).

29. For further information on arguments for the existence of God, see Norman Geisler, *Philosophy of Religion* (Grand Rapids: Zondervan, 1974).

30. *Buddhism: The Living Philosophy,* op. cit., pp. 25-26.
31. Ibid., pp. 26-28.
32. Ibid., p. 29.
33. *Seikyo Times,* March 1973, p. 59.
34. Ibid., Oct. 1972, p. 44.
35. Ibid., Oct. 1972, p. 37.
36. Anonymous, *The East* (Tokyo: The East Publications, n.d.), p. 26.
37. *NSA Quarterly,* op. cit., Fall 1973, p. 126.
38. *Seikyo Times,* March 1973, pp. 23, 24, 49, 50-51, 53, 54, 58; October 1971, p. 55; *NSA Quarterly,* Spring 1974, p. 43; Spring 1973, p. 87.
39. *Seikyo Times,* Oct. 1972, p. 37; *NSA Quarterly,* Fall 1973, p. 50.
40. *Nichiren Shoshu and Soka Gakkai,* op. cit., p. 3.
41. *Buddhism: The Living Philosophy,* op. cit., p. 59.
42. Ibid., p. 94.
43. *Seikyo Times,* op. cit., Nov. 1972, p. 45.
44. *NSA Quarterly,* op. cit., Spring 1973, p. 24.
45. Nichiren Daishonin, quoted on a bulletin board at NSA headquarters in Santa Monica, CA. Written in 1272 A.D.
46. *Seikyo Times,* op. cit., March 1973, p. 59.
47. Ibid., Oct. 1972, p. 44.
48. *The Future Is Your Responsibility,* op. cit., p. 15.
49. *NSA Quarterly,* op. cit., Spring 1974, p. 28.
50. *Buddhism: The Living Philosophy,* op. cit., pp. 34-36.
51. *Seikyo Times,* March 1973, p. 57.
52. Ibid., Oct. 1972, p. 44.
53. Ibid., Oct. 1972, p. 16.
54. *Buddhism: The Living Philosophy,* op. cit., pp. 59, 30-32.
55. *Seikyo Times,* Nov. 1972, p. 45.; *NSA Quarterly,* op. cit., Fall 1973, p. 18; *Seikyo Times,* op. cit., Oct. 1972, p. 37.
56. *NSA Quarterly,* op. cit., Spring 1974, pp. 140-41.
57. *NSA Quarterly,* Spring 1973, p. 24.
58. *Seikyo Times,* op. cit., Nov. 1972, p. 45.
59. Ibid., March 1973, p. 58.
60. *The Future Is Your Responsibility,* op. cit., p. 5.
61. *Buddhism: The Living Philosophy,* op. cit., p. 56.
62. Ibid., p. 39.
63. *Seikyo Times,* op. cit., Oct. 1972, p. 50.
64. *NSA Quarterly,* Fall 1973, pp. 30-32.
65. Ibid., Spring 1973, p. 45.
66. *Seikyo Times,* op. cit., March 1973, p. 24.
67. Ibid., Sept. 1972, p. 51.

11

THE RIDDLE OF REINCARNATION*

HISTORY

Reincarnation is the widely held belief that one's soul lives a succession of lives, gradually evolving into a perfect state, usually reached when a person becomes one with the infinite and impersonal God of pantheism. One lives his life on this earth, dies, and then is reincarnated (assumes a new body and new life). Hopefully each new incarnation gives the soul a moral and spiritual advantage over his previous life and enables him to move closer to oneness (nirvana in Eastern thought), when he will finally be released from the cycle of reincarnation.

Although modern beliefs in reincarnation generally find their origin in Eastern thought, we must distinguish between reincarnation and transmigration of the soul (sometimes called metempsychosis). Transmigration of the soul allows for the soul to live successively in any number of different bodies in addition to human bodies. The soul may be incarnated in animals and plants, and in some religions even in inanimate objects (such as rocks, etc.). Although transmigration is probably the earlier of these two Eastern

---

* Researched by Cal Beisner.

beliefs, reincarnation as its successor has met with considerably more Western acceptance than has transmigration.

Most ancient religions taught reincarnation, except those which were purely theistic, like Judaism (as well as Christianity, Islam, and Zoroastrianism). Most religions which have taught reincarnation have also believed in a pantheistic or polytheistic God. (Some forms of Hinduism attempt to hold both polytheism and pantheism.) Transmigration is still the teaching of pure Hinduism, but many offshoots of Hinduism and most Western proponents of such ideas have rejected transmigration and now embrace only reincarnation.

Reincarnation was never a part of early Christianity or even of Judaism. However, in later centuries cultic offshoots of Christianity and Judaism embraced reincarnation, among other heretical doctrines. Cabalistic Judaism (a medieval occultic Jewish cult based on the Cabala) and some forms of cultic Christian gnosticism held a belief in reincarnation.[1]

The majority of the cultic Christian gnostics today (Christian Science is excepted) teach reincarnation. It is on these cults that we shall focus our attention in this chapter. Gnosticism is generally described as a belief in emanations or hierarchies of communicants between the supreme God and base evil. Gnostics usually believe in an impersonal God which is pure spirit and completely good. Ranging down from God are emanations (sometimes called angels) who are progressively farther from God and closer to material existence, which is generally considered evil or fallen. Since man is material, but possesses a soul or spirit, the common gnostic believes that man is on his way to regaining his lost station, returning to spirit, and shedding evil for divine good. Gnosticism, like reincarnation, presupposes salvation by works. Since one must work to regain his divine stature as one with the divine spirit of the universe, he is hard-pressed to accomplish the requisite good works in only one lifetime. In reincarnation, one is given many lifetimes. Thus is accomplished the close marriage between gnosticism and reincarnation.*

There are many modern cults which teach and believe reincarnation. Aside from the many sects which are parts of Hinduism and are indigenous to India, the following are some of the groups which teach reincarnation today: Theosophy, the Unity School of Christianity, Edgar Cayce and the Association for Research and Enlightenment, Hare Krishna, Transcendental Meditation, Self-Realization Fellowship, the Vedanta Society, many Spiritist or Spiritualist sects,† and the Rosicrucian Fellowship. As representative of reincarnation beliefs, we will discuss Theosophy and the Association for Research and Enlightenment (A.R.E.) in this chapter.

THEOSOPHY

The Theosophical Society was founded in 1886 by Mme. Helena Petrovna Blavatsky (1831-91). Of Russian background, this woman left her husband and wandered the world for 20 years, saying that she was seeking spiritual truth. She especially studied spiritualism and other occultic cults and practices. She claimed to have received the truth of the ages, explaining the mysteries of the world, from the spiritual "masters" she visited in Tibet. When Blavatsky died in 1891, her Theosophical movement was directed by Annie Wood Besant and C.W. Leadbeater. The Theosophical Society now claims a U.S. membership of 6000.†[2]

The Association for Research and Enlightenment

---

* For additional information on more traditional gnostic cults, see Walter Martin, *Kingdom of the Cults*, especially Chapters 5, 9, and 14.

† See Walter Martin, *Rise of the Cults,* Chapter 7, for further information on spiritism.

‡ See Chapter 6 for other information on Theosophy.

(A.R.E.) was founded in 1931 by Edgar Cayce (1877-1945). Cayce was an American psychic whose powers apparently gave him the ability to diagnose and treat illnesses far in advance of the medical knowledge of his time. Known as the "sleeping prophet," Cayce would go into a trance and give "readings" on individuals. The "readings" might be medical (for which he is the best-known) but also concerned religion and reincarnation. Cayce claimed to be a devout Christian and aligned himself with parts of Protestantism through most of his life.

> Far from discouraging my work in giving readings, my studies of the Bible have given me greater understanding of the true meaning and significance of my experiences, and I certainly believe that the information contained in hundreds of readings in our files helps to clarify and explain my Bible for me. I consider the Bible the greatest of all records of psychic experiences.[3]

> The information which has come through my readings has always stimulated me to greater studies of the Scriptures and applications of the truths which they contain.[4]

The entity speaking through Cayce during his "readings" appeared to be different from Cayce himself. The voice was different, the personality was different, and the beliefs espoused by the voice were often contrary to Cayce's original tenets. However, when Cayce was later informed of the beliefs taught during his readings, he abandoned his own more-orthodox beliefs in favor of the mystical beliefs of his spirit companion.[5]

> In 1923, Cayce awoke from a trance in Dayton, Ohio, to be told that he had asserted the reality of reincarnation: that man is born in many different bodies. At that time Cayce did not himself believe in reincarnation; but when his sleeping self had repeatedly affirmed its reality, he came to terms with it, and incorporated it into his orthodox Christian doctrine.[6]

The paradox exists in the fact that much of the information

which came through the sleeping Cayce was extremely alien to the awakened Edgar Cayce's manner of thinking—and especially contrary to his fundamentalist Christian background. This is the foundation of our discussion. As such, the paradox presented Cayce himself with both an unceasing burden and still an undeniable appeal for further search and enlightenment.[7]

...the comments which came through the Life Readings on such subjects as akashic records, planetary sojourns, and past incarnations with their related karmic implications were decidedly alien to the awakened Cayce's manner of thinking. Nevertheless, the Life Readings were pursued from 1923 onward and comprise a major portion of the material in the Cayce files.[8]

SOURCES OF AUTHORITY

All of the Westernized cultic systems which teach reincarnation believe that the Bible contains spiritual truth. However, the Bible is not considered the infallible Word of God, is not considered complete, is not considered the only source of spiritual authority, and is usually alleged to teach or at least mention reincarnation.

Coupled with this reduced view of Scripture is the almost-mystical reliance on individual special revelation. Most reincarnationists inject such special revelation into their religious systems. In this way a whole religious and doctrinal system can evolve almost entirely from "messages from beyond"—whether alleged to be from God, departed spirits, aliens from other planets, or angels.

Closely related to this extrabiblical revelation is the attempt of most reincarnationists to deny the uniqueness of Christ as the only way to God. On the contrary, the reincarnationist will take what he likes from any and all religious systems, claiming that all are in one way or another representing spiritual truth. As rational thinkers, it is hard for us to understand how the unequivocal and exclusive claims of Christianity can possibly be harmonized with other religious systems and with reincarnation itself. The reincarnationist accomplishes this by adopting a theory of truth which in essence makes all language and words completely subjective in meaning. Truth becomes relevant on a purely personal level.

We often say that any movement, of any character, succeeds in so far as it has a portion of the truth. We may be sure *that's* the truth. Then don't worry because you disagree with any individual as to what your conception of any movement may be—don't think anyone is going to hell because he doesn't think as you do! Remember the three blind men who went to see the elephant! Just *know* that people may be right, but wrong as *you* would see it, with your eyes wide open.[9]

Then if this be true, it is possible that truth is a changeable thing—is a growth. Will it be possible for us to find something of which we can say *"This is Truth"* and know that it will answer in everything or in every way that life may present itself to us? I believe that we can.

...but *this is Truth:*
That which, kept before your mental mind, your spiritual mind, will continue to develop you upward!

...All right, then: what do we mean by developing upward? That which will enable you to hold the vision of what *you* worship as *your* God.

Every man, every individual, every object has its conception of its superior position. We would ask, then, "Well, would it answer the Indian who is looking for his Happy Hunting Ground?" Why wouldn't it answer? That which will enable him to hold before him what *he* worships as *his* God is Truth, to him.[10]

Truth to the reincarnationist is relative. What may be true for me may not be true for you. What the Bible asserts in one place may be denied in another, the argument goes, and thus the reincarnationist is able to assert how "Christian" his beliefs are while at the same time denying the cardinal doctrines of the Bible.

The extrabiblical special revelations associated with reincarnationists allegedly come from extraterrestrials, or God, or the divinity within the self, or angels, and/or departed spirits. The most common source of communication from beyond is from those souls who have "ascended"§ and who are willing to impart the special knowledge they have obtained in their many incarnations. Theosophy holds to this primary source for its extrabiblical authority. Such pronouncements from these ascended masters is considered infallible.

Moreover, if a student wants to make a serious study of the subject, and to be trained to respond to vibrations, he must, as we have seen before, place himself under discipleship in the inner school. This involves a position of absolute loyalty to the Head of the school, and a recognition of the unimpeachable nature of the knowledge dispensed in the school.[11]

The term Theosophy, in the modern sense of the word, is a highly comprehensive one. It 'may be described to the outside world,' according to one of its chief exponents, 'as an intelligent theory of the universe.' It is claimed that there exists, and has existed for untold ages, a body of supermen, adepts, initiates, the Brotherhood of the Great White Lodge (they are known by various names), who are possessed of all knowledge on every subject....From time to time, some parts of this knowledge have been revealed to such men as were found developed enough to receive it.[12]

According to the literature of the Theosophical cult...there is a great fraternity of 'Mahatmas' or 'Masters,' who are highly evolved examples of advanced reincarnations whose dwelling place is somewhere in the far reaches of remote Tibet. These divine beings possessed Madam Blavatsky, and utilized her services to reach the generations now living upon the earth with the restored truths of the great religions of the world, which have been perverted by mankind. In this highly

---

§ See Chapter 6 on the Ascended Masters.

imaginative picture the Theosophists add seven planes of progression previously noted, through which the souls of men must progress, on their way to the Theosophist's 'heaven' or Devachan.[13]

Although this special revelation was supposed to come from disembodied spirits, the Theosophists' methods for receiving messages were sometimes open to suspicion.

> The story of the investigation by the [Society for Psychical Research] of the phenomena connected with the famous 'shrine' at Madras in 1884 is now an old one; but, unfortunately, it is still significant....This shrine was a case built into the wall between two rooms in the house inhabited by Mme Blavatsky. Letters were placed in it addressed to the Masters; it was then kept locked, and answers from the Masters were in due course found in it, 'precipitated,' it was said, from their distant abode in Tibet. During the absence of Mme Blavatsky in England, certain employees of the Society brought various allegations of bad faith against her, including charges of tampering with the shrine. It was then discovered that there was a false back to the shrine and a secret way of access to it from the room behind, which was Mme Blavatsky's bedroom.[14]

Cayce and the A.R.E. hold a similar view of Scripture and extrabiblical authority. Although Cayce claimed to accept the Bible as God's Word, he subjected his Scripture reading to his psychic experiences, instead of the other way around. Instead of letting the Bible interpret or denounce his psychic experiences, he used his psychic experiences to "understand" and "interpret" his Bible. As noted previously, Cayce tended to reject what he had previously learned from the Bible in favor of what his psychic experiences taught him. He also pursued occultic practices that were explicitly forbidden by Scripture.

> Dreams, astrology, numerology, the vibrations from metal, stones, and so on, should be considered only as lights or signs in our experiences.[17]

Since reincarnationists deny the sole and absolute authority of the Bible, it is no wonder that their beliefs concerning the essential doctrines of the Christian faith are also perverted.

REINCARNATIONIST DOCTRINES

God

Most reincarnationists believe in a pantheistic, impersonal God. They believe that God (Greek *theos*) is in all (Greek *pan*) things—hence the word *pantheistic*. It follows naturally from this belief that, if God is all, and God is good, then all is good. Evil does not really exist, or is illusionary. It also means that each man is part of God and in that sense is divine. Such a fragmented God is not capable of independent personality. In fact, it is the ultimate aim of most Eastern religions to achieve oneness with the Ultimate by denying one's own personality.

>...the undifferentiated monadic essence originally breathed out by our Solar Logos through and by the countless experiences it has to undergo, gradually achieves differentiation, and gradually develops self-consciousness. Slowly, and through the infinite ages, that which was the mineral becomes the plant, that which was the plant passes into the animal kingdom, that which was the animal passes into the human kingdom, while the man is destined to become the god.[18]

>Matter must not be thought of as external to Deity. God being the one fundamental reality must necessarily embrace all that exists.[19]

>GOD. Creative Energy; Universal Mind; Universal Force; Father; Lord; Jehovah; Allah; Yah; etc.[20]

>God is not a person in the sense that we think of persons; yet to those of us who seek His presence, He is very personal. He is God to all—Father, to those who seek.[21]

In the universe all manifestations are of God and are one with Him...How wonderful to realize that there is only one force, one power, one presence, and that is God, the Father.[22]

The God of the reincarnationist is not the God of the biblical revelation. Throughout Scripture we find assertions that God is both personal and intelligent.

The accounts of Genesis concerning the creation presuppose and support that God is personal and not a part of His creation. Genesis 1:31 declares, "God saw all that he had made, and it was very good." God *made* the universe; He is not part of this created universe. In the discourses between God and Adam in Genesis chapters 1, 2, and 3 we see the subject-object distinction between God and man. As Adam was an individual person, so God is personal and distinct from Adam and all men.

However, we do not mean that God is just a big man or an anthropomorphic force. On the contrary, man is made in the image of God—not God in the image of man. By saying that man is in the image of God, we mean at least that man is spiritual and personal—he has will, intellect, reason, emotion: he can dialogue meaningfully with other personalities. We are not saying that man's physical body is in the image of God, which would necessitate that God also had material form, contrary to what is stated by Christ in John 4:24.

Personal pronouns are ascribed to God, and He is directly quoted in many Old and New Testament verses. One of the strongest assertions of the independent personality and the eternity of God is in Exodus 3:14, where God says to Moses, "I am who I am. This is what you are to say to the Israelites: 'I AM has sent me to you.'"

It is not the spiritually *elite* who conceive of God as part of His own creation; it is the spiritually *corrupt*.

For although they knew God, they neither glorified him as God nor gave thanks to him, but their thinking became futile and their foolish hearts were darkened. Although they claimed to be wise, they became fools and exchanged the glory of the immortal God for images made to look like mortal man and birds and animals and reptiles.[23]

The God of the Christian faith is so superior to the god of reincarnation that one wonders how people could prefer such impotence on the part of the reincarnationist's god to the majesty and splendor of the God of the Bible!

The God who made the world and everything in it is the Lord of heaven and earth and does not live in temples built by hands. And he is not served by human hands, as if he needed anything, because he himself gives all men life and breath and everything else. From one man he made every nation of men, that they should inhabit the whole earth; and he determined the times set for them and the exact places where they should live. God did this so that men would seek him and perhaps reach out for him and find him, though he is not far from each one of us.[24]

It is impossible for man to reach God on his own. No system of reincarnation or karma or good works can overcome the great gap between the created and the Creator. Job 37:23,24 describes this gap: "The Almighty is beyond our reach and exalted in power; in his justice and great righeousness he does not oppress. Therefore, men revere him, for does he not have regard for all the wise in heart?" The created cannot reach up and touch the Creator. Praise God that in Christianity God has reached down and touched us, and brought us close to Him with the love He expressed through the sacrifice of His own Son (John 3:16; Acts 20:28)!

The Trinity

Like most cultists, reincarnationists redefine the Trinity, believing in a triad of gods rather than in one God in three Persons. Reincarnationists also parallel gnostics in identifying the Holy Spirit as the female mother member of their Trinity.

Trinity. Everyone knows the Christian dogma of the 'three in one' and 'one in three'; therefore it is useless to repeat that which may be found in every catechism. Athanasius, the Church Father who defined the Trinity as a dogma, had little necessity of drawing upon inspiration or his own brain power; he had but to turn to one of the innumerable trinities of the heathen creeds, or to the Egyptian priests, in whose country he had lived all his life. He modified slightly only one of the 'persons'. All the triads of the Gentiles were composed of the Father, Mother, and the Son. By making it 'Father, Son, and Holy Ghost', he changed the dogma only outwardly, as the Holy Ghost had always been feminine, and Jesus is made to address the Holy Ghost as his 'mother' in every Gnostic Gospel.[25]

The Christian doctrine of the Trinity is not like pagan "trinities" (so-called). As Christians we believe that within the nature of the one eternal God are three distinct Persons—the Father, the Son, and the Holy Spirit. We do not believe in three gods. We do not anthropomorphize our God so that the Trinity imitates the human family of father, mother, and child. The three Persons of the Trinity are without sex and without origin (James 1:17; John 8:58; Hebrews 9;14). Although each Person expresses the full nature of the one true God, we do not confound the Persons. The Father is not the Son, the Son is not the Holy Spirit, and the Holy Spirit is neither the Son nor the Father.

That the Bible asserts the existence of only one true God is abundantly clear from many Old and New Testament verses. Isaiah 45:22 is representative: "Turn to me and be saved, all you ends of the earth; for I am God, and there is no other."

The Father is called "God" many times in Scripture, and is distinct from the Person of the Son and of the Spirit (John 14:16,17). The Son's deity is repeatedly upheld in the Bible (John 1:1; Colossians 2:9), and yet His personal distinction from the Father and the Holy Spirit is also evident (John 14:26). From a careful and objective study of the Bible, we conclude that within the nature of the one true God (Isaiah 43:10) are three distinct Persons (Luke 3:22)—the Father (2 Peter 1:17), the Son (John 20:28), and the Holy Spirit (Acts 5:3,4). These three Persons are the one God (Matthew 28:19).

The trinity of theosophy, A.R.E., and other reincarnationist groups is not the Trinity revealed in the Bible.

Christ

When reincarnationists approach the Person of Christ, they devise almost every belief about Him except that which is biblical. As we shall see more fully in our discussion of the reincarnationist doctrine of sin and salvation, most reincarnationists believe that Christ's main role is not as a Savior, but rather as an example.

> It is to His life as an example and to His explanations of the Creative Force that we may turn with a feeling of complete faith for understanding. Jesus demonstrated in a very practical manner the Oneness of God as related to each individual soul. He showed us what could be attained by an individual who was willing to make his will one with that of the Father. He promised us that He would make intercession for us, opening a way for all who seek to be drawn to the Father.[26]

> [Also] as was shown by the Son of Man, Jesus ...each and every soul must become, must be, the savior of some soul, must comprehend the purpose of the entrance of the Son into the earth: that man might have the closer walk with, yea the open door to, the very heart of the Living God![27]

Since reincarnation teaches a pantheistic, impersonal God, it follows that reincarnation also teaches that we can become God (realize our deity), just as Jesus did. For them, Jesus Christ was not unique in His deity: He was representative of what all of us can realize.

> He came in the flesh to show that we in the flesh could become as He, God in Spirit; and taught that we may be one,

364 / THE NEW CULTS

even as He and the Father are one.[28]

The message of The Revelation is that each of us, through a proper approach to the body, mind, spirit principle of the body as the Temple of the Living God, can attain the Christhood even as He did. And that 'Even greater things shall we do' because He has prepared the Way to the Father.[29]

Of course, as the ideal example, Jesus Christ supposedly went through many incarnations. Reincarnationists usually attribute all of history's religious leaders to previous incarnations of Jesus Christ. Coupled with this is the common gnostic separation of the "Christ" from "Jesus." Gnosticism declares that Jesus was only a man, and that "the Christ" was His divinity.

Hast thou not found that the essence, the truth, the real truth is One? Mercy and justice; peace and harmony. For without Moses and his leader Joshua (that was bodily Jesus at another time in the earth) there *is* no Christ. Christ is not a man! Jesus was the man; Christ, the messenger; Christ in all ages: Jesus in one, Joshua in another, Melchizedek in another; these be those that led Judaism![30]

Since the entire framework of Edgar Cayce's story of Jesus is based upon reincarnation, it should be noted that according to the Readings the Master possibly had some thirty incarnations during His development in becoming the Christ.[31]

Q. Please give the important incarnations of Jesus in the world's history.

A. In the beginning as Amilius, as Adam, as Melchizedek, as Zend, as ur, as Asaph, as Jeshua—Joseph—(Joshus)—Jesus.[32]

Recognizing the dichotomy between this view of Jesus Christ and the biblical and Christian view of Jesus Christ, Furst described Cayce's initial reactions to such ideas:

Surely the sincere and devout Cayce must have trembled fully inside upon hearing these accounts and then prayed long and hard concerning the source.[33]

The Jesus of the reincarnationists is not the Jesus of history or the Jesus of the Bible. The Bible teaches us that Jesus is the *only* way to salvation. He is much more than an example to us: He is our Savior, the One who gave his life to save us while we were still sinners (Romans 5:6-8). He is the only One who can offer us full and free salvation, cleansing us from our sins (Acts 4:12). In John 14:6 Jesus declared that He is the only way: "Jesus answered, 'I am the way and the truth and the life. No one comes to the Father except through me.'" Those who would say that Jesus is not the unique way to fellowship with God fall under the condemnation of Jesus' words: "If you really knew me, you would know my Father as well" (John 14:7).

Jesus did much more than give us an example: "How much more did God's grace and the gift that came by the grace of the one man, Jesus Christ, overflow to the many!" (Romans 5:15b). Romans 5, the great atonement chapter, declares the importance of Christ's atonement for us: "The result of one act of righteousness was justification that brings life for all men" (v. 18). Righteousness does not come from mimicking Jesus: grace reigns "through righteousness to bring eternal life through Jesus Christ our Lord" (Romans 5:21).

We do not become Christs, or God. We do not realize our own innate deity. We are creatures who can be made whole in the sight of God through the sacrifice of His Son. We cannot attain Christhood. Jesus Christ was the only God-man (Romans 1:3,4). The divine Person, the eternal Word, possessed all the attributes of the one true God as fully as did the Father and the Holy Spirit. But Jesus Christ also took on an additional nature, that of man. He was truly man and truly God. This unique event became the means of our reconciliation to God. Philippians 2:5-11 describes the incarnation of Christ, asserting both His divine nature and His human nature. We as created beings will never become God; instead, those of us who have received Christ will in the future receive glorified human bodies and live forever with God, worshiping and serving Him (1 Corinthians 15:42-56; Revelation 22:1-5).

The Bible does not separate the Christ from Jesus. Jesus *is* the Christ. First John 5:1 states, "Everyone who believes that Jesus is the Christ is born of God, and everyone who loves the father loves his child as well." Jesus was born the Christ (Luke 2:11). Simeon, the devout man to whom had been promised the seeing of "the Lord's Christ," counted that promise of God to be fulfilled when he saw the eight-day-old baby Jesus (Luke 2:26-32). There has never been, nor will there ever be, a time when "Jesus" can be separated from "Christ." This one Person with two natures, human and divine, is called *Jesus Christ.* The terms are often interchangeable. We are promised in 1 Timothy 2:5,6 that our Mediator is "the man Christ Jesus, who gave himself as a ransom for all men." God has pronounced Jesus the Christ: "Therefore let all Israel be assured of this: God has made this Jesus, whom you crucified, both Lord and Christ" (Acts 2:36).

The Jesus we trust for our salvation was not the product of successive incarnations through the ages. His soul had no need to work out its own sin (karma in Eastern terminology). As the divine Logos, He never sinned; when He was incarnated as Jesus Christ, He never sinned (Hebrews 4:15; 13:8). Hebrews 9:26 declares that Christ's incarnation was the only one necessary to accomplish our redemption: "He has appeared once for all at the end of the ages to do away with sin by the sacrifice of himself."

The men mentioned by Cayce as previous incarnations were as corruptible as we are. They were not sinless, like Jesus, although they did trust in God for their redemption and were used by God in mighty ways. When they died, their bodies turned to dust. The Apostle Peter declared that "the patriarch David died and was buried, and his tomb is here to this day" (Acts 2:29). By contrast, Jesus Christ rose from the dead victorious, in a glorified body. "He was not abandoned to the grave, nor did his body see decay" (Acts 2:31). Christ's resurrection body was tangible (Luke 24:39), glorified, and incorruptible (1 Corinthians 15:42-55; Romans 8:11; Philippians 3:21). Philippians 2:5-11, which describes Jesus' incarnation and death and resurrection, asserts only one incarnation, not many. Jesus was not the product of successful reincarnation. As we shall see in our discussion of salvation, reincarnation does not answer the question of sin. It is a false hope based on the false reasonings of men rather than on the wisdom of God. Isaiah 55:6-9 declares:

> Seek the Lord while he may be found; call on him while he is near. let the wicked forsake his way and the evil man his thoughts. Let him turn to the Lord, and he will have mercy on him, and to our God, for he will freely pardon. "For my thoughts are not your thoughts, neither are your ways my ways," declares the Lord. "As the heavens are higher than the earth, so are my ways higher than your ways and my thoughts than your thoughts."

Mankind

Reincarnation usually conceives man as divided between body and soul: the body is a limiting, harmful sheath of matter which imprisons the soul. The soul is an emanation from God, divine in its own right, but through disobedience it is chained to matter until it can restore its perfection and once again be lost in the mass of spirit and divinity. Man himself is not evil; he is divine. Man has rebelled against God (the question of how a part of God can rebel against itself is not answered) and so must pass through successions of incarnations which become progressively more pure and good until the individual is absorbed in the divine mass, the all-pervading spirit of God. (Also not answered by reincarnationists is the question of how, if everything in the universe is part of God, any of it—matter particularly—could be evil or separated from God. If all is God, then what happens when the successful soul finally rids itself of its restrictive body? Is the body part of God? Then how could it be bad? Reincarnation is basically illogical.)

Man is 'an emanation from the Logos, a spark of the Divine fire.' But that which came forth from the Divine was not yet man—not yet even a spark; for there was no developed individualisation in it. It was simply a cloud of Divine Essence, though capable of condensing eventually into many sparks.[34]

As we were created for companionship with the Father, being a portion of First Cause, it behooves us in materiality to manifest more and more our awareness of this relationship in our mental, physical and spiritual bodies.[35]

The soul is of God. It had its beginning in God and its ending is only in Him. To name the name of God is to recognize that we are a part of the Whole, and we know, because we are of the Whole, Our soul, as a part of Creative Force, came into being, and was given breath, by the will of the father, that it might be a companion with Him in his activity. Our soul is everlasting, containing eternal creative power, and through expressions of this power we may come to know ourselves to be one with Him. Then the destiny of the soul, as of all creation, is to become one with the Creator.[36]

...Spirit is Life and Consciousness—the absolute Consciousness which is God, or the rays of consciousness sent forth by Him, which form the individualities of men; which Matter is that other pole of the one universal Substance, through and by means of which consciousness can alone function.[37]

It should be understood that Life is One, that each soul, each entity is a part of the Whole, able, capable of being one with the Source, or the Universal Power, God, yet capable of being individual, independent entities in their own selves.[38]

As has been indicated by some, ye are part and parcel of all

Universal Consciousness, or God. And thus [part] of all that is within, the Universal Consciousness, or Universal Awareness: as are the stars, the planets, the Sun and the Moon....For ye are as a corpuscle in the body of God; thus a co-creator with Him, in what ye think and in what ye do.[39]

Error came into existence before the earth, the heavens, or space were created. Using free will, expressing selfish desire, spiritual beings (souls) separated themselves from a consciousness of Oneness with Creative Will. Life, in material bodies, is the reflection of this separation in this state of consciousness.[40]

The sum total of the beginning and end of our early existence is that we may fully realize that we are one with the Father and worthy to be companions with Him in glory.[41]

And, according to the Readings—*all sin*, all error, all evil, indeed *the only sin, is self!*[42]

In such a system as this there is no room for the idea of sin. What seem like temptations to evil are really only the downward pull of the grosser material of the outer vehicles. The matter of which they are composed is 'at a stage of evolution much earlier than our own....The tendency is always to press downwards toward the grosser material and coarser vibrations which mean progress for it, but retrogression for us; and so it happens that the interest of the true man sometimes comes into collision with that of the living matter in some of his vehicles.' Thus is the whole problem of evil summarily disposed of, or at least deprived of its moral aspect.[43]

In contrast to this, God tells us that man is not an emanation from God. We are not part of God, but are created by God to worship and serve Him (Genesis 1:26,27; 2:8; John 6:29). If the substance of God is indivisible (if God is all), then souls cannot emanate out from Him in some mystical way. Either God is one or He is not. The reincarnationist has an inconsistent system which simultaneously affirms one thing and yet denies it. God is said to be all, and yet human souls are said to have rebelled against God. God is said to be all and to be good, and yet man's rebellion is considered evil and the base material world his prison. And at the same time the reincarnationist denies that evil exists.

But the Scriptures teach that man is not eternal. He is a direct creation of God (Psalm 139:13; Genesis 1:26,27). He is not incarnated successively, forced to physically atone for sins of a previous life that he does not even remember. Hebrews 9:26-28 categorically denies such ideas and instead asserts the justice of God: "But now he [Christ] has appeared once for all at the end of the ages to do away with sin by the sacrifice of himself. Just as man is destined to die once, and after that to face judgment, so Christ was sacrificed once to take away the sins of many people; and he will appear a second time, not to bear sin, but to bring salvation to those who are waiting for him."

One of reincarnation's main beliefs concerning man is that man is basically good. After all, he is part of the divine and as such is exempt from sin. (Perhaps reincarnationists have neglected to note that this eliminates any need for reincarnation as a way of salvation.) But Scripture says that man is thoroughly sinful. He is separated from God by his sin and is unable to atone for his own sin.

> ...How then can we be saved? All of us have become like one who is unclean, and all our righteous acts are like filthy rags; we all shrivel up like a leaf, and like the wind our sins sweep us away. No one calls on your name or strives to lay hold of you; for you have hidden your face from us and made us waste away because of our sins.[44]

The Prophet Isaiah continues with the answer to man's sin problem. It is not by his own effort that he comes to God, because "We are the clay, you are the potter; we are all the work of your hand" (Isaiah 64:8). Salvation comes through the grace and mercy of the Lord, expressed in the sacrifice of His Son (Romans 3:21,22). We will discuss this further when we discuss the doctrine of salvation.

Job 33:12 denies that man is part of God: "But I tell you, in this you are not right, for God is greater than man." The distance between the Creator and the created is infinite. That which is created can never achieve a state of being uncreated. We are adopted sons of God (Romans 8:23); we are received by His grace. Only Jesus can claim to the true Son of God, one in nature with His Father (John 1:14; 5:18).

Salvation

Reincarnationism, like most other cults, teaches salvation by works. This self-salvation (autosoterism) is accomplished through the inexorable law of karma. Karma, an Eastern term, refers to the principle that one must atone for his own sins throughout successive incarnations. This is the backbone of the teaching of reincarnation. Since the weight of sin is so heavy on each individual, the reincarnationist reasons that no one life is long enough to work one's way out of the depths of such sin. Therefore, reasons the reincarnationist, man has many lives. He is reincarnated.

Theosophy offers no forgiveness for sin except through myriads of reincarnations ever progressing toward Davachan, and no eternal retribution for man's rebellion or sin, only the evolutionary terrors of Kamaloka.[45]

The Law of Karma, in its broadest sense, is the law of equilibrium, or re-adjustment, of cause and effect...while the function of the Law of Karma is to readjust the results ensuing from desires and thoughts and motives as well as from speech and action on the physical plane. Its operation as bearing on the individual has thus a twofold aspect, internal as regards character, external as regards circumstance and environment.[46]

The doctrine of *karma* in Hinduism is pitilessly and unflinchingly logical. This works itself out in two directions. First, since all suffering is the result of evil done in a former life, a sufferer is something akin to a criminal....Secondly, the law of *karma* is inexorable. If a man is born an outcaste or a leper, or if he falls into some great calamity, he has brought it on himself; and since his *karma* must work itself out, it is useless or worse to try to help him.... This is orthodox Hinduism, as believed and practised in India today; but the English Theosophist, brought up in a Christian atmosphere and impregnated with Christian ethical standards, stops short of the logical deductions from his own premises. 'Every one with whom we are brought into contact is a soul who may be helped,' says Mr. Leadbeater; but in order to say it, he must abandon the very doctrine of karma on which he and all Theosophists so much insist.[47]

It is clear that reincarnation answers many questions religion has left unanswered; for example, why people suffer terribly in their lifetimes when they are patently innocent of any wrongdoing, or when they are trying very hard to accomplish things and yet fail. To an average person, this seems unjust, unfair; and only reincarnation and the religions based upon it have an answer: what one has done in one lifetime may very well reflect upon the results one obtains in another lifetime. That is the law of just retribution, which extends over one's entire life cycle: the soul may reap in one lifetime what it has sown in another, and vice versa.[48]

After countless ages, the man becomes an Adept, 'capable of himself developing into a Logos'; the end is absorption into the Divine Essence from which he emanated: 'the dewdrop slips into the shining sea.'[49]

Salvation to the reincarnationist involves working out one's own karma. God is not sufficiently strong to save one apart from a man's own works.

The God, the Father, the Spirit, the Ohm, the influencing force in every activity, is not wholly sufficient unto man's salvation, in that he, man, is a free-will being, as intimated—Alpha, beginning; Omega, ending; for the separating, the confirmation, the segregation, the building, the adding to, are necessary in relation to those activities that lie between the beginning and the end.[50]

...each must return in *His way*—through the crucifixion of self. The possibilities commensurate with this return to the Creator are what can be termed (with some inadequacy) as 'God's Grace'.[51]

The hypothesis of reincarnation shows our inherent divinity, and the method by which the latent becomes the actual. Instead of the ignoble belief that we can fling our sins upon another, it makes personal responsibility the keynote of life. It is the ethics of self-help. It is the moral code of self-reliance. It is the religion of self-respect![52]

The mission of man's life is to move towards perfection, towards God. This is his *dharma,* his duty. In this struggle the forces of evil are bound to be defeated. This has been the case all along, and history will repeat itself.

You have no right to rest until you have fulfilled your mission of being perfect, of being divine, of establishing yourself in perfection.[53]

As we develop our spiritual forces, our soul forces within, we fan this spark into a flame which brings realization of our oneness and fellowship with the Creator of all things.[54]

'Thou shalt not make unto thee any graven image.' Why not? Because if you make an image, it becomes your God. But if you have for your God that which is within your own individual self—you yourself being a portion of the Creator—you will continue to build upward, to it![55]

The doctrine of karma is not found in the Bible. God is just, but He is also loving and merciful. Man's sin must be atoned for; in this one respect the reincarnationists are right. However, *God* is the One who has the right to decree the method of payment. After all, He is the one against whom we sin! God has not decreed the "inexorable law of karma." Instead, He has decreed that our sins can be atoned for only in the Person of His Son on the cross: "After he had provided purification for sins, he sat down at the right hand of the Majesty in heaven" (Hebrews 1:3). The reincarnationist is right in saying that man cannot atone for all of his sins in one lifetime. The Bible says that man could not atone for his own sins if he had thousands of lifetimes (Romans 3:10-12). Christians do not look forward to reincarnation; we look forward to *resurrection,* when Christ will return and clothe us with glorified bodies so that we may eternally serve and worship God (1 Corinthians 15:42-57). Our glorification is not accomplished by our own efforts, but by "victory through our Lord Jesus Christ" (1 Corinthians 15:57).

Observing the divine law can never save anyone, for the Scriptures clearly teach that men can never observe the law perfectly, and are consequently condemned by the law (Galatians 3:10-12). On the contrary, "Christ redeemed us from the curse of the law by becoming a curse for us, for it is written: 'Cursed is everyone who is hung on a tree.' He redeemed us in order that the blessing given to Abraham might come to the Gentiles through Christ Jesus, so that by faith we might receive the promise of the Spirit" (Galatians 3:13,14).

Ephesians 2:8-10 makes it clear that salvation comes not by working out one's karma, but comes instead by the grace of God: "For it is by grace you have been saved, through faith—and this not from yourselves, it is the gift of God—not by works, so that no one can boast. For we are God's workmanship, created in Christ Jesus to do good works, which God prepared in advance for us to do."

There are only two kinds of people recognized in the Bible: those who have been redeemed by the grace and sacrifice of Christ, and those who have rejected God's gift of salvation. By choice, Christians remain with God forever. By choice, nonbelievers remain alienated from God in judgment forever. (See Revelation 20:11-15 for details.) Reincarnationists recognize that their system is not the biblical revelation.

The doctrine of reincarnation, as found among the Hindus and Buddhists, is in some ways a flat contradiction of the

Christian notion that eternal bliss or eternal punishment may be the outcome of a man's activities during a single lifetime.[56]

But with Judaeo-Christian monotheism, the life cycle ends right then and there. You go to heaven or you go to hell, and that's where you stay. True, there is resurrection, but resurrection comes at one particular time for everyone in exactly the same way.[57]

Christians have the assurance from God's Word through the Holy Spirit that "If the Spirit of him who raised Jesus from the dead is living in you, he who raised Christ from the dead will also give life to your mortal bodies through his Spirit, who lives in you" (Romans 8:11).

Cases of Reincarnation

In recent years a spate of "documented" cases of alleged reincarnation have appeared in books, magazines, and films. Some of these cases seem extremely convincing on the surface. How are we to evaluate these cases of apparent past lives that seem to be validated by objective researchers and honest witnesses?

The answer lies in the fact that reincarnation denies the complete and exclusive value of the atonement of Christ. Thus reincarnation receives its supporting power from a source other than God. We must not forget that there is a malevolent personal being who has lived down through the ages and is designated "the god of this age" and "the ruler of this world" (2 Corinthians 4:4; John 14:30). This personal being could easily provide "evidence" from historical records (or even from living persons) that would seem to confirm reincarnation. But note that when such "evidence" is presented it is often associated with either non-Christian religious backgrounds or the world of the occult.

By asserting the false doctrine of reincarnation, Satan as the master counterfeiter attacks the value of Christ's sacrifice at Calvary, and teaches that man can do for himself through "cycles of reincarnation" what Christ could not do for him at Calvary. This is a compelling condemnation of the so-called "evidence" in favor of reincarnation.

CONCLUSION

What can we say about the psychic wonders performed by many people who believe in reincarnation? Can such miraculous things as Cayce's prophecies and "cures" be explained apart from God? As Christians, we believe in the spiritual dimension—the dimension of angels and demons. It is possible for demons to work through willing men who are not submitted to the power of the Holy Spirit (Romans 8:9; 1 John 4:4). Deuteronomy 13:1-5 gives solemn warning to those who would follow a teacher who performs miracles but denies the God of the Bible:

> If a prophet, or one who foretells by dreams, appears among you and announces to you a miraculous sign or wonder, and if the sign or wonder of which he has spoken takes place, and he says, "Let us follow other gods" (gods you have not known) "and let us worship them," you must not listen to the words of that prophet or dreamer. The Lord your God is testing you to find out whether you love him with all your heart and with all your soul. It is the Lord your God you must follow, and him you must revere. Keep his commands and obey him; serve him and hold fast to him. That prophet or dreamer must be put to death, because he preached rebellion against the Lord your God, who brought you out of Egypt and redeemed you from the land of slavery; he has tried to turn you from the way the Lord your God commanded you to follow. You must purge the evil from among you.

CHAPTER NOTES

1. Carpocrates was an early leader of a gnostic sect which believed in reincarnation. See discussion of him in Philip Schaff, *History of the Christian Church* (Wilmington, Delaware: AP&A, no date), Vol. II, p. 219; G. Kruger, "Carpocrates and the Carpocratians," in S.M. Jackson, ed., *The New Schaff-Herzog Encyclopedia of Religious Knowledge* (Grand Rapids: Baker, 1977), Vol. II, p. 423.

2. *Encyclopedia of Associations,* 1977 edition.

3. Quoted in Jeffrey Furst, ed., *Edgar Cayce's Story of Jesus* (New York: Coward-McCann, 1969), p. 346.

4. Ibid., p. 343.

5. Ibid., pp. 220, 324.

6. Colin Wilson, *The Occult: A History* (New York: Random House, 1971), p. 168.

7. Furst, op. cit., p. 10.

8. Ibid., p. 24.

9. Hugh Lynn Cayce, ed., *The Cayce Reader* (New York: Paperback Library, 1969), p. 30.

10. Ibid., pp. 32-33.

11. E.R. McNeile, *From Theosophy to Christian Faith: A Comparison of Theosophy with Christianity* (London: Longmans, Green, and Co., 1919), p. 51.

12. Ibid., p. 1.

13. Martin, *Kingdom of the Cults,* op. cit., p. 225.

14. McNeile, op. cit., pp. 37-38.

15. Furst, op. cit., p. 346.

16. Wilson, op. cit., p. 168.

17. Association for Research and Enlightenment, ed., *A Search for God,* Book II (Virginia Beach: A.R.E., 1968), pp. 47-48.

18. Anonymous ("By the Author of The Story of Atlantis"), *Man's Place in the Universe: A Summary of Theosophic Study* (London: Theosophical Publishing Society, 1902), p. 24.

19. Ibid., p. 16.

20. Association for Research and Enlightenment, *A Search for God,* Book I (Virginia Beach: A.R.E., 1969), p. 133.

21. Ibid., p. 93.

22. Ibid., p. 115.

23. Romans 1:21-23.

24. Acts 17:24-27.

25. Helena Petrovna Blavatsky, *The Theosophical Glossary* (Los Angeles: The Theosophy Company, 1966), p. 341.

26. *A Search for God,* op. cit., Book I, pp. 117-18.

27. Furst, op. cit., pp. 301-02.

28. *A Search for God,* op. cit., Book 1, p. 108.

29. Furst, op. cit., p. 72.
30. Ibid., pp. 172-73.
31. Ibid., p. 71.
32. Ibid., p. 38.
33. Ibid., p. 30.
34. McNeile, op. cit., p. 7.
35. *A Search for God,* op. cit., Book II, p. 109.
36. Ibid., pp. 63-64.
37. *Man's Place in the Universe,* op. cit., pp. 5-6.
38. Furst, op. cit., p. 362.
39. Ibid., p. 52.
40. *A Search for God,* Book II, p. 108.
41. Ibid., p. 18.
42. Furst, op. cit., p. 52.
43. McNeile, op. cit., p. 8.
44. Isaiah 64:5b-7.
45. *Kingdom of the Cults,* op. cit., p. 226.
46. *Man's Place in the Universe,* op. cit., pp. 7-8.
47. McNeile, op. cit., p. 11.
48. Hans Holzer, *Born Again—The Truth about Reincarnation* (Garden City, NY: Doubleday, 1970), p. xiii.
49. McNeile, op. cit., p. 8.
50. *A Search for God,* op. cit., Book II, p. 18.
51. Furst, op. cit., p. 52.
52. Quoted in *Kingdom of the Cults,* op. cit., p. 230, from L.W. Rogers, *Elementary Theosophy* (Wheaton: Theosophical Press, 1956), pp. 205-06.
53. Shrii Shrii Anandamurti, *Baba's Grace: Discourses of Shrii Shrii Anandamurti* (Ananda Marga Publications, 1973), pp. 150-51.
54. *A Search for God,* op. cit., Book I, p. 63.
55. Cayce, ed., op. cit., p. 34.
56. Wilson, op. cit., p. 513.
57. Holzer, op. cit., p. 41.

APPENDIX

THE LOCAL CHURCH OF WITNESS LEE*

It should be mentioned at the outset that the Local Church and its leader, Witness Lee, are different from the other groups we are dealing with in this book in that by and large the Local Church is composed of Christians who have been confused about major areas of doctrine and Christian practice. We must be sure to distinguish between the *doctrines and practices* of this group, which are not in harmony with the Bible, and the *members* of the Local Church, who are confused Christians. Technically speaking, the Local Church of Witness Lee cannot be called a non-Christian cult, but it has strong elements of cultism in some of its theology and practices.

HISTORY

The Local Church sect, under the direction and leadership of an elderly Chinese man, Witness Lee, has a 30-year history which began in the Orient and came to the Western world in the early sixties.

Lee began his religious career in China, under the direc-

★ Researched by Cal Beisner and Robert and Gretchen Passantino.

tion of the Chinese Christian mystic, Watchman Nee. Nee headed what he called "the Little Flock Movement," a Christian pietistic movement with roots starting in 1923 in China. During the time that Lee worked in the churches under Watchman Nee, he rose through the ranks to become the senior worker in Shanghai and the Philippines.[1]

Lee was born in 1905 in the Chefoo region of China. He was raised under both Christian and Buddhistic influences, and he made his public decision for Christ in 1925.[2] In 1927, Witness Lee began studying the magazine published by Watchman Nee's group, and later began preaching for the movement. For several years after that time, Lee presided at the "Little Flock" in Chefoo, until he was asked to move to Foochow to help Watchman Nee in the work there in 1946.[3]

According to the well-known Watchman Nee biographer, Angus Kinnear, Witness Lee—

...is energetic and authoritarian, thriving on large numbers, and has a flair for organizing people....Witness Lee was careful, of course, to disown the concept of "organization.'...But he exhorted everyone in the church to be submissive. "Do nothing without first asking," he urged. "Since the Fall, man does as he pleases. Here there is order. Here there is authority. The Church is a place of strict discipline."[4]

Some differences in doctrine and practice led to a split between Witness Lee and other leaders of the "Little Flock" after Watchman Nee was imprisoned. Lee finally struck out on his own, in the early 1950s, taking with him many of the Church members from Taiwan and the Philippines.

Witness Lee patterned his movement after the Little Flock movement plan used in China by Watchman Nee and his followers. The churches are based on the idea that the body of Christ can only be expressed in one gathering of believers in each city. This is often referred to as a "locality" doctrine, and is the trait by which the name "Local Church" was acquired.

In 1962 Lee founded the first American Local Church, in Los Angeles. Since then the movement has grown steadily but not dramatically, until some membership was lost in 1978 in a split.* Some Local Church spokesmen have claimed worldwide membership of 60,000, but the more likely figure is closer to 20,000. We know that there are 7000 members in Taiwan and the Philippines, 5000 members in the United States, and an additional 8000 members in other parts of the world.

The founding of the Local Church in Los Angeles was called "a new move of the Lord,"[5] and marked the Americanization of Lee's movement. For the first time, active recruitment was attempted with non-Chinese people. The individual churches call themselves after the name of the town in which they meet. The Church in Anaheim is considered the worldwide headquarters, and it is from there that Lee presides as leader.† Living Stream Ministries is the publishing arm of the movement and is also located in Anaheim.

Problems between the Local Church and other Christians were slight and scattered until 1974. In 1974, the churches following Lee began to proselytize much more openly than before, and to make their disdain of "organized Christianity" much more plain. Church members in the Southern California area began to disrupt other church's services, and to call other Christians members of "Babylon." These practices soon spread to the other Local Churches.

During the summer of 1974, Robert and Gretchen Passantino (researchers with Christian Research Institute and Christian Apologetics: Research and Information Service) researched the teachings and practices of the Local Church and lectured on their findings. Spiritual Counterfeits Project (in Berkeley, California) and indepen-

---

* More about the split later in this chapter.

† Although the churches claim no "leadership," "headquarters" or even "membership," such is not the case.

dent researcher Jack Sparks also produced material critical of the movement. In addition to the Passantino lectures, CARIS devoted several radio programs to discussions by the Passantinos on the Local Church. Jack Sparks's book *The Mindbenders* and Spiritual Counterfeit Project's book *The God-Men* later dealt with the erroneous teachings of the group.

Christian Research Institute published a booklet on the teachings of the Local Church and followed that up with a longer written treatment in 1978. All of these efforts by Christians to expose the errors of the movement were quickly attacked by members of the Local Church.

The debate erupted into the media in October 1977, when the Local Church published large advertisements in major newspapers throughout the country, challenging the allegations of Prof. Walter Martin, whose own allegations had been made in a lecture at Melodyland Christian Center on the first Sunday in October. The first advertisements spawned additional ones, until some observers estimated that over $50,000 had been spent by the Local Church in advertising solely for the purpose of denying the claims of Martin, the Passantinos, Sparks, and SCP, CRI, and CARIS.

However, the media blitz of the Local Church was less than successful in assuring its members of the truth of Witness Lee's teachings. In September 1978, Max Rappoport, then reputedly the number two man in the Local Church (and considered by some as most likely to succeed Lee in the event of Lee's death), defected from the Local Church. This powerful blow to Lee's authority was followed by the defections of two other trusted leaders, Gene Ford and Sal Benoit. In leaving, the three church officials convinced quite a few local members to follow them. Sal Benoit, former leader of the Boston Local Church, declared, "You don't know how insidious it is until you come out, and then you are amazed you could have been in it and not seen through it."[6]

Today, although the sect has suffered severe damage from internal problems and from the loss of so many members through defection, the Local Church is still run personally by Lee, and still disseminates mountains of literature and tapes to its members.

CHURCH STRUCTURE

As we said earlier, one of the cardinal tenets of the Local Church is the idea that the body of Christ can only be expressed in one gathering of believers in each city. This "locality" doctrine caused problems when Watchman Nee first promoted it in a mild form in China,[7] and the problems continue today under Witness Lee.

When the Local Church says that there is only one expression of the Body of Christ in any locality, it is not saying that there are many gatherings in one city that are harmonious. There is *no other meeting* of God's people in a city, in essence, except for the Local Church meeting. Lee states that his followers are the only ones in a given city who are representing the body of Christ. He says, "Roman Catholicism and Protestantism, as well as Judaism, all fall into this category, becoming an organization of Satan as his tool to damage God's economy [the Local Church]."[8]

[Satan] has taken another step by creating all the sects, denominations and divisions in the Body of Christ....God is moving in these days to recover. What is the way of His recovery?...the recovery of the proper unity. Not until these three things are recovered among us will we have a proper and adequate church life.[9]

...Thus, two cities, Babylon and Jerusalem, are opposed to each other. These two lines continue to the present day. The [Local] church is today's Jerusalem, and the Roman Catholic Church is today's Babel, Babylon....Only the pure, genuine local churches are in the line of Jerusalem today.[10]

What is this great Babylon? It is the mixture of Christianity. The great Babylon is a harlot mother with many harlot daughters. The Roman Catholic Church is the mother, and the denominations are the daughters.[11]

...Through all the centuries since then, religious people have followed in their steps, persecuting the genuine seekers and followers of the Lord in spirit and life, while still considering themselves to be defending the interests of God. Roman Catholicism and Protestantism, as well as Judaism, all fall into this category, becoming an organization of Satan as his tool to damage God's economy [the Local Church].[12]

Do not be cheated by today's Christianity. In Christianity there is a great deal of vain talk, especially regarding the church, but little of this talk is practical....If you do not have the local church, you do not have the church. God is expressed in Christ, Christ is expressed in the church,‡ and the church is expressed in the local churches.[13]

...Consider all the denominations. They only have division and confusion. Every denomination is a deviation from God's center lane. Some denominations are larger and others are smaller, some are farther away and some are closer, but none of them is in the center lane.[14]

Judaism is Satanic, Catholicism is demonic, and Protestantism is without Christ. They teach Christ's name, but He is not there. Do you really believe that today the living Lord Jesus is in the Protestant churches? Whether you believe it or not, the Lord says that He is outside the door.

We must all realize that there are four things on the earth today: Satanic Judaism, worldliness, demonic Catholicism, and Christless Protestantism....

...We must be saved from Satanic Judaism, demonic Catholicism, Christless Protestantism, and worldliness.[15]

This divisiveness is not the biblical teaching. The most obvious contradiction to localism found in the Bible is expressed in Romans 16:5. Paul, writing to the church in Rome,

---

‡ Further comments later about the Local Church doctrine that the church is becoming God.

asked the members there to greet the church which was meeting in the home of his friends, Aquila and Priscilla. Although they too lived in Rome, they evidently had a church that was meeting independently from the one Paul was writing to, since he specifically asked his readers to greet the two laborers. If Priscilla and Aquila had been members of that church, or even if their congregation had been in subjection to it, they would have been present at the reading of the letter. There would have been no need to send someone to them with Paul's greetings.[16]

The Local Church teaches that the ground of unity is localism, but Jesus said that the ground is Himself. Matthew 7:24-27 says:

> Therefore everyone who hears these words of mine and puts them into practice is like a wise man who built his house on the rock. The rain came down, and the streams rose, and the winds blew and beat against that house; yet it did not fall, because it had its foundation on the rock. But everyone who hears these words of mine and does not put them into practice is like a foolish man who built his house on sand. The rain came down, the streams rose, and the winds blew and beat against that house, and it fell with a great crash.

In other words, if our "ground" of faith is a living faith in Jesus Christ, we cannot fail. But if our "ground" of faith is anything else, even localism, we will not be able to last.

Matthew 16:16,18 confirms this by saying, "Simon Peter answered, 'You are the Christ, the Son of the living God.'" Jesus replied, "On this rock I will build my church, and the gates of Hades will not overcome it."

Lee would have us believe that the Church is only represented in one gathering in any given locality. In other words, since there is a Local Church of Witness Lee in Los Angeles, there cannot be any other church in Los Angeles.

Jesus refutes this in Matthew 18:15-20. He is talking about dealing with a problem between brothers. He tells how to solve the problem within the context of the church.

386 / THE NEW CULTS

That the context of this entire section is the church is evident from verse 17, which says, "If he refuses to listen to them, tell it to the church; and if he refuses to listen even to the church, treat him as you would a pagan or a tax collector." Then, in verses 18 and 19, Jesus gives the source of the authority for the judgment of verse 17. He states that the church has God's blessing from heaven for this judgment.

Finally, Jesus defines just what the church is, so that concerned Christians can discern whether they have the authority to make such judgments. Jesus' definition of the church is clear (v. 20): "For where two or three come together in my name, there am I with them."

The great church historian of the last century, Philip Schaff, noted the form of the early Christian church in Volume 1 of his monumental *History of the Christian Church*.

> We have no reason to suppose that it was at once fully organized and consolidated into one community. The Christians were scattered all over the immense city [of Rome], and held their devotional meetings in different localities. The Jewish and the Gentile converts may have formed distinct communities, or rather two sections of one Christian community.[17]

> ...In larger cities, as in Rome, the Christian community divided itself into several such assemblies at private houses, which, however, are always addressed in the epistles as a unit.[18]

Even Witness Lee's predecessor, Watchman Nee, did not go as far in his exclusivism as the Local Church does today. Nee declared:

> It is not my desire here to attack denominational Christianity as wrong. I only say again that, for the Body of Christ to find effective local expression, the basis of fellowship must be a true one. And that basis is the life-relation of the members to their Lord and their willing submission to Him as Head. Nor am I pleading for those who will make a fresh sect of

something called 'localism'—that is, the strict demarcation of churches by localities. For such a thing could easily happen. If what we are doing to-day in life becomes to-morrow a mere method, so that by its very character some of His own are excluded from it, may God have mercy upon us and break it up![19]

AUTHORITARIAN RULE

Part of the Local Church structure concerns the authoritarian system rigidly administered by Lee. This authoritarianism produces negative psychological results in many Local Church members.

Local Church members are taught to put the church before anything else in their lives. As is common to most cults, denial of self and exaltation of the organization are rampant.

> ...The church should be our only interest. What is your interest today—school? business? family? My only interest is the church. We all need to be such "drunkards" for the church.[20]

In the Local Church, members are kept so busy with church functions that they have almost no time for their families and, of course, no time to reflect on what they are taught.§

> We all need to devote more time for contacting people. One evening out of the week should be used for your personal affairs, three nights for the church meetings, and the three remaining nights for contacting people. In addition to these three nights, I hope that you will use every lunch hour for this purpose. Make an appointment with people to have lunch or dinner with them.[21]

Of course, as the head of the Local Church, Witness Lee is regarded as the church's supreme commander. He is considered specially led by God and to be obeyed implicitly. Lee

---

§ See this topic in Chapter 1.

once described the proper attitude toward himself by Local Church members:

> Let me tell you the secret to being solidly perfected to be a strong pillar for the Lord's move. Brothers like Benson Phillips and John So have been perfected because they have had no concepts of their own. Recently, Brother Benson declared strongly that he only knows to follow the ministry of Brother Lee. When John So stayed with us in Los Angeles, he knew nothing except to absorb everything of this ministry....Even when they saw mistakes, they forgot about them, having no time to waste discussing them.[22]

Lee expects his teachings to be followed as if they were from God Himself. He is confident that his years as a leader in God's organization have given him the necessary credentials to demand the obedience of his followers.

> These words are not merely a teaching, but a strong testimony to what I have been practicing and experiencing for more than 35 years. I have been captured by this vision. By the mercy of the Lord I have never changed my way or my tone. ☆[23]

Concerning the whole concept of the Local Church and Lee's direction of it, Lee said, "Do not think this is my teaching; it is the Lord's revelation."[24] We see, then, that the structure of the Local Church is completely authoritarian, with the wishes of the Church, determined by Witness Lee, the all-important goal toward which every Local Church member should strive.

LOCAL CHURCH MEMBERS

The Local Church attracts all types of individuals—simple, intellectual, emotional, depressed, joyful, etc. However, as diversified as those are who attach themselves to the movement, there is one basic psychological common

---

☆ Contrary to this claim, Lee contradicts himself numerous times in his writings.

denominator among the members: all seem to have some emotional need in their own lives that was not previously met. Often this need is simply a desire to feel needed and loved.

Through the many Local Church functions, this need often appears to be met. However, many people outside the group, especially the families of the ones involved, notice a very *unhealthy* change. Not only does it appear to them that the emotional need has not been met, but it appears that the member has been presented with a whole new set of problems. Several families have contacted us that had seriously contemplated obtaining professional therapy for these family members who were in the Local Church, since the members now seemed unable to cope with reality as they had been able to do before joining the Local Church.

From the outside, the Local Church appears very loving and considerate of its members. This is true. It is considerate of its own members, as long as those members are cooperative. However, we have already seen the Local Church attitude toward nonmembers, and the group's complete rejection of any other churches. However, if one tries to leave the Local Church, he is often told that God will punish him, that he has committed the unforgivable sin, or that he might die by God's judgment. The authors have on file testimonies from ex-Local Church members to whom these "divine threats" were made.

One of the characteristics of the cults that we discussed in Chapter 1 of this book is the inculcation of a paranoia in the individual members—a fear of persecution. This is true in the Local Church. Members are taught that all who are not in "the Lord's Recovery," another name for the Local Church, are "tools of Satan."

However, before we go further, we should point out one important difference between the Local Church and the other groups discussed in this book. At this time in its development, the majority of the members of the Local

Church are born-again Christians who have been swept into this group because they have not critically thought about what they have joined. Partly responsible for this phenomenon is the fact that most of the evangelism done by the Local Church is to people who are already Christians. Comparatively little is done to evangelize non-Christians.

The members' concentration on the Church sometimes even seems to obliterate their relationship to Christ. For example, when Gene Ford was still a leader in the Local Church, he gave his "testimony" twice in a small booklet which was published in response to the first CRI booklet exposing the group. These "testimonies" are *not* about Jesus: they are about the "the Church life." Each member talks about how empty his life was before he found the church, before he joined "the Lord's Recovery."

> ...let me tell you a little about myself. I graduated from a fundamental Presbyterian college and from the School of Theology of Drew University. I was a minister in the Methodist Church from 1949 to 1958. In 1958 I became an Episcopalian for doctrinal reasons and was ordained to the priesthood of that denomination....Through the testimony of Father Dennis Bennett of Seattle, I was introduced into the charismatic revival in 1962 and was active in the so-called "Pentecostal Revival" for several years. At the end of 1968, through the gracious mercy of God, my eyes were opened to see the Lord's up-to-date move on the earth today. Since that time I have been fully given to the Lord's recovery.[25]
>
> Allow me to give a word of personal testimony....I was not born yesterday. I am forty-six years old, with a certain amount of experience. I have a respectable amount of education. I have also spent a number of years in Christian work. Also, I am reasonably well acquainted with the Word of God. I saw the truth of the Lord's Recovery in 1968, and when I saw it, I took this way. Since being under the ministry of Witness Lee, I have enjoyed riches of Christ I never knew existed. Do you think I would be so foolish as to give up my future in the ministry if I had not found something worth giv-

ing it up for?[26]

Paul's testimonies in the New Testament are a striking contrast to Local Church testimonies. In 1 Corinthians 2:2 he said, "For I resolved to know nothing while I was with you except Jesus Christ and him crucified."

THE LOCAL CHURCH AND THE MIND

Local Church members have been taught not to be "in the mind" or to question anything they are taught, since to do so would be to act like the pagan world. The Local Church does not have any individualized Bible study. All study is exactly in harmony with what Witness Lee says. The Local Church "Bible studies" are actually studies of Local Church teachings, with the Bible used as backup material. Individuals studying the Bible have no need of any study books or even any thinking. Instead of using the intellect which God gave us to understand His Word, Lee tells us to "close our minds" when we approach the Bible.

As long as [Jesus] is with us, we need no regulations, no rituals, no doctrines or forms....Do you come to the meetings for teaching or for learning? We must come to the meetings for [spiritual] feasting.[27]

...there is no need for us to close our eyes to pray. It is better for us to close our mind!...Do not try only to learn the Bible. We must realize that this is a book of life, not a book of knowledge. This book is the divine embodiment of the living Spirit, and he is life.[28]

Simply pick up the Word and pray-read a few verses in the morning and in the evening. There is no need for you to exercise your mind in order to squeeze out some utterance, and it is unnecessary to think over that you read....It is better for us to close our mind!...There is no need for you to compose any sentences or create a prayer. Just pray-read the Word. Pray the words of the Bible exactly as they read. Eventually, you will see that the whole Bible is a prayer book! You can open to any page of the Bible and start to pray with any portion of the Word....There is no need to explain or expound the Word! Simply pray with the Word. Forget about reading, researching, understanding, and learning the Word. You must pray-read the Word.[29]

The Bible completely condemns this practice. Matthew 6:7 declares, "And when you pray, do not keep on babbling like pagans, for they think they will be heard because of their many words." Second Timothy 2:15 exhorts all Christians, "Do your best to present yourself to God as one approved, a workman who does not need to be ashamed and who correctly handles the word of truth." In Acts 17:11 the Bereans are commended for their diligent study: "Now the Bereans were of more noble character than the Thessalonians, for they received the message with great eagerness and examined the Scriptures every day to see if what Paul said was true."

Unfortunately, members of the Local Church act as though *experience* is the test for truth and the way to sure knowledge. Reasoning, logic, and intellect have nothing to do with knowledge; if one's reason contradicts one's experience in the Local Church, his reason must be wrong.

The Local Church structure and organization fits the criteria of a cult in several respects. However, we should be careful to reiterate that many of the members of the Local Church are Christians who have been drawn away from their original Christian churches and into the false system of the Local Church. Let us now look at the doctrines of the Local Church, which also conform to the characteristics of cultic doctrines.

DOCTRINE

Several cardinal doctrines of the Bible have been changed by the Local Church. While claiming to be representing biblical Christianity, the Local Church at the same time confuses the biblical doctrine of the Trinity, the nature of Jesus Christ, the nature of man, the biblical process of salvation, and the doctrine of the church. Although most of the present members of the Local Church are Christians (and, we believe, can have assurance of their faith), we must not forget that the doctrines they promulgate are not biblical and cannot in themselves draw a person to biblical faith. The majority of Local Church members are Christians, not because of the Local Church, but because they came to a saving knowledge of Christ *before* they became members of Witness Lee's movement.

The Trinity

The doctrine taught by the Local Church on the Trinity is known generally in church history as monarchianistic modalism. This doctrine arose in the third century A.D. as the result of the teachings of a man named Sabellius. Sabellius was not the only man who believed in a modalistic Trinity. Before him were Noetus, Praxeas, Epigonus, Cleomenes, Calistus, and Beryllus. Philip Schaff, noted church historian, observed that these forerunners of Sabellius were properly called Patripassians (meaning that they believed the Father suffered on the cross) rather than classic modalists. As he said, the Patripassians were embryonic modalists. Sabellius was the one who logically complicated the doctrine.

Although the Local Church does not believe everything that Sabellius taught in exactly the same way that Sabellius believed it, its understanding of the Trinity comes under the general category of what is known theologically as "Sabellianism" or modalism, which identifies the Person of the Father with the Person of the Son (and identifies the Person of the Holy Spirit with the Persons of the Father and the Son). The modalist generally describes God as one Nature and one individual Person who projects Himself in three distinct modes or aspects of His Being. Although a modalist may say that he believes in three Persons, he has merely redefined the word "persons" and still has an "economic" Trinity rather than the genuine biblical Trinity.

There are two major types of modalists. There are the "logical" ones, who claim that God cannot be both Father and Son and Holy Spirit at the same time and who therefore say that God was first the Father, became the Son, and then became the Holy Spirit. The illogical modalists recognize that often the Father, Son, and Holy Spirit are spoken of at the same time. These modalists try to say that the Father, Son, and Holy Spirit somehow exist at the same time and yet are each other.

Witness Lee and the Local Church teach *both* kinds of modalism. They teach that God was the Father, became the Son, and then became the Holy Spirit (and even that the Holy Spirit is becoming the Church—a topic we will deal with later). Witness Lee says:

> Thus, the three Persons of the Trinity become the *three successive steps* in the process of God's economy.#[30]

> In the heavens, where man cannot see Him, God is the Father; when He is expressed among men, He is the Son; and when He comes into men, He is the Spirit. The Father was expressed among men in the Son, and the Son became the Spirit to come into men. The Father is in the Son, and the Son became the Spirit—the three are just one God.[31]

> Likewise, the Father, Son, and Spirit are not three Gods, but *three stages of one God* for us to possess and enjoy.[32]

> The Father as the inexhaustible source of everything is embodied in the Son.... In the place where no man can approach Him (I Tim. 6:16), God is the Father. When He comes forth to manifest Himself, He is the Son.... We know the Lord is the Son and that He is also called the Father.... Now we read that He is the Spirit. So we must be clear that Christ the Lord is the Spirit, too.... As the source, God is the Father. As the expression, He is the Son. As the transmission, He is the

---

All emphasis is ours.

Spirit. The Father is the source, the Son is the expression, and the Spirit is the transmission, the communion. This is the triune God....[33]

Such views are clearly unscriptural. They present a changing God, contrary to Malachi 3:6 ("I the Lord do not change") and Hebrews 13:8 ("Jesus Christ is the same yesterday and today and forever"). Even the Holy Spirit is called the "eternal Spirit" in Hebrews 9:14. The three Persons of the Trinity are eternally coexistent, and no one of them becomes another Person at any time.

Shortly after the first booklet by the Passantinos on the Local Church appeared, in which this error was pointed out, the Local Church tried to avoid the label of Sabellianism by indicating that Lee did not believe in successionism, but that he believed that all three Persons existed at the same time. The Local Church, however, did not change any of its previous statements, and Lee did not retract any of the quotes which were used by Christian researchers to prove that he believed in successionism. Both sets of statements continued to deny a real distinction among the Persons, teaching that the Father in His Person was the Person of the Son, and that the Person of the Son was the Person of the Holy Spirit.

> Although He is one God, yet there is the matter of threefoldness, that is, the threefold Person—the Father, the Son, and the Spirit....[34]

> The Son who prays is the Father who listens....[35]

> ...the Son is the Father, and the Son is also the Spirit. Otherwise, how could these three be one God?[36]

> The Son is the Father, and the Son is also the Spirit.[37]

While Lee thus tried to escape the charge of Sabellianism (without denying his previous assertions), he merely affirmed his support of another modalistic heresy, Patripassianism, which taught (as Lee does) that the Father and the

Son are actually the same Person at the same time. (Few Patripassians of the third and fourth centuries said much about the Spirit; one who did, Marcellus of Ancyra, taught the personal identity of the Spirit with the Father and Son, just as Lee does.)[38]

Even in this form, Lee's teaching is clearly unscriptural. That the Father, the Son, and the Spirit are distinct Persons is obvious in Scripture. They have separate, though never conflicting, wills (Luke 22:42; 1 Corinthians 12:11). Jesus is sent by the Father, and He and the Father send the Spirit (John 17:8; 15:26; 16:7; 14:26; 20:21). The Father speaks to to the Son employing the second-person pronoun "you": "You are my beloved Son..." (Luke 3:22). Jesus offered Himself to the Father through the Spirit (Hebrews 9:14). We should remember Jesus' words when He said that He came *not* to testify of *Himself,* but of Him who sent Him.

It is true that the Local Church and Witness Lee say that they somehow believe in the "three-and-one" God. This is their attempt to say that they believe as we do; yet they believe in the merging of the Persons of the Trinity, too. Gene Ford, a former Local Church spokesman, said, "We say unequivocally that God being three is one, and that God being one is three."[39] However, the word "unequivocal" means "admitting of no doubt or misunderstanding; clear." The Local Church's position on the "three and one" is anything but unequivocal. They have used the terms "one" and "three" without defining what they mean. God is one. One what? One Person? One God? One body? One principle? God is three. Three what? Mary Baker Eddy, the founder of Christian Science, believed that "God is three." Her problem was that she believed that "three" referred to the "three divine principles" of "love, truth, and life." The Local Church means by three "the matter of threefoldness, that is the threefold Person...."[40] Notice that they believe that the one *Person* has "threefoldness"—not that there are three eternal and distinct Persons, as the Bible teaches.

Fortunately, the great early-church theologian, Augustine, did not suffer from such ambiguity.

> But when it is asked three what, then the great poverty from which our language suffers becomes apparent. But the formula "three persons" has been coined, not in order to give a complete explanation by means of it, but in order that we might not be obliged to remain silent.[41]

> But on the other hand it could not say that they were not three somethings (tria quaedam), since by denying this Sabellius fell into heresy. From the Scriptures we learn with absolute certainty that which we must piously believe, and the eye of the mind perceives it with its unfailing perception, namely, that there is the Father, the Son, and the Holy Spirit, that the Son is not the same as the Father, and that the Holy Spirit is not the same as the Father and the Son. When asked to explain what these three were, it answered substances or persons.[42]

The biblical Trinity may be defined as follows: within the nature of the one eternal God are three distinct Persons—the Father, the Son, and the Holy Spirit. These three Persons are the one God.

How can we demonstrate from the Bible that the Trinity is not an "economic" Trinity but a Trinity of three eternally distinct Persons in the one essential Being? The easiest way is to demonstrate each part of our definition in order to substantiate the definition as a whole.

The Bible teaches that there is only one God. We can see this from countless verses, such as Isaiah 43:10, Deuteronomy 6:4, 1 Corinthians 8:4-6, and 1 Timothy 2:5.

Our second step in testing our definition is to see if the Bible teaches that there is an eternal Person called the Father who is distinct from the Son, who is called God. Second Peter 1:17 calls the Father "God" and clearly distinguishes Him from the Son. First Corinthians 8:6 emphatically states that there is "one God, the Father."

After we have determined that there is an eternal, distinct

Person called the Father, we must see if there is a Person who is called the Word or Son in Scripture who is also called God and is distinguished from the Father. John 1:1 states of the Son, "In the beginning was the Word, and the Word was with God, and the Word was God." Hebrews 1:8 quotes the Father speaking to the Son, showing a distinction between the two and yet calling the Son "God." Hebrews 13:8 says, "Jesus Christ is the same yesterday and today and forever."

Finally, the Bible also teaches that there is an eternal and distinct Person called the Holy Spirit who is neither the Son nor the Father, but who is called God. Hebrews 9:14 talks of the eternal Spirit who worked in offering up Christ for our sins. In John 14:16 Jesus, speaking of the Holy Spirit, called him "another Comforter," which according to the original Greek word means another Person of the same nature or kind.

After careful study of these and many other passages, we can clearly see that there are three *distinct* Persons within the nature of the one God. We are forced by the Bible to the conclusion that these three distinct Persons are the one God. In Jesus' baptism, we see this distinctness illustrated: the Son came up from the water, the Holy Spirit descended as a dove, and the Father spoke from heaven.

Regardless of our reasoning, if the Bible teaches a certain doctrine, then as Christians we must believe it. We should discard our presuppositions and see what the Bible teaches. If the Bible teaches the doctrine of the Trinity as outlined above—that there are three eternally distinct Persons within the nature of the one God—then that is what we must believe as Christians. We cannot try to simplify this doctrine or try to make it easy to understand. We see what the Bible teaches and we believe it because it is the Word of God. We must never base our faith in God on experience alone, because experience can lie. We can only fully trust the Word of God.

Christ

The Local Church doctrine of Christ has been covered to some extent in the preceding section on the doctrine of the Trinity. We have seen that the Local Church has taken away Christ's unique existence as the beloved of the Father and the sender of the Comforter. He becomes, in Local Church theology, merely one of three aspects of the one Person of God.

However, the Local Church also misinterprets other aspects of Christ. They teach the error that, when the Word of God was incarnated, He "mingled" His two natures and became neither distinctly man nor distinctly God but a new nature, a mixture of God and man.

> Formerly it was impossible for man to contact the Father. He was exclusively God and His nature was exclusively divine. There was nothing in the Father to bridge the gap between God and man....But now He has...become incarnate in human nature. The Father was pleased to combine His own divinity with humanity in the Son.[43]

> With the Incarnation a dispensation began in which God and man, man and God were blended into one.[44]

This doctrine can be answered by many passages of Scripture, but one is sufficient. The clearest teaching on the two natures of Christ, known as the hypostatic union, is found in Philippians 2:5-7:

> Your attitude should be the same as that of Christ Jesus: Who, being in very nature God, did not consider equality with God something to be grasped, but made himself nothing, taking the very nature of a servant, being made in human likeness....

This clearly teaches that Christ was both man *and* God, not a strange mixture of the two. He was truly God, according to verse 6, and, since we know from Malachi 3:6 that God never changes, we know that when He emptied himself and became a man, He could not have stopped possessing the nature of God. He assumed an *additional* nature—that of a human. The Christian church has consistently taught that Christ had two natures, human and divine, which were in submission to one Person, the eternal Logos or Word. These two natures were *never* mingled.

Romans 9:5, speaking of all the blessings that Israel has had, culminates by declaring that Christ was the greatest blessing they had ever received: "...from [the Jews] is traced the human ancestry of Christ, who is God over all, forever praised!"

Mankind

The Local Church doctrine of mankind is affected by the Church's doctrine of Christ, already discussed, and its doctrine of the church, which will be discussed later.

Man as He was Created

At the very beginning of the Scriptures, God is seen creating man as the center of the whole creation for the purpose of expressing Himself. In His economy God intended that man should express Himself as the center of His whole universe.[45]

Lee also teaches that "flesh" is bad in itself. This is known as asceticism and is also related to "docetic gnosticism." (That ancient heresy taught that Jesus had no flesh, since flesh was bad; Jesus, being good, was pure spirit.) Lee says:

Man's body as originally created by God was something very good, but it has now become the flesh. The body was pure, since it was created good, but when the body was corrupted by Satan, it became flesh.[46]

Nowhere does Lee clarify what he means by "flesh" as opposed to a "body," although he does refer to becoming flesh as obtaining a damaged, ruined body.

The Local Church doctrine of man (as it concerns man

after the fall in Eden) is closely affiliated with the Church's strange doctrine of sin (and Satan). For this reason, we will suspend discussion of the doctrine of man for a short space and deal with the doctrine of sin.

Sin

Sin, to the Local Church, is nothing more or less than "the embodiment of Satan." After we define the Local Church concept of sin, we will discuss its doctrine of the fall of man and how sin affected that event.

> The body simply became the residence of Sin, which is the embodiment of Satan.... Sin is the embodiment of Satan and death is the issue or effect of Satan. This corrupted, transmuted body is called the 'body of sin,' and the 'body of death,' because this body became the very residence of Satan.[47]

According to the Local Church, the original sin of man was *not* a matter of ethics or doing good, but was a matter of choosing to be mingled with either God or Satan. The tree of life represented God (see *The Economy of God,* pages 105-06) or Christ (who is nothing more than the embodiment of the Father). The tree of knowledge represented Satan, with the result of death from mingling Satan with man. Man chose the tree of knowledge (that is one reason knowledge is so disparaged in the group today) and thus became mingled with Satan, also known as Sin.

> The significance of Adam taking the fruit of the tree of knowledge was that he received Satan into himself.... When he took the fruit of the tree of knowledge into himself...he received Satan, who then grew in him...thus, Satan grew in Adam and became a part of him.[48]

This doctrine actually takes away from the personality of Satan and makes him little more than a force. The Bible teaches clearly that Satan is a person and is distinct from man, even fallen man. In Matthew 4:1-11 Jesus was tempted by Satan (he is even called the tempter), and there is dialogue between them. If both were merely forces, they could not communicate at all. If Satan were a mere force, Jesus could not hold a conversation with him. This shows that Satan has independent personality, apart from any personality that he may demonstrate through a person who is Satan-possessed.

The distinction between Satan and fallen man is clearly shown in Revelation 20:10, where Satan is cast into the lake of fire, but not until verse 15 do we find that fallen men are also cast there. This succession of events necessitates a distinction between Satan and unsaved men.

Lee's insistence that the "body" is corrupt because the Bible calls the "flesh" corrupt displays his complete ignorance of the Bible's use of the literary device called metonymy. "Flesh" is used biblically to mean "sin." It does not necessarily bear any relatinship to the actual body that man possesses, any more than calling a king the "Crown" (a common example of metonymy) makes the king become the crown.

Before we return to the doctrine of man and see the different kinds of man that the Local Church envisions, we should deal with the Local Church doctrine of salvation, since that doctrine directly affects the doctrine of man held by the group.

Salvation

The doctrine of salvation in Local Church theology is closely linked with its doctrines of man and of the church. Since we need to return to our discussion of man, we will discuss only one aspect of the doctrine of salvation at this point and will discuss the other aspects and its ultimate implications under the section on church theology.

Lee teaches that in the same way that man fell, he was saved. He fell when Satan mingled with him, and he was saved when God mingled Himself, first in Jesus and then subsequently in each man who becomes a Christian. This goes into the doctrine of the deification of the church, or the church becoming God. Lee said:

> [After the fall] Satan was joyful, boasting that he had succeeded in taking over man. But God, who was still outside of man, seemed to say: 'I will also become incarnated. If Satan wrought himself into man, then let Me enter man and put man upon Myself.'[49]

> ...Subsequently, the Lord came and put man upon Himself to bring him to the cross....At the same time, Satan within this fallen man was put to death also....Christ brought man with Satan into death and the grave and brought man without Satan out of death and the grave. He left Satan buried in the grave....Now this resurrected man is one with Christ...through this resurrection man with God became one. By incarnation God came into man, and by resurrection man with God became one. Now God is in man's spirit.[50]

Since Lee has identified sin with Satan, he has detracted from the biblical value of the cross. We know that sin is disobedience to *God*—not Satan. According to the Bible, God did *not* mingle Himself with man in Christ (see the previous section on the doctrine of Christ), and it was *not* Satan who was put to death on the cross.

Romans 5:9,10 shows us that Christ died instead to *justify* us and to *reconcile* us: "Since we have now been justified by his blood, how much more shall we be saved from God's wrath through Him!...We were reconciled to [God] through the death of His Son...." Acts 20:28 shows us that it was God Himself who made the perfect sacrifice and who was sacrificed on the cross for our benefit—not some impersonal divinity mingled with a humanness: "...the church...which he bought with His own blood...." Finally, Hebrews 9:14 shows us that Christ's sacrifice was made *to God,* and not as some trick to trap and kill Satan: "...Christ, who through the eternal Spirit offered himself unblemished to God...." Hebrews 10:10 tells us that the cross sanctifies us: "by [God's] will we have been made holy through the sacrifice of the body of Jesus Christ once for all."

The Natures of Man

The Local Church teaches that man, at various times, has different natures. It teaches that the first man, before the fall, was "neutral," containing only human elements, but was created for the purpose of expressing God throughout the universe if he chose to "eat God" as represented in the tree of life. If that had happened, God would have immediately mingled with man and this new manifestation would have expressed God to the universe. However, man chose to "eat Satan" by taking the fruit of the tree of knowledge, and therefore man and Satan (also known as Sin) were mingled and became one. When Christ was incarnated, this "Sinman" clothed the divinity of Christ, allowing God to "trap" Satan and kill him (it) on the cross. This enabled God to return to His original plan of mingling Himself with man. Since that time, men who have come to Christ have lost their mingling with Satan and are now mingled with God in the same way. We are now ready to discuss Witness Lee's complicated and confusing doctrine of the church.

The Church

The Local Church teaches not only that it is the only true church, but also that the church is of a nature not usually taught in history. We shall see that it is not taught in the Bible, either!

Witness Lee teaches that the church, the Body of Christ, *is* Christ, and is becoming more and more "full" of God, to the point where eventually the church *is* God manifest in the flesh, fulfilling God's original intention to "work Himself into man."

Prior to the Incarnation God was God and man was man....The two were quite separate....With the incarnation a dispensation began in which God and man, man and God were blended into one...the very nature of God may be wrought into the nature of man...the life of the creature is blended with the life of the Creator....He invariably chooses the lot of each [Christian] with this goal in view—an increase of the divine content in our lives.[51]

The Father is in the Son, the Son is in the Spirit, and the Spirit is now in the Body. They are now four in one: the Father, the Son, the Spirit, and the Body.[52]

Speaking of the Church and Christ: "In number we are different, but in nature we are exactly the same.[53]

This Christ has expanded from one Person to thousands and thousands of persons. He was once the individual Christ, but in Acts He has become a corporate Christ.[54]

Then the day will come when the Triune God and the resurrected man will be one expression....[55]

Eventually, God will become us.[56]

The Bible says that man can never become God or a part of God. There is only one God, who is eternally the same. He will not become one in essence with us. Isaiah 43:10 declares, "You are my witnesses, declares the Lord, and my servant whom I have chosen, so that you may know and believe me and understand that I am he. Before me no god was formed, nor will there be one after me."

CONCLUSION

We have seen that Witness Lee and the Local Church teach error conerning the doctrines of God, Christ, man, sin, salvation, and the church. Witness Lee is *not* a sound Bible teacher, and the Local Church is cultic in many ways, both doctrinally and in structure, even though many of its members are Christians. One cannot be truly obedient to

God and join or remain in the Local Church or support the teachings we have critically analyzed here.

The fact that many immature Christians have been deceived into joining this group does not mean that the Local Church is close to orthodoxy, but only that it has become a clever counterfeit of the truth. Although we cannot and will not pass judgment on the souls of Local Church members, we can pass judgment on a number of Local Church teachings, which are not biblical. The Book of Acts describes the type of situation we find in the Local Church: "Even from your own number men will arise and distort the truth in order to draw away disciples after them" (Acts 20:30).

APPENDIX NOTES

1. Angus Kinnear, *Against the Tide* (Fort Washington, PA: Christian Literature Crusade, 1973), p. xiv.

2. Ibid., p. 88.

3. Ibid., p. 130.

4. Ibid., pp. 132-33.

5. Witness Lee, *The All-Inclusive Christ* (Anaheim: Stream Publishers, 1969), p. 5.

6. John Dart, "Cult Defector Warns Parents," in *Los Angeles Times,* December 11, 1978.

7. Kinnear, op. cit., pp. viii, ix.

8. *Recovery Version of Revelation* (Stream Publishers, n.d.), p. 17.

9. *Satan's Strategy Against the Church* (Stream Publishers, 1977), pp. 6, 8.

10. *Life-Study of Revelation* (Stream Publishers, 1977), p. 608 (Message Fifty-three).

11. *The Stream Magazine,* Vol. 7, no. 4, November 1, 1969, p. 19.

12. *Recovery Version of Revelation,* op. cit., p. 17.

13. *Young People's Training, Message Eight* (Stream Publishers, n.d.), p. 103.

14. *Young People's Training, Message Two* (Stream Publishers, n.d.), p. 24.

15. *The Stream Magazine,* Vol. 14, no. 4, November 1976, p. 12.

16. See A.T. Robertson, *Word Pictures in the New Testament: Romans* (Nashville: Broadman Press, 1931), p. 426.

17. Philip Schaff, *History of the Christian Church,* vol. 1 (Grand Rapids: Eerdmans, n.d.), p. 173.

18. Ibid., p. 220.

19. Watchman Nee, *What Shall This Man Do?* (Christian Literature Crusade, n.d.), pp. 133, 134.

20. Lee, *Life-Study of Genesis, Message Eighty-nine* (Stream Publishers, 1977), p. 1157.

21. Lee, *Young People's Training, Message Four* (Stream Publishers, n.d.), p. 51.

22. Lee, *Life-Study of Genesis, Message Eighty-Eight* (Stream Publishers, n.d.), pp. 1144-45.

23. Lee, *The Vision of the Church* (Stream Publishers), p. 10.

24. Lee, *Christ Versus Religion* (Stream Publishers), p. 13.

25. Gene Ford, *A Reply to the Tract Against Witness Lee and the Local Church* (Stream Publishers, 1977), p. 2.

26. Ibid., p. 40.

27. Lee, *Christ versus Religion,* op. cit., pp. 14-15.

28. Lee, *A Time With the Lord* (Stream Publishers), pp. 10, 11.

29. Lee, *Pray-Reading the Word* (Stream Publishers), pp. 8-12.

30. Lee, *The Economy of God* (Stream Publishers), p. 10.

31. Lee, *Concerning the Triune God* (Stream Publishers), pp. 8-9.

32. Ibid., p. 31.

33. *The Economy of God,* op. cit., p. 111; Witness Lee, *The All-Inclusive Spirit of Christ* (Stream Publishers), pp. 4, 6, 8.

34. Lee, *Concerning the Triune God* (Stream Publishers), p. 11.

35. Ibid., p. 25.

36. Ibid., p. 23.

37. Ibid., p. 17.

38. See Louis Berkhof, *The History of Christian Doctrines* (Carlisle, PA: Banner of Truth Trust, 1975), pp. 78-79.

39. *A Reply to the Tract Against Witness Lee and the Local Church,* op. cit., p. 16.

40. *Concerning the Triune God,* op. cit., p. 11.

41. Augustine, *The Trinity,* Book V, pages 18-88.

42. Augustine, *The Trinity,* Book VIII, page 233.

43. *The Economy of God,* op. cit., p. 11.

44. Lee, *The God of Resurrection* (Stream Publishers), p. 4.

45. *The Economy of God,* op. cit., p. 105.

46. *The Economy of God,* op. cit., p. 108.

47. Ibid., p. 109.

48. Ibid., p. 107.

49. Ibid., p. 109.

50. Ibid., pp. 109-12.

51. *The God of Resurrection,* op. cit., pp. 12-16.

52. Lee, *The Practical Expression of the Church* (Stream Publishers), p. 43.

53. Lee, *The All-Inclusive Christ,* op. cit., p. 103.

54. *Life-Study in Matthew, Message One* (Stream Publishers), p. 3.

55. *The Economy of God,* op. cit., p. 113.

56. Lee, *Life-Study in Genesis, Message Ten,* pp. 121-22.

CREDITS

PROFESSOR WALTER MARTIN is the Founder and Director of the Christian Research Institute in Anaheim, California. He is also Professor of Comparative Religions and Apologetics at Melodyland School of Theology and School of the Bible, host of the radio program "The Bible Answer Man," and the best-known authority on the cults and the occult in the United States today.

Dr. Martin's extensive ministry spans thirty years and the length and breadth of this country, as well as abroad. His unique work with the cults and Christian apologetics has earned him the respect and compliments of many of the church's prominent leaders, including Dr. Billy Graham, the late Dr. Donald Grey Barnhouse, and Dr. Bill Bright, President of Campus Crusade for Christ.

Dr. Martin has received recognition for his work from *Time, Christianity Today, Eternity, Moody Monthly, Logos Journal,* and many other Christian and non-Christian periodicals. He is the author of more than a dozen books, has contributed to many periodicals, and presents his specialized teachings of cult apologetics through ten sets of teaching cassettes and many individual teaching cassettes. His best-selling *Kingdom of the Cults* has been reprinted over thirty times and is considered the standard reference work on the major cults of our time.

The researchers who contributed their research to this book are all experts in their respective fields of research. Cal Beisner, a University of Southern California graduate, has studied cult apologetics for nine years and worked with Christian Research Institute and Dr. Martin for four years. He is now with Christian Apologetics: Research and Information Service. Todd Ehrenborg is a Rockmont Bible College graduate and Fuller Seminary student whose specialized research in the cult of Christian Science prepared him for work with the Christian Research Institute spanning two years. Carole Hausmann, a graduate of California State University at Long Beach, participated in several cult ministries for several years before joining the research team at Christian Research Institute for a one-year tenure. Elliott Miller came to Christ out of occultism, drug abuse, and Eastern thought. He has spent ten years in cult and apologetic research and ministry, four years of which were at Christian

Research Institute.

Robert Passantino is the director of Christian Apologetics: Research and Information Service. He has spent nine years in cult apologetics and general apologetics, has previously published his research projects, and frequently lectures on cults, apologetics, and the Bible. Kurt Van Gordon is Director of Practical Apologetics and Christian Evangelism and is an expert on Mormonism as well as some of the new cults, including The Way and the Unification Church. He was a missionary for Christian Research Institute for over three years. John Weldon is a veteran researcher and author who provided research for Christian Research Institute for more than seven years. His several books are well-respected in Christian circles.

Gretchen Passantino contributed significantly to the research of this book, and also contributed the writing of the manuscript. She completed her bachelor's work in comparative literature at the University of California at Irvine before joining Christian Research Institute as the senior research consultant, a position she held for five years while also pursuing her dedication toward writing. In addition to *The New Cults,* she has written articles for periodicals, pamphlets, and booklets, coauthored *Who Really Wrote the Book of Mormon?* and edited the Christian Research Institute periodical, *Forward.* She has written scripts for radio programs and edited the publications of the Christian Research Institute during her time there. She is currently the Research Department Director for Christian Apologetics: Research and Information Service, and continues to be active in free-lance writing and editing.

Thanks are also due to editor Raymond Schafer for his dedication and skill in preparing this manuscript for publication, and to Robert Passantino and Cal Beisner for their extra help on the Bibliography.

BIBLIOGRAPHY

General Works

Anderson, Sir Norman, ed. *The World's Religions.* Grand Rapids: Eerdmans, 1974.

Berkhof, Louis. *The History of Christian Doctrines.* Carlisle, PA: Banner of Truth Trust, 1975.

Buswell, James Oliver, Jr. *A Systematic Theology of the Christian Religion,* 2 vols. in 1. Grand Rapids: Zondervan, 1962.

Encyclopedia of Associations. Detroit: Gale Research Co., 1977 edition.

Enroth, Ronald M., and Ericson, Edward E., and Peters, C. Breckinridge. *The Jesus People.* Grand Rapids: Eerdmans, 1972.

Geisler, Norman L. *Philosophy of Religion.* Grand Rapids: Zondervan, 1974.

Guinness, Os. *The East: No Exit.* Downers Grove, IL: InterVarsity Press, 1974.

Harris, R. Laird. *Man: God's Eternal Creation.* Chicago: Moody Press, 1971.

Klotz, John W. *Genes, Genesis, and Evolution.* St. Louis: Concordia, 1955.

Lenski, Richard C. H. *The Interpretation of St. Paul's Epistles to the Galatians, Ephesians and Philippians.* Minneapolis: Augsburg, 1961.

Lewis, Gordon R. *What Everyone Should Know About Transcendental Meditation.* Glendale: Gospel Light, 1975.

Machen, J. Gresham. *The Virgin Birth of Christ.* Grand Rapids: Baker, 1930.

Martin, Walter R. *Essential Christianity.* Santa Ana: Vision House, rev. 1975.

————. *Jehovah of the Watchtower.* Chicago: Moody Press, rev. 1975.

————. *The Kingdom of the Cults.* Minneapolis: Bethany Fellowship, 1980.

————. *The Maze of Mormonism.* Santa Ana: Vision House, rev. 1978.

————. *The Rise of the Cults.* Santa Ana: Vision House, rev. 1980.

Means, Pat. *The Mystical Maze.* San Bernardino, CA: Campus Crusade for Christ, 1976.

Orwell, George. *Nineteen Eighty-four.* New York: New American Library, Signet Classics Edition, 1961.

Radhakrishnan. *Indian Philosophy.* London: George, Allen, and Unwin, Ltd., 1923.

Ramacharaka, Yogi. *The Philosophies and Religions of India.* Chicago: The Yogi Publication Society, 1930.

Robertson, A.T. *Word Pictures in the New Testament,* 6 vols. Nashville: Broadman Press, 1931.

Schaff, Philip. *History of the Christian Church,* 8 vols. Grand Rapids: Eerdmans, n.d.

Smith, Huston. *Religions of Man.* New York: Harper & Row, 1958.

Torrey, R.A. *What the Bible Teaches.* Old Tappan, NJ: Fleming H. Revell, 1933.

Vine, W.E. *Expository Dictionary of New Testament Words.* Old Tappan, NJ: Revell, 1940.

West, L.J., and Delgado, R. "Psyching Out the Cults' Collective Mania," in *Los Angeles Times,* October 26, 1978.

Wilder-Smith, A.E. *Man's Origin, Man's Destiny.* Minneapolis: Bethany Fellowship, 1960.

Wilson, Colin. *The Occult: A History.* New York: Random House, 1971.

Wuest, Kenneth. *The New Testament: An Expanded Translation.* Grand Rapids: Eerdmans, 1961.

Young, Warren. *A Christian Approach to Philosophy.* Grand Rapids: Baker, 1954.

Zaretsky, Irving, and Leone, Mark. *Religious Movements in Contemporary America*. Princeton, NJ: Princeton University Press, 1974.

Chapter 2: The Way International

Anonymous. *This is the Way*. New Knoxville, OH: The Way, n.d.

Anonymous. *Twenty-fifth Anniversary Souvenir Booklet*. New Knoxville, OH: The Way, 1967.

The Way Magazine, New Knoxville, OH: 1970-76.

Whiteside, Elena. *The Way: Living in Love*. New Knoxville, OH: American Christian Press, 1970.

Wierwille, Victor Paul. *Jesus Christ Is Not God*. New Knoxville, OH: American Christian Press, 1975.

——————. *The New Dynamic Church*. New Knoxville, OH: American Christian Press, 1971.

——————. *Power for Abundant Living*. New Knoxville, OH: American Christian Press, 1971.

——————. *Receiving the Holy Spirit Today*. New Knoxville, OH: American Christian Press, n.d.

——————. *The Word's Way*. New Knoxville, OH: American Christian Press, n.d.

Chapter 3: Hinduism: Hare Krishna and Transcendental Meditation (TM)

Anonymous, trans. *An English Translation of Transcendental Meditation's Initiatory Puja*. Berkeley, CA: Spiritual Counterfeits Project, n.d.

Back to Godhead (The Magazine of the Hare Krishna Movement). Bhaktivedanta Book Trust, 3764 Watseka Ave., Los Angeles, CA 90034.

Domino, George. "Transcendental Meditation and Creativity: An Empirical Investigation," in *Journal of Applied Psychology*, June 1977.

Embree, Ainslie T., ed. *The Hindu Tradition*. New York: The Modern Library, 1966.

Forem, Jack. *Transcendental Meditation, Maharishi Mahesh Yogi and the Science of Creative Intelligence*. New York: E.P. Dutton, 1974.

Goswami, Siddha Swarup Ananda. *Jesus Loves KRSNA*. Vedic Christian Committee and Life Force, Krsnan Yoga Viewpoint, 1975.

Haddon, David, and Hamilton, Vail. *TM Wants You! A Christian Response to Transcendental Meditation*. Grand Rapids: Baker, 1976.

Lewis, Gordon R. *What Everyone Should Know About Transcendental Meditation*. New York: Pillar Books/Gospel Light, 1975.

Mahesh Yogi, Maharishi. *Maharishi Mahesh Yogi on the Bhagavad-Gita*. New York: Penguin, 1967.

Mahesh Yogi, Maharishi. *Meditations of Maharishi Mahesh Yogi*. New York: Bantam, 1968.

Mahesh Yogi, Maharishi. *The Science of Being and Art of Living*. New York: New American Library, 1968.

Nicholls, Bruce J. "Hinduism," in Sir Norman Anderson, ed., *The World's Religions*. Grand Rapids: Eerdmans, 1974.

Prabhavananda, Swami, and Manchest, Frederick, transs. *The Upanishads: Breath of the Eternal*. New York: New American Library, 1948.

Prabhupada. *On Chanting the Hare Krsna Mantra*. Boston: ISKCON Press,

n.d.
Prabhupada, A.C. Bhaktivedanta Swami. *Bhagavad-Gita As It Is.* New York: Bhaktivedanta Book Trust, 1968.
——. *The Nectar of Devotion.* New York: The Bhaktivedanta Book Trust, 1970.
Towery, Jeanette. "The Impact of Transcendental Meditation on Cognitive Flexibility, Field Dependence, and Directional Priorities in Attention Deployment," reviewed in *Dissertation Abstracts,* July 1976, pp. 475-76.
Zander, Hans Conrad. "My Brief Life As a Hare Krishna," in *Atlas World Press Review,* September 1974.

Chapter 4: EST: Erhard Seminars Training

Anonymous. "Forum: *est,* Who Got What?" in *The East-West Journal,* December 15, 1975.
Anonymous. "Werner Erhard: All I Can Do Is Lie," in *The East-West Journal,* September 1974.
Anonymous. "Werner Erhard—An Interview with the Source of EST," Part 1, in *The New Age Journal,* September 15, 1975.
Anonymous. "Werner Erhard Live!" Part 2, in *The New Age Journal,* October 15, 1975.
Bry, Adelaide. *EST: 60 Hours That Transform Your Life.* New York: Avon, 1976.
Clarke, Gary. "The Struggle to Share It," in *The Graduate Review,* February 1977.
Erhard, Werner. "Life, Living, and Winning the Game," in *The Graduate Review,* July 1976.
——. "The Transformation of EST," in *The Graduate Review,* November 1976.
Frederick, Carl. *est: Playing the Game the New Way.* New York: Delta, 1976.
Gordon, Suzanne. *Lonely in America.* New York: Simon and Schuster, 1976.
Green, William. *est: 4 Days to Make Your Life Work.* New York: Simon and Schuster (Pocket Books Edition), 1976.
Hargrove, Robert. *est: Making Life Work.* New York: Dell, 1976.
Heck, R.C., and Thompson, J.L. "Est: Salvation or Swindle," in *San Francisco Magazine,* January 1976.
Kettle, James. *The est Experience.* New York: Kensington Corporation, Zebra Books Edition, 1976.
Kornbluth, Jesse. "The Fuhrer Over Est," in *New Times,* March 19, 1976.
Marks, Pat. *est: The Movement and the Man.* Chicago: Playboy Press, 1976.
Orth, Maureen. "The Sunshine Boy," in *Newsweek,* December 20, 1976.
Porter, Donald, and Taxson, Diane. *The EST Experience.* New York Award Books, 1976.
Rajneesh, Bhagwan Shree. Unnamed article in *The Graduate Review,* July 1977, explaining Werner Erhard's Aphorisms.
Rhinehart, Luke. *The Book of est.* New York: Holt, Rinehart and Winston 1976.
Rogin, Neil. "A Trainer Is a Graduate Who Does the Training," Part 1, in *The*

Graduate Review, May 1977.

Rubin, Jerry. "The est Things in Life Aren't Free," in *Crawdaddy,* February 1976.

Seligson, Marcia. "EST" in *New Times,* October 18, 1974.

Miscellaneous est Publications

"What Is the Purpose of the *est* Training?"

"Werner's Aphorisms"

est graduation booklet

"What's So"

Chapter 5: The Children of God

David, Faith. *Pioneering, Popularity, and Persecution.* London: Children of God, October 25, 1973.

——————. *Talk to the Translators.* London: Children of God, November 1972.

David, Moses. *Afflictions.* No city named: Children of God, November 25, 1976.

——————. *Alexander the Evil Magician!* Rome: Family of Love, February 7, 1978.

——————. *Atlanta!—Goddess of Atlantis!* Rome: Children of God, October 2, 1974.

——————. *The Basic Mo Letters.* Hong Kong: Children of God, 1976.

——————. *Come on Ma!—Burn Your Bra!* No city named: Children of God, December 22, 1973.

——————. *Communicate!* Rome: Children of God, April 25, 1977.

——————. *The Crystal Pyramid.* Dallas: Children of God, 1973.

——————. *Daily Might: Readings from the Mo Letters, Compiled by Justus Pound & Adar David.* Hong Kong: Family of Love, 1977.

——————. *40 Days! And Nineveh Shall Be Destroyed!* London: Children of God, November 12, 1973.

——————. *Death in Your Arms!* Rome: Family of Love, December 24, 1976.

——————. *Do You Want a Penis?—Or a Sword?* Rome: Children of God, July 19, 1976.

——————. *The Elixir of Love!* Rome: Family of Love, January 20, 1976.

—————— (aka. Father David). *Excommunication!* Rome: Family of Love, March 13, 1978.

——————. *The Fan.* Rome: Children of God, May 22, 1975.

——————. *The FF Revolution!* Rome: Children of God, August 7, 1976.

——————. *FF-er's Handbook!—Condensed Selected Quotes from More than 50 FF Letters!* Ed. by Justus Ashtree. Rome: Children of God, January 1977.

——————. "The Flirty Little Fish," in *The Basic Mo Letters.* Hong Kong: Children of God, 1976.

——————. *Flying Saucers! UFO's! Spiritual Vehicles?* Rome: Children of God, September 30, 1973.

——————. *God's Love Slave!* No city named: Children of God, April 21, 1974.

——————. *God's Whore?* Rome: Children of God, April 26, 1976.

——————. *Grace vs. Law.* Rome: Children of God, November 1977.

—————. *He Stands in the Gap.* London: Children of God, May 20, 1971.

—————. *Heavenly Homes!* Children of God, October 21, 1974.

—————. *Islam! (Chapter One).* Rome: Children of God, May 18, 1975.

—————. *The Kingdom, A Prophecy.* No city named: Children of God, August 20, 1971.

—————. *The Lit Revolution!—But Where Is the Harvest?* London: Children of God, February 17, 1975.

—————. *Love vs. Law.* Rome: Children of God, July 23, 1977.

—————. *Married to Jesus.* London: Children of God, December 1973.

—————. *More Truth!* Rome: Children of God, August 23, 1977.

—————. *Mountainslide.* Dallas: Children of God, October 21, 1971.

————— (aka. Father David). *Nationalisation—Indegenuity at Last!* Lima, Peru: Children of God, January 1978.

—————. "One Wife," in *Leader's Book.* London: Children of God, 1974.

—————. *Our Message.* London: Children of God, September 1974.

—————. *A Prayer for the Poor!* Rome: Family of Love, March 19, 1978.

—————. *Re-Organization, Nationalization, Revolution!* Children of God, January 1978.

—————. *Revolutionary New Life!* London: Children of God, June 1974.

—————. *The Revolutionary Rules.* London: Children of God, March 1972.

—————. *Revolutionary Sex.* London: Children of God, March 27, 1973.

—————. *The Shepherd's Rod!* Rome: Family of Love, March 13, 1978.

—————. *Shiners—Or Shamers!* No city named: Children of God, June 26, 1973.

—————. *Snowman.* London: Children of God, December 26, 1972.

—————. *Spaceship!* Rome: Children of God, December 17, 1976.

—————. *The Spirit World.* Rome: Children of God, November 1977.

—————. *7 Supporters!* Rome: Children of God, February 1978.

—————. *Survival.* Hong Kong: Children of God, 1976.

—————. *Taurig!* Rome: Children of God, October 5, 1977.

—————. *Teamwork!—The Gaffers!—Mo 'FF Tips!* Rome: Children of God, May 1976.

—————. *Winning the System.* Rome: Children of God, November 25, 1976.

—————. *The Word—New and Old (Mt. 13:52).* London: Children of God, September 1974.

—————. *The Wrath of God!* Rome: Children of God, March 5, 1977.

Hopkins, Joseph M. "The Children of God: Disciples of Deception," in *Christianity Today,* February 18, 1977.

Knoblock, James. *The Children of David: A Biblical Examination of Moses David and the Children of God.* Unpublished research paper. Available from the author: P.O. Box 711, Escondido, CA, 1977-78.

Moriconi, John. *Children of God, Family of Love.* Downers Grove, IL: InterVarsity Press, 1980.

Wallenstein, Herbert J., Assistant Attorney General in Charge. *Final Report on the Activities of the Children of God to Hon. Louis J. Lefkowitz, Attorney General of the State of New York.* Charity Frauds Bureau, September 30, 1974.

Chapter 6: The "I AM" Ascended Masters

Anonymous. *Man's Place in the Universe.* London: Theosophical Publishing Society 1902.

Ballard, Mrs. G.W., and Donald. *I AM Decrees for Ascended Masters Supply of All Good Things—Including Money.* Chicago: Saint Germain Press, n.d.

—————. *Purpose of the Ascended Masters "I AM" Activity.* Chicago: Saint Germain Press, 1942.

Jinarajadas, C.M.A. edition. *The Early Teachings of the Masters.* Chicago: Theosophical Press, 1881 and 1923.

King, Godfre Ray. *Unveiled Mysteries.* Chicago: Saint Germain Press, 1939.

Kuthumi. *Studies of the Human Aura.* Colorado Springs, CO: Summit University Press, 1971.

McNeile, E.R. *From Theosophy to Christian Faith.* London: Longmans, Green, and Co., 1919.

Morya, El. *The Chela and the Path.* Colorado Springs, CO: Summit Lighthouse, 1975.

Prophet, Elizabeth Clare. *Cosmic Consciousness: the Putting On of the Garment of the Lord.* Colorado Springs, CO: Summit University Press, 1974.

Prophet, Mark and Elizabeth. *Climb the Highest Mountain.* Los Angeles: Summit Lighthouse, 1975.

Spalding, Baird T. *Life and Teachings of the Masters of the Far East.* Santa Monica, CA: De Vorss and Co., 1924.

Spiritual Counterfeits Project Newsletter, II (9), December/January 1977. Spiritual Counterfeits Project, P.O. Box 4308, Berkeley, CA 94704.

Chapter 7: Silva Mind Control

Gross, Amy. "Mind Control: Four Days that Shook My Head," in *Mademoiselle Magazine,* March 1972.

McKnight, Harry. *Silva Mind Control: Key to Inner Kingdoms Through Psychorientology.* Laredo, TX: Institute of Psychorientology, Inc., 1972.

Merrill, Sam. "Under Control," in *New Times,* May 2, 1975.

Pellegrino, Victoria Y. "Getting High on Silva Mind Control," in *Today's Health,* November 1975.

Sylva, Jose, and Miele, Philip. *The Silva Mind Control Method.* New York: Simon and Schuster, 1977.

Taylor, Robert. "The Descent into Alpha," in *The Boston Globe,* August 20, 1972.

Chapter 8: The Church of the Living Word

Stevens, John Robert. *Apostolic Directives.* North Hollywood, CA: Living Word, 1976.

—————. *As Though Some Strange Thing Were Happening.* North Hollywood, CA: Living Word, 1973.

—————. *Beyond Passover.* North Hollywood, CA: Living Word, 1977.

—————. *Continuing in the Apostles' Teaching.* North Hollywood, CA: Living Word, 1976.

————. *Dedicated to Total Loss.* North Hollywood, CA: Living Word, 1976.

————. *The Delightful Bride.* North Hollywood, CA: Living Word, 1975.

————. *Every Blow Has to Count.* North Hollywood, CA: Living Word, 1978.

————. *First Principles.* North Hollywood, CA: Living Word, 1970.

————. *From Many Comes One.* North Hollywood, CA: Living Word, 1977.

————. *Lord, Make Me Overflow.* North Hollywood, CA: Living Word, 1975.

————. *Lord, What Do You Think About Babylon?* North Hollywood, CA: Living Word, 1975.

————. *The ManChild.* North Hollywood, CA: Living Word, 1972.

————. *New Testament Church.* North Hollywood, CA: Living Word, 1968.

————. *Plumb Perfect.* North Hollywood, CA: Living Word, 1977.

————. *The Prophet-Priest of the Kingdom.* North Hollywood, CA: Living Word, 1977.

————. *The Right to Become.* North Hollywood, CA: Living Word, n.d.

————. *Speak the Word of the Lord.* North Hollywood, CA: Living Word, 1971.

————. *To Every Man that Asketh.* North Hollywood, CA: Living Word, 1975.

————. *Very Legally Yours.* North Hollywood, CA: Living Word, 1974.

————. *Whole and Complete—At His Presence.* North Hollywood, CA: Living Word, 1977.

Chapter 9: Roy Masters: Foundation of Human Understanding

Anonymous. *Foundation of Human Understanding.* Los Angeles: Foundation of Human Understanding, n.d. (publicity pamphlet).

Chandler, Russell. "Radio Mystic 'Dehypnotizes' Followers," in *Los Angeles Times,* July 16, 1977.

Masters, Roy. *Be Still and Know.* Los Angeles: Foundation Press, 1976.

————. *The God Game.* Los Angeles: Foundation Press, 1977.

————. "Guilt" (cassette tape). Los Angeles: Foundation Press, n.d.

————. *How Your Mind Can Keep You Well.* Los Angeles: Foundation Press, 1971.

————. *Hypno-Christianity.* Los Angeles: Foundation Press, 1977.

————. *Hypnosis of Dying and Death.* Los Angeles: Foundation Press, 1977.

————. "Principles of Salvation" (cassette tape). Los Angeles: Foundation Press, n.d.

————. *The Secret of Life and Death.* Los Angeles: Foundation Press, 1964.

————. *Sex: The Substitute Love.* Los Angeles: Foundation Press, 1976.

Chapter 10: Nichiren Shoshu Buddhism

Anonymous. *Nichiren Shoshu and Soka Gakkai.* Nichiren Shoshu Association, n.d.

Ikeda, Daisaku. *Buddhism: The Living Philosophy.* Tokyo: The East Publications, 1974.

Ikeda, Daisaku. *The Future Is Your Responsibility.* Nichiren Shoshu Association, n.d.

Latourette, Kenneth Scott. *Introducing Buddhism.* New York: Friendship Press, 1963.

Murata, K. *Japan's New Buddhism.* New York: Weatherhill, 1969.

NSB Quarterly, Spring 1973. (A periodical of Nichiren Shoshu Buddhism.)

Seikyo Times, October 1971. (A periodical of the Nichiren Shoshu Association.)

Thomas, Edward J. *The Life of Buddha As Legend and History.* New York: Barnes & Noble, 1956.

Chapter 11: The Riddle of Reincarnation

Anadamurti, Shrii Shrii. *Baba's Grace: Discourses of Shrii Shrii Ananadamurti.* Los Altos Hills, CA: Anada Marga Publications, 1973.

Anonymous (by the author of "The Story of Atlantis"). *Man's Place in the Universe, A Summary of Theosophic Study.* London: Theosophical Publishing Society, 1902.

Association for Research and Enlightenment, ed. *A Search for God,* 2 vols. Virginia Beach, VA: Association for Research and Enlightenment, 1968.

Blavatsky, Helene Petrovna. *The Theosophical Glossary.* Los Angeles: Theosophy Company, 1966.

Cayce, Hugh Lynn, ed. *The Cayce Reader.* New York: Paperback Library, 1969.

Furst, Jeffrey, ed. *Edgar Cayce's Story of Jesus.* New York: Coward-McCann, 1969.

Holzer, Hans. *Born Again—The Truth About Reincarnation.* Garden City, NY: Doubleday, 1970.

Kruger, G. "Carpocrates, and the Carpocratians," in S.M. Jackson, ed., *The New Schaff-Herzog Encyclopedia of Religious Knowledge.* Grand Rapids: Baker, 1977 rpt.

McNeile, E.R. *From Theosophy to Christian Faith: A Comparison of Theosophy with Christianity.* London: Longmans, Green, and Co., 1919.

Rogers, L.W. *Elementary Theosophy.* Wheaton, IL: Theosophical Press, 1956.

Appendix: The Local Church of Witness Lee

Anonymous. *Recovery Version of Revelation.* Anaheim: Stream Publishers, n.d.

Anonymous. *Satan's Strategy Against the Church.* Anaheim: Stream Publishers, n.d.

Augustine. *The Trinity,* Vol. 10, Book 5, pages 187-88. Harvard Classic Reprints.

Dart, John. "Cult Defector Warns Parents," in *Los Angeles Times*, December 11, 1978.

Ford, Gene. *A Reply to the Tract Against Witness Lee and the Local Church*. Anaheim: Stream, 1977.

Kinnear, Angus. *Against the Tide*. Fort Washington, PA: Christian Literature Crusade, n.d.

Lee, Witness. *The All-Inclusive Christ*. Anaheim: Stream, n.d.

—————. *The All-Inclusive Spirit of Christ*. Anaheim: Stream, n.d.

—————. *Christ Versus Religion*. Anaheim: Stream, n.d.

—————. *Concerning the Triune God*. Anaheim: Stream, n.d.

—————. *The Economy of God*. Los Angeles: Stream, 1968.

—————. *The God of Resurrection*. Anaheim: Stream, n.d.

—————. *Life-Study in Genesis, Message Ten*. Anaheim: Stream, n.d.

—————. *Life-Study in Genesis, Message Eighty-eight*. Anaheim: Stream, n.d.

—————. *Life-Study of Genesis, Message Eighty-nine*. Anaheim: Stream, 1977.

—————. *Life-Study of Matthew, Message One*. Anaheim: Stream, n.d.

—————. *Life-Study of Revelation*. Anaheim: Stream, 1977.

—————. *The Practical Expression of the Church*. Anaheim: Stream, n.d.

—————. *Pray-Reading the Word*. Anaheim: Stream, n.d.

—————. *A Time with the Lord*. Anaheim: Stream, n.d.

—————. *The Vision of the Church*. Anaheim: Stream, n.d.

—————. *Young People's Training, Message Two*. Anaheim: Stream, n.d.

—————. *Young People's Training, Message Four*. Anaheim: Stream, n.d.

—————. *Young People's Training, Message Eight*. Anaheim: Stream, n.d.

Nee, Watchman. *What Shall This Man Do?* Fort Washington, PA: CLC, n.d.

Sparks, Jack. *The Mindbenders*. Nashville: Thomas Nelson Inc., 1977.

The Stream Magazine (a periodical publication of the Local Church). Anaheim: Stream Publishers.

The New Cults

by Dr. Walter Martin

Dr. Martin exposes the spiritually and psychologically dangerous games that modern-day "prophets" are playing with unwary followers. **The Truth about Rev. Sun Myung Moon**—A careful examination of the appeal of Sun Myung Moon, contradictions in Unification theology, and Biblical arguments refuting Moon's claims and methods. ■ **Reverend Ike—the Monetary Messiah?**—Reverend Ike maintains that "lack of money is the root of all evil," and he has accumulated quite a following to back him up! Dr. Martin sorts through the persuasive claims of this misleading mind science; one of the most rapidly growing non-Christian cults in America today. ■ **The Way**—This new and burgeoning pseudo-Christian movement is characterized by counterfeit charismatic manifestations, super sales pressure techniques and a questionable scholarship that erodes the basic doctrine of the deity of Christ. Dr. Martin presents a concise and thoroughly doctrinated analysis of The Way Biblical Foundation and its leader, Victor Paul Wierwille. ■ **EST**—The greatest consumer rip-off in years, says Dr. Martin! EST and its prophet, Werner Erhardt, seek to solicit the unwary (for an astronomical fee, of course) in a diabolical system of pseudo-psychological and spiritual exercises designed to "enlighten" the participant.
4 Tapes $23.98 A284509

How to Witness to Jehovah's Witnesses

by Dr. Walter Martin

When the knock comes, will you be able to answer the claim? With profound insight and compassion, Dr. Martin constructs a firm base from which you will be able to communicate the truth of Scripture to Jehovah's Witnesses.

Tape Titles:
Jehovah's Witnesses and the Real Jesus—Part 1
Jehovah's Witnesses and the Real Jesus—Part 2
Text and Terms Twisted by the Watchtower—Part 1
Text and Terms Twisted by the Watchtower—Part 2

4 Tapes $23.98 A284002

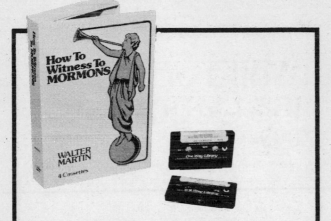

How to Witness to Mormons

by Dr. Walter Martin

This series is a must for anyone who wants to effectively communicate the Gospel to Mormons.
- Is there more than one God?
- Who is the Jesus of the Mormons?
- Can we become gods ourselves?

These and other questions are answered in detail by Martin. He untangles the knot of double meaning words and opens the door to meaningful discussion.

Tape Titles: Meeting Mormon Missionaries—Do's and Don'ts · The Priesthood—Who Has the Authority? · The Key to Mormon Theology—Romance of the Gods · The Bible vs. Joseph Smith, Brigham Young and Mormon Doctrine

4 Tapes $23.98 A284118

REVISED & UPDATED

Rise of the Cults

by Dr. Walter Martin

A highly informative and often startling handbook on the history, theology and practices of some of today's major cultic systems.

Rise of the Cults represents a revised and updated analysis of cultic problems—to assist pastors and concerned laymen!

Chapters include: Jehovah's Witnesses and the Dawn Bible Students, Mormonism, Spiritism, Baha'ism, Christian Science and the Unity School of Christianity, and Herbert Armstrong's Worldwide Church of God.

Paper $3.95 A424394

Seven Campus Curses
by Dr. Walter Martin

The seven most common objections to the
Christian faith are dealt with, in a hard-hitting,
lively discussion on the existence of God,
miracles, creation, Biblical inspiration, and other
issues crucial to the faith.
Single Cassette $5.98 A126679

Do's & Don't's of Witnessing
by Dr. Walter Martin

A practical, down-to-earth approach for sharing
your faith with others. Teaches you how to gain
the attention of the cults instead of losing the
opportunity to witness.
Single Cassette $5.98 A126586

Charisma
by Dr. Walter Martin

The surprising answers from Evangelical
Christianity which have been hailed by
charismatics and dispensationalists alike as an
authoritative discussion on this controversial
issue. (From his album *The World of the
Occult, Vol. I*).
Single Cassette $5.98 A126571

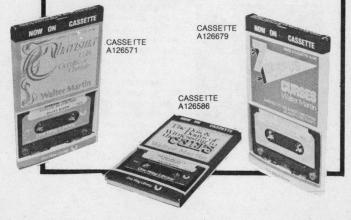

CASSETTE
A126571

CASSETTE
A126679

CASSETTE
A126586